ANSWERS FROM "THE WORKING ACTOR"

For nearly a decade, Jackie Apodaca and Michael Kostroff shared duties as advice columnists for the actors' trade paper, *Backstage*. Their highly popular weekly feature, "The Working Actor," fielded questions from actors all over the country. A cross between "Dear Abby" and *The Hollywood Reporter*, their column was a fact-based, humorous, compassionate take on the questions actors most wanted answered. Using some of their most interesting, entertaining, and informative columns as launch points, *Answers from "The Working Actor"* guides readers through the ins and outs (and ups and downs) of the acting industry.

Apodaca and Kostroff share an approach that is decidedly "on the ground." They've both labored in the trenches just like their readers—dealing with auditions, classes, photos, résumés, rehearsals, contract negotiations, representatives, jobs, challenging colleagues, and the search for that elusive life/career balance. There are few absolutes in the acting profession and virtually no proven and reliable steps. Unlike books that claim to offer "Quick Steps to a Successful Acting Career," *Answers from "The Working Actor"* deals honestly with the realities, providing facts, options, strategies, stories, points of view, and the wisdom of experience, while ultimately challenging readers to make their own decisions. This book will give new actors a head start on their journeys and remind experienced professionals that, in the acting business, there is never only one answer to any question.

Jackie Apodaca is a professor of theatre at Southern Oregon University. She has worked as an actor, director, and producer in theatre, film, and media, with companies such as the Roundabout, Denver Center, National Geographic, filmscience, Modern Media (head of production), Venice Theatre Works (associate artistic director), Shakespeare Santa Barbara (producing director), and Ashland New Plays Festival (associate artistic director). She spent more than a decade at *Backstage*, where she was a contributing editor and wrote the advice column "The Working Actor." Jackie earned an MFA from the National Theatre Conservatory, under the guidance of RSC founding member, Tony Church.

Michael Kostroff is an established actor best known for his five seasons on HBO's *The Wire* and a long list of other television roles. He's toured nationally in *The Producers* and *Les Misérables*, an experience which he chronicled in his book, *Letters from Backstage* (Allworth Press, 2005). From 2006 to 2012, he shared writing duties with Jackie Apodaca on *Backstage*'s advice column, "The Working Actor." A teacher as well as an actor and writer, he's presented his popular Audition Psych 101 workshop all over the country, and recently authored a book by the same name (Dog Ear Publishing, 2017).

ANSWERS FROM "THE WORKING ACTOR"

Two *Backstage* Columnists Share Ten Years of Advice

Jackie Apodaca and Michael Kostroff

Routledge
Taylor & Francis Group

NEW YORK AND LONDON

First published 2018
by Routledge
711 Third Avenue, New York, NY 10017

and by Routledge
2 Park Square, Milton Park, Abingdon, Oxon OX14 4RN

Routledge is an imprint of the Taylor & Francis Group, an informa business

Library of Congress Cataloging-in-Publication Data
A catalog record has been requested for this book

ISBN: 978-0-415-39442-0 (hbk)
ISBN: 978-0-415-39482-6 (pbk)
ISBN: 978-1-315-22285-1 (ebk)

Typeset in Bembo
by Apex CoVantage, LLC

To the hundreds of actors who've written to us over the years asking for our advice, only to learn that there's "no one answer." Sorry about that.

CONTENTS

ACKNOWLEDGMENTS

The authors would like to thank *Backstage* editors Jamie Painter-Young and Dany Margolies, spouses Greg Eliason and Jenny Kostroff, the many *Backstage* readers, and our students from around the country, who taught us most of what we know. And finally, our deepest thanks to Rob Weinert-Kendt who, many years ago, assigned Jackie to review Michael's first book and unknowingly put this whole thing into motion.

PREFACE

The choice to turn your art into a business is a crucial, difficult, and often under-analyzed decision. Many actors step blithely into the acting profession, expecting to do what they have done throughout their educations—after all, it's worked so far. You go to class, work on your craft, audition, get cast, and do a show. Then you do it again. Unfortunately, adding elements like money and real-world competition to the equation changes it entirely. While talent, training, and enthusiasm remain assets in the professional world, they're only part of the picture.

For actors, there's an inherent conflict: The *art* of acting requires vulnerability, openness, and sensitivity. You create a performance using your own mind, heart, and body—it's an incredibly personal endeavor. The *business* of acting, on the other hand, requires steely headed pragmatism, self-motivation, savvy, and grit. In order to thrive, you can't be ruled by the very sensitivity needed in your craft. Managing these two opposing pulls can be difficult and even debilitating. Some of the best actors we have ever known have long since quit the profession—not because they weren't talented and hard-working, but because the profession did not suit them. They wanted to act, but were unprepared for the attendant puzzle of managing an acting *career*. It was that part—the non-artistic part—which, it turned out, was simply not for them. Liking—even loving—to act, and enjoying the process of putting on a show, isn't a reliable indicator of whether you'll actually enjoy pursuing, or maintaining, an acting career.

For many years, the two of us fielded questions from professional actors of all levels in our capacities as advice columnists for the popular actors' newspaper and website, *Backstage*. Our column, "The Working Actor," was a weekly feature, affording us the opportunity to address myriad topics, both general and specific, on all aspects of the acting business. As working actors ourselves, we had years of experience in the trenches to draw upon. And as journalists, we had direct access to industry insiders and experts. These resources allowed us to answer readers' questions using a combination of research, interviews, and our own first-hand knowledge.

This book compiles some of our favorites from among those many questions and answers. It's our hope that this collection of "Working Actor" columns will offer readers an advance look at some of the challenges that may arise as they navigate the life of a professional actor. Throughout the chapters that follow, we'll orient you to the business so that you can make a more informed decision about whether to pursue an acting career. And if you choose to do so, this book will help you to embark on this path better educated about the profession, more savvy about opportunities as well as scams, and more prepared for the marathon that will be your career. As you explore the concepts and information here, we offer this advice: bring only your brain to this work. Leave your heart outside.

Perhaps the biggest truth we hope to convey—one that we have rediscovered again and again both in our careers and in years of writing the "Working Actor" column—is that in this profession there are virtually no absolutes, few reliable rules, and a stunning absence of consistency. Sooner or later, all advice can be contradicted and all theories proven wrong. Again and again, you'll see us answer that there is no one answer. Accepting the unpredictable and inconsistent nature of the industry is crucial to your professional survival. And while it's always valuable and wise to seek advice from those who've hacked through the thicket ahead, it's important to remember that, in the strange world of professional acting, you are blazing your own trail, a trail where you can expect the unexpected. That unpredictability can be alternately enchanting and maddening, but for the working actor, it's about the only thing that's guaranteed.

—Jackie Apodaca and Michael Kostroff

1

STARTING OUT

Going into acting as a career means entering a profession in which supply will always outweigh demand—by an enormous ratio—and in which unemployment and unpredictability will, in all likelihood, be constant norms.

All that uncertainty leaves many nascent professionals in a fog as they ponder the question of *how* to begin. Most professions have some sort of acknowledged entry procedure—steps one can take towards becoming employed in that field. There's no such norm in acting. Careers begin in any number of ways, and no method is proven to work consistently. Getting your foot in the door and actually launching a career is a process that is mysterious at best, impossible at worst.

Here is one very encouraging fact: All the most famous and accomplished actors we could name, were, at one time or another, beginners, not knowing what to do first or how to build their careers. As daunting as a professional acting career may seem, there's living proof that it can be done.

When starting out, it's common to feel lost, discouraged, or overwhelmed. Many actors spend more time drowning in worry and questions than taking concrete steps towards their goals. It's wiser to embrace the randomness and lack of structure, and simply pursue leads and opportunities as you unearth them. Adhere to a healthy sense of skepticism about anything that seems dicey or too easy. Exchange information with fellow actors and avoid those that waste time wallowing in frustration. Work hard, but avoid obsession. Replenish by doing things that inspire you and reignite your artistic passion. And finally, relish the journey. In the acting profession, there will always be something you haven't yet achieved. Perpetually looking to the future, while negating what is happening now, can lead to madness, while focusing on the present and investing in your current opportunities—big or small—will make starting out far less daunting.

Questions and Answers

Dear Michael,

I'm new to LA, and I'm not sure where to begin. It's such a big place, and being new is a bit overwhelming. What do I do first? I know some things just come with time, but I'm a proactive type, and I don't just want to sit around waiting for something to happen. Do you have any suggestions on how to get started here?

—New Girl in Town

Dear New Girl,

Moving to any new city can be a challenging transition for an actor. It can be even more challenging without help from those who know the lay of the land. So, assuming you've already found an apartment, a car, a day job, your supermarket, Starbucks, and all the other basic necessities, your next priority should be building a network of fellow actors—for the camaraderie and for the connections. Your new showbiz neighbors can guide you to local opportunities, connect you with contacts, and provide the kind of support that can only come from those who are on the same path. But how do you connect? Meeting peers can be a challenge, especially in LA, where things are so spread out and people spend so much time in their cars. Here are suggestions for places where you can make a start.

—Join a theatre company. This one offers multiple benefits. You make friends, which is of no small value when you've recently arrived and don't know a lot of people. Your fellow members—professional performers, like you—will know more about the LA acting scene and can fill you in. You get to keep your chops up by working on plays. And if it's a respected company, you'll start having opportunities to be seen by casting people.

—Take classes. In addition to the obvious benefits of training, acting classes are great places to get to know fellow actors. Meeting at a party is one thing, but when actors study together, they bond in a deeper and more substantial way. What's more, if you're agent hunting, a fellow actor is far more likely to recommend you if he or she has seen your work in class.

—See plays. You want to gather where the actors gather, and smaller theatres are great places to find your peers.

—If you're a union member, take advantage of the programs, workshops, and seminars. These are well worth attending for their own merits, but an added advantage is that these events facilitate gatherings of actors, and they do so in an atmosphere of learning and solidarity.

—Find a support job where you'll meet fellow performers. When I moved to LA I was lucky enough to find a job at one of the theme parks and was impressed to discover that my coworkers had major Broadway and regional theatre credits. It was one of the best support jobs I could ever hope for. I made a living performing, and I made friends and contacts—lots of them, many of whom I'm still in touch with.

—Many actors find each other and stay in touch via various apps and websites, where you can communicate with peers, ask for advice, promote shows you're in, organize gatherings, read reviews, and get information on classes, teachers, theatre companies, and just about any other actor-related topic you can think of.

Some actors choose to commune away from their professional settings.

—If you're spiritually inclined, why not choose a house of worship where you can attend alongside fellow artists? Agape, described on its website, agapelive.com, as a "transdenominational spiritual community," seems to be a popular actors' church, frequented even by those who don't consider themselves religious. The Synagogue for the Performing Arts, sftpa.com, speaks for itself, and Valley Beth Shalom, vbs.org, attracts industry types as well. There's also Act One, actoneprogram.com, an interdenominational organization for Christians in the entertainment industry. Several Christian churches cater to the industry as well, such as Ecclesia Hollywood (ecclesiahollywood.org), and Mosaic (mosaic.org). Obviously, you shouldn't go to these places to shmooze . . . unless it's with your higher power.

—You really want to meet actors? Go to a twelve-step program. That's not a joke, a recommendation, or a judgment. I'm just saying that if you choose to go, you'll find comrades there. And because of the nature of these groups, twelve-steppers also tend to be more supportive than competitive, and willing to help you get acclimated. Not that you should use these groups for those purposes. But if there's one that addresses an issue for you, you'll be enhancing both yourself and your circle.

—Donate your time to a good cause. You know what they say: if you want to get something, give something . . . or something like that. Volunteering is good for the soul, good for the world, and a good way to connect. And since two out of every three Los Angelenos seem to be actors, you're bound to meet some along the way.

When not working on their careers, actors are often at the gym, at the coffee house, or engaged in our favorite pastime: eating and talking. The hike at Runyon Canyon seems designed for reunions, as you'll rarely get to the top without running into someone you know. (For New Yorkers, the equivalent seems to be 9th Avenue in the Theatre District.) Some gravitate toward the Farmers' Market on Fairfax, some gather at the Aroma Café in Studio City. The point is, you'll meet more of your fellow artistes if you leave your house. MK

Dear Jackie,

I'm in New Jersey and just getting started in the business. My résumé at this point consists of training and some plays I did in college. I want to get an agent. My question is what should the cover letter consist of? Also, should I seek out an agent before I join a union or wait until after?

—Beginner

Dear Beginner,

Why do you want an agent right now? With your minimal résumé, now is not a time for results, but for process. Get into a good acting class. Begin auditioning for student films, low-budget commercials, and plays—all the things you don't need an agent to get you in the door for. Build up your credits and begin to network in your field. Right now, all you could say in a cover letter is "I am just starting out and have only done plays in college." Unless you have a very marketable look, you aren't likely to garner much attention with that. If you book a few small jobs on your own—a low-budget film here, a play there—and begin studying with reputable teachers, you'll have something more interesting to include.

Similarly, you, as a relatively unproven actor without representation, aren't going to be greatly helped by joining an actors' union. The unions were constructed to provide bargaining power and safeguards for professional actors. I'm not saying that SAG-AFTRA[1] and AEA[2] are only meant for good actors or real actors or worthy actors, just that they can't serve you until you are regularly getting paid for acting—or at least auditioning for roles in union gigs. Once you join, you will be limiting your work opportunities. An unrepresented actor of your experience level needs to be competing for every available acting job—including those that are smaller and less glamorous. Don't undervalue legitimate nonunion work. Such projects can provide valuable knowledge and footage for your reel.[3] You may even make a buck or two.

I'm not suggesting that you hold off on pursuing an agent or getting your union cards for very long. It makes sense that you are eager to get knee-deep into your chosen profession, and the sooner you are prepared to do so, the better. But prepare you must. Reps and unions are only part of the picture. JA

Dear Michael,

I always want to know if there's something more that I can do to cultivate my career, other than checking websites, reading plays, watching great films, etc. Is it okay to send my résumé, headshot, and cover letter to a casting office that I know is casting a project, even if it hasn't posted a casting notice? Being that I'm young and new to this, I don't want to look unprofessional or annoy anyone.

—Searching Starlet

Dear Starlet,

Yes, it is absolutely appropriate to mail your headshot, résumé, and a brief cover letter or note to casting people. Now, whether or not it's effective is another story. Some offices don't even open that mail. But even if it doesn't immediately result in an audition, the cumulative effect of those mailings could be an audition down the line. It never hurts to be *appropriately* proactive. One caution about mailings, though: don't call to follow up. That's strongly discouraged by casting offices. And that makes sense when you think of how many actors there are out there; the casting folks would be on the phone with actors all day long, and wouldn't be able to do any casting. You sort of have to send it and forget it. MK

Dear Jackie,

I'm 21, and have had an interest in acting my whole life. I passed up theatre classes in high school—which I now regret—but I have taken classes at my local junior college. I went into those knowing that I would not be the most attractive or seasoned person there, but simply with the goal of having fun. I had so much fun that I have now taken all the classes offered at my school! I have a very flexible job, and am applying to four-year universities. No luck yet, but I don't plan on letting that get me down.

In the meantime, what can I do to get more experience here in Virginia? I always wanted to do film, but was told I should start off with theatre. I realize I have very little experience and will never be the most talented person, but I really loved all of my time in the theatre department and want to keep going.

—Virginia Voyager

Dear Virginia,

Don't worry about theatre vs. film, or whether you're as good as the people playing the leads at your college. There are many acting opportunities out there, especially if your goal is simply to have fun and explore. While states like Virginia don't offer the bang for your buck of California and New York, they can present friendlier, less competitive environments in which to gain experience. You mentioned exhausting your college's acting class offerings, but have you gotten all your acting teachers have to offer? Speak to your favorites and see whether they have any local ideas for you. Maybe one of them teaches privately, or works with a summer company you could audition or volunteer for.

Next, check out your state resources. Start with the Virginia Film Office[4] and local film festivals.[5] Many state film commission websites list local opportunities and even auditions, and festivals and screenings are great places to connect with others in your local market. Look, too, at the Virginia Production Alliance. Many communities have their own versions of this kind of group, a collection of filmmakers and production personnel who want to network, share job news, and find collaborators. Some hold auditions to connect directors with promising local actors. On the theatre front, Virginia—like most states—has no shortage of venues. Local nonunion, community, and dinner theatres, as well as summer stock companies, are all great places to learn the ropes. Much of casting is based on who you know and whether you're in the right place at the right time. Get out there and begin meeting people who work. JA

Dear Michael,

I didn't just start wanting to be an actor. I've wanted to do this since I was around 5, but life has gotten in the way. I'm now 22, and for nearly the past two years, I've been actively searching for any auditions for theatre and film that I can get into, and I've spent every weekend out auditioning, but have only gotten parts as an extra for a short internet series and a nonunion film. I live in Davenport, Florida, and aside from musical theatre (which I don't do, since I don't have a singing voice), there's practically nothing here. Another problem for me is that I have utterly no experience and no training, and casting directors down around here don't take a serious look at someone like me. I'd like to be able to move to New York or California where auditions for movies and theatre are more abundant than they are here, but, alas, I lack the money to do such a thing. What would your advice be to go from here?
—Starting Out

Dear Starting,

Take heart. You've been at this a whopping two years. It takes a minute or two. But if this is what you really want to do, there are several actions you can take right now:

—Your lack of training is something you can fix. Wherever you are, there's a class you can take. Choose one that teaches you about the *craft of acting*, not one that offers to teach you how to break into the business. You'll be tempted, I know. But there are no shortcuts. Work on your technique, so you'll be more prepared when legitimate opportunities arise. Study with someone who's recommended and very experienced. If funds are tight, consider taking classes at a community college. They're inexpensive, and sometimes really good.
—Since there's more musical theatre where you are, why not study voice? You may not be a great singer now, but most people can be taught to sing. Try. You might just open up a whole new market for yourself.

—Learn to use the English language properly. I had to correct your letter so our readers would understand what you were saying. It was misspelled, improperly punctuated, and incoherently worded. You may think I'm picking on you, but hear me out: Carpenters use hammers and saws. Plumbers use pipes and wrenches. Actors use language. We spend much of our time discussing and analyzing what specific words mean, why characters say them, and why writers chose them. If you want people to believe you can act, I encourage you to develop a great respect for the tool of language. Things like failing to capitalize "Florida" or misspelling "advice" make people think you don't pay attention to your work. I recommend reading more—a lot more; reading teaches you better writing. And be sure to proofread before you send anything out. You'll improve your chances of being taken seriously.

What you *shouldn't* do is make the mistake of thinking that moving to New York or California will suddenly put you on track for a great acting career. Yes, opportunities are more abundant in those places . . . and so are actors—actors with training and professional credits. You think it's tough in Davenport? Kid stuff.

You're just discovering what many of us know: it's hard to be an actor, especially at the beginning. But don't discount the baby steps. A friend of mine was a psychology student. Every year at her school, they'd do the same experiment; they'd play ring toss. You know how it works: toss the ring three feet, you get three points; five feet, five points; ten feet, ten points. And every year they had the same results: without fail, the people who went for the three-foot toss again and again—the easiest one—walked away with the most points. It became their shorthand. When someone faced a problem, fellow students would ask, "What's the three-foot toss?" This advice will serve you well in all areas of life: don't focus on the mountain. Just take the small, easy step you see before you—the three-foot toss—and before you know it, you'll be looking for the next mountain. MK

Dear Jackie,

I have a friend who suggests I do background work to get my SAG-AFTRA card and start my acting career. He has been doing it for years and swears by it. What do you think?

—Newbie

Dear Newbie,

Background work can provide a helpful glimpse into the film and television industry, and some find its proximity to professional acting inspiring, informational, and even a little bit thrilling. But your friend would do well to remember that that's all it is: proximity.

A couple of weeks is about as much background work as I would suggest. Some actors use the occasional background gig as a day job, and this might work for you now and then, but if you rely on it week after week, you'll have to start making sacrifices to be there. And those sacrifices will include your availability to seek acting gigs. Background actors put in long hours, and they often work days—prime auditioning time. They also spend a lot of time in a fairly insular environment, socializing mainly with other background actors. Better to get another day job—one that's flexible or allows you to work nights—and get into an acting class where you'll meet other actors who share your long-term goals.

Getting into SAG-AFTRA or AEA is not where your focus—as a beginning actor—should be. Focus on acting classes, submissions, auditioning, researching, networking, and performing. Leave full-time background work to full-time background actors, like your friend. You did, I hope, notice the irony of his advice. If background work swiftly launches acting careers, why is your friend still doing it? JA

Dear Michael,

I've auditioned for two talent agencies in NYC, but didn't get signed to either. Is there something I'm doing wrong?

—Out of Ideas

Dear Out of Ideas,

Don't panic. Agencies pass on signing actors all the time. It doesn't mean you're doing anything wrong. Finding an agent is one of the hardest tasks actors face. So take heart: your situation isn't uncommon.

Each agent has his or her own taste regarding who might be marketable, but they all look for clients who they think will make money for the agency. There's no way to become that, so don't stress over it. They're also obligated to serve their existing clients by not signing too many actors of similar type.[6] And it's also possible that you're not quite ready for professional representation yet, and that's OK too. Just keep working at your craft and getting better. And keep in mind that it often takes meeting with lots of agencies before you find one that's the right match. MK

Dear Jackie,

I'm a director, but have found it really easy to get cast in shows at my college. I was thinking of doing acting as a back-up profession since it comes so easy to me and pays so well. What do you think?

—Back-Up Plan

Dear Back-Up,

I suggest you go ahead and become an astronaut and a figure skating gold medalist as well. Oh, and a senator.

Okay look: acting is not something to pursue as a survival job. It's the job you get a survival job in order to pursue. Your logic is skewed. You have been lucky enough to land a few roles at school, but unless you are drop-dead gorgeous and have an uncle who's an agent at CAA[7] you will find professional work a wee bit harder to come by. I'm not saying that only "the chosen few" should pursue acting or that you don't have a chance at making a little cash here and there if you don't commit to making acting your life's work. You should, however, talk to some actors outside of your college to get a clearer idea of how much effort landing an acting role really takes.

By the way, I wouldn't mention using acting as a "back up" to these actors if I were you. JA

Dear Michael,

I was wondering what's the best way to make the most of pilot[8] season. Do most actors go to LA for that period? I'd like to get my name out there and be in the mix for some series, especially like a cop or detective show, but I'm not sure of the first step (or even the exact dates when pilot season takes place). Can you give me the rundown?
—Parts and Rec

Dear P&R,

Sure thing. Pilot season isn't as clear cut as it once was. Back in the day, TV networks all cast and produced their pilots around the same time—roughly between February and April—so they'd be ready for presentation at what's known as "the upfronts"—a week-long spring event at which networks pitch shows to advertisers. But the rise of cable and digital media opened up not only the playing field but also the schedule. What that means is that pilots are now cast and produced year round, though the largest concentration is still during the traditional season.

Yes, a lot of actors make pilgrimage to LA. But keep in mind, pilot season is not a magical time during which previously-closed casting doors are suddenly wide open to all. Unless you're represented by a well-established agent—not just any agent—you won't have access to pilot auditions. Networks keep lists of recognizable, pilot-ready actors; they're at the top of the pile of possible casting choices. Next come working actors who are with the A-list agencies. Very rarely does the search go beyond those top tiers. Often, young actors will come to LA pre-season to secure representation so they can get seen; with the majority of roles going to young talent, agencies will sometimes rep such types for the season. But there are always actors without any connections who come to LA thinking that just by virtue of being in town for pilot season, something will happen. Well . . . I hope they enjoy the beach. MK

Dear Jackie,

I recently graduated with a BA in acting but didn't take the film acting class because I never considered myself a film and television person. I've been too self-conscious about whether I have the right "look" to pursue it professionally. However, I was recently called into work as an extra for a film and am now intrigued. I am aware that background work is quite a different thing altogether, but I loved being on a set. It's exhausting but fascinating work. How do I go about breaking into film and TV with no experience and no credits on my résumé?

Before you say, "Go take classes at a film and TV school," I need to tell you that I'm really struggling financially, and still paying off student loans. I honestly don't have the money to spend on classes even though I know they would be really helpful in terms of learning this whole other world of acting. I know I have a more natural style and was once mock auditioning for a television casting director (in a workshop) who said I had great style, but how do I get real auditions? I am worried because I have heard that undergraduate degrees in theatre are warning signs to film/TV people.

I don't necessarily even want an agent or manager unless it's virtually impossible to break into TV/film without them. You see, I am more than happy to do any and all legwork because I feel productive when I'm doing the research. But I fear there is only so far I can get without them. Are my suspicions true?
—Moving into Moving Pictures

Dear Moving,

While your eagerness to do your own legwork is admirable, your suspicions are correct. Getting in the film and television doors is usually managed with the help of a respected and aggressive agent. There is, of course, the occasional small, indie film[9] that thwarts expectations and boosts an actor into notoriety, but those are the exceptions.

It often works something like this: a well-prepared actor courts and eventually lands an agent. With the help of this first agent, she begins getting auditions. With hard work and continued training, she begins to book jobs and eventually nabs a big enough gig for her to sign with a bigger agent. This second agent has the wherewithal to get her into bigger auditions. With hard work and continued training, she begins to book these bigger jobs . . . and so on and so forth. The process is not as linear as I have made it sound—the path to acting success looks more like jungle gym than a ladder—but this is one of the general scenarios.

I understand how, as a recent grad, taking more classes can seem unappealing. It's frustrating to be paying off loans to one school and told to shell out cash for another. But you have chosen a field that is tremendously competitive and requires workers to constantly better themselves. You'll have to invest in the business you are creating, paying not only for more classes, but to submit yourself via casting sites, get good headshots, buy an audition wardrobe, and—eventually—to join SAG-AFTRA and AEA—which require hefty initiation fees and yearly dues. Luckily you don't need to do all these things at once, but you shouldn't kid yourself into thinking your startup won't cost you.

It's not the end of the world that you didn't take film acting in college—in fact, some college-level Acting for Camera classes are not up to snuff on a professional level and can do more harm than good. As you save for classes, audition for student films and every on-camera job you can find. Drop your headshot/résumé off at local film schools for their casting files. Get out your camera or phone and do some preliminary self-training by taping yourself doing a monologue and then watching the result. If you're anything like I was when I first dared to look, what you see will horrify you. (My eyebrows! Why were they moving so much!) But with practice and focused relaxation you can begin to tone down those overactive shoulders or twitchy ears. Rent Michael Caine's *Acting for the Camera* for some practical advice and a few laughs. (Just skip the part where he directs the students; that's pretty painful.)

Go ahead and begin submitting to agents. And don't worry, your education won't work against you. Many actors land their first agent off a university showcase,[10] at least at the MFA level. And submitting yourself to casting directors is not a bad idea either, though at this point your headshot will most likely end up in the trash—which might be a blessing in disguise. It may be better not to be seen than to be seen before you are ready. You say you have never considered yourself a film and television person—why would anyone else? Instead of trying to break into something you've just discovered an interest in, take stock in where you are and set goals for the coming year. There'll be plenty of time to focus on landing those "real" auditions once you've built up your confidence in the medium. JA

Dear Michael,

I came into the industry knowing absolutely nothing, so I began interning for a boutique talent management company. It's been an excellent experience and has taught me a lot in a short amount of time. I know most of the industry jargon. I'm even given the great privilege of submitting myself through The Breakdowns.[11] But entering the business still seems like a huge paradox to me: you have to be in a union project to join the union, but if you're not in the union, union productions won't hire you. Even getting under-five roles[12] is extremely difficult without first having credits. I've heard a lot lately that casting directors are only looking at those with credits. What should I do?

And what about my reel? I know that casting directors hardly look at people without them, but I'm new and have nothing to work with. Even student films offer stiff competition. And I'm not even getting auditions for those, because they want to see some sort of reel. I'm extremely enthusiastic about becoming a working actress, but it seems impossible. I've been at this for six months and I've only been called on one audition. What can I do to get myself in a casting room? Is there anything special I can do to make myself stand out? Maybe I'm just being impatient—you tell me.

—What Am I Missing?

Dear What Am I Missing,

Okay, I'll tell you: you're being impatient. My goodness! You've been pursuing a professional acting career for *six months* and you *still* don't have a reel or a résumé? Do yourself a favor: sit down with someone who's been at this a decade or two and hear what he or she has to say. Most actors can tell you stories that would curl your hair about how long it can take to get a career off the ground. Now, I'm not trying to scare you—quite the opposite. I'm saying get comfortable; you're going to be here a while.

Meanwhile, you have correctly identified one of our biggest conundrums: often, to get your foot in the door, you have to already be successful. And how can you already be successful if you can't get your foot in the door? That equation is, of course, impossible—except in those rare instances when it isn't. And it's that tiny sliver of a flicker of a percentage of a chance that keeps us all going. As impossible as it sounds, we're all assuming there are gaps in the wall somewhere. Otherwise, why bother?

But the way to avoid going nuts in this business is to look at things as they really are, rather than as we think they should be. So know that an acting career is a long shot, embrace it as such, keep pursuing it anyway, and don't waste a single second bemoaning the unfairness of it all. That's not going to change, and believe me, no one cares about one more actor who thinks the system is unfair. Soldier on, keep that enthusiasm, and enjoy the journey. I really believe that's the key.

Now let me tell you what you've done that's brilliant. By interning at a management office and seeing its inner workings, you've given yourself a free advanced education in an important area of the business—actors' representation. Most actors go their whole careers missing the knowledge you already have. And hold on a second. Did I read that correctly? You get to submit yourself? Maybe you're too new at this to grasp how fortunate you are. So just trust the old pro here: you're very fortunate—fortunate enough that some of your contemporaries would probably line up to smack you. So, well done! Other than that, all you can do is continue to get the lay of the land. I promise, things get clearer. MK

Dear Jackie,

I am interested in becoming an actor. Let's say I know I have a gimmick that will open doors for me, and not to try and get into a movie with this would be stupid. I have no experience at acting or at preparing a portfolio to send to television or movie studios. I was wondering if you could tell me what I need to do to make a portfolio or send me in the right direction to people who know how to make one.
—Guaranteed Gimmick

Dear Guaranteed,

I am dying to know what your surefire gimmick could be. Actors everywhere would be willing to pay cash for such a secret. Here's an idea, package and sell your gimmick and use the proceeds to fund your own film. If it's good enough to open doors for someone with no acting experience, it should earn you enough to finance your own project.

Although . . . no acting experience? How do you know you want to act? Why seek something you don't know the first thing about? Are you attracted to the fame? The imagined money? The house in the hills? There are hundreds of well-trained, hard-working, deserving actors out there looking for big breaks that may never come. I fully understand the joy actors take in performing and their desire to make a living at something they love. But I also know the road is long and can be full of frustration and rejection. You seem not to realize this very essential truth.

If you think you want to give acting a shot, take an acting class. Audition for a local play or student film. Read an acting book. After you've spent some time trying the craft on for size, get back to me and I'll help you sort out your whole "portfolio" confusion. JA

Dear Michael,

I'm a beginning actor with a little community-college experience and an interest in theatre. I decided, since I had a headshot done in one of my acting classes, to send out a few to agents and casting offices in my area. The problem is that although I like my headshot, I do not currently have any full-body shots, something a lot of the casting agents ask for. I also was accepted by an agency, but they have been sending me emails every few weeks asking for a one-time payment to "make my online profile public." Am I wasting my time even looking for work via casting agents and talent agencies? Is it worth getting professional full-body shots done at this time, or is it better for me to wait?
—Looking for Advice

Dear Looking,

The most important thing I need to tell you is this: never pay for representation under any circumstances. No legitimate agents or managers charge up-front fees. They work on commission. If you book a job, they negotiate for you, then take a percentage of what you earn—usually ten percent for agents, fifteen percent for managers. Newcomers like you can always find someone willing to take your money, enticing you with promises of work on film and TV. They're scam artists.[13]

While you're in the learning phase, I advise you to carefully weigh each expenditure before whipping out the credit card. Be frugal. For example, you don't have to get full-body shots just because a casting director requests them. I don't have any, and I'm a working pro. Remember: having an office doesn't make someone an expert, and you don't have to do everything every casting person or agent suggests. If you start booking work, that will justify greater investments as you direct more of your focus to these pursuits. Until then, keep a firm grip on your wallet. MK

Dear Jackie,

I'm young and have pretty good film and theatre credits, a great body, and am flawless with dialects. I won the Best Actor award in The Strawberry One-Act Theatre Festival and I've been reviewed by NYTheatre.com, Off-Offonline.com, and Showbiz weekly. Also, something I'm very proud of in my skills section (besides others) is my background in gymnastics, martial arts, and Olympic diving. I was a national competitor in martial arts and diving. I know with my physical background I may be at an advantage over others.

Now that I'm getting opportunities to meet with industry, how can I come off as a kick-ass package, acting-wise and physical-wise without coming off cocky?

—Confident Enough

Dear Confident,

Based on your letter, your fear of coming off "cocky" is well-founded. Here's the problem: your experience doesn't seem to merit the bravado with which it's presented.

When you meet industry professionals, present yourself for what you are—a young actor with passion and drive—rather than for what you hope to become. And relax. An agent recently complained to me about an actor who came in to meet with her like a "ball-buster," which turned her off. She was uninterested in working with someone so aggressively sure of himself, even if that aggressiveness was put on for her benefit. Anyone in the business of representing actors knows that such meetings are nerve-wracking and can be hard to come by. Don't feel as though you have to prove otherwise. As for your physical attributes, let's hope the representatives you meet with will see those for themselves.

Not to say your confidence won't serve you. You'll need it, and plenty of fortitude, to deal with the inevitable rejection all actors face. And you do have great selling points in the physical skill arena—not many actors can claim Olympic diving on their résumés. But in order to be taken seriously as more than just a "great body" you'll need to train, just like an athlete. JA

Dear Michael,

Are there any ways to get an audition for a film without having an agent? I completely understand the general way of going about things—I'm currently doing student films to build up my résumé and create a reel and then submit to agents, and I'm now SAG-AFTRA. However, there's an upcoming movie, which is an adaptation of a book, with a character that fits me very well. I'm not what you'd call a classical leading lady type so roles that fit my description and type this well are not easy to come by (plus I just love the character) . . . and I thought it would be amazing to just get to audition for the project. I could even have a chance, but I don't have any chance at all if I don't get in the room. I just figured it's not impossible. Do I just somehow find out the casting director on IMDbPro[14] and submit my headshot to them? Target them by meeting them at a CD workshop? Or is there a better way?

—Picture Perfect

Dear Picture Perfect,

There is indeed a better way.

Given your specific connection with the project—your love of the original material, your rightness for the role, and your fondness for the character—instead of sending a headshot to the casting director, I think you should research who the director is, and write him or her a letter. Not an email. A letter. Trust me, people don't do this very often, so it will stand out.

Attending a workshop to meet a casting director, on the other hand, is what everyone does. And I believe it's highly unlikely that a casting director will pick you out of the crowd for a major film role when you're paying him or her for the meeting. Your very attendance is a signal that you're not at the major motion picture level. Similarly, I think the likelihood of getting an appointment for this kind of role from an unsolicited mailing is pretty slim. Here's why: the casting director wants to present actors who'll make him or her look good to the director and producer, so he or she will be looking for those with substantial credits, rather than the needle-in-the-haystack beginner who might be perfect for the part.

So do something different, something dignified, something special. Do something that says you're unique, and well worth looking at. Write a letter. Tell the director about your love for the story and the character, and how much you'd love to get to read for the role. Go into detail about your reaction to the book, and why it appealed to you so much. Remember to also present yourself as an actor who possesses the necessary chops for the job. And while you're at it, you might write similar letters to the producer, the screenwriter and the author of the book. Any of these folks can request that you be seen. A unique goal merits a unique approach. MK

Dear Jackie,

I have always wanted to act professionally, but lack of self-confidence kept me from pursuing this goal. Over the years I have taken many acting classes, gone on several auditions, acted in student films, off-off Broadway plays, and two Equity showcases.[15] I feel ready at last to try for some professional work. The only problem is, I sometimes feel too old to enter the world of show business. I'm a 40-year-old woman. Has my time passed?

—Over the Hill?

Dear Over,

I'm not going to pretend that there aren't more opportunities for very young men and women than for those of us over, say, 25. SAG-AFTRA statistics (and being awake and alive) show that women over 40 have a much tougher road than men and younger women—there just aren't as many roles out there for women in this category. Still, you have to remember that there are more actors in their early 20s competing for that larger percentage of parts. By the time actors reach 40, many have called it quits. Not to say there isn't fierce competition—those still in the field are there because they have found some success. But if you are realistic and willing to work like the professional newcomer you are, you may find opportunities. For example, many working actors your age have already joined the unions. If you are nonunion you will discover the competition for nonunion jobs is much less daunting.

Be realistic about your credits and what kinds of roles you are suited for. You aren't likely to be up for series leads with a résumé as lean as yours, so target smaller, less glamorous roles. If you show casting people and representatives that you don't expect to jump to the front of the line, they may be more receptive. As you build your résumé and your experience, you may be able to stair-step up the credit ladder.

And don't despair. Look at Emmy Award winner Kathryn Joosten, who began acting at 42. "I never saw age as an impediment," she said. Her advice to other actors getting what some might call a late start? "Get as much experience as you can locally, on stage, in industrials, and whatever else is open to you and don't try to compete with the younger set. Determine who *you* are and sell that." JA

Dear Michael,

I've done a fair bit of stage acting and been encouraged for years by many friends to pursue it seriously, but I've been fearful of making the professional plunge before. But now, at 28, feel I'm ready to make that commitment to pursuing acting in film and television as a full-time vocation.

Am I too old to embark on a serious acting career? I've heard that one can expect to invest at least five years before making a dent in the business. Hence, my concern is that by the time I would have made significant strides I would be at the age where there are very minimal roles. Also, it seems that age can be a prohibitive factor when trying to get an agent. I've been told, and have read, that agents prefer to invest in talent under the age of 25. No agent equals no work!

I think I should be better informed before making such a serious investment of both time and funds. So, what are my chances?
—Too Old?

Dear Too Old?

You seem to be trying to nail things down, map out a reliable plan, and assess things like your chances of success or of getting an agent. While I admire your almost scientific approach, I can tell you that if you're looking for a calculable business model, this profession never fares very well. Acting careers just aren't that predictable. Yes, starting later than most could present significant challenges, and maybe prove prohibitive. On the other hand, some working actors—even some very successful ones—began careers later in life. There's no telling how it'll go for you.

I would gently suggest that if you're looking for assurances of success before you can feel comfortable committing, then maybe this profession isn't for you—and I don't say that as a put-down. You ask whether you're too old to embark on a serious acting career. My friend, embarking on an acting career is impractical at any age. Your friends are probably right about your talent, but they won't have to face your career challenges, live through your disappointments, or pay your bills while you find your way through the maze. So before you sign on, investing your time, money, and soul, make absolutely sure you're ready to embrace the whole thing. If you're sure acting is the career you want, then don't allow the impracticality or unpredictability to stop you. That yearning will sustain you when the going gets tough. Go forward. Learn. Audition. Experience yourself as an artist, and let the showbiz fates take care of the results. Maybe you'll have no success at all. And that has to be OK with you before you even start. MK

Dear Jackie,

I moved to NYC eleven years ago to attend college, majoring in musical theatre. After graduating with honors, I quickly landed my first national tour. I spent much of the next five years on the road with nonunion shows and a few regional theatres. After a very long stint on the road with the last show, I felt burnt out and exhausted from being away from NYC. I decided to take a year off and just have a regular life as an out-of-work actor/waiter. It was absolutely great.

Well, that one year turned into six and I'm still waiting tables. My old headshots look like a different person, my audition music is outdated, and I'm not even sure I would know how to turn out a decent dance combo. I haven't sung a note since I started my self-proclaimed hiatus and I'm sure the vocals are pretty out of shape.

The itch is there to get back out and start auditioning again. However, I have no clue as to what kind of "type" I am anymore. At 21 years old I was the tall, funny, supporting male character actor. Now at 30, I've got a lot less hair and a few more lines on the face—I couldn't tell you where I fit in on stage. I feel as if everyone out there is so much younger than I am. I don't even know where to start—it's all so overwhelming that I can't make a move. Where do I begin?
   —Lost in Transition

Dear Lost,
   Everyone out there is "so much younger" than you? You're only 30! Stage is traditionally less age-phobic than screen, especially for men, so you should stop worrying about the years you took off. Since you play funny supporting characters—and not young, debonair leading men—you may have actually aged further into the sweet spot of your type.

Don't worry about where you "should" be—embrace this new beginning and jump into what any beginner should do. Get into acting, singing, and dancing classes, get new headshots, research updated singing selections, and begin auditioning. Your past experience will help you conquer hurdles much faster this time around. Set clear goals for yourself based on where you are right now. Don't set goals you can't control—like booking three tours next year or making it to Broadway before you're 35. Try something along the lines of getting into a class and auditioning for at least five shows before the month is out.

As you gear up for round two, take some time to think through the reasons for your extended break. Why were your six years off so "great"? What was so overwhelming about touring? What did you dislike about your life as a working actor—and what will you do differently this time around to avoid burning out and needing another 1/2 decade away? Although you are yearning to get back into the grind, you may need to impose limits on what kind or how much work you will accept.

Six years is a long time. It seems probable that you took that time off for good reason. Until you figure out what that was, and how you can mediate such things in the future, you'll have trouble creating an enduring career. JA

Dear Michael,

I'm an actor who was born with a mild disability and was hoping you could give me some ideas for building my career. I've been in a few indie projects so far and taken classes and workshops with casting directors. I also mail out headshots and résumés every other month. I feel I have something to offer, my physical uniqueness, along with my talent of course. I know that in most cases it would hurt my chances but it's what I have, and damn it—I'm going to work it. Plus, with mainstream shows like *Glee* depicting actors with disabilities I think we're on the rise to seeing more people on TV with a variety of so-called "shortcomings." There's going to be a new perception of the word "disability," and I'm going to be it!
—Ready, Willing, and Able

Dear Ready,

I love your enthusiasm and determination, and I think your assessment is balanced and realistic: having an evident disability limits the roles you're right for, but it certainly needn't discourage you from pursuing an acting career, particularly with your terrific, go-get-'em attitude.

While there doesn't seem to be a US equivalent of the UK's VisABLE People (visablepeople.com), a talent agency that specializes in repping actors with disabilities, some will surely appreciate the potential value of your uniqueness, and some even have performers-with-disabilities departments. I asked manager Eric Stevens to give me his take. He agreed that while opportunities are limited, they're out there.

> There are calls for these roles on occasion, and some directors want an actor with real-life experience with those physical challenges. Also, some roles can be altered accordingly if the director and producer are open-minded. If an agent has the vision to see the big picture, she'll see the potential.

Luckily, you have some great resources in your corner, like the Media Access Office (found on the site, disabled-world.com), UCLA's National Arts and Disability Center (nadc.ucla.edu/theatre.cfm), and the Alliance for Inclusion in the Arts (www.inclusioninthearts.org). The unions are also mindful of the cause. SAG-AFTRA and AEA share the I AM PWD (Inclusion in the Arts and Media for Performers With Disabilities) campaign.

If your disability is a visible one, the best plan may be to boldly emphasize it in your photos, reel, cover letter, and other materials. Recently, a director I know raved about a wonderful actor she saw at an audition. His résumé said, on the top and in bold, "The actor has cerebral palsy which results in unique physicality and mannerisms. No accommodation is needed." I don't want to paint an overly-rosy picture; the roles are still scarce. But as you well understand, someone will play those roles. It may as well be you. MK

Dear Jackie,

Since deciding to actively pursue acting after graduating high school, I have been truly blessed. In the past six months I've booked three modeling jobs via an agency, auditioned for an NBC pilot, and have met with over fifty New York casting directors and agents.

I'm young and everyone says, "You have plenty of time!" My agents want to send me out on big auditions. I have up to two new modeling agents calling me weekly to work with them. Now I want to pursue commercial auditions and land national spots. My worry is, is it all too much? Am I spreading myself too thin?

I took a hiatus from legit[16] auditions because I want to hone my craft by taking acting classes. I thought I was making the right choice, but some agents and managers are telling me otherwise. Am I selling myself short by not pursuing legit auditions? Am I pursuing too much, too quickly?

This is a dilemma I'm sure other actors would love, however, instead of having a steady acting career, I want to have a phenomenal one.
—Prince of Gotham

Dear Prince,

You're right. Many actors would sell a kidney to have your problems. You can't work unless you get cast, and you can't get cast unless you get seen—something you're doing in spades.

Look, all jobs don't require the same level of proficiency in your craft. You probably *shouldn't* be seen for projects that require significant technique until you get some basics under your belt. How much skill is enough? That depends on the job at hand. Performing *Othello* for The Public Theater in New York is going to require a different level of acting technique than starring in a Bud Light commercial. You'll have to figure out which jobs you feel ready to tackle.

Many reps and casting people will see you once based on your look or a manager's recommendation, but if you can't deliver, they will be hesitant to see you again. You don't want to hurry out there just to make a bad first impression. Then again, it would be all kinds of ironic if you put off auditioning until you felt you were "ready," only to have such opportunities dry up and float away. And what's "ready," anyway? Your best bet may be to avoid a black-and-white perspective. While you solidify your technique, you might tackle modeling, commercials, films, television, and contemporary pieces in which the character is a lot like yourself, but hold off on roles requiring you to stretch beyond your comfort level. But don't wait too long. In art, there's no such thing as "practice makes perfect." JA

What Do You Think?

1 Why do experienced actors often discourage newcomers from entering the profession?
2 What are some of the most common career challenges new actors face?
3 Explain five steps you can take to begin your career as a professional actor.
4 What are some ways to learn more about the business of acting?
5 What are some pros and cons of doing background work?
6 Should you go to LA for pilot season? Why or why not?
7 How long does it take to build a successful acting career?
8 When is it too late to start acting? Start an acting career?
9 Do actors need to move to one of the major acting hubs (like New York or Los Angeles) before beginning a career? Why or why not?
10 What are some qualities or personality traits that would be valuable for a beginning actor to possess?

Notes

1 SAG-AFTRA—Screen Actors Guild-American Federation of Television and Radio Artists. See Chapter 9, "Unions."
2 AEA (Actors' Equity Association, often called Equity), is the actors and stage managers union for theatre projects. See Chapter 9, "Unions."
3 A "reel" is an edited collection of clips of an actor's work. These are often submitted to casting personnel who are unfamiliar with the actor.
4 Most states have a film commission website with local opportunities. Many offices can be found by a simple web search or via the directory of Association of Film Commissions International (afci) at www.afci.org/jurisdiction/wo/all
5 Most states have at least one film festival with similar opportunities.
6 In acting, "type" refers to the kinds of roles a particular actor is most likely to play. Appearance, vocal quality, and one's overall essence all have a bearing on type. More on this throughout the book.
7 CAA (Creative Artists Agency), formed in 1975, is in the very top echelon of influential and powerful talent agencies, representing A-list actors, sports figures, musicians, and other celebrities.
8 Pilot—a single episode of a proposed series, filmed as a selling tool for the show.
9 "Indie films" (also, "indies")—independent films, not produced by studios or networks.
10 University showcase—many university programs culminate in a New York and/or LA industry talent showcase for agents, managers, and other industry professionals. For more, see Chapter 2, "Training and Craft."
11 The Breakdowns are a daily listing of roles that's sent out to talent reps. See Chapter 7, "Auditions and the Casting Process."

12 An "under-five" is an on-camera role with five lines or fewer. At one point, it was an official category, with its own payscale. Now, it's used generally to describe smaller principal (speaking) roles.
13 See Chapter 10, "Scams, Shams, and Ripoffs."
14 IMDb, or Internet Movie Database, is used by many actors as a research and marketing tool. The Pro subscription grants a user more access to detailed information about listings.
15 "Equity Showcase" (or "Equity Waiver") productions fall under the union's Showcase Code, which allows Equity actors to work without pay in order to showcase themselves.
16 In the industry, "legit" refers to theatre, film, and television.

2

TRAINING AND CRAFT

Training is a vital, ongoing necessity to maintaining not only your career but your craft. Like a musician and his instrument, or an athlete and her sport, an actor must practice regularly to stay in peak shape. Acting education takes many forms, each with its own advantages.

A university education which includes acting classes can of course have general career benefits as it awards an undergraduate degree, a basic necessity for many jobs in any industry. A Bachelor of Arts, a Bachelor of Science, or a Bachelor of Fine Arts degree all meet the prerequisite for graduate school. While some actors prefer the more intensive pre-professional acting training inherent in most BFA programs, a BS or BA degree track offers a wider humanities education and leaves time to take on specialized minors that can prove helpful down the line. A widely held belief is that the specific degree you earn will affect your future employment as an actor. That is, with few exceptions, untrue. Casting professionals and agents don't take those with BFAs more seriously than those with BAs or BSs or even those with no degree at all, so don't get caught up in the letters.

Many actors continue their college training in graduate programs, earning masters of fine arts degrees. An MFA in acting is what's known as a "terminal degree"—the highest academic degree available in the field—and is a minimum requirement for most academic jobs, including university faculty positions. Some programs, like Yale School of Drama, are widely respected and do open doors. Most are lesser-known and don't provide graduates with powerful name recognition. Training varies widely and—as we will discuss—it's important to look closely into what a program has on offer before signing up. Many MFA programs will arrange industry showcase performances, introducing their graduates to talent representatives and casting professionals through an evening of scenes, monologues, and songs. These are not all created equally (more prestigious schools draw more attendees) so again, it's important to do specific research before enrolling.

There are, of course, alternatives to the college route. Industry hubs (like New York, Los Angeles, and Chicago) are bursting with private acting classes, offering ongoing training in scene study, auditioning, on-camera, improv, and other specific techniques. Some actors find it advantageous to skip graduate school—or even undergrad—and head straight into the trenches, training privately and on the job.

Most markets also offer numerous types of one-night, weekend, or day-long classes. While some of these provide valuable training by experts, others (often advertised as casting director or agent "workshops") serve as paid meet-and-greets, regarding which there has been a long, passionate debate over ethics and legality. More on that in Chapter 6, "Marketing: Promotion and Networking."

Training is an ongoing focus for many performers, but there is no one-size-fits-all solution.

Questions and Answers

Dear Jackie,

I was wondering, what schools do you recommend for acting training? I got accepted into a well-known Los Angeles acting school. I did my homework on the school and looked at the alumni who went there and they are working, but I have heard some negative reviews about it. How do I know where to study?

—Choices

Dear Choices,

I don't recommend specific acting schools because I know—from experience—that what works for one artist may be anathema for another. When I graduated college I set out for a "top ten" MFA program. The university and its acting program were well-known, well-reviewed, and offered me a fellowship to boot. Unfortunately, I hated the program. It wasn't that the school lacked interesting and relevant courses, or that the training wasn't decent, but I could not stand the general "vibe" of the place—for lack of a better word. The school and I were not a good match.

The next year I began a different MFA program, at a similarly ranked school in another state. My experience was entirely different, and entirely positive.

I can't say exactly why the second school was so much better than the first and I am well aware that others might disagree. I just know I was going insane at school #1 and thrived at school #2.

In your decision, research—the homework you mentioned—is crucial. Remember that the alumni a school touts as representative are really the lucky few with recognizable faces. Dig deeper. Along with reading all you can about a program, talk to both graduates and current students to get their input. Exactly what are you after in your training? Do you want a school that devotes years to classical material or one that offers intensive on-camera work? Compare prices. Many public institutions offer conservatory-style training at a fraction of the cost of private conservatories, while some private schools do not grant academic degrees.

Perhaps the most valuable commodity an acting program can offer is connectivity. After graduating from an institution, you will know the instructors—who, presumably will have their own contacts and do at least occasional professional work—and more importantly, other up-and-coming actors. It may seem counterintuitive that bonding with a bunch of other starving-artists-to-be will help your career, but there's really nothing else as valuable. After several years of intense joint training, your future class is very likely to advocate for each other as they climb the professional ladder; doing shows together, referring each other to agents and directors, casting each other in projects, and introducing each other to connections. You'll also hold a soft spot in the heart of your school's alumni who are probably several rungs up that ladder, if not at the top.

What about location? Consider choosing a school inside an entertainment industry hub. Studying in the city you want to work in assures that any non-school contacts you make can benefit you after graduation.

My final piece of advice is the most essential. Visit any school in which you consider enrolling. Audit classes, take a tour, and chat with faculty, staff, and administrators. Watch the students as they move from class to class. Even just parking in the school's lot or taking the subway to its stop will be an education. Listen to your instincts. And be on guard for a hard sell. If you get one, walk away. JA

Dear Michael,

I'm going to be a junior in college, studying for my BFA in Theatre Arts. I love my program. It gets me on stage in multiple shows a semester and gives me opportunities to grow as much as possible. There's only one problem: it's in the middle of the USA (in Lincoln, NE), far from the coasts and professional acting opportunities. I live in Wisconsin, which has more theatre opportunities, but I'm only there in summer. I see people my age on TV and in films and wonder, if

I was in New York or LA, if that couldn't be me. Might it be more advantageous for me to attempt to get closer to the centers of industry? I could either transfer to a different college, or just quit school and start my career. I've heard of people being able to jump right into the game, get a support job, and make it without a degree. But it also seems like getting a college degree in NY would give me a foot in the door when I graduate.

Sometimes I feel like everything I'm learning in class is useless when I seem unable to apply it to getting a job.
  —Ready to Move

Dear Ready,
  I say it a lot, because people need the reminder: our business is unpredictable, everyone's experience is different, and it's rare to find a reliable, scientific pattern. You ask whether to continue at your college, transfer, or drop out and seek work. There are actors who've found success along each of those paths, and actors who've found failure. So, no conclusions to be drawn there, I'm afraid.

But let's assess. Here's what you've got: a known versus an unknown. You've told me that you *love* your current college program, and that it gets you on stage a lot. And you wonder whether that training will have value when it comes time to audition for paying work? Of course it will. Each time you play a role, you solve acting challenges. You improve the skills you need for auditioning: breaking down scenes, figuring out what drives characters, making choices, the whole process! You're becoming more and more adept at playing various kinds of material. You're building your confidence, gaining authority as an actor. All that will *undoubtedly* serve you in your career.

You're right: moving to a major market would put you near opportunities you now lack. You're also right that some actors your age are already working. You never know; maybe you're missing all kinds of opportunities. Or—more likely, I'm afraid—you could move to the big city, and sit in your apartment, wondering how to get seen amidst the vast sea of actors.

Keep in mind, moving presents a new set of challenges: Those cities are expensive; you'd need a plan for paying the bills. Yes, auditions might be happening, but would you have access to them? You might need an agent who can get you in the door, and finding an agent is among the more challenging tasks beginning actors face. There's also more competition, and of a higher caliber. I'm not suggesting for a moment that it's a bad idea. Only that you take a realistic look at what you'd gain and what you wouldn't. In spite of the daunting challenges, young actors who choose this path are sometimes overjoyed to have done so.

But with just two years to go, finishing college sounds to me like a much better idea than jumping ship and diving into the deep ocean of professional show business. As far as whether to transfer to a college in New York or LA, why not do some research, narrow down your choices, apply, and see where you're accepted? Transferring might indeed be a great step toward that transition. Then, by the time you graduate, you'll know the city, and you will have learned a bit about how the business operates there. And if you're not accepted to the school you want, stay put, and trust that the training you're getting will serve you well when you make the big move later on.

If I've succeeded in confusing you, you're probably getting a much clearer sense of just how unpredictable the actor's life can be. Ultimately, you have to make choices by educated guess without necessarily knowing the results. MK

Dear Jackie,
I am currently a student at a university in Los Angeles. I have always wanted to pursue acting and theatre. Do nonunion play directors usually work around the actor's schedule, or would I have to work around their schedules? Wouldn't it be best to leave school for a semester and see what may come my way? I am worried about risking tarnishing my transcript, because acting is such an unstable profession.
—Beckoned by Break

Dear Break,
Most non-Equity—which usually means non-paying—theatre gigs do make an effort to work within the constraints of actors' schedules. The difficulty comes from the diversity of those schedules. Many actors wait tables or bartend, leaving them free to rehearse during the day. Others, like yourself, are students or work at offices and have free time in the evening. For the low-budget production, creating a rehearsal schedule that will work for everyone is a puzzle.

However, there is no reason for you to feel compelled to take time off of school as you begin auditioning. Any rational, non-paying producer will expect you to have other commitments and ask for your rehearsal conflicts at the initial audition or callback. If not, ask about the rehearsal schedule yourself. In the rare case that it is set in stone, you will need to carefully consider what accepting a role in the production would mean for your school commitments. Would the show cause you to miss just two or three sessions or numerous weeks of class? If the latter, perhaps it would be better to thank the producers, value your audition experience, and keep submitting.

If you are fortunate enough to be cast in a well-paying or more visible production, your choice may be more difficult. It will depend on the role, the pay, and most importantly, where you are in your education. But don't worry too much about such a choice right now; weigh the specifics when you get the opportunity. JA

Dear Michael,

My agent recently sent out a referral to a group of teachers who call themselves "master talent teachers." I know there are classes on every corner and I need to do my *own* homework before selecting which ones to check out. But aside from popularity, what criteria should I look for in acting teachers? And are they required to have credentials?

—Torn About Teachers

Dear TAT,

When an agent or manager recommends a particular teacher, coach, photographer, or any other service, my eyebrow arches just a tad. It's not necessarily a sign of something unethical, but it is something to be viewed judiciously—perhaps even skeptically. The time-honored rule is, it's fine for agents to offer *lists* of their preferred teachers, coaches, photographers, and so on. But if they're sending all their clients to the same providers, well . . . that can raise suspicions of nasty things like kickbacks, nepotism, bartering, and other unseemly practices. I briefly had a less-than-reputable agent who made all his clients get their headshots retouched by the same person. It was all very clandestine: leave the shots and payment outside the door, collect the photos a few days later. No one-on-one contact with the retoucher. Big surprise, she was the agent's girlfriend.

Acting teachers don't need to be certified, credentialed, or vetted. Anyone can hang out a shingle. And there's nothing regulating price. So it's the old Latin adage, *caveat emptor* ("let the buyer beware") that applies. While I'm certainly not suggesting anything sinister about these recommended instructors, I do suggest checking out *any* potential teachers for yourself, applying your own criteria. Ask around, and audit classes that interest you.

What should you look for? Look for an atmosphere where you think you can grow—make sure you're not the most accomplished student in class; you want to study alongside at least a few people who have more experience and training than you have. Look for a teacher who speaks a language you understand; a style and technique that make sense to you. And look for a dynamic that'll be conducive to learning. For example, if the teacher intimidates you, or doesn't inspire your respect, you might have a difficult time absorbing what he or she has to teach. The teacher may have a reputation for brilliance and amazing results, but if you're uncomfortable, untrusting, or unimpressed, all the reputation or popularity in the world isn't going to enable you to learn. On the other hand, if a class makes you feel challenged and a bit nervous, it's well worth considering. MK

Dear Jackie,

I recently took a commercial acting class and the casting director told me, "the camera doesn't catch a commercial sparkle on you." What did he mean and how can I get better?

—Dull

Dear Dull,

To be blunt about your so-called feedback: it was stupid.

Find a supportive, skilled teacher whose comments will actually stimulate your growth. Stay away from anyone offering tired clichés instead of active assistance. The last thing any actor needs is to be told they lack some ephemeral, mysterious quality that the "teacher" is too inexperienced to put into workable, active instruction. JA

Dear Jackie,

I feel like taking classes is a great way to exercise my acting muscles when I'm not working. I often take one class that lasts six-to-ten weeks right after another, and do casting director workshops in between. But the cost is adding up and the training section of my résumé is starting to get longer than my credits. I feel isolated if I'm not taking a class, but I feel like new headshots or a new reel might be more beneficial. What do you suggest?

—Too Much Training

Dear Training,

In a perfect world where money was no object, I'd say you should always be in an ongoing, intensive technique class as well as a rotating rep of courses designed to help you with specific skills like sitcom, commercial, voice-over, and singing. But while classes are crucial in keeping performers well-tuned, headshots and reels aren't luxuries. If you need to update your marketing tools, do it.

To combat the isolation you mentioned, join a theatre company. Beyond providing an artistic outlet and introducing you to like-minded artists, some companies offer member benefits such as workshops and readings. Even going to company meetings and taking tickets at performances can yield surprising educational opportunities. Spend some time researching companies in your area. Look for groups that are open to new members, do work you respect, and express an artistic point of view you want to get behind. Ask how you can get involved. While you'll want to get back into class when finances permit, it's possible your theatre company will keep your acting muscles in shape during your break. JA

Dear Jackie,

My biggest worry when I act is that it doesn't sound right, and today during rehearsal my fear was confirmed. During notes my director—who is also my acting teacher—told me to work on sounding less "acty." I nodded graciously and wrote down the note on my script. After notes, I left for my car and tried not to cry.

This is something I love doing and I really want to be good at it. It means a lot to me. How do you work on sounding more natural, or conversational? People tell me to think of how I sound in real life, but when I talk to my friends I get carried away in the actual conversation and forget to take notes on it.
   —Acty

Dear Acty,

"Sound less 'acty'" is not an act-able instruction. It's rather harsh criticism, actually, which is why you felt so bad. And it's a result-oriented direction, which took you out of your work and put your attention on yourself instead of on what you—or your character—was doing in the world of the script. You shouldn't be worrying about what you sound like, just focusing with all your might on what your character wants and how you can get it. The less you focus on yourself and the more you focus on your scene partner the better.

Reread the last sentence of your question: "People tell me to think of how I sound in real life, but when I talk to my friends I get carried away in the actual conversation and I forget to take notes on it." There's your answer. When you are as carried away with your scene as you are with your life, you'll sound natural.

In the meantime, consider adding another teacher to your class load. I'm not saying to drop this one yet; maybe he was just having a bad day. But branch out in your attack on your craft. You need someone who can help you stop watching, and listening, to yourself. JA

Dear Michael,

I've heard again and again that funny can't be taught. As a not-that-funny actor myself, I find that theory pretty frustrating. Are there no comedic acting classes? There has to be a way for me to at least improve. And meanwhile, if I get an audition for something that's supposed to be funny, what do I do? Turn it down?
   —Drama Queen

Dear DQ,

No! As an audition coach, I often have the enjoyable task of helping clients work on comedic material. Like you, some don't think of themselves as funny. But I'm stubborn in my belief that there's more than one key to the comedy door, and I love helping actors solve that puzzle. Though there are things that can't be taught (some actors are just instinctively funny), here are some things to consider as you work on comedic material:

First and foremost, find the honesty. Truthful commitment to comedic circumstances is funny. Some actors think playing comedy means forgoing basic acting homework. Not so. Knowing and inhabiting your character's objectives, stakes, obstacles, state of mind, philosophy, relationships, and circumstances is crucial. You must also understand the time period, location, and attendant customs. Good comedy honors these fundamentals.

Figure out your character's job in the story. This is important. The humor might depend on your character's cleverness or, conversely, his gullibility. You might be driving the comedy, or just reacting to a funny character. Look at the big picture and see what best serves the comedic equation.

And then, there are certain recurring elements in comedy. Once you understand what particular devices are being used in the writing, you'll know better how to play a scene. Here are but a few of the many possibilities to look for when you dive into your script:

- —Disproportion (an extreme reaction to a small problem; a small reaction to a huge problem; lots of effort for an easy task; little effort for a great task)
- —Lack of self-awareness (an unattractive character who thinks he's irresistibly good looking; a drunk who thinks she's behaving normally)
- —Awkwardness created by societal expectations (trying to stay awake while a talkative dinner guest overstays his welcome, hiding an embarrassing stain at an important job interview)
- —Skewed status (a bossy secretary, a wimpy king, a snobby beggar)
- —Someone in the wrong job (a self-centered psychotherapist, a squeamish nurse, a tone-deaf back-up singer)
- —Incongruity—qualities that don't seem to match (a nun who swears, a sensitive gang member)
- —Recognizable human foibles (nervousness about asking someone out, melting at the sight of a baby, craving food while on a diet, not making sense first thing in the morning)
- —Non-compatibility/cultural differences (*The Odd Couple*, *My Cousin Vinny*, a hippie type in an Amish home, a shy tech nerd in a rap battle)

—Dealing with temporary afflictions (drunkenness, sunburn, allergic reactions, tooth pain)
—Neuroses (irrational fears, insecurities, schizophrenia, obsessions, control issues)

It's a fascinating and never-ending study. Comedic acting classes exist, but they're not as common as others. For now, start by watching comedies analytically and figuring out what makes a funny situation funny. And by all means, don't decline comedic auditions. You might be funnier than you think. MK

Dear Jackie,

I am in a really expensive, very demanding scene study class with a well-respected teacher. Right now, I am teamed up with another actor who is beloved of the teacher. Everything he does is gold in her eyes. Whenever he presents a scene, she praises him to high heaven and pretty much ignores the other actor.

I'm not really a jealous person and this wouldn't usually bug me very much, but this actor is being really flakey about rehearsing. He's already cancelled our rehearsals two times, and the one time we did meet he left after forty-five minutes because he said he had other plans. He is one of those people who thinks they are extremely talented and after only a few run-throughs is like, "Okay that was great, we got it, bye!" I'm not a rehearsal Nazi, but at the same time I know when a scene is garbage, and I don't like getting up in front of people and just embarrassing myself.

I guess he isn't worried about getting grilled by the teacher since he's her pet, but I am! Also I am really frustrated about not getting my money's worth for my work in the class. Is there anything I can do to fix this?
—Frustrated

Dear Frustrated,

It sounds like it's too late for me to help with your current rehearsal situation, which is headed—you guessed it—to a presentation of an ill-rehearsed scene in which your partner is praised and you are ignored.

For the sake of argument however: is that really so bad? It's not unlike the proverbial "real world"—unfair! In the course of your career, you'll be paired up with all sorts of folks—flakey, driven, narcissistic, generous, and downright abusive. That's the nature of freelance work, especially for actors, and one of a working actor's skills needs to be navigating the tricky terrain of other performers. Many will be focused and hardworking, but others will stretch your patience. Some will insist you rehearse for days on end and kill all spontaneity in a scene, while others will need to "keep it fresh" beyond your comfort level. Some will be just plain bad. Sometimes you'll be auditioning with casting assistants or interns who rush and stumble through every line. Even after landing a role, you may be asked to do your close-ups talking to a stand-in, or a C-stand.[1] In other words, you have to forget about everyone else and worry about your own performance in your professional life—you may as well start now.

Use this situation to practice preparing a scene without a scene partner— something you *will* have to do in the future, especially if you go on to a film and television career. Prep your role meticulously with maximum flexibility, since your presentation is likely to be heavy on spontaneity. It's kind of like an improv scene with scripted dialogue—what a good challenge.

You didn't mention whether you choose your own scene partners in this class, or if the teacher pairs you up. If the latter, wait until the scene is over and then tactfully approach the teacher and explain the situation. Don't "tattle" on your partner, just let her know that you'd like to work with someone else in the future. If she excuses his behavior or, worse, suggests you take your chances to bask in his glory, you'll know it's time to find another course. From what you've said about her attitude about her star pupil, it may be that time already. JA

Dear Jackie,

My acting teacher spends a lot of time talking to us about our personal lives and figuring out how to use them in our monologues and scenes. Sometimes I feel like he goes too far in his questioning. I think he's a nice person, and really felt connected when he was working with me, but I worry that this is not a healthy situation.

—It's Personal

Dear Personal,

Generally I'd say that if you feel like a teacher is going "too far" in the personal arena, you're probably right.

Many popular acting techniques employ delving into one's feelings and history, but in the wrong hands such methods can be destructive. Requiring actors to reveal the specifics of painful events is wrong-headed and possibly dangerous. Yes, using affective memory,[2] an actor might reveal that he is using a painful event from his past, but he doesn't sit down and tell the story. He doesn't say, "I am using the time that my father beat me." The instructor doesn't say, "A painful experience? Tell us all about it!"

Working responsibly, a teacher might help an actor make a connection between a past event and his work by having him recall the color of the carpet and the smell of the coffee on that painful day—the basis of sense memory is the recall of these sensory experiences that hold our emotions—but the student shouldn't be asked, or permitted, to reveal personal details. The instructor should by no means act as therapist, psychoanalyzing the past of the student, or prescribing remedies for emotional trauma. Beware of instructors who say things like, "Perhaps that's why you're so guarded. Just let that old hurt go!"

I have witnessed several such inappropriate interactions. In one, a guest teacher pushed a classmate of mine to talk about the recent death of a parent. The student repeatedly refused to use the event, saying he wasn't ready, but the instructor shamed him into giving it a try by saying things like, "What are you afraid of?" The result: the scene was extremely moving and emotional, but it wasn't acting. Watching it, I felt sick. In another class I observed, the instructor had the students pick real fights with one another and when they were fully engaged in lambasting each other's failures as actors and shortcomings as scene partners, he shouted, "Go!" and they began the scene. Again, those actors were feeling lots and lots of stuff—but it wasn't acting.

You say that you have felt connected to your work under this teacher. Is this connection something you can create in future performances or was it a one-time provocation? Anyone can make someone cry. It takes a lot more skill to teach someone to act. JA

Dear Jackie,

I recently graduated from a college that has a small acting conservatory within its theatre major. It's a really competitive program, and they cut people along the way. If you get cut, you end up with a BA in theatre. If you finish the conservatory, you get a BFA in acting. The teachers would always tell us that the "cream rises to the top." Well, I got cut, so I guess I'm not the cream. Nonetheless, I have just graduated with a BA and am determined to make it.

What do I do about my degree? I feel like I need to go to graduate school so I can show people I have had good training and that I can compete with the actors who didn't get cut. What do you think?

—Missing the F

Dear Missing,

Almost no one outside of your campus knows anything about the way your department rewards its degrees or manages its actors' training program. And even if they did, I can't imagine they would care.

If you'd like to focus solely on your craft for a few years, or really want the conservatory experience you missed, an MFA program might suit you. But if you are just looking for good, solid training, there's no reason you can't get that through private acting classes—and you can take those while pursuing your career. While a BFA program might seem like a résumé booster, the name of a respected acting coach would do just as much to show you are serious about your work.

Consider too, that while you've been in college you may have begun to see the world from the perspective of your acting teachers and peers. Being "cut" was probably a pretty unhappy experience—one that likely took a toll on your confidence. Remember though, that any college or institution is just a tiny, random sampling of the varied opinions and values of the larger acting community. You may not have been a big fish in that little pond, but you learned valuable lessons about rejection and perseverance that will serve you.

As for the cream rising to the top? That's hogwash. That tired old phrase is just another unfortunate and meaningless cliché perpetuated to make those doing the choosing feel better about themselves. After all, if the cream rises to the top, their actions aren't to blame for your disappointment—their choices are just part of natural selection! Humbug.

Look, you aren't competing against those other actors—the ones who didn't get cut—anymore. You're now competing with every other actor on the face of the planet. And guess what? You have just as much right to be here as anyone else. JA

Dear Michael,

For so many years, I've been looking for ways to be an actor. That wasn't that easy seeing that I live in Conyers, Georgia. Well fortunately for me, this year I got lucky. Over the summer, I visited New York. One of my dad's friends there happened to be a member of SAG-AFTRA (just my luck!), and gave me some information about acting opportunities in NY. I did my research and went on a few auditions and got cast in a student film, a few extras jobs, and a nonunion play, and I also took a few classes and attended seminars. I was psyched! I couldn't believe that in a blink of an eye I had so many opportunities at my fingertips.

But I have a dilemma. I have so many family members giving me different advice that I'm confused. I don't want to take out a million loans to finish my degree in acting when I can just attend classes in New York, and I definitely don't want college to get in the way of what I love to do. I'm also back in Georgia where there aren't as many opportunities, and the last thing I want is for things to stall, especially seeing that I've waited so long to even get this far! How do I keep this momentum going?

—Beyond Confused

Dear Beyond Confused,

I need to caution you: the opportunities you've described, while wonderful, aren't the equivalent of a blinking neon light declaring, YOU DON'T NEED COLLEGE! YOU'RE ON YOUR WAY! Extra work, student films and a non-union play are great, accessible gigs for beginners. Be careful about interpreting them as signs from the heavens. This is a moment in your life when it would be very wise to step back and assess the big picture.

While I have no wish to demean the input from your family, it's far more ben-eficial for you to gather information from working professional actors. And even with them, take each opinion with a grain of salt—actors love to express ideas, informed or otherwise. But I believe you may be able to get some very valuable insight from fellow actors who've faced similar decisions so you can pursue your calling . . . judiciously. MK

Dear Jackie,

I'm 21 years old and going into my final year of college. If everything goes well, I'll be graduating as a theatre major this summer. I'm curious to hear your input as to where I should go from there. Do you see much difference in actors who have gone to graduate school as opposed to the ones who don't?

I don't feel like I learned enough in college to be competitive in the real world. That could be my neurosis talking, but I'm curious. Would I learn more taking the plunge into working-actor-land, or continuing on with some post-graduate work?
—Grad School or School of Life

Dear Grad or Life,

It depends on what you want to learn.

It's likely you'll learn more about acting technique, history, voice, speech, move-ment, dialects, and dance in a graduate program. There, you'll have the chance to study nothing but your craft all day long—and half the night too. Besides what you'll learn, the simple opportunity to put your head and your heart fully into acting—without the pressures of making a living breathing down your neck—is an incredible gift. It may be some time before you can devote yourself so whole-heartedly to acting again. Some schools offer stipends and grants, so don't let money deter you from auditioning. But this is not a "now or never" situation. If more school doesn't excite you right now, you can always apply at a later time. You may actually get more out of it with a little life experience under your belt.

Launching straight into "working-actor-land," as you put it, sends you right into the midst of your own professional trajectory. Certainly you'll learn much more about the *business* of acting outside of a school setting. Another perk to jumping into the professional waters early? Your youth. Not to say you'll be over the hill at 24 (most grad programs are three years), but 21 is a very marketable age.

You said you don't feel as if you've learned enough in your undergrad program to be competitive in the "real world." That's probably the best argument you could make for more training. Whether in an academic setting or through private classes in the city of your choice, keep studying your craft. JA

Dear Jackie,

After finishing college I planned on taking a year off to act but now I'm really considering applying for MFA programs. What is the audition process like? Is there an interview involved? If so, what are some of the typical interview questions that are asked? Do you have any audition tips?

—Making it to MFA

Dear MFA,

The most expansive MFA audition is through the University/Resident Theatre Association, or U/RTA. This audition gives you the most bang for your buck, with a flat fee of about $100 to audition in front of numerous MFA program representatives. Individual schools outside of U/RTA, like NYU and Columbia, usually charge about $80–$100 apiece and some require on-campus callbacks, which means plane tickets and hotels. While a top school, like Yale, might be worth the extra expense, audition costs can add up quickly.

My problem with U/RTA is the very thing that makes it convenient and affordable—it's so darn big. You can't be sure the school you are targeting has a representative in the room during your read. That's because U/RTA auditions go on for hours, and auditors leave the auditorium to go to the bathroom, get coffee, and make calls. Reps from some schools may actually skip West Coast auditions if they've filled their upcoming classes on the New York and Chicago stops. Still, if the schools you are interested in are members, U/RTAs provide massive exposure and may present opportunities that would otherwise have remained unknown. Go to urta.com to see a list of participating programs.

Actor Elizabeth Taheri says,

> My biggest piece of advice—I wish I knew it then—is to focus on schools that are in the part of the country where you want to work. Not just the region—but right there. My school in South Carolina gave me a pitch about being on the East Coast and said they got a lot of NY actors down as guest teachers. And yes, we had a few people from NY come down, but if I were to move to NY and think my school had any pull, I'd be sorely mistaken.

As far as auditioning, she continues, "Start with your strongest piece and show off your strengths."

I couldn't agree more. Auditors are more interested in your essential qualities than seeing you stretch. Why watch a 20-year-old struggling with Lady Macbeth when they could see her excel at Juliet?

Whatever you do, please—for the love of god—don't do a "climactic moment" piece for this or any audition, monologuing the emotional peak of a play with lots of crying or yelling. Skip hot-button issues and pieces about breasts, penises, vaginas, rape, abortion, suicide, assault, abuse, murder, genocide, infanticide, or incest. Trust me. Your auditors haven't been on the play's journey with you and can't "get there" in one minute (and neither, probably, can you).

Most auditions will limit your overall time to three or four minutes, meaning each piece should be two minutes or less. Choose pieces well within the limit so you aren't hurrying nervously along—some will cut you off. Better to leave them wanting more than wondering when you will stop talking.

Unlike auditions for single projects, MFA auditors are selecting students for three-year programs in which they will spend countless hours with their chosen class. They are looking for talent, but they are also trying to put together an amiable, exciting ensemble that will be able to work well together—and with themselves—over the long haul. This means no matter how good you are, you might not be chosen if you seem high-maintenance or are too similar to other students they have chosen. You can't control the latter, but you can be sure to present yourself in a positive light. You want to be seen as an energetic and enthusiastic optimist. This applies to your audition persona, but more importantly, to your interview.

If you get a chance to sit down with representatives from a few schools, be sure to research them beforehand so you can have a well-informed and productive conversation. Prepare, too, for the standard questions like, "What kind of program are you looking for?" and "Tell us a little bit about yourself." They'll want to get to know you and what it would be like to work with you for three long years. Whatever you do, be sure not to complain about anyone or anything. Negativity is a big turn off. Instead, use the time to express your excitement. Don't play it cool. Go ahead and gush about how wonderful their program is and what a great thrill it would be for you to attend. It may sound cheesy, but if it's true, why hide it? When push comes to shove, they'll know that you—unlike some other actors they meet—really, really want to work with them. That may go a long way.

Finally, make sure an MFA is what you really want. "I think it's really important to ask yourself why you're going to graduate school and what you hope to get out of it," says actor Gwyn Fawcett McColl:

I knew a number of students who were really hoping for business information, but our program was all about the training and truthful acting. We didn't have a great on-camera class and our Preparing for the Profession class was geared towards careers in regional theatre. I was thrilled with what I took away in terms of my craft, but I didn't really feel prepared for the business.

This is a common complaint. I don't know of a single graduate program that makes the profession a serious focus of their curriculum. Many do graduation showcases, which vary in quality and success, but generally MFA programs are all about acting. Before you decide to enroll, be sure you are after further training as a craftsman, and not hoping for an industry edge.

As for your erstwhile plan to take a year off before applying to graduate school, you may have been onto something there. Many programs prefer actors with a little real-world experience under their belts. And after a year in the field, you're likely to have a better handle on whether grad school is truly your best option and, if so, which programs you want to pursue. JA

Dear Jackie,

I am looking into apprenticeships/internships and trying to figure out their costs. Programs like Actor's Theatre of Louisville are tuition-free, but cost of living is not covered. Are there scholarship or loan options for people like me, who would love the experience and networking opportunities of an apprenticeship, but can't live off of savings for ten months? There are two others in particular I am interested in: the Acting Fellowship at The Shakespeare Theatre Company in D.C. and the Emerging Professional Residency program at the Milwaukee Repertory.

—Apprentice in Waiting

Dear Apprentice,

There doesn't appear to be a quick and easy solution for actors pursuing a year of networking and training in an apprenticeship, internship, or fellowship. I spoke to a few actors who have completed such programs and they all talked about it being a hard but worthwhile experience. It sounds like most actors either save up enough money ahead of time to get them through the season or pull in extra money through side jobs—whether doing non-acting work at the theatre company or waiting tables on their limited time off. Some even seek public assistance, like food stamps.

I contacted the three companies you mentioned to get more specifics.

"I believe that internships and apprenticeships are an amazing way to bridge the gap between educational theatre and the professional world," says Michael

Legg, the director of the Professional Training Company at the Actors Theatre of Louisville:

> I understand that the commitment to programs like ours can be a financial burden on the young artists who choose to undertake them. However, when looked at as an investment, the returns—the contacts, experience and, in our case, a full season of shows, including a specially commissioned work for the apprentices in the Humana Festival of New American Plays—can be huge.

The Louisville program charges no tuition of any sort, so there are no direct costs to its apprentices and interns. The program has also received a generous gift from the Roy Cockrum foundation which gives every member of the company $5000 to cover expenses for the year, with no strings attached. Louisville helps actors find convenient, low-cost housing (within walking distance to the theatre) and, if necessary, assists recent graduates in getting their student loans deferred while they complete the program.

Dat Ngo, the Associate Director of Education at the Shakespeare Theatre Company in D.C. says that in his five seasons with the company, he has yet to see an acting Fellow fail to make the arrangement work:

> Some find Monday night gigs—in our call center or with special events. Some look outside of the company for work in the service industry. Others come prepared with a savvy financial plan to survive on the small stipend provided and company-furnished, rent-free housing.

Even with free housing, Ngo acknowledges balancing the fellowship requirements with financial needs can be hard work:

> It's an Equity rehearsal and performance schedule and it can prove quite challenging for young and early career actors, but the payoff is significant. Fellows get to work under directors like Michael Kahn, Gale Edwards, and Robert Falls and alongside artists such as Stacy Keach, Elizabeth Ashley, and Michael Hayden. They get a full season of mainstage acting credits and numerous opportunities for mentorship.

The internship program at Milwaukee Rep also offers a stipend and free housing within walking distance to the theatre, but as Associate Artistic Director Brent Hazelton explains,

> The schedule is quite demanding at upwards of 60 hours per week, which allows no time for any kind of outside employment. The program is

designed to be one of complete immersion in the season of a major regional theatre, so taking time away from that to work also waters down the experience for the individual intern.

Even so, Hazelton points out that there are occasionally ways to make a few extra bucks through opportunities with the theatre:

> We have a nice relationship with a local commercial agency, and many interns are able to bolster their finances by pursuing some of that work. The cost of living in Milwaukee is significantly lower than that on the coasts or in Chicago. Most interns spend the summers before they join us establishing a financial cushion, and everyone finds a way to make it work.

If you get a chance to do so, I'm sure you will too. JA

Dear Michael,

I wanted to ask for your advice on researching and joining theatre companies. For all the positive things I hear about joining a theatre company (camaraderie, common goals, honing your craft), I've also heard about scams and dues, and honestly, I don't know where to start. Any advice for an unrepresented actor looking for a theatre company and how to join?

—Orphan Artist

Dear Orphan,

As with so many things in our profession, quizzing colleagues you respect is the very best place to start. Our network is pretty amazing, and I find it usually doesn't take much more than three degrees of separation before you track down just the source or recommendation you're seeking. It's pretty difficult to evaluate a theatre company based on just an ad or a website, but someone acquainted with it firsthand can really lay out its assets and deficits for you.

Failing that, there are other ways to check out your potential theatre family. Look up the company's online reviews; consistent pans or raves can tell you a lot. Go see a show or two. If possible, speak with the artistic director or a current member. Ask about membership requirements and benefits—dues aren't uncommon, but you'll want to know whether they're affordable before growing too attached. See if there are perks like access to rehearsal space, or opportunities to write, direct, or produce. And if there's anything unethical going on, it can be unearthed by a bit of investigating.

Not only does the company need to be legit, affordable, and penetrable (some of them are locked up tight and it's nearly impossible to get in) but it has to be a match in terms of style. Some companies emphasize the classics; some focus on being socially conscious; some tend to do original plays; some like the more experimental, abstract stuff. Do you like the company's productions? Its level of talent? Its performance space? Its mission statement? It may take a bit of work, but the research is pretty fun.

Once you find a company or companies you like, you have to see whether they like you. There's usually an audition involved, and you may need to volunteer for a while (ushering or working in the box office, for example) before becoming eligible to join. This is a good way to get to know the company and see if it's a match. Often your best way in is by recommendation, which also means you'll have at least one friend in the group.

There are pros and cons to joining a theatre company. On the one hand, there might be dues, and you can pretty much be assured you'll never get paid. On the other hand, you might get to do great work with great actors, develop your abilities, and feel like part of a family. MK

Dear Jackie,

I have heard that having a respected acting coach on your résumé is very important as far as agents and casting directors go. I am in New York City and I attended a respected acting studio long ago, but I don't have any well-known teacher names on my résumé. Although I have been at this for quite a while, it's very difficult to understand exactly what the CDs and the agents are looking for.

—Nameless

Dear Nameless,

CDs and agents usually care very little about where and with whom you've studied. They're more interested in whether you can deliver a competent, marketable performance and are a sane and professional human being. But having a well-known teacher on your résumé might occasionally get you a second look—even shuffle you into the "yes" pile—so it's a question worth asking.

There's a difference between lining your résumé with well-respected names and finding a teacher who fits your learning style, with enough time to give you individual attention. Some big-name acting coaches teach in large group settings, where individual actors get very little personal attention. While watching and listening are important parts of training, it's hard to learn acting with a predominantly hands-off approach. Most people in the industry know about these lecture-style classes, and take these teachers' names on a résumé with a grain of salt. Besides, the acting world is very small. It's best that a follow-up call made by a casting director to a teacher on your résumé isn't met with, "Who?"

As for finding out which teachers are viewed with respect, you'll have to do some legwork. New York, Los Angeles, Austin, Denver, Seattle . . . every city has its list—and that list is constantly changing. The best way to find a great teacher who fits your learning style is to ask around, look up possibilities online on sites like backstage.com, and to audit (that is, sit in on a class—usually free of charge—to get a better idea of how the teacher operates before you plunk down your cash).

I contacted an acting teacher who recently managed a private studio in New York. He warned against seeking out someone for the benefit of your résumé. "It's been my experience that a CD is just as likely to be turned off because of a specific name on a résumé as turned on," he says.

> I always caution against trying to figure out who the latest 'hot' teacher is. You might think you're studying with someone trendy—but maybe the CD just saw one of your classmates audition and it was awful. I believe that a teacher's reputation among their students is much more valuable than trying to figure out the reaction of a casting director, who for the most part doesn't care who you have studied with as long as you appear professional and show some imagination.

"Putting down the name of a teacher is much like putting down the name of a director, theatre company, or college," he continued.

> If the CD knows the name, it's likely to produce a bit of conversation that will help the CD remember your name and face ('Oh, she was the girl who went to Northwestern' or 'He's the guy who studied voice with Kristin Linklater'). It's potentially helpful, but there is no 'magic' name, person, or institution that is going to get your name to the top of the list. And take into account that 'hot' may equal hype. If you're studying with a teacher who has been around a long time—Michael Howard, William Esper, Ivana Chubbuck, Larry Moss, Terry Schreiber—that would certainly indicate to a CD that you are serious about your craft, but if you are in one of those classes then you've likely already got a fairly impressive résumé to begin with.

You mentioned studying acting "long ago." No line on a résumé is going to make up for what you'll lack in the room if you don't keep in practice. Do your research, pick five possible teachers based on your personal criteria, audit, and get into a class before the end of the month. JA

Dear Jackie,
   I have been taking acting and vocal classes with the same instructor for about a year, but now I want to do vocals with him and study acting with another instructor.

This person was my first acting teacher and I like him a lot on a personal level, but I feel stagnant in the class. Thinking about leaving gives me this immense feeling of betrayal. He has done an awful lot for me and even though I will still be working with him I feel bad. Does everyone get this feeling when changing instructors? This new acting teacher I am considering comes very highly recommended. I am excited about seeing if he can take me to another level or give me a different perspective, but I feel guilty.

—Climbing

Dear Climbing,

Choosing an acting teacher, and managing that relationship for better or worse, is a highly personal affair, between you and your teacher, and perhaps, eventually, your representative. If you feel stagnant in your current class, it's probably time to make a change. I asked a few highly esteemed instructors to comment on your moving-on guilt.

Well-known Los Angeles acting teacher and author of *The Power of the Actor: The Chubbuck Technique*, Ivana Chubbuck says,

> There's a special bond an acting teacher has with their students. An acting teacher requires, even more than a therapist, access into an actor's private and most innermost secrets. Not to heal, as a therapist would, but rather to use [these aspects] as 'colors' for the canvas that is creating a character in a role. That being the case, when an actor leaves to explore another teacher, it can feel like your mate or child is abandoning you.

Does that mean an actor should never move on? Of course not. Chubbuck continues: "Even though that feeling has occurred to me, my students' welfare and skill level is more important than my personal attachment."

Los Angeles-based commercial casting director, teacher, and actor Carolyne Barry recommends these steps to ease the transition:

> I suggest you know who you will be studying with before you leave so there won't be a long lapse in your training. Then, give the teacher a month's notice, maybe buy a small thank you gift, and write a very nice note thanking them for contributing to your life and career. You might also say that you may like to come back in a year or so and would like the door to be open.

Many teachers recognize that students need a variety of influences to become the best artist they can be. Barry continues:

I usually urge students to move on after two or three years. I believe that when an actor gets too comfortable in a training environment, they are probably not being challenged enough. And, after a solid foundation has been created, it is very beneficial to get another point of view.

You have every right and responsibility to get the best education you can find. Yes, goodbyes can be painful for both student and teacher, but your path is singular—it's your own. No teacher, no matter how great, can chart your course. You aren't the first student this teacher has bid farewell and you won't be the last. JA

Dear Jackie,

Last year I auditioned for a very well-known New York acting academy that was on an audition tour. They accepted me into their summer program, but I wasn't able to attend because I couldn't afford it. I felt horrible about that but it was out-of-control expensive. I hate that a lack of money stood in my way. I am thinking about saving up, taking out loans, asking for help from my parents, and auditioning for this famous academy again next year. Do you think that's a good idea?

—In Need of Great Advice

Dear In Need,

How did you set your sights on this particular program? Is this a place you've heard first-hand raves about or you assuming the program's marketing materials are true? There are many unaccredited "conservatories" and "academies" that audition hopeful talent all over the country (and world), luring them to study in the "big city" for outrageous sums of money. Before you go on beating yourself up for not being able to afford what seems like the best, make sure it's actually all it's cracked up to be.

Training is important, but no one should be buried in debt (or ask their parents to mortgage the house) to pay for any acting program. Our work just isn't consistent enough to merit a huge financial risk. Student loans can be taken out responsibly— just make sure the total is an amount you can repay, no matter what your career brings. And be sure the school you choose offers more than promises of fame and industry exposure. If the admissions officer says anything along the lines of, "How much is your future worth to you?" you should walk away fast.

I can understand how disappointing it must have been not to get to go to a program you had your heart set on, but perhaps it was a blessing in disguise. JA

Dear Jackie,

I'm sick of going to acting classes. I got an MFA a few years back, and then moved out to Los Angeles to pursue my career. Everything I read and everyone

I spoke to kept telling me to keep training—so I did, even though it was the last thing I wanted to do. I'm burnt out! When can I stop going to class?

—No More Teachers, No More Books

Dear No More,

Now. Take some time off and when you find yourself eager for a workout, look for alternatives to traditional acting classes. If you have trouble staying in the moment, why not try meditation? Want to loosen up your physicality? How about practicing yoga or salsa dancing? Vocal problems? Maybe a singing class would help. There's no reason to limit yourself to the same old classes, year after year.

Eventually, you're likely to find yourself ready to get back into a straightforward scene study class again. Take care to look for one that juices you up. I'd wager your current burnout might have as much to do with your recent teachers as with your résumé. With as much training as you've had, it matters less that you follow some standardized curriculum than that you continue to feed the fires of your talent. JA

What Do You Think?

1 Is training necessary in order to have a successful career? If not, what are other reasons to study?
2 Does an actor need to get a college degree? Why or why not? If so, what kind of degree(s) should they pursue and why?
3 Explain five benefits of going to graduate school and earning an MFA.
4 Explain five benefits of skipping a formal education and heading straight into the career.
5 How do you get into graduate school?
6 How do you know it's time to move on from a particular teacher or training modality? How can you do so in a professional manner?
7 What are some ways poor training might be detrimental to your growth as an actor? How can you know whether you are getting "good" training?
8 Do casting professionals care about your education? Who you've trained with? Your degrees? Explain.
9 How does a fellowship, internship, or apprenticeship work? How might this type of educational program serve your career and craft?
10 What are three ways you can continue to train, or "work out" as an actor, throughout your career?

Notes

1 C-stand—a standard piece of equipment on a film set, most often used to position light modifiers (such as silks, nets, or flags) in front of light sources.
2 Affective memory—an early element of Stanislavski's acting system, it is the use of the actor's memory to draw upon similar events (or experiences that brought up similar emotions) for utilization in a scene. The terms emotional memory, emotional recall, and sense memory refer to similar techniques.

3

WHERE TO LIVE

Where is the very best place to live to pursue your career? As with so many things in our world, the answer is simply this: no one knows. If a particular city boasted a higher ratio of successful actors, we'd all move there. And as soon as we did, the ratio would shift.

Actors need to go where the work is. Los Angeles and New York remain major hubs for our industry, but there's lots going on in Chicago, Toronto, Vancouver, Seattle, San Francisco, Pittsburgh, Baltimore, Boston . . . the list goes on, and is far from static. For a time, Wilmington, NC was the new "in" spot. Then suddenly, it was all about New Mexico . . . then Atlanta, GA. Actor-friendly cities are ever-changing, along with state tax incentives, the real estate market, and other trends.

Here are some things to consider when deciding where to put down roots:

—Smaller markets mean less competition and, possibly, more opportunities to build up professional credits, while larger markets have more activity, and more competition.

—Part of the decision of where to live should be made based on personal preferences. Hate driving? LA isn't for you. Can't stand crowds? You won't like New York. Since we spend much of our time unemployed, it's important to be in an environment that doesn't work against your sense of wellbeing.

—The decision to move somewhere isn't permanent. They don't lock the doors behind you. Many actors have experimented with living in different locations. Sometimes, those moves were prompted by work—a job took them someplace, and they stayed. Other times, they were prompted by *lack* of work.

—When it comes to choosing a place to live, no decision is wrong, except the decision to stay somewhere that isn't working for you. Rather than trying to predict which place will offer the most success—something that, *once again, no one can predict*—think in terms of having experiences that offer growth as an artist. In that sense, even someplace that doesn't end up holding the keys to your future may nonetheless offer valuable benefits.

—Most importantly, consider where you are drawn to spend your time. If your career were not a factor, where would you go? Yes, challenging yourself to try something new can be important, but your choice of location is personal and does not have to be entirely logical. Since there is not one path to one homogeneous form of success, you are not bound to any one location.

Questions and Answers

Dear Michael,

I'm graduating in three months and there's nothing else I want to do in this world but be part of a movie. The problem is I don't know if I can handle moving to LA by myself even though I have a burning desire to do so. I have done a couple of films here in Dallas but nothing extravagant, because there's not much work here. Should I move to LA after graduating, or not?

—Texas Exit

Dear TE,

On the one hand, you know the odds. You certainly can't move to LA with the assumption you'll get acting work. In such a major show business hub, the pursuit of an acting career requires a lot of patience—maybe more than you think. Yes, there's more film work in LA, but there are also more actors, so there's major competition to even get an audition, let alone an acting gig. There are more agents, but it's hard to land a good one. So for some people, it's better to stay where they are and build some credits and experience before testing the waters in a bigger market.

On the other hand, you're young. This could be a great time for crazy experiments like moving to LA for a while. These decisions get more complicated as you get older. Jobs, relationships, kids, and increased financial responsibilities can bog down your freedom to pick up and move around. Besides, what are you going to do, spend your life not doing things because they're long shots? What's the worst that can happen? You run out of money and go home. Meanwhile, you will have had a great adventure.

So you see: there's a case to be made for staying put, and a case to be made for diving in and giving it a shot.

What should you do? I have no idea. But I'll say this: if you do decide to make the move, do it wisely. Figure out what you're going to do for work. Cultivate job leads. If you can, arrange to stay with friends. Make sure you can afford a car. Be skeptical so you don't fall for scams; they're everywhere. And research, research, research. Read through the many, many columns and articles on this popular subject to see what others have written. If you go, go for the joy of the pursuit, rather than for the result. That way, you can't lose. MK

Dear Jackie,

I'm a struggling actor living in Arizona with my 4-month-old daughter. How can I get more involved in theatre and acting when I have a child and live in a place with very few opportunities to advance my passion? Do I quit my mainstream job as a sales rep, pack up my things, and move to California? What is the best thing for me and my family? How can I pursue my dreams without living in a cardboard box?

—Struggling in AZ

Dear Struggling,

When did this idea of California pop up? Has it always been in your plans or has it recently become more alluring? Could the hurdles of parenthood—lack of sleep, emotional turmoil, intense responsibilities that stretch far out into the foreseeable future—have anything to do with your desire to steep yourself in the acting pursuit in a faraway land?

The last thing you and your baby need is to toss the stability you have earned into the trash. The second to last thing you need is to move to California with so little idea of what would happen next. You are in Arizona, presumably, because it's your home. You have friends, a job, and probably family nearby. In these first few years of parenthood, you have to take very good care of your child, of course, but just as importantly, you need to be good to yourself. While pursuing an acting career might be something you want deeply and truly, ditching your current digs for an unknown coast is unnecessary and probably unwise. And that advice applies to any new parent, no matter their gender or background.

Fortunately, neither parenthood nor holding off on a move to the left coast means you have to wait to begin your actor's journey. Arizona, like each and every state, is home to plenty of opportunities of its own.

You can find some of these on durantcom.com—which has been listing weekly audition notices for the Arizona market since 2001. Founder Laura Durant says,

> There has never been a fee for actors to subscribe to the service or to see the listings in their entirety. Notices are posted online each Monday as well as distributed to a listserv of 7000 subscribers. The types of notices are a mix of film, stage, industrial, and commercial.

The Arizona Film Office, Independent Film Project: Phoenix, Arizona Theatre Company, and Arizona Broadway Theatre are all in your backyard. SAG-AFTRA and AEA offer local opportunities and links to numerous acting and theatrical organizations as well.

Start where you are. Explore your local market, build your résumé, improve your craft, save your money, and enjoy your daughter's babyhood. When you're ready, revisit the California plan with a lot more knowledge, and sleep, under your belt. JA

Dear Michael,
   I'm an unrepresented actor currently living in Philadelphia. I make a decent living as a bartender, and the scheduling is flexible enough to do local theatre. However, it's become increasingly obvious to me that most of the acting work that pays anything is in New York.

Since (for a variety of reasons) it's not an ideal time for me to move, what kind of professional hurdles would I face staying here and trying to get work in NYC? Lots of actors are based in NY but work all over the country. Is it possible to do the reverse?

I've worked exclusively in theatre, and I'm unfamiliar with the practical mechanics of how film and television work. Will an agent not be interested in me if I'm based out of town? Are there certain days of the week that TV and film auditions are most likely to happen? What could I do down here to help me succeed up there?
   —Pulled in Two Directions

Dear Pulled,
   I hate to be discouraging, but your situation presents a number of substantial challenges. Yes, there are more acting jobs in New York, but there are also more actors—plenty of them. So New York casting directors very rarely have incentive to look beyond the local talent pool. The reason you hear about NY-based actors being able to work elsewhere is that out-of-town producers often come here to cast. The same isn't true in reverse. You're not likely to hear of a NY-based production holding auditions in Philly.

New York agents generally aren't interested in actors who aren't local, and you'd definitely need a New York agent. Trying to score well-paying acting work without one is difficult. Trying to do so from out of town is even harder.

Add in that you've never done TV or film, and your chances for success drop even further. You'd be vying for the attention of casting directors who have access to lots of local actors with on-camera credits, followed by scores of actors with fewer or no credits—but who are at least available at a moment's notice because they, too, are local. I'm sure you can see the difficulty of muscling your way in from afar.

Even if you land a New York agent, you can spend a lot of money commuting back and forth to audition for roles that are likely to go to a more experienced actor. I'm concerned that you'd find this pursuit disappointing and frustrating.

If I were in your circumstances, I'd put all my efforts into finding representation in Philadelphia so you can start accumulating some on-camera credits. Build your résumé and your reel, and hoard those bartending dollars. Then, when the time is right, make the big move, prepared to be patient while people get to know you. Once you're a New Yorker, you can pursue agents from the much more favorable position of having credits and a local address. MK

Dear Jackie,

I've just moved back to Milwaukee, WI. Because of recent tax breaks, we're already catching the eye of production companies. How can I find out who is casting a project? I am signed with the only SAG-AFTRA franchised agent in the Milwaukee area.

I had worked in Los Angeles for twelve years, and am very aware of the casting protocol. However, my thought is if I could just let the casting company know that I (a union actor with years of experience on set) am here, it might be to their benefit to see me rather than bringing someone up from Chicago for a one- or two-day shoot.

—Local Hire

Dear Local,

Jennifer Berg of Jennifer's Talent, a SAG-AFTRA Franchised Milwaukee agency, offers this insight:

> Since we are in a very small market we do not have casting companies here. Each agency does its own casting so the actor would have to be represented by an agency in Milwaukee. When looking for actors, a production company may contact us or all local agencies or they may work through a Chicago casting company.

It looks as if you're halfway home being represented by a legitimate, franchised agency. Since the town is so small, and opportunities so few, you may find your frustration comes not from lack of access to casting information, but from lack of casting opportunities.

Stay current on what's being shot in town through the traditional trades and the state Film Commission's office.[1] On its website (filmwisconsin.net) there is a "casting call" section as well as news on recent productions (although the day I looked both sections were empty). When upcoming projects are listed, it doesn't hurt to submit. While it's not likely to yield results often, local casting does have its monetary advantages, and you may at least spur an occasional call to your agent.

The quickest, and perhaps most fun, way to find opportunities in your new home is to go where the actors are. Get familiar with your local union branches and attend their events, screenings, and workshops. Sign up for a class. Audition for local theatres, such as Milwaukee Rep. The more you immerse yourself in the Milwaukee scene, the easier it will be to navigate. JA

Dear Jackie,

To bi-coast or not to bi-coast! I moved to New York from Chicago to build my career as an actor and was there for two years. Then I moved to LA and wow, what a difference. In New York I lived in a closet, which was a "rented room." I moved from downtown Brooklyn to east Flatbush Brooklyn on the F train, which took about seven trips. I would read monologues and prepare scenes on the daily train rides to and from class. I didn't even know what "jaywalking" was until I moved to LA, since pedestrians in NY cross whenever they can and you watch out for your life while doing it!

The crazy thing is that I sort of miss New York and want to go back, at least for six months, to connect with agents, CDs, producers, managers, and actors to network and build relationships. Plus, I just miss perusing the city and the theatres.

However, after living in LA for the last several years, I've built a home for myself here. I'm concerned about the practicalities of going to NY. What about my life in LA? Do I just pay rent at my apartment here in advance and cancel the electricity or do I sublet? Part of me wants to just dive back into NY like I did when I was 18, but I'm older and wiser now and know I need a plan. I have friends in NY who I would be able to crash with for a week max, but six months would require a place of my own. I was asking a fellow actor friend in LA if he wanted to go as well and we could rent a place that has a month-to-month lease. Or maybe I can rent a hostel room. What about money? I would have to get a survival job just for a few months.

A part of me is saying forget about NY for now and focus on getting more work in LA and allow my career to take me to NY later.
—Stuck in the Middle

Dear Stuck,

It sounds as if you are feeling some perfectly understandable New York nostalgia, but I wonder about the logic of a six-month visit. Seeing friends, reconnecting with contacts, and soaking up the sights doesn't need to take months, while pursuing acting work is going to take considerably longer. To be truly bicoastal, you'd need to commit to a more regular, consistent stay or be able to afford frequent cross-country flights. You'd also need a housing/work plan in place. I'm not saying that's a bad idea but before you have an established career, it will take some real planning and some very understanding agents.

To more fully investigate the option, start with finding a bicoastal day job. Many temp agencies have offices on both coasts, and you may be able to register with several that can employ you in both cities. Some national chains, such as Starbucks, may have the ability to help employees transfer from city to city (and back again) as well. Or you might also look into seasonal employment in hotels, restaurants, stores, or attractions, since the coasts appeal to tourists at different times of year. Housing-wise, subletting can be a great way to cover some of your hometown expenses while traveling for work. You might also find a roommate situation where you pay a lower rent in exchange for only partial year occupancy. There are plenty of guesthouses and guest rooms in LA where an owner might appreciate semi-vacancy. Think too about acting training. Could you enroll in short term acting intensives in each city, as opposed to one long scene study course?

If you have an agent, this is obviously something you'll want to discuss with him or her but if you are unrepresented, consider how you'll present your situation to prospective reps. Yes, some agencies are bicoastal, but most successful agent–client relationships require personal development and tending. This will be harder to achieve if you're a geographically inconsistent client. And what about your personal life? It may quickly become frustrating to jump in and out of in-person friendships and relationships.

For now, why not head out to New York on a two- or three-week working vacation? Instead of worrying about practicalities, you can use your prep time to save money and plan for optimal social and professional activity. You might arrange your visit around shows you want to see, workshops you want to attend, or events with friends. Put the money you'll save on trying to rent a short-term apartment towards a decent hotel and splurges that will help you enjoy your trip. When you return to Los Angeles, you'll be able to reconsider whether your yearning for New York needs further attention or if it has been sated. JA

Dear Michael,

I recently graduated with my BFA in film/TV (directing and screenwriting) and a double minor in producing and entertainment business from a university in New York. When I first moved to the Big Apple, I didn't like it. I missed my home state and the place I spent most of my high school years, Los Angeles. Well, I finished school a year-and-a-half early and moved back to LA a week after graduation. And now . . . I'm really missing New York.

I'm a SAG-AFTRA member with ambitions that are exclusively film/TV/ commercial. I was accepted into a prestigious BFA drama program in New York as well, but decided to transfer to directing because I really disdain theatre. While I was there, I met with four agents, who passed on me. In LA, I got offers from two. Do you think I have more chances to get auditions or get cast in New York or LA? My lease expires five months from today.

—Empire State of Mind

Dear Empire State of Mind,

I'm often baffled that people actually think I can tell them which coast will yield them greater success. Sans psychic powers, it's impossible to predict such things. And as it turns out, I'm not even a little bit psychic.

That said, you've already given two indications of which city might be a better fit: 1) You disdain theatre. 2) You want to do on-camera work. While both media exist in both places, in general, LA has the greater film/TV emphasis. So it's kind of a no-brainer. Regardless, moving back and forth is never a good plan, because it usually takes a while before folks catch on that you're around and capable. And so I think that patience—that *awful, awful* concept—is the name of the game.

Missing New York isn't a good enough reason to leave your agents and set the career dial back to zero. I miss Venice, Italy, but it's damn short on acting opportunities. So, let's visit those places and keep our careers on track. MK

Dear Jackie,

After ten years and a consistent off-off-Broadway career in New York, my husband and I are moving to LA. Although I'm more of a theatre gal, I'm excited about this move for many reasons. I'm hoping you can give me some advice on establishing a foothold in the LA scene. I have a lot of experience with Shakespeare and that is my forte, but I have hardly any film experience (believe me it's not for lack of trying, I'm just not a typical babe).

Is it unrealistic to think I can focus on theatre in LA? And how can I use my non-hot-chick status to my best advantage if I do go after film and TV roles?

—Non-Hot Chick

Dear Non-Hot Chick,

There are, contrary to popular mythology, more actual theatre spaces in Los Angeles than in NYC. There are tons of plays being produced all year long—many classical. While LA theatre gets a bad rap for being "showcase-ey"—meaning actors do it only to get agents and not for its own sake—when you take a look around at the variety of material being performed, it becomes clear that's not the case. LA theatre is alive and well and could keep you plenty busy.

Now, if there was a hidden question in your question—something like, "Can I make money doing theatre in LA?" you're in for some bad news. To make more than a few bucks a week, you'll need to work in one of LA's few Equity houses. And if you want to earn a consistent living, you'll need something akin to divine intervention. There just aren't that many big shows casting out of and performing in LA.

As for your question about Hollywood's beauty bias, rest assured that there are plenty of roles for "non-hot" actors. Count yourself lucky that you know your type, understand the market, and can avoid competing in the saturated 20-something-hot-girl category.

I want to leave you with a few theatre companies a new-to-town classics lover should know: Shakespeare Orange County, Shakespeare in LA, Los Angeles Women's Shakespeare Company, Long Beach Shakespeare Company, ARK Theatre Company, Fountain Theatre, East LA Classic Theatre Company, Pacific Resident Theatre, and A Noise Within are—amongst many others—worth looking into. JA

Dear Jackie,

I'm moving to New York in a couple months. What should I do first?
—Ready to Rule

Dear Ready,

Get a subway map. JA

Dear Jackie,

I don't know what to do! I'm an actor on the East Coast and I was offered a sweet sublet deal in New York to start in January for several months. Then literally an hour later, I got a call from a management company in LA and they are interested in representing me. Do I go to New York and pound the pavement there or go to LA with this manager? I am so confused, and literally an hour ago I thought I had it all figured out.
—So Close to a Solution

Dear So Close,

My strong feeling about this is you should live in the place you want to live. If you have a manager in Los Angeles interested in you, it's likely you'll end up with interest in New York too. Which do you prefer?

When I finished graduate school I thought I was headed right back to Los Angeles, which is where I'm from. I was really looking forward to going home. Like most MFA programs, my school did a showcase in both New York and LA. Our New York show was packed, with representatives and casting people standing in back. Our LA show? It was filled with my personal friends with just a few scattered agents in the mix. I got a callback with an LA agency, but no bite. In New York, however, I got numerous callbacks and landed both an agent and a job. It seemed to me that the choice was made. LA didn't want me—New York was my town! I did the job and worked for a while with the New York agent before it hit me. I really did want to move back to Los Angeles and I wasn't going to let one audition (the showcase) decide something that important for me. I bid my agency farewell and got on a plane. And you know what? Within a year I had another agent, in LA.

If you were already an established commodity in one city and thinking of starting anew in another, I might pause, but then I'd give you the exact same advice. Building and maintaining an acting career is hard work—don't add living someplace you don't want to be to your struggles. JA

Dear Michael,

I'm an aspiring actor living in Chicago who wants to move to NY (after more training and saving) to pursue it seriously. I've been looking to find figures on how many actors there are in NY, to get some kind of estimate for how many people I will be competing against. Obviously that won't include females, or males not in my age range (I'm 22, but look 17–20). Is there a source for those numbers?

—What Are the Odds?

Dear Odds,

Unfortunately, answers to these statistical questions are harder to nail down than you might imagine. Here's why: there are plenty of New Yorkers who'd answer "yes" to the question, "Are you an actor?" But within that group, you'll find everyone from the established, trained, steadily working SAG-AFTRA member to the crackpot at Coney Island Beach who says he's an actor because the people in his head told him so, and who also claims to be able to control the outcome of TV game shows with his mind. There are people who have never taken an acting class or appeared in a play who just like how it sounds; there are guys who take acting classes to meet women; and then there are aspiring professionals like you who work hard, study, and are building careers. It's impossible to figure how many of those people are "real" actors (or how one might even make that determination), but we do know this: there are a lot of them in New York—both union and nonunion—many of whom could be considered your competition.

SAG-AFTRA doesn't do breakdowns by age, but Todd Amorde, the Guild's former national director of organizing, sent along these thoughts in response to your question:

> There are a lot of opportunities for someone your age. That's the good news. The bad news is that you are also among one of the largest groups of actors in Hollywood and New York, but it's probably best not to dwell on the competition. What's more important is how prepared you are. You can probably count on three-to-five years minimum to get established, and you will want to make sure you are prepared to work hard. Don't be overly concerned about what the industry might be looking for. Rather, focus on your craft, your process, your ability to deliver, and above all your experience and confidence. The most compelling auditions happen when you understand the role and can give the producers a viable option for how it should be played. Ultimately you will get hired because of your own uniqueness.

I'll add that there seem to be far more roles for young, white male actors than for those in any other group. And actors who are over 18 but can play younger are especially valuable to producers, because, unlike minors, they don't have to be tutored on set and can work full days and even go into overtime. All of that saves producers money. Even still, as much as you might want a clear picture of your chances, it's always going to be a guess. At a certain point, you just have to roll the dice. MK

Dear Jackie,

I'm a recent college graduate planning to move to New York to pursue my acting career. I've visited a few times, but I can't figure out how to find an apartment. It seems totally impossible to find a place to live in Manhattan! I can't afford to deal with a broker, and it seems like there aren't any apartments around for people making an average living, let alone struggling actors without any long-term job security. Should I just move to New Jersey and commute?

—Housing Crisis

Dear Housing,

Don't despair. Apartment deals in New York City are out there. It's just a matter of time and, like everything, who you know. If you're new to the city, that might not sound very encouraging, but remember, you won't be new for long. Do you have a family member or classmate with whom you could crash for a month or two while you look? If not, try Gypsy Housing on Facebook for short-term sublets while you get acclimated.

During my time in New York I lived in four great apartments—two in Manhattan and two in Park Slope, Brooklyn. Of those, three I found through friends or friends of friends; the fourth—a long-term sublet—I found through an ad. With that one, I only got the place because it turned out that the actor doing the subletting and I shared the same agent, which made him feel like he and I had a coincidental "friend" in common. Many New Yorkers tell similar stories. The more people you meet—at your temp job, in a play, through friends or your alumni association—the more chances you'll have to find that elusive space.

The Actors Fund Housing Development Corp. has plans, according to a press release, to "build hundreds of low-income housing units in urban centers across the country over the next few years." Go to actorsfund.org to learn more. Also, check out the New York Housing Development Corporation website at nychdc. com and click on Now Renting. If you are union, or as soon as you join, inquire about union-run housing programs. And don't neglect to put yourself on waiting lists for affordable artist housing. Most of the lists are long, so the sooner you get on, the sooner your number might come up. Each housing complex has its own rules, so do your research now.

My actor friend Kent, who is a current tenant of Manhattan Plaza, gave me the scoop on that artist-subsidized housing:

> Manhattan Plaza was started in the 1970s, and people ranging from Angela Lansbury to Alicia Keys have lived here. That makes it sound much swankier than it really is, but for performers and artists, it's really the best deal in Manhattan. To calculate your rent payment, they have you project how much you think you'll make in the next year and pay 30 percent of that as your rent. Then, at the end of that year, they look at your tax return and see whether you paid too much or too little, and they credit or bill you as need be. They also allow performers to deduct performance expenses from their rent—after filling out what feels like never-ending paperwork.

Want to sign up? "You have to get your name on 'the list to get on the list,'" Kent continues,

> Then, whenever the list is opened, they put all the names that were on 'the list to get on the list' onto the *actual* list in a random order. Then you wait.

Years later, they contact you and you have to fill out a bunch of paperwork to be sure you qualify. It took about five and a half years for my name to come up, but I was pretty lucky—most people wait about seven years.

Seven years? Before you write this opportunity off, listen to Kent's final words of wisdom:

People say, 'Seven years to wait for an apartment? In seven years, I'll be able to afford something better than Manhattan Plaza.' Then seven years come and go, and they say, 'I wish I had put my name on the list seven years ago.'

Like acting, apartment hunting in New York requires determination and luck. JA

Dear Jackie,

I've been an actor living in New York City for three years. I moved here from Colorado just out of college and I've seen my career progress in the right direction. I got my SAG-AFTRA card and have been working union background jobs in television and film. Also I've gotten several callbacks for Equity productions and companies.

I'm very proud of all that I've accomplished and I want to continue building a career as an actor, but I have decided that I'd like to do it in Colorado. A city lifestyle just isn't who I am and I love Colorado too much to let it go.

What can I expect when I head back home? I plan on creating my own projects just to keep my creative juices flowing. Will being part of SAG-AFTRA and getting my Equity card serve any purpose there or should I pursue my passion nonunion? Are there any reputable agencies in Denver that you are aware of? I have heard that many of them have bad reputations. Am I making a horrible mistake?
   —Rocky Mountain High

Dear Rocky Mountain High,

Congratulations for finding clarity on where you'd like to be. Many actors spend years sampling the coasts and trying to find a home—you're lucky to be putting down roots someplace as gorgeous as Colorado. But make no mistake, the career implications of your choice are serious. Unlike in New York, Colorado acting opportunities—especially the paying kind—are comparatively scarce.

I asked local acting teacher Dan O'Neill—once a classmate of mine at the National Theatre Conservatory in Denver—what he thought of making a career in Colorado. He, apologizing for his cynicism, replied,

I would like to act on the moon, because I hear it's nice there and the views are pretty. However, I'm prevented from my goal by lack of a rocket, rocket fuel, and an audience. I'm afraid your reader is in a similar boat/rocket. Colorado is a very difficult joint in which to make a living in the entertainment business. I am proudly a full-time drama teacher at a wonderful private school in Denver and I am occasionally seen on experimental, nonunion stages here and there, when I feel the urge to practice what I preach. For me, it is deeply personal when I act now—which means I don't think about the dough.

I contacted one of Colorado's most successful working actors, who had this to say in response to your union query:

In general, I am a pro-union person. However, here in Colorado, it doesn't make much sense. SAG-AFTRA work is rare. Once in awhile, there's a union commercial but the vast majority of film work here is nonunion. Colorado gets a major motion picture shooting here maybe once every few years. There are no TV shows that shoot here regularly. If you come, honestly, you should probably quit the union and do nonunion work, which actually in many cases pays better than union work, although there will be no pension or benefits. Or you can stay union and audition about three times a year. And there are only a few nearby AEA theatres that pay a livable wage: The Denver Center Theatre Company and the Arvada Center. The others have limited AEA contracts and don't pay very much, if you manage to get the job. But there aren't that many AEA members here, so the competition for AEA jobs is nothing like in New York.

Denver's got just three SAG-AFTRA franchised agencies, and none listed with ATA/NATR.[2]

I checked the website for the Colorado local SAG-AFTRA branch and it lists local programs such as the Colorado Conservatory and Denver Film Society. The Local Resources link has but one listing, which is, I think, a payroll servicing company for film productions . . . not very encouraging. Upcoming events were listed as . . . nil. As consolation, it looks like there were a few last year.

Colorado Film Commission (coloradofilm.org) representative Kevin Shand says: "Colorado has been fortunate in that we have a strong local production community producing a variety of films, television shows, and commercials. We are projecting there will be over $50 million in spending in Colorado this year." Despite this upbeat message, the online filmography is sparse. Take a look for yourself.

Does all this mean I think you should stay in New York? No. Actors, like all artists, need to follow their hearts. Is Colorado the right place to make an acting fortune? Probably not. Is it the right place for you to find your niche, your home, even your place as an artist in the world? It most definitely could be. JA

Dear Jackie,

I'd like to become a member of a theatre company that has a core family of actors they use for their productions. Are there companies that hire actors to be members for an entire season, or even longer, as opposed to hiring only on an as-needed basis? I'm willing to look outside the major industry hubs to find a permanent home. I have my MFA, and can teach for the educational division of the company or at a nearby college or university during the day while performing at night. I can accept the fact that the career I envisioned as a kid may not become a reality. What I can't accept, however, is that just because my career didn't work out in one way, I have to give up the craft that I have practiced, trained in, and grown to love so much.

—Actor for Life

Dear Actor,

The span of a theatre actor's career is closely tied to how long they are willing to live a gypsy lifestyle. I'm not saying a steady regional living can't be made, but it's a very difficult feat to pull off. Most of the working regional theatre actors I know continuously hopscotch the country, going from job to job. Most don't own homes, have children, or plan much farther than a season ahead.

"Most regional theatres don't use a permanent company anymore," says one successful regional theatre actor I spoke to,

> I freelance out of NYC, and the theatres I work for job in their actors from NY or LA. A few theatres that seem to have a relatively steady company with consistent casting are Oregon Shakespeare, Trinity Rep, Alabama Shakes, Utah Shakes, Steppenwolf, Milwaukee Rep, and Seattle Rep, but even these seem to be relying more and more on New York and LA actors. And Pacific Conservatory Theatre (PCPA) is one of the only theatres I've come across to have a full-time faculty that teaches at their conservatory and also composes the core acting company. That's very rare. Unfortunately, with shrinking budgets and shrinking audiences, more and more theatres are doing co-productions and using smaller casts.

Jerry Lapidus, who spent years working with developing theatres for Actors' Equity Association, was similarly discouraging:

> This was the idea behind the whole regional theatre movement, and in fact, the organization now known as the League of Regional Theatres

(LORT)[3] was once the League of *Resident* Theatres. The concept was that theatres would hire permanent companies of actors who would move to the surrounding cities, work regularly at the theatre and have, y'know, a real life, rather than just being hired as 'stock' players for a show or a tour. This is pretty much gone, even for the few theatres that once had it. Some theatres today at least try to hire for a season, if not individual shows, but that's usually the best one can hope for.

Bleak, I know. But there are tons of companies out there that operate in all sorts of ways so don't throw in the towel just yet. And there *are* actually companies loyal to a consistent group of talent on the smaller, lower-budget end of the spectrum. You may be able to find an artistic, if not financial, home. Can you make a situation like that work? You can pursue a scaled-down theatre career anywhere in the country. If money isn't your driver, you might find settling into a nice acting scene easier than it sounds.

To begin your own research on possible home bases check out the Theatre Communications Group website at tcg.org. TCG, which publishes *American Theatre* Magazine, lists member theatres on its website, where you'll find recent and upcoming seasons. LORT also has a member listing at lort.org. While Actors' Equity Association doesn't have a simple list of all Equity theatres on its site, you can search open job announcements by region at actorsequity.org, under Casting Call. If you are nonunion, or willing to give up your union status, check out AACT, the American Association of Community Theatre at aact. org. You can use its search feature to find member companies by state, name, or keyword.

You may not end up with the career you envisioned, but with some research, flexibility, and creative thinking you might end up with one you love. Your career is important, but your life is . . . your life. My truest, simplest advice is that you should go where you will be happy. JA

What Do You Think?

1   Should beginning actors move to New York, LA, or begin at home? Why?
2   Name five pros and five cons of living in Los Angeles. Do the same for New York City.
3   What are some of the challenges "bicoastal" actors face?
4   Is it impractical to try to cultivate a New York or LA career if you don't live in either of those cities? Why or why not?
5   In addition to New York and Los Angeles, name three cities that offer ample acting opportunities for upcoming artists.
6   Describe at least five specific ways to learn about a potential home base.

7 Could you have an acting career outside of a large city? Does that ideal appeal to you? Why or why not?

8 Name five criteria, *other* than career potential, that you could use in choosing someplace to call home.

9 Name three ways to research acting opportunities in smaller markets.

10 What are some reasons a working actor might choose to relocate?

Notes

1 Most states have official film commissions or offices devoted to promoting local film, television, and commercial work and bringing productions (and revenue) to their communities.

2 ATA/NATR—Association of Talent Agents/National Association of Talent Representatives. Much more on this in Chapter 8, "Agents and Managers."

3 LORT (League of Resident Theatres)—a particular type of Equity contract.

4

MARKETING: BRANDING

In many ways, the business of being an actor is similar to working in sales. Sales-people must know their product, brand accordingly, learn the market, connect with potential buyers, create visibility, and track trends. What can be hard to come to terms with, however, is that for actors, the product is *themselves*. All sales folk face rejection, but it can be especially tough when the commodity is you.

Before an actor makes decisions about headshots, a website, or any other market-ing materials, she must first develop a clear and unvarnished understanding of her brand, or, as it's commonly referred to in the profession, "type." When we talk about type, we mean an actor's *perceived* identity—not necessarily who he really is—and the kinds of roles he's most likely to play. Factors that may affect type include the actor's perceived age, ethnicity, sexuality, gender, size, vocal quality, personality, and general "vibe."

Understanding type is a crucial step in effective self-marketing. This is why (although we deal in fantasy) an actor cannot afford to have an unrealistic self-image. We must operate in the bright light of honest self-assessment and develop a realistic grasp of how people see us. Many actors in training are told they should be versatile enough to "play anything" and are concerned about getting "type-cast" (becoming known for playing only one type of role, and finding themselves limited to those roles). While a fine approach to learning the craft, this perspec-tive is misguided in the pursuit of a career. It can lead to endless frustration.

Like it or not, we all make snap decisions about people based on their appearance. In real life, this may be unfair and limiting. But in storytelling, it can be valuable.

An in-shape physique might suggest discipline or focus; obesity might suggest indulgence; low voices could suggest authority; small voices could suggest humility or kindness; English accents might suggest class or coldness. Writers often use characters as devices, with the primary function of furthering the plot. Thus, typecasting these roles provides clues for viewers that help them follow the story.

The practice is also useful in characters the viewer *isn't* supposed to follow. Imagine, if you will, a scene about a movie's leading character under interrogation by police after being wrongly accused of a crime. Our hero sits, scared, as the police officer badgers him in a dimly lit room. If you were casting this scene, you'd need to keep the viewer's focus on the protagonist—on the plot. If you cast "against type" and creatively chose an 80-year-old, grey-haired woman with a whispery voice to play the cop, your casting would pull focus from the scene. The audience might stop thinking about the hero and wonder, instead, about grandma's backstory. Does this mean grandmas can't be cops? Of course not! But storytelling in our visual media plays inside simpler parameters than real life.

Occasionally, directors will cast "against type" for a unique take on a character. Even still, it's a device that makes use of the audience's preconceptions.

An understanding of one's type is key to an actor's self-branding, affecting decisions about headshots, résumés, website design, demo reels, social media presence, hairstyle, attire, and occasionally even one's professional name.

Questions and Answers

Dear Michael,

I'm having trouble figuring out my "type." I'm sort of ethnic looking, though no one can ever figure out what I am. An acting teacher told me that though I was beautiful, I wasn't "classic looking" and I should market myself towards character parts. I have no problem with that, but when I've asked others to honestly tell me what they see me playing, I've gotten "doctor," "funny, cute-yet-awkward type," "dark roles, like a drug addict," and "definitely an ingénue." One casting person said I was "too girl-next-door," another said I was "too exotic"! I always thought it was good to be able to play many different parts but now I hear that you should play one type well initially, then, once you're established, explore others. How should I market myself? Do I leave it up to agents and casting directors? And should I even bother with commercials?

—Confused-Yet-Determined

Dear Confused-Yet-Determined,

There are several questions here. Let's work backwards.

Yes, you should pursue commercials. Ethnically ambiguous is in. Yes, you should look to the people who deal most often with casting to guide your ideas about your castability. And yes, while you may have a wide range, as casting director Gwen Hiller and I agree, "No one is shopping for versatile." So it's important— particularly early in your career—to aim for the types of roles that people can *most easily* see you playing. Let's look at how to figure that out.

First, disregard the opinions of non-professionals, inexperienced peers, and anyone outside of the business. Uninformed input can drive you crazy. Now, I understand that even the *professional* feedback you've gotten has been all over the place, but narrowing this puzzle down to just those opinions makes it easier to solve. Follow the actors to whom you're most often compared. Note the roles they play. As you begin to get called back and/or cast professionally, those roles will provide more reliable indications of type. I promise you, in time, a pattern will emerge.

Get a range of top-notch, professional-quality headshots that suggest your most viable types—what I call your "A market." Then, use the one that best fits each role for which you audition. You may need a quirky/funny look, a lower class look, a professional look, and one that suggests exotic ethnicity. (Important: don't dress in costume or portray characters. Headshots should always present a side of your real-life self.)

In a flooded market like ours, there's no room for vague branding. We need to look like how we sound, like how we behave, like how we dress, and have shots to match. Figuring out your type is a process. If you're represented, listen to your agent or manager on this one. If not, submit for whatever you think you can play, and see how people respond. Think of it as a fun experiment, and let time and experience provide clarity. MK

Dear Jackie,

I know that the industry is notorious for being nicer to guys with quirky looks than it is with imperfect ladies, but how much do looks really matter? I don't really care if I'm the leading lady type. Truthfully I'd rather be a character actor because I think they have better chances at longevity.

Regardless of the answer, I know that I will achieve success as a film/TV actor because I happen to think that it doesn't matter what you look like. I know I have talent, a great personality, and good personal magnetism. All it takes is that one big break. Still, I'd like to get a professional opinion on how much looks really matter.

—Looking into Looks

Dear Looking,

It sounds as if you have already assured yourself of your inevitable success and discounted the meaningfulness of looks in the equation. And yet, you asked for my opinion—so here it is.

Looks do matter. A whole lot. No matter how much we want to believe that our personal auras or shining talent can shield us from this reality, we can't escape that film, TV, and even stage are visual media in which what we look like becomes part of the story. Yes, we can on occasion transcend our physical appearances if given the chance by the casting people, producers, and directors—as well as viewers—but generally, actors are cast based on how they fit a particular role, both internally and externally. We are all, in a sense, beneficiaries and victims of our "type."

There is no "right" look for working in television and film. But the more we know about which jobs others view us as "right" for, the easier our early acting years will be. You can, of course, work against type whenever the opportunity arises and once you've established your career. JA

Dear Jackie,

I just did a showcase with my graduating class and I got very little interest from agents. I'm not conventionally good-looking, but have an alternative look and vibe that's very hard to sell. I have the kind of mind and face that would probably sell really well in Europe—a kind of soft-spoken, subtle, non-flamboyant demeanor—but that doesn't help me any as a young American actor. While I know artistry and commercialism actually don't have to be mutually exclusive in this business, it seems like you have to be good-looking, charming, and tremendously social to even be seen.

Does this industry prefer a certain type of package, talent and physical, over others? And what can I do to incite interest in my very complex persona as an actor? Please just tell me you can be a working actor and an artist at the same time.
   —Folk Actor

Dear Folk,

Sure, it's easier to get noticed if you are beautiful. Does that mean you have to be beautiful? No. Do all gorgeous actors get noticed? Nope. Does that mean you can't be an artist and a working actor? Of course not. Does superior artistry mean you'll be successful in the acting marketplace? Nyet.

There's nothing to hold you back from being an artist. Merriam-Webster defines "artist" as "one who professes and practices an imaginative art," or, "a skilled performer." Your identity as an artist hinges on your continuing to practice the art of acting. Making money as an artist, however, is much harder—you are held back by the immense competition and the need to fill others' perceptions about you and the roles in their projects. And sadly, the amount of talent you possess doesn't directly correlate to the size of your paycheck.

However, as a recent graduate, you may be worrying too much about your perceived non-commercialism and "complex persona." One showcase is hardly a wide net, and you'll need to do a lot more fishing before making any assumptions about your viability in the marketplace. There are lots of successful "alternative" looking and intelligent actors out there.

You may, too, be taking on ideas about yourself from your teachers and others in your college setting, as opposed to looking at where you might fit in the professional world. Here's what I mean: I know a young actor who is getting primed to play the complex artist, much like yourself. His college instructors repeatedly cast him as the tortured young man, and he's highly valued for his ability to play those parts. Unfortunately, with all that praise and repetition, he may be missing out on learning how to play who he actually is—a relatively carefree, young guy. You can't always play Hamlet. JA

Dear Michael,

I'm an actor working in NYC. However, I happen to be in the most crowded category: early-to-mid-20s Caucasian female. I'm incredibly driven, and know one day I'll have a successful career, but in the meantime, it is pretty difficult to even get an audition. I have technique, a great look, and what I am told is a pretty charming personality. The only thing lacking is experience. For right now, I'm going to keep pushing forward in creating my own work and opportunities and try and be patient, rather than complaining that it's tough to get an audition or job because there are so many people my type (I am the only me, you know?). But how can I make myself stand out even more in this very crowded crowd?

—Ingé-new

Dear Ingé-new,

You're right. You're in a very competitive category. But it sounds like you've got the right attitude in terms of patience, creating your own work and the fact that, no matter how many young women are in your category, there's only one of you.

What'll help even further is to get very, very specific about the kinds of parts you play. Remember, it's someone *else* who lumps you together in the same group as everyone your age and gender. You don't have to. Think about what makes you unique; what sides of you might surprise people.

There's a "typing" exercise I do in some of my audition classes. It works best with a group, so see if you can convince some actor pals to make an evening of it: Pose and answer questions that narrow down your specific qualities. For example, if you were playing a student, what major might the character be likely to have? Would you be more likely to play a good student? A prankster? A bad influence? Troubled? Well-adjusted? Ambitious? Popular? Or a misfit? Do you play the best friend? What kind of friend are you? Reliable? Flaky? The leader of the pack, or a follower? Without knowing you, would people guess that you like to dance? Travel? Read? Collect things? What kind of family would your character come from? If you did this with a group of strangers, as I do in my class, you'd be surprised by how often the whole group agreed on their answers.

Now, this is not at all designed to *limit* your thinking about roles you could play, but rather to build your sense of your individuality in a sea of young women. And when you're going in for something that calls for those specifics, you'll have greater confidence, knowing that people are already inclined to see you that way. MK

Dear Michael,

   Here's my dilemma. I'm a Mexican actress, but ninety percent of the people I meet say that I don't look Mexican. I have light skin, light eyes, and dark hair. Plus, there's my name (Katya Fitzpatrick), which doesn't sound Mexican at all. So I'm really having a hard time with my headshots and the roles that I should be applying for.

Should I play up the European features in my pictures and apply for these kinds of roles? In the past, I've been applying for a lot of roles that call for Latinas, but I never seem to get a call since I don't fit the typical Latina look.
   —Mistaken Identity

Dear Mistaken Identity,

   It is a fine thing to celebrate and express one's ethnic heritage: speaking the language, taking part in holidays, sharing traditions, and so forth. But marketing for the actor is another matter entirely. In that arena, as you've often heard, you're selling a product—you—and often, perceptions of that product are far more important than realities. You may not end up playing roles that accurately reflect your ethnicity, and there's nothing wrong with that. You're not betraying your culture by portraying other races, you're just being a sensible marketer. A good friend of mine who's gay, big-hearted, and sensitive in real life is cast almost exclusively as straight, macho, hardened tough guys. It has nothing to do with who he really is; that's just his market. Me, I play mostly losers and jerks. Okay, so that part is accurate, but still, you see my point.

If you're not perceived as Mexican, then essentially, as far as casting is concerned, you're not. That doesn't mean you'll never play a Mexican character. But what it does mean is that it's not who you're *most* likely to play, especially with a name like Katya Fitzpatrick. Between your appearance and your name, it's not surprising that people are disinclined to buy you as Mexican.

You could try changing your name and your look, but why not go where the doors are open? You have a European look and a Russian-Irish name. Run with it. When casting people ask your nationality, don't confuse them with the truth. Tell them you're a melting pot, and let them assume you have the heritage they're looking for. Or lie. Whatever works. Offer them a clear, simple, digestible concept, and you'll find yourself working a lot more. Just ask Ramón Gerardo Antonio Estévez, who changed his name to fit his appearance—and found much more success as Martin Sheen. MK

Dear Jackie,

I'm in my late thirties, but look younger. I've been paying a lot of attention to commercials lately, and I haven't seen any "hip" young-looking moms like myself. Most of the "mom" actors I see are in their forties and look overweight and matronly. Do you think I should target that look for an option in my upcoming headshot shoot?

—Hip, Not Haggard

Dear Hip,

If you are a young, hip 30-something, I can't imagine why you would transform yourself into a 40-something, dowdy matron. I understand that acting is playing different characters and creating different looks, but I would argue that commercial acting—especially for the type you would play—is much more about using what you've got. Commercials tend to rely less on acting prowess and more on looks, so casting doesn't look for actors who can dress up to look like a role— they cast actors who fit that role to a T. Besides, commercial auditions—especially with the help of a good representative—can be frequent, with some actors going out ten times a week. Could you get your frumpy mum act together on short notice that frequently?

Luckily, this is all a moot point. I disagree with your assessment of the common "mom" type. In my experience, commercial moms are usually late 20s–early 30s, thin, and pretty. Their children are too old for them and their husbands are in their mid-to-late 40s, balding, and slightly overweight. I've done my share of mom commercials and when I was about 28, I was cast alongside a 14-year-old daughter and a 40-something husband. This was not uncommon.

Don't try and reshape and age yourself to make it work. Figure out where you fit. JA

Dear Michael,

For some reason, I can barely get any auditions, even though I apply for everything—student films, music videos, commercials, films, TV—everything. The thing is, I have an accent and Eastern European features, so I might have a "non-marketable" look, if such a thing exists—does it? I mean, there has to be a reason why I'm not getting auditions, apart from lack of experience and no reel.

I enjoy the craft all too much to just leave it at this stage, so I'm pushing, but not getting anywhere. I was also planning to move to LA, but I do have doubts; what am I going to do if nobody would like to cast me?
—Stressed and Lost

Dear Stressed and Lost,

No, I don't think there's any such thing as an unmarketable look that would make one completely uncastable, though some looks are more marketable than others. I think you're glossing over the more immediate issue: you're a beginner, with little experience, and no reel. That's why auditions are scarce. Surely, it's too soon to give up; this stuff takes a while. While you wait, you can work on learning to speak without an accent, which will definitely increase the number of roles you can play.

It's really no more mysterious than this: getting auditions is hard—harder for you than for some others. But what's the alternative? Quit acting? Waste your energy on worrying? Just trust those opportunities to increase with experience, perseverance and—we hope—an ever-expanding palette of characters. MK

Dear Michael,

I have an upcoming commercial audition to play a sales representative, but I feel like I don't fit the breakdown. Although I'm 19, I look even younger. My headshots look exactly like me (I recently got them done because I had this problem before where I was going out for college type roles). It just seems like I'm wrong for the part. What should I do in this situation?
—Not the Type

Dear Not the Type,

Here's my short answer: go.

I've had those auditions myself, where I was completely wrong for the part and I knew it. There was one where I was called in to audition to play the friendly checkout register guy who represented the store the commercial was for. I never play that guy. I play the untrustworthy competitor, or the dumb neighbor who doesn't get it, or some weird character part. This role called for a nice, normal, friendly, helpful spokesperson type. I couldn't imagine what the casting people were thinking.

So I went, grumbling the whole time . . . and got a callback. In fact, I was the only person called back for my role. They were matching up the other actors to me. That's how sure they were that I was their choice. You guessed it: I booked the damned thing. Now . . . granted . . . a few months after the spot aired the store went out of business, but that's beside the point. For whatever reason, the advertising folks wanted someone like me to represent this particular product.

Trust the expertise of the casting folks. They know what they're looking for, and who they want to see. And if—worst case scenario—they've made a mistake by calling you in to audition, they still get to see you give it your best shot. And that's an ad for a different product: you. MK

Postscript: Sure enough, "Not the Type" wrote back to let us know he'd gotten a callback for the role he wasn't right for.

Dear Jackie,

I've noticed that, even in movies about cavemen, the actors have perfect teeth. How do they do it? I am not poor enough to qualify for special assistance, and I am not wealthy enough to obtain the cosmetic dentistry I need to give me a great smile. I'm a singer and I've got all sorts of mercury fillings that are too large to be replaced with white fillings, and I need some bonding on four teeth in the front. According to my dentist, we're talking about thousands upon thousands of dollars. Recently, I read something about a union program to offer discounted dentistry, but they wanted to hold the offer to really young actors in their 20s and 30s. Do you have any suggestions?

—Desperately Seeking Dentistry

Dear Desperately,

I never thought much about the origin of all those gleaming white smiles, but you're right, television is apparently the mecca of the dentally advanced. Unfortunately, I couldn't find any resources for actors wanting cosmetic dentistry. There are programs for dental health, but elective dentistry—for looks alone—is not at the top of any charity list.

Even Uncle Sam turns a blind eye to aspiring actors in need of whitening and bonding. IRS materials state:

> A deduction is allowed only for expenses paid for the prevention or alle-
> viation of a physical or mental defect or illness . . . You may not deduct
> funeral or burial expenses, health club dues, over-the-counter medicines,

toothpaste, toiletries, cosmetics, a trip or program for the general improvement of your health, or most cosmetic surgery.

So, unfortunately, you'll probably need to throw down for the procedures yourself. At several hundred dollars per tooth it won't be easy, but you're likely to be able to set up a decent payment plan with one of the numerous dentists catering to actors on either coast. Or take a look at the Actors Federal Credit Union, which has a loan category for just this kind of expense—the Actors Body Image Loan—with a limit of $10,000.

The silver lining is that today's dentistry options are much improved over the choices available in the not-too-distant past. Actors of the 1920s and 1930s would sometimes have all of their teeth removed and replaced with fake teeth to give them a movie star smile. I'll take a ding on the credit card over dentures any day. JA

Dear Michael,

I'm an actor planning to move to LA. But I started losing my hair about a year ago, at 22, and now I see that in one more year, I'll be half bald. It's hard to get noticed in LA when you're young and attractive, but when you're not even attractive (which, for me, is not having hair), it makes it barely possible. I even tried to find actors who made it who are bald, but there aren't that many. And I'm no Paul Giamatti.

Is being bald a big issue when you're just "another actor in the city"? I know that if you're the next Marlon Brando, maybe people won't care about your lost hair, but let's not kid ourselves.
—Too Naïve

Dear Too Naïve,

Being "half bald" myself, you can imagine my disappointment upon learning, from your letter, that this renders one completely unattractive and uncastable. I'll inform my wife and my agent at once. Thank the Lord I'm funny, so at least I have that.

I guess you'd better give up, cancel your move to LA and take up goat farming in some nice, isolated village where no one will have to gaze upon the horror of your half-bald head. I mean, what are the alternatives, unless you're Marlon Brando?

OK. I'm teasing (no pun intended). But you might be shocked to learn that there are some rare, rare cases in which being bald, or balding, doesn't completely squash an acting career. Patrick Stewart comes to mind. Ed Harris,

John Malkovich, David Hyde Pierce, Jason Alexander, Nicolas Cage, Anthony Edwards, Bruce Willis . . . and that's not to mention the guys with transplants or hairpieces, like Hugh Laurie, Jeremy Piven, Matthew McConaughey, Brendan Fraser . . . I could go on, but I don't want to reveal too many Hollywood secrets.

Hair loss can even be a plus, depending on your type. As a character actor, my career didn't really take off until I started losing hair and gaining weight. When I had a huge mop of gorgeous hair and a thirty-two-inch waist, no one knew what to do with me. Now, I work like crazy.

Actor Michael Thomas Holmes had a similar experience. At 20, he started losing his hair. After seven years of using Rogaine[1] and waiting for his big break, he began to get discouraged. "I told my girlfriend, 'I always wanted to make it while I still had hair,'" says Holmes,

> Her response: 'Don't you know that you'll only make it when you *lose* it?' I stopped using the Rogaine. In seven months, my hair went away, and in about nine months, I began to be cast consistently. I believe two things happened: With less hair, casting people started to see me as falling firmly into the 'character man' type, while simultaneously, I began *accepting* that I was falling firmly in the 'character man' type. No one likes losing their hair—it's like watching your young self go away—but the greatest strength we have as actors is that the person auditioning is *us*. When we can incorporate all aspects of us into our 'package,' that package will be unique and, as I found, castable. It's a challenge to make young and bald work in this business, but it can be done, through acceptance and the right haircut.

Now, this is all great for us character guys. If you're a young leading man type, maybe it's more advisable to sustain the appearance of having hair, in which case, there are products and procedures to research: transplants, growth stimulants (McConaughey publicly touted such a product), hair pieces, etc. The better ones can be expensive, so save your pennies. Or, you could let nature take its course and see what happens. You want something that sets you apart? You might have found it. A receding hairline didn't seem to hurt leading man Jude Law's career.

Whatever you decide, be sure you don't present a false image in your headshots. If you start wearing a hairpiece in real life, then sure, wear it in photos. But don't Photoshop or retouch in a way that falsely advertises your product. Cleaning up blemishes, smudges or shadows is fine. But making it look like you have hair you don't have is a waste of time for you and casting people alike. MK

Dear Jackie,

I have two tattoos, a small one on my right upper arm, and a smaller one on the back of my neck. These have never been a problem for me in landing roles, but I recently decided that I want to get some more, and I'd like to know what you think. I'm not talking about going overboard, because I'm not looking to be cast in "tattooed guy" roles or anything. I just want to get a few more pieces, all of which would be coverable by a t-shirt. Do you recommend that actors stay tattoo-free? How much do you think this extra artwork will limit my castability?

—Inky

Dear Inky,

Tattoos have become more common in recent years, and what was once considered taboo is now fairly mainstream. A 2015 Harris Poll showed that three in ten Americans now have at least one tattoo. That doesn't mean the stigma has vanished. Of the "tattooless" who were surveyed: 47% admitted thinking people with tattoos were less attractive and 29% suggested those people were less intelligent.

Despite such opinions, tattoos that are coverable by short-sleeved shirts aren't likely to limit you, and—depending on your type—may give you an edge. A little ink can seem alternative and hip. The same poll showed that 45% of people surveyed believed people with tattoos to be more rebellious than those without.

One CSA[2] casting director had this to say:

> There are many actors these days who have opted for body art and it doesn't seem to have hurt their careers. Angelina Jolie, Johnny Depp, Evan Rachel Wood, Zoe Saldana, Jason Momoa, and dozens more—all have conspicuous body art, and it doesn't seem to have stopped the plum roles from coming their way. These days, make-up technology is truly state-of-the-art in tattoo concealment, so if you get a shot at that big role where visible tattoos may be inappropriate—unless you have a scorpion on your forehead—you should be able to make your tats 'disappear' with little or no trouble.

Jolie herself, in a 2001 interview with *The New York Times* said,

> When you're a young actor, they tell you not to get tattoos or cut your hair, don't do anything, just try to remain a blank canvas. But I couldn't get a part as a girlfriend on a television show to save my life, anyway. So it was great to say, 'I'm going to shave my head and get tattoos in

places you can't hide. Then if I'm going to work, I'm going to work.' I wanted to have a self that was really strong and really me, and that I felt comfortable in.

This approach works well when a professional make-up artist is on hand, although if you want to play more straight-laced types or do lots of classics, especially in situations where shirts are going to come off with frequency, you might want to avoid what can be a bother. Most nonunion plays and some indie film projects can't afford make-up professionals, so you'll be spending time and money covering your tattoos yourself. While lighter artwork might be hidden under simple foundation, large dark designs will be harder to disguise. And if you're working under hot lights, or in a play with lots of action, you may run into trouble as your make-up washes away under the sweat. JA

Dear Jackie,

I would really like to pursue an acting career, but I don't go to many auditions because I am embarrassed about my scars. When I was five I was staying in a summerhouse in Pennsylvania and two girls about 10 years old were driving a large lawnmower and began to fight over the wheel. They ended up driving over my right leg and even though I still have my leg, the entire backside of my right calf and my ankle has a huge scar. I've also had skin grafts so I have a thin scar across my left shoulder blade and a patch of uneven looking skin on my right thigh. I'm self-conscious about them and I'm really scared I'll be rejected for all the jobs I try out for because of them. Should I just not waste my time? If I do audition, should I show or tell them about my scars?
—Self-Conscious

Dear Self,

Forget about your scars and move forward. I'd bet that in about 99 out of 100 auditions you go on, your scars will be as irrelevant as your eye color. Yes, there will be the occasional job where they really want someone with silky-smooth calves, but actors lose out on jobs for having brown hair, blue eyes, large hands, short eyelashes, knobby knees, and dry elbows.

Your scars are much bigger deals to you than they will ever be to anyone for whom you audition. Whether film or stage, actors have access to wonderful make-up to conceal whatever they choose—auditors realize this. Sometimes your scar itself might even be an asset.

In a 2001 *Vogue* interview, Padma Lakshmi, model and host of *Top Chef*, talked about coming to terms with the large scar on her arm. While there was a time she shied away from the camera, it was a world-famous photographer who finally encouraged her to embrace her appearance. "People have told me that my scar makes me seem more approachable, more vulnerable; that it inspires a certain tenderness . . . I love my scar," she said,

> It is so much a part of me. I'm not sure I would remove it even if a doctor could wave a magic wand and delete it from my arm. The scar has singled me out and made me who I am.

JA

Dear Jackie,

I'm a working actor who has been very fortunate to land many a role in lower-budget film and television. I am now working towards jobs in series television and larger-budget films and finding that there is great interest in my work but I'm not "sealing the deal."

I was recently smacked into reality when my friend, who has been a TV series regular, told me she's flat out being told she's too fat for lead roles. She's seriously being informed she'd have the lead if she was, and I quote, "lead weight." She's my weight and body type and I haven't ever been told I am "fat" but I'm most certainly not skinny and could do with getting in what I call, "film shape," meaning zero fat on the body. I'm often curious if my lack of bookings at this level is due to my being a size 6 rather than a 2. Let's not kid ourselves. Look at the women on TV—even the "quirky girl next door" is uber-skinny. Imagine how skinny she is in real life without the extra pounds TV adds. I want to focus on the art but I'm realizing perhaps those "unsaids" in my meetings have been my inability to fit into what co-star[3] and leading actors often are—a size many times smaller than me.

The hardest part is that it's a huge lifestyle choice to be "underweight." In the past, it's required a trainer, food coach, and what felt like a team behind my skinny body. But if it means the difference between getting the role and not getting the role, I'd rather be working. Let's be frank here, I don't believe it when people say that weight doesn't matter. Watch TV and tell me that's true.
   —Practical About Pounds

Dear Practical,

I'm torn between telling you to screw stereotypes and ignore the scale or agreeing that your weight may well be a factor in your lack of bookings. It's no secret that physical attributes are important factors in an industry where so much of our marketing power depends on our looks. It may seem unfair to say that, for many television and film roles, a size 2 has an advantage over a size 6, but, as we all know, this industry is not about fair. It's about capturing audiences in a competitive marketplace. When the "in" look is very thin, very thin actors have the advantage.

Here are some thoughts from others in the industry: "I was told by my old manager that 120 pounds was 'a lot,' and that itself was a lie on my résumé," says one LA-based performer,

> At meetings, she would make me turn around in a circle 'to see what kind of shape' I was in and determined that I was 'hippy.' I've been told on set that they would go get a 'large' size to accommodate my shape and, on seeing me in a pair of my favorite pants I'd brought as a wardrobe option to a fitting, I've been told, 'Well, those aren't flattering, are they?' If I was wealthy, I would get liposuction. That's the truth. I think it would at least give me a boost of confidence, which would help me book. By the way, I'm a size 6 or 8, depending on the brand.

Another actor, who works frequently in television and film, including as a series regular, shares,

> Early on in my career, I was told by one manager not to eat for two weeks and by another that I needed to 'starve' myself. I ignored them. I knew that I didn't look good at the weight I was at and I didn't feel good about myself, but I wasn't ready to make a change. When I finally got to a healthy place, spiritually and emotionally, I lost weight and started to work. I never starved myself. Every woman on the planet has to come to a place where she can accept and love her body and be healthy and radiant in her own skin. Period. Live in the reality, but don't be a slave to it. You are in charge of your body and you need to do what is best for you.

And finally, some thoughts from a feature film casting director:

> A hard-and-fast rule about weight and career success doesn't exist. Casting decisions can be political, sometimes counterintuitive, and usually a reflection of the taste of whomever is in power. Inequities are inevitable, and one actor's ability to lose or maintain a certain weight is another's ability to do a flawless British accent on the spot. The cold truth of this business is that you are surrounded by people who are willing to sacrifice a lot to achieve their goals. But if you were to ask the actor with multiple plastic surgeries on the front page of the tabloids and the actor who's a company member of a theatre in the Berkshires if they'd change the level

of sacrifice they were willing to make for their careers, I'd bet they'd have the same answer.

JA

Dear Michael,

I'm about to graduate from a prominent conservatory program in New York, and I have a question about stage names. My background is very international; I've lived in six different countries and speak five languages. Although my "neutral American" accent is nearly flawless, my very European name is likely to scare off anyone looking for American talent. In fact, it's so misleading that my first name—Jan—tells any English speaker I'm a female (I'm not), and my last name is unpronounceable to anyone outside my country of origin.

Now, thinking from a business point of view, a name is a big part of branding, and a good, marketable name will definitely help to pave the way to success—people in the industry will easily remember it. Do you think Americanizing my name would help me get into the room?

—It's Hard to Say

Dear Hard to Say,

For all the reasons you've listed, I agree that changing your name professionally is a great idea. And now is the time to do it, before you've accumulated a substantial number of credits and contacts associated with your real name.

As you've said, having a foreign or ethnic name can put you in a casting box that doesn't consider your range. Marlene Forte, a successful "ethnic" actor says,

> I use my mom's maiden name, Forte, because it could be anything. My daughter's last name is Rodriguez, but they were typecasting her so I told her to change it to Forte as well. Whatever it takes to get you in the room. You can't work if you don't get in that room. An ambiguous name is the best!

In addition to the problems you've already mentioned—all of which are completely valid—I'd be concerned that people who've mispronounced your name or gotten your gender wrong might thereafter subconsciously associate you with their own feelings of awkwardness. They may even feel nervous or intimidated about pronouncing your name. And you don't want any of that. Those subconscious negatives can mean the difference between getting an audition and not getting an audition, and affect whether an agent feels comfortable pitching you.

So I say do it—go American, and make it easier for people to know who you are. And don't worry about losing your identity. Your friends can still call you Jan. MK

Dear Jackie,

I am certain that I will be changing my last name because anyone trying to pronounce it butchers it. I've decided on one that I'm pleased with and have been mulling it around in my head for about a month now to make sure I can move forward with it. Having decided, am I free to use this name on my head-shots, web listings, etc.? I've looked up the name on a few of the major acting websites and can't seem to find anyone else with it. Is there any other factor I should be considering before I officially put myself out there under this name—legally speaking?

—TBA

Dear TBA,

You can call yourself anything you want on your headshots and listings. What's important is to decide whether you want to legally change your name or just use a stage name for acting and keep your legal name intact. If you change your legal name, you'll be able to simplify any confusion with paperwork, payroll, and so on, but you'll also lose what might be an important part of your identity. How do you think your family will react to the news that you've ditched their moniker?

The procedures for legal name changes vary by state, but the information is easy to find online on your state government's website. Most likely you won't need to pay for help from a service or lawyer. And if you decide to keep your name but use another for your career, you won't be alone. Stage names aren't uncommon—many people change their acting names to better fit the persona they are selling and some do so because another actor has already registered their name with SAG-AFTRA or AEA.

As for butchered pronunciation? That might not be as bad as you think. I have actually benefited from an unusual, hard to pronounce, and ethnically ambiguous name. Apodaca is Basque—but people think it's Greek, Latin, Portuguese—you name it. They see what they want to see and it's quite a conversation starter. JA

What Do You Think?

1 What is a type?
2 Why is it important for actors to understand their type? What are the possible hazards of misunderstanding or working against your type?
3 Name three methods you could use to help figure out your type.

4 How will knowledge of your type affect decisions on headshots, websites, reels, and other marketing materials?

5 How might your particular looks influence your career? Be as specific as you can.

6 Does your current "look" (body shape, height, hair color and style, make-up, etc.) align with the roles you expect to play? Why or why not?

7 How might tattoos affect actor branding? What about your own brand in particular?

8 How might aging affect your brand?

9 Are there things about your appearance you might want to change for professional reasons? If so, why?

10 Would you consider using a "stage name"? Why or why not?

Notes

1 Rogaine—one brand of Minoxidil, a hair-regrowth medication.
2 CSA—Casting Society of America.
3 Co-star is an official designation in TV casting that indicates role size and pay rates.

5

MARKETING: MATERIALS

Once actors get clarity on how they want to present and sell themselves in the industry, they must pull together the marketing materials needed for doing business as professional performers. An actor's standard toolkit includes a headshot, résumé, website, and reel, all used to introduce and promote your brand. There are, of course, other creative ways to market yourself, including social media and independent projects.

Headshots

Headshots should be professionally photographed and clearly show what an actor currently looks like. Excessive retouching, filtering, and other "tricks" are discouraged, as they can produce an image that doesn't match one's real-life appearance. A good headshot may also subtly suggest the actor's personality and how he or she might be cast. In addition to the digital files, an actor will also need a supply of physical 8x10 photos for auditions that require them.

Headshot styles change periodically. They've gone from black-and-white to color, from glossy finish to matte. In the 90s, there was a trend of showing three-quarters of the body and in the early 2000s it was modish to frame the photo with a "sloppy border." Now, we're back to full-face shots, to accommodate the smaller online "thumbnails."[1] It's important to work with a photographer who knows the current industry standard. You can also research trends with a quick browse through online portfolios of professional headshot photographers.

Résumés

The actor's résumé lists credits, training, and other pertinent information. The classic layout is a three-column format, with credits sorted under headings for

Theatre, Film, and Television (sometimes these last two are combined as Film/Television). Occasionally, there may be other categories of credits, such as Concert, Cruise Ship, or Stand-Up. There should also be headings for Training and Special Skills. The résumé must be formatted to line up correctly when the page is cut to 8 × 10 and attached to the back of a headshot. You can see an example of a typical résumé in the Appendix.

There is, among actors, a misconception that résumé credits need to be in chronological order. Not so. A résumé is neither a historical document nor a sworn statement. The idea is to help the people who are reading it understand the actor's experience level. Keep your more impressive credits close to the top, so those doing a quick scan will be sure to see them. Staged readings, school productions, and student films can live further down the page. As you earn better credits, your less impressive ones can be dropped from the bottom of the list.

Reels

An actor's reel is a short collection of clips from his or her on-camera work. Some actors keep these clips as individual files so they (or their agents) can choose which ones to send in for specific projects. Others create separate reels for drama and comedy, so they can be submitted accordingly. Beginning actors who've yet to acquire professional on-camera footage sometimes record their own scenes or pay for content through a reel-making company. While these types of footage can sometimes be the only options available to the less-experienced performer, they can be of poor quality. And sometimes, a bad reel can be worse than no reel at all.

Websites

An actor's website hosts all their materials in one location, making it convenient for representatives and casting directors to view everything at once. Links to websites can be shared easily via email, on business cards, on postcards, on other websites, or in play programs, giving people a quick and easy way to find the actor. Websites also contribute to the actor's online "findability." Google yourself. What's the first thing to pop up? You'll want that search to take interested parties to a promotional site, supporting your "brand," which should be reflected in the site's color choices, font, images, and layout style.

Social Media

While used primarily for networking, Facebook, Twitter, Instagram, Pinterest, LinkedIn, Snapchat, and other social media should be considered marketing tools as well. They are public forums, easily viewed by possible employers, casting directors, agents, and colleagues—whether we like it or not. Actors must decide whether to open their personal accounts up to professional scrutiny or create separate accounts to avoid mixing business with pleasure. In either case, all *public* posts should reflect an actor's brand.

Questions and Answers

Dear Jackie,

    I took a chance on an unknown photographer who was recommended by the school I go to, but I was unhappy with the results. I am now spending endless hours on photographer websites trying to choose one for my next shoot. I've narrowed it down to two well-known photographers, but how do I know which one is best?

    —Undecided

Dear Undecided,

    The two most important factors in choosing a photographer are their portfolio and an in-person interview. You need to be sure the photographer is someone you can be at ease in front of—someone you can show yourself to. Even a photographer with a wonderful reputation and website crammed with star-shots may put you off if they are abrupt or condescending. You know that old saying—the camera doesn't lie? No matter how skilled an actor you are, you aren't going to be able to look relaxed and natural while feeling uncomfortable.

As for the portfolio—look at more than just the very best shots on the photographer's website. You need to see examples of photo shoots with people like yourself. Someone who takes great shots of pretty, young women may not be adept at capturing characters. Someone who's been around for years may have lost touch with the times, and someone who seems flashy and hip may have no insight into industry standards. And remember, the priciest session isn't necessarily the best. A shoot with my favorite photographer is far less than one with some of her peers.

Choosing a photographer is a little bit like choosing a restaurant. Yes, there are things we can all agree on—the restaurant should meet health department standards, for example—but there is a lot left to personal taste. JA

Dear Jackie,

    I just chose a photographer and am getting my headshots done next week. I was wondering if you could give me some tips to make the headshots perfect!

    —Perfect Pics

Dear Perfect,

    Now that you've chosen who will take your shots, you can—almost—relax. Here are a few final steps:

—Get plenty of sleep the night before your shoot.

—Choose and prepare your photo session clothes in advance. You don't want to rely on the "1-hour dry cleaning" promise or realize you don't still fit into your little red dress while you are pulling it up in the photographer's changing room. Prep and bring numerous options so you can swap out easily if there's a last minute snafu.

—When you arrive at your session, take the time you need to be sure you are comfortable. (Making sure you'll have enough time is something you should have discussed at your photographer interview.) If you don't like your make-up, ask the make-up artist to fix it. If the photographer wants you to pose in a way that makes you feel stiff or uncomfortable, ask for an alternative. Great shots are ones in which you—the relaxed, confident, and real you—shines through.

—Finally, let go of the notion that your headshots have even the slightest chance of being perfect. They won't be—I guarantee it. Aim for high-quality pictures that help you feel confident in the way you look. Be sure that the photo represents the real you—flatteringly but accurately. And before you settle on one particular shot, make sure it gets great responses from other professionals. JA

Dear Michael,

I live in Phoenix now, but plan to move to LA within the next year. I've had this question for the longest time but no one seems to have an answer: I have current headshots, but I've been told that they have to look a lot different in the big market (aka Hollywood) than they do in my smaller market. What are the casting people and agents/managers looking for?

—Airheaded in Arizona

Dear Airheaded,

This is going to sound a little snobby, but it's the truth: photographers in the larger markets of LA and New York are more on the cutting edge of headshot trends.

"You only have a few resources to market yourself," advises New York photographer Sean Turi,

> Each of these carries significant weight when approaching casting directors, agents, and managers. Headshots are tricky because the style is constantly evolving within the New York and LA markets. It doesn't take a whole lot to make a headshot really great, really bad, or simply dated in style. Investing in quality headshots, within your targeted market, shows the rest of the industry that you care about what you do and that you take

your career seriously. Remember, you only get one shot to make a first impression. Make it count.

"The smaller market photographer may be a good shooter with good technical skills," adds photographer Rick Stockwell,

> but he's rarely knowledgeable about good headshot photography because that specialty is something you can only make money at if you live in one of the entertainment capitals. There's a look to a headshot that's different from portraiture, which is how most of these guys in smaller cities are trained.

While your current photo may be OK to start with, eventually, you'll almost definitely want new shots. A headshot taken in Phoenix will look less-than-professional to a New York or LA casting director. MK

Dear Jackie,

With regards to looking like my headshots, I feel like I will be stuck with the same hairstyle for the rest of my life. I don't want to make any changes that will make casting directors do a double take and I don't want to hurt my chances at being cast. Is it acceptable to change your look even though your headshots won't match? Are haircuts and dyes acceptable after you have taken your headshots?

—OCD

Dear OCD,

Small changes to your look shouldn't cause alarm. Growing out your bangs, adding a few highlights, layering, growing out layers, or even cutting off a couple inches of hair should all be fine. Feel free to wear it up or down, and style it appropriately for the role you are auditioning for. You need to look like your headshot, but you needn't be your picture come to life—that would be scary.

If you want to change your hair's base color or go from Rapunzel to Pixie, start saving your money. You shouldn't feel locked into the look you had on picture day—it sounds as if you need some variety—but when you plan a big change, you'll need to change your photos as well. JA

Dear Jackie,

Is it better to staple, glue, or print your résumé on the back of your headshot?

—Need Specifics

Dear Specifics,

Feel free to staple, glue, two-sided print, or otherwise attach your résumé any way you like. Yes, there will be a few casting types—the 2% with too much time on their hands—who may criticize your methods, but for the most part no one cares about these details. Casting director Billy DaMota points out:

> Preferences can be good but in this case, it's much ado about diddly. There's probably one casting director who prefers that résumés be attached with chewing gum or that the paper is made from bark of only California-grown Knotty Pine. It gets pretty silly sometimes.

Instead of fetishizing tiny details, make sure your pictures are fantastic and that they work online—where they need to "pop" off a computer screen filled with thumbnail images. And attach your résumé thoroughly, anyway you please. JA

Dear Michael,

On my résumé, what exactly is supposed to go under Special Skills? I just finished school so I actually have a lot of things I can do but I'm not sure which ones are relevant. So far the definites are dance, directing, writing, and a couple of sports. What else?

—Résumé Riter

Dear RR,

Special Skills is a résumé heading that allows actors to share abilities that might be valuable to those doing the casting. Some of the most common include dialects, foreign languages, sports, martial arts, stunts, singing, and improvisation. It's good to be specific. If you include "dialects," then list them; "dancing" is too general; "ballet: intermediate" is better. Some actors also use the Special Skills section to share their funny or unusual talents, particularly those that might spark conversations, like "amateur magician," "licensed yodeler," or "horse impressions." Go easy on these, and keep in mind that you have to be able to *do* whatever you list, on demand—people can and will ask!

Things to leave *off* your list: anything that doesn't apply to performing. Adding that you write or direct muddles your message; have separate résumés for those endeavors. And omit anything that's too wacky or even remotely controversial, as these can be offputting. MK

Dear Jackie,

I'm just wondering if it is necessary to put your weight on your résumé. Can't weight be seen from a picture? Mine is quickly changing, as I have been dieting and working out and I really don't want to list it. It's kind of a touchy subject for me, and I feel like I will lose prospective acting jobs over it. I am losing a few pounds a week, and am rather muscular—so I weigh more than I appear. Is there anything else I should list?

—Not a Number

Dear Not,

Your weight is your weight—own it, and own your image. As actors we are selling, in a sense, who we are. We must be prepared to present that package in its most flattering but honest light. It can be hard sometimes to look at ourselves from the outside, truly assessing our attributes and flaws, but the better we understand our "product" the better we can promote it.

Accuracy is required even if it may sometimes cost you an audition. Yes, we've all heard stories about those one-in-ten-thousand cases in which a misleading headshot/résumé followed by a knockout audition has yielded an actor a role, but for the most part gaining access to an audition under false pretenses is just a plain old waste of time—for everyone involved. Spend that time looking for auditions where your traits will pay off.

If you are rapidly losing weight, you can easily change your résumé to reflect that as you go. And of course you don't have to be accurate to the ounce—use your average weight within about 10 pounds. You should know, though, that at many commercial auditions you'll have to fill out a size card. This demands up-to-date information as it goes directly to the wardrobe department. The last thing you want is to show up to a fitting and face a rack of clothes a size too small.

As for what else to list, your height ought to do it. List your eye and hair color if you'd like but since your shots are color, those will be evident.

Remember that your stats are just numbers, there to give the casting people a general idea of your physical stature. Unfortunately, most of us are too hard on ourselves—our perceptions skewed by self-consciousness and old embarrassments. Try not to give this more importance than it deserves. JA

Dear Michael,

I am an actress from central Pennsylvania, currently starring in my first full-time professional production. I'm so excited to be living my dream, and I'm trying to book more shows with this company and others. However, I'm afraid to submit to things outside of Pennsylvania because of my résumé. Most of my credits are from community theatre, and my education section is extremely lacking. I have a few community-college-level classes that I took years ago, voice lessons, and some workshops. I know that I have a long and hard journey ahead of me, and I've started to travel to take as many classes as possible. What can I do to make my résumé pop?
  —Little Fish in a Big Pond

Dear Little Fish,

Don't try to be a casting director. Submit, submit, submit, and let the people receiving those submissions decide whether to call you in. It's not our job to evaluate whether our credits merit an audition. That's what casting people do.

As for making your résumé "pop," you're at the perfect point in your career to learn a few tricky tricks of the trade—things many beginning actors do to maximize their credits, but few talk about publicly. So, let's be bold, and lay it all out there.

—Don't lie, but do "fudge." Welcome to the gray area. No one needs to know that community theatres are community theatres. If the name of the place is The Whatchamacallit Community Theatre, omit the word "Community." Next, eliminate credits for roles you couldn't realistically play in the professional world. If you played Medea when you were 16, leave that off. Blur school theatre credits by using the name of the school's theatre, rather than the name of the school. Of course, the savvy résumé reader knows how to spot gussied-up amateur or small-time credits. But removing the repeated stamps of "community" or "college" helps reduce the impression that you're a complete beginner.

—In your "Training" section, treat community college courses like independent classes, listing only the subjects and the instructors (e.g. Diction: Mike Clearspeaker, Dance: Grace Tourjeté). Also include seminars, lectures, and workshops you've attended; those provide training as well.

—Next, remove telltale amateur giveaways: only kids need to list their birthdates. And never include your address or Social Security number. (Yes, believe it or not, people do.) If you have no agent or manager, it's appropriate to list your website, email, and phone number.

This whole endeavor calls for nuance and creativity. Don't lie—that can easily backfire. (If you do, be very careful; make sure you know all about the production with which you're claiming to be experienced, in case you're asked. Better still: *don't lie!*)

There's no crime in being a beginner (everyone was at one point) so don't be ashamed. Present whatever experience you have in its best light, and put yourself out there. MK

Dear Jackie,

I have been cast in the Brecht play, *The Caucasian Chalk Circle*. I am playing multiple small roles without actual character names, except for one (Ludovica), who only has a couple of lines. I have been told that when playing multiple characters without names that it is better to list "Ensemble" on a résumé.

I have always wondered if "Ensemble" looks unimpressive. I already have two ensemble credits on my résumé. Should I list the character that has an actual name instead?

—Need a Name?

Dear Need a Name,
One So-Cal theatre coach and director responded to your query this way:

> If you are playing 'Ensemble' at A Noise Within or PCPA Theaterfest, it informs me that you were good enough to get into a decent professional production and are steadily making your way up the ranks. If I read multiple 'Ensemble' listings at minor community theatres, I believe that you are limited and perpetually stuck at this level. In your case, I would definitely list 'Ludovica' over 'Ensemble.' The majority of casting directors who know this play are usually only vaguely familiar with it and . . . chances are they won't remember names. Unlike familiar iconic names like Willy Loman, 'Ludovica' could be any number of mid-sized characters. Additionally, listing 'Ensemble' on your résumé again does not tell me anything new about your ability. If all three listings are in the same venue, it could make you look like you are stuck at the lower end of the talent pool.

Ensemble roles are often challenging and your experience speaks to your versatility and ability to work well in a team. My only concern is that "Ensemble" sometimes indicates that you were more of a background player. You may want to limit its use to shows in which the playwright actually calls for an ensemble. You can try "Multiple Roles" for productions in which you had numerous small parts. JA

Dear Michael,
Several months ago, when I met with a career coach (with a very impressive résumé, including seven Broadway shows), he suggested that in light of my interest in both legit and musical theatre, I should use two separate résumés. This is, according to him, because of the perception of the industry—you're either this or that. Where non-musical plays are concerned, if they see a résumé of mostly musicals, they will not be inclined to cast you.

At one point when I went to a seminar, still using the one résumé, the casting director said, "You do both. That is *so* interesting." This may demonstrate this perception. I often hear people say, "Your résumé doesn't mean anything. It's what you do in the room." Well, is that so?
—Guided by the Light

Dear Guided,
Whoever told you your résumé doesn't mean anything was mistaken. These are the kinds of sweeping generalizations I find completely baffling. Certainly, your résumé matters. In some cases, its content may determine whether you even *see* the inside of that audition room.

I agree with your career coach's suggestion. My philosophy is this: do everything you can to help those doing the casting to feel comfortable hiring you. If you're auditioning for a drama, and a résumé that features musical theatre is going to make them nervous, you can help them by instead presenting one that features your non-musicals. Now, that doesn't mean there shouldn't be overlap. Your musical theatre résumé should include some straight plays, and vice versa, to show that you're well-rounded. And your most impressive credits should appear on both.

I use the two-résumé plan myself. In my case, the division is between stage and television. I know some TV folks are dismissive of theatre actors, and some theatre folks are dismissive of TV actors, so I have two résumés, one emphasizing stage, one emphasizing screen. It seems to make both groups more comfortable. MK

Dear Michael,

I just landed an agent a while ago. I'm curious, when I go to networking activities like casting director workshops, meet-and-greets, showcases, or parties, should I give out résumés with my agent contact info, my personal contact info, or both? I've heard people telling me to print the agency info only, because it makes you look more legit, and the fact that you have an agent will mean something to the casting director, especially if they have a good relationship with the agent. However, I have also heard people telling me that at meetings initiated by me, it would be better to hand out my direct personal contact only. Because, in case I've moved to another agency, the casting directors would still be able to contact me, and I'd also get to build a more personal relationship with them. Which is a more appropriate way of networking?

Also, let's say I want to look for another agent. Should I send a headshot and résumé to another agent that lists my current agency info?
   —Hardworking Actor

Dear Hardworking,

Represented actors should never omit their agent's info from their résumés. That's a signal that they're either agentless, untrusting of their agent, or unaware of the protocol. It's considered unprofessional. Those who told you that having only your agent's information on your résumé demonstrates legitimacy were correct. However, there are some occasions when *adding* your personal information (by hand) is advisable, such as when you're auditioning for non-paying acting gigs, or those that are so low-paying that your agent may not want to be bothered with the administrative details. Even still, you should consult with your agent to see how she'd like you to handle such opportunities.

Building more personal relationships with casting people shouldn't be your goal. Meeting them is fine, but those interactions are for cultivating *professional* relationships, not personal ones. Leaving your agent completely out of that equation looks bad for the agent and bad for you, and confuses the casting person. (And confusion is the last thing you want to create.) Your agent won't appreciate it either. If you try to deal directly with casting personnel, you're doing the agent's job, and the agent may think your plan is to avoid paying a commission. Bad!

If you move to another agency, and a casting director wants to find you, there are ways to do that. He or she can call the good people at SAG-AFTRA, and, if you're a member, they'll know who represents you and provide that information. Or he or she can contact your old agent. Standard professional courtesy dictates that your former agents will do their best to direct casting people to your new representation. And most will. Only the pettiest, most small-time agents would sabotage a former client's opportunities. That's rare, so don't worry about it.

When seeking a new agent (which I hope you won't have to do for a while), yes, you should send a résumé imprinted with your current agent's info. That shows that someone else was interested in representing you, and makes you more appealing. But in that situation, again, it's absolutely appropriate—necessary even—to provide your personal contact info at the top of the résumé. That way, interested agents can contact you directly. MK

Dear Michael,

I need some résumé help. My look and voice both fit very naturally into the musical theatre ingénue roles. However, in every musical I've ever been in (in school and the few local theatres in my small town), I've always played the character who's supposed to look older, be funny, and who normally sings in the mezzo-soprano or brassy alto range. Though I always enjoy the challenge, I feel like these roles are hurting my résumé rather than helping. At one college theatre audition I attended, the teacher questioned why I was so miscast and had played all of these older, mostly alto roles when she couldn't see me playing anything but a young, innocent soprano. I felt strangely guilty, like it was my fault I hadn't been cast in her idea of the "correct" roles.

Unfortunately, these are the only roles I have to list on my résumé, and strange or seemingly miscast credits are better than no credits at all, right? Will this turn into a problem that could hurt my chances at future professional auditions? Should I wait and see what types of roles I may be asked to play in the future before I really start to worry?

—Concerned About "Correct" Casting

Dear Concerned,

It isn't a crisis, but your concern is legitimate. At the moment, your résumé may be confusing to people, which can be bad for business. However, one advantage of your youth and inexperience is that you have time to fix the problem.

Here are a few suggestions:

> —Make it your mission to rack up some credits that more accurately reflect
> your type. Whether it's at school, church, community theatre or someplace
> more professional, keep a watchful eye out for all opportunities to *shape* your
> résumé, rather than being at the mercy of someone else's shortage of charac-
> ter women. That might mean turning down roles that are against type, but
> you have enough of those. Once you've amassed a few credits that better
> suit your voice and appearance, the character roles will become pleasant sur-
> prises on your résumé that show you can do more than what meets the eye.
> —Have a really good answer ready for when someone questions you about
> your credits, as the teacher at the college theatre audition did. I think
> you could simply say, "They had a lot of leading ladies at that particular
> theatre, so I ended up playing the character roles, since they said I had the
> range to do it." Uh-oh! See what I just did? Suddenly, you're the hero-
> ine who took one for the team, pinch hitting and knocking it out of the
> park while the frilly divas, limited to their ingénue roles, minced around
> the stage warbling vapid love songs. Or, you could just laugh and say,
> "I honestly don't know. I've been trying to figure that out," and leave it
> at that. Just don't apologize or show embarrassment. Make it a positive.

You're very early in your career, and you've been wise enough to identify a
potential problem early on. So now, just leave Gooch to the Gooches,[2] and start
"typing" yourself. MK

Dear Jackie,

I've begun trying to collect all the film work I've done for my reel. I recently
shot a short scene with an acquaintance from acting school. I had agreed to do
it on the presumption that I would receive a copy. I've contacted her multiple
times via phone and email without receiving any response. I never signed a
contract or any legally binding agreement that she can be compelled to follow
through on, but I spent a whole day shooting this and feel it's the least I deserve.
This has happened to me before and I don't know what to do. Do I have any
recourse to get my work without making more threatening phone calls!?

—Scene-Less

Dear Scene-less,

Unfortunately, I don't see any way to compel someone to give you a copy of
your work, especially when the initial arrangement was so informal, and threatening phone calls aren't likely to do much more than annoy her.

Give the calls a rest for a couple weeks, and then return with a new, improved
demeanor. Ask her for a copy of the material in its current state and on the simplest medium. She may not want to give it to you before "she finishes editing,"

which may never happen, so explain that's not necessary. Full sequences that you can edit yourself give you the best shot at playing up your own best acting moments anyway. I once used clips from a film in which I had an important but non-speaking role. With all the footage to pull from, I turned a scene about a guy being beat up, as I watched, into a scene about me, as I watched a guy being beat up.

Most likely, your material is just sitting on a drive or memory card somewhere and your acquaintance isn't following through because it's simply easier not to. Offer to do all the work (pick it up, copy, and edit it) and share the outcome (a nicely edited reel piece she can also use). But if no amount of cajoling, begging, wrangling, or pleading gets you your tape, take heart in three facts. One: you only spent one day on this piece, and hopefully you learned a few things in the process. Two: anything you shot with your classmate in one day is unlikely to be good enough for your reel anyway. And finally: you learned a very valuable lesson. Clarify any agreements you make up front and in writing (at least in an email). Don't assume or presume—ask, discuss, and come to an understanding.

Even when working professionally, actors are still sometimes left without anything to show for a long day's work. When I used to produce commercials, I hated those calls from actors requesting copies because I was busy and the request got in the way of the million other things I had to do, on a deadline. That is the single biggest reason actors don't end up with tape they were promised, whether from national commercials, television shows, student films, or nonunion re-enactments. Overworked production people suffer no consequence for not getting you your tape. They don't have to follow through, so they don't. And what can you do? Sue them? Yell at them? Refuse to work for them again?

I hope you're still learning and enjoying the process so much that a little free on-camera practice doesn't feel like wasted time. JA

Dear Michael,

Can you give us some hints on making the best presentation with our reels? And do I need to be concerned about copyrights, since I'm using clips from things that aired on TV?

—Ready for My Close-Up

Dear Ready,

Here are a few tips, from various sources:

A casting director I spoke with says,

> Put your best, most substantial stuff up front, and go from there. Don't try to show us everything. Short is great. And avoid those montages. They're

sort of passé. Too many fast clips can be tiresome and don't necessarily help us get to know you. Also, if the sound or picture is bad, it's better not to include the clip. It's hard to watch and makes you look bad.

Matt Draper of SpeedReels suggests that you feature clips that show you playing the kinds of roles in which you're most likely to be cast—in other words, your type. "Don't make the casting director play detective to figure out who you are," he says.

Seasoned editor Stephen Pillster of V4 Video reminds us,

> Keep it short. There are no reels that are too short, but there are many that are too long. Don't worry about telling a story. Stay focused on you—the actor you're trying to market. Always start and end with yourself.

He also advises, "Change the bait from time to time. Update your reel as often as you have new, worthy material."

When I last edited my own reel, I made a lot of internal cuts to each scene, shortening other actors' lines—and even some of mine—to make the whole thing zip along more quickly. It's a very effective technique, and it makes for a shorter reel. It can also make you look like the star of every scene, which isn't a bad way to present yourself.

Don't worry about copyright issues. You are free to use excerpts for personal, professional marketing. As long as you don't begin charging admission for screenings or selling copies on the internet, you're fine.

One last thing: if you're hiring an editor, preparation will save you money. Before your editing session, watch your clips, jotting down potential cuts, noting the time where they occur and thinking about the order in which you want to assemble the clips. This helps you avoid spending time hunting around for things in the middle of an editing session, which can run up your bill. Happy cutting. MK

Dear Michael,

I'm currently in the process of creating my reel. I have some really great footage from multiple projects that I feel will help me land representation. The footage from one of my projects, however, brings up a concern. In this footage, my character curses. A couple of my other projects were silent films, thus the amount of dialog would be very minimal if I left this scene out. So should I include it? It does fit the character and the situation perfectly, and to me it's not an extremely offensive curse word, though I do say it twice. The word, if you'd like to know, starts with "bull" . . . and I bet you can finish the rest. I'm just not sure if this would be considered an extremely bad decision within the industry.

—Reely Looking for Advice

Dear Reely,

I wish all questions were as easy to answer as yours. Leave the @*!&%$ clip alone.

People who are offended by profanity usually don't last long in show business. For one thing, some of the stories we tell are about people who use that kind of language. (Indeed, you've said that the profane word in question fits your character in the clip.) But besides that, even off-screen, off-stage, in the suites of agents and casting people and producers and writers everywhere, among actors and dancers and scene painters and musicians and any other show folk you can name, "purple" vocabulary is almost an imbedded, time-honored feature of the lingo. I think it's highly unlikely that anyone will say, "Well, we *were* going to call Reely in for a meeting . . . but that *language!*"

Here's a little trivia. Did you know that in the old days, backstage crews were mostly staffed by sailors? Ever hear the expression, "She swears like a sailor"? No wonder we curse. It's part of our theatrical tradition.

Now, I know there are some writers and performers who choose not to use profanity, and I mean no disrespect to those people. I'm only saying that anyone in a position to view your reel will not be hearing "bull@*!#" for the first time. In fact, they deal with bull@*!# every #%*@#!% day. MK

Dear Jackie,

I paid a friend to help me get my acting website up and running. It looks pretty good, but it's not finished and I am not sure when I will have the time (and money) to complete it. I have a main page with my headshot, a bio page, a résumé page, a page with a lot of photos of me in different shows, a page for a reel (although I don't have a reel completed yet), an audition blog (in the works), and a page for contact information. What other pages should I add? I want to be ready to finish this thing as soon as I have the funds.

—On the Way to the Web

Dear On the Way,

I'd say you should actually consolidate a few pages. Make navigating your website easy for all viewers—streamline instead of piling on. Why not put your headshot, bio, and contact information all on the main page? Remove pages for unwritten blogs and unfinished reels, as well as links that lead nowhere or take your visitor to an error message, which can drive casting people crazy. You don't want interested parties spending more time clicking around on your site than looking at what you have to offer.

Once you have the wherewithal to make improvements, begin by fleshing out the pages you already have. Many actors list their current and upcoming projects on their homepage, with links to the theatre or film website. Others include positive quotes from reviewers or even colleagues. Want more ideas? Spend some time looking up the sites of actors you admire. And don't feel like you have to launch your entire site at once. Begin with a well-crafted homepage and add to it when you have the time and money to do it right.

And finally, you may not need to pay your friend for help down the line. Most do-it-yourself website builders, like Wix, Squarespace, and WordPress, are extremely user-friendly, requiring users to do little more than drag and drop. JA

Dear Michael,

I have an all-purpose website I like a lot, but I use it for stuff like family photos and just silly things I find on the internet. I also have a blog page about my various adventures (mostly bad dates!). Recently, an actor friend gave me a big lecture about how it wasn't the "right" kind of site. But if a website is to show who I am, well . . . this is me. What's the deal?

—Never Ashamed

Dear Never,

I agree with your friend. You're squandering an opportunity. I've known many a casting director who, when seeking a particular actor, will look first for a website, hoping to find agency info, a link to reels, a résumé, and so forth, all in one place. So I strongly urge you to put your fun stuff on a second, less searchable site (*not* simply a "yourname.com"), and use your main site for your "product." Make it professional, polished, not overly personal, and a great representation of you as an actor. Pick colors and fonts that match your brand, use professional photos only, and *please* omit any juicy dating stories. MK

Dear Jackie,

I've managed to add some top casting directors as friends on Facebook. I haven't met them, I took a chance and just added them and they accepted me. However, I am not sure if I should message them.

I've been to so many workshops where CDs say they hate when actors add or message them on Facebook and that they hate being bugged unless it's necessary. So with these CDs who are currently casting huge network shows, what do I do? Do I take the risk and say hello and ask if they would consider casting me on their television show?

Also I am wondering if these CDs are adding me because they are actually interested in networking or just for the sake of adding. Maybe they don't know I'm just another struggling actor who is desperate for serious auditions.

—Friendly

Dear Friendly,

   I think what you've been hearing is pretty accurate. Yes, lots of casting people love Facebook and no, they don't want you to message them with requests for auditions.

While many casting directors, agents, and managers have social media presences, their reasons for accepting friend requests from strangers vary. Some want to promote books or workshops, others see it as free publicity, and some might just like feeling popular.

I thought it only fair to get Facebook opinions from Facebook users, so I reached out to a couple of casting directors and a manager from my own friend list. (I kept their names out of print so I wouldn't be responsible for any unwanted friend requests.) Here are a few of their replies:

"I don't think Facebook is the best way to introduce yourself to me," wrote a talent manager,

> It's much better if I have already met you. I have my Facebook on high privacy settings so I don't get too many strange requests anymore. If I don't know someone already then most likely I won't accept the request. I guess for me Facebook is a 'stage two' networking tool.

"I know it's a social networking site," begins a casting director,

> But when an actor asks to be my friend and then incessantly bombards me with messages like 'What are you working on?' or their every post is about 'looking for an agent' or 'What do you think about my new photos?' Well, I tend to unfriend pretty fast. Also, what's up with actors (nonunion, no agent, no credits) asking me to join their fan pages? They also go away almost immediately.

Facebook *can* be used to advance your career goals—just not as baldly as you suggest. In my opinion you should not "friend" anyone just to get something from them. It's obvious and tactless. Instead, use Facebook and similar sites to keep in touch with existing off-line contacts. Look for opportunities to connect with actual friends and acquaintances—even those you've lost touch with. What about your college roommate who's finally making his film, or the director you worked with a couple years back who has now moved to your hometown? What about the casting assistant who's always coming to chat with you in the waiting room? Sometimes, just being accessible sparks new collaborations.

"While striking up a new relationship is possible, social networking may be more useful in developing already existing, if tentative, connections," agrees another manager,

> Just like at a party you go to in real life, you have to have tact. You have to think: Whose party is this? What's my relationship to this person? You can't just butt into a conversation. You need to use social etiquette.

Another Casting Director, who has used social networking sites like Instagram and Facebook to fill hard-to-cast roles agrees,

> I have a personal Facebook (which I don't allow actors to friend) and a work Facebook, to which I do allow actors to send materials. However, some are so obnoxious that I ban them permanently. Be careful about how much nonsense you send out and don't share app invites or game stats—that's the quickest way to get blocked. Be professional.

Kevin E. West, actor and founder of The Actors Network puts it this way:

> Just because something is possible doesn't make it a good idea. The thing I see that's a tragedy with actors using social media is that you can't control your audience—there's just no filter. You can easily come across on Facebook or Twitter as someone I wouldn't want on my set. And it's very easy now to shoot a moving picture—on a phone, whatever—and put it in front of people, but badly made stuff is just unprofessional. Do you really want to show that to everyone?

As you move ahead, don't rely on Facebook to sort your friends into "close" and "acquaintances." Create a new "Industry" list and add everyone you want to see you in a professional light, sharing only appropriate content with them. You'll have to keep on top of the ever-changing privacy options, adjusting which photo albums and other content your list can access. You don't have to limit access to acting-only topics—you can share other items that promote your "brand." But as you friend powerful strangers, remember that—even with strict privacy controls in place—it's near impossible to rein in every careless comment or awkward junior high school photo. The last thing you need is a potential agent seeing you "performing" a keg stand. JA

Dear Jackie,

I have heard about actors getting auditions or meetings through Twitter. I don't currently use Twitter, because it can be so political and obnoxious, but I am willing to join if it will help my career.

—Reluctant Tweeter

Dear Reluctant,

Many Twitter-using actors have seized the opportunity to connect, however distantly, with people who had previously seemed out of reach and follow successful actors, agents, managers, and casting directors. A few talent reps and casting directors will occasionally tweet tips, advice, and lists (such as their favorite gifts—hint, hint—or pet peeves) to their largely actor-based following. This arrangement builds the rep or casting director's user base, therefore their sphere of influence, and maybe their egos. As for tangible results, the evidence of social media providing real acting opportunities is, at best, anecdotal.

It's possible that the meetings you heard about may have been part of the "Generals in July" experiment. A few years ago, a Twitter feud about the value and legality of paid casting director workshops heated up between some Hollywood based actors and the representatives they followed. It played out in quickly volleyed, 140-character tweets.

The most vocal of the anonymous actors in the discussion was "ActorwithaChip," who issued a challenge: "I think @commeagent & the other agents/CDs here should try an experiment:" "Set aside four Fridays in a row [for generals given to actors on Twitter]. First come, first served. Actors get five minutes. Bring in a scene. Bring in a monologue. Leave a headshot. Go home."

Commeagent, Abrams Artists agent Mark Measures, agreed: "You have a deal @ActorwithaChip. I am more then happy to meet 10 actors a week for a month & then give you the results on Twitter as to how many we felt were worth signing."

Rapidly, via Twitter, several more talent reps joined the challenge. Besides Measures, Phil Brock of Studio Talent Group, and agents from Lemon Lime and Brick signed on. All that month, the agents tweeted out opportunities for actors to land coveted meeting spots, usually on a first-comment-first-served basis.

"Twitter is a good resource to keep in touch with agents and see what everyone is doing," said Rich Liu, an actor who nabbed one of the Twitter meetings. "I never thought they'd do a Twitter general or anything like this, but I'm new to LA so it made sense for me."

The experiment made less sense, as it turned out, for agent Mark Measures.

"I think that any time you are just randomly picking people out of a pile it's a waste of time, to be honest." Over the month, Measures held short, one-on-one meetings with about forty-two actors. Asked if he would do it again, he was unequivocal:

> No, no. It's just not an effective business model. I could do the same thing with a stack of pictures and just randomly grab ten, but this business isn't a lottery. And it's not like actors can't get to me in other ways. Anyone

who submits to me personally gets a response from my office. We're always attending showcases and plays and seeing actors through client referrals.

Phil Brock organized his sessions more like free workshops—and had a very different experience:

> We did a group session in mid-July, similar to what I would do if I were doing a seminar. We had fifteen actors in, they each got to do a monologue if they wanted to, or they could just meet on our patio for a talk. We actually thought it was going to be horrible, but in reality we ended up signing two actors from it. One was an actor who had actually submitted to me three times before and we had not seen him—it turned out he was good.

For better or worse, the experiment was short-lived and these generals are largely extinct. Twitter, like all social media, remains a noisy, imperfect platform. If you do choose to join, heed active Twitter user and actor CaroleAnne Johnson's warning:

> Tweeting can make you feel like you're doing something to further your career, but so much of it can be a waste of time. I see actors who tweet a dozen or more times a day, and have to wonder, who is reading all of that information? If it's not real news about their career, I don't see how it's helping them move forward. There's so much web "noise" out there. Just like speaking, I think it's best to speak only when you have something to say.

JA

Dear Jackie,

I think we all know the benefits of using postcards to publicize an upcoming gig or to follow up after a meeting with an agent, but what about to thank someone after an audition? Are postcards a polite and practical follow-up or just a waste of money?

—Willing but not Wasteful

Dear Willing,

Personalized postcards, with a small version of your headshot and a few of your impressive credits or a press quote, make great casual, repeatable marketing tools. Since you are trying to create relationships with casting people, any legitimate chance you have to get your face in front of them is one you should take. The thank-you is better than a general introduction postcard or mailing because it reminds the casting folks that (a) they liked you enough to bring you in for an audition, (b) you are a thoughtful and professional person, and (c) you still exist.

While you probably won't forget to thank casting directors and assistants, agents and managers, and directors who book you on jobs, it doesn't hurt to send a note to someone for giving you the chance to read for something in the first place. And what about teachers, castmates, stage managers, and that lovely make-up artist who made you look like a dream? Don't be stingy, but calibrate your thank-yous to the relationship: it might seem odd if your thank-yous stack up taller than you.

How you choose to format your thank-you is up to you. Postcards are good tools: they advertise your face as well as your name. Personally, I like actual thank-you cards, perhaps containing a postcard to remind the recipient who you are. A real card seems more personal and less like a marketing ploy—even though that, of course, is what it is.

There is a ton of marketing an actor must do from which they will see no direct response. That doesn't make it a waste of money. Postcards, continuous targeted submissions, industry events, and thank-yous are just part of the investment you need to make in your fledgling business. The hope is that consistent nurturing and tireless marketing will pay off. Besides, you're probably thankful when you get a chance to audition; why not say so? JA

Dear Jackie,

For creative marketing purposes, I think a photo on a milk carton, like they do with missing children, is likely to be saved and put on a bulletin board. It's such an original way to get my face out there. What do you think?

—Original

Dear Original,

I've heard about lots of "get noticed" gimmicks, but never heard a single story in which said gimmick yielded a desirable result.

In his book, *An Agent Tells All*, agent Tony Martinez writes about one such gimmick:

> Years ago, every agent in town received the same submission. It was a box with a picture and résumé attached to it. Inside there was a human foot. Not a real one, but an exact copy, the kind you'd find in a doctor's office. The note said, 'I'm just trying to get my foot in the door.' Funny, right? Everyone I know still remembers that submission. But as far as I know, no one ever signed the actor. Gimmicks don't work.

What's more, your idea may actually offend some recipients. Cutesy self-promotion that references missing children? Ahem. Instead of concocting gimmicks, focus on the things that might actually help you land a representative: build your résumé, experience, abilities, contacts, and confidence. JA

What Do You Think?

1   What are the standard actor marketing materials? Can you think of any creative tools to add to that list?
2   How do you choose a headshot photographer?
3   What should your headshots look like? What should you avoid?
4   How can you choose which credits to include on your résumé? What about your special skills? What should you list?
5   Is it OK to lie on your résumé? Why or why not? Explain the "gray area."
6   How do you get footage for your reel? What footage should be included?
7   What makes a great reel? How long should it be and what should it showcase?
8   Why do actors need websites?
9   What makes a great website? Do you have ideas for your own?
10   Do you have ideas for marketing material not presented in this chapter? What are they and why do you think they will work?

Notes

1 Thumbnail—a reduced-size version of a photo, prevalent on casting websites.
2 Agnes Gooch is a character role in both *Auntie Mame*, and the musical version, *Mame*. Gooch is a secretary, and therefore presumably acquainted with typing, hence the reference.

6

MARKETING: PROMOTION AND NETWORKING

Once you know your product and have created your marketing materials, you need to figure out how to publicize yourself and build your "customer" base—a challenging endeavor for actors. How do you sell a product in a market that is glutted to bursting? If no one needs another aspiring actor, how can you cultivate awareness of your presence and find clients in our crowded marketplace?

Simply put, promotion is advertising. From getting the word out about a show you're in to sending an agent an introductory letter, it's everything you do to get people's attention and let them know who you are and what you do. Networking simply means interacting with other people to exchange information and develop contacts. Because we are "selling ourselves," these can sometimes feel like vulgar endeavors, but in the broadest sense, everyone promotes and networks.

The dictionary defines networking as, "the exchange of information or services among individuals, groups, or institutions; *specifically*: the cultivation of productive relationships for employment or business." Actors are their own products, and cultivating "productive business relationships for employment" requires putting themselves out there—through auditions, yes, but also through a variety of other means.

That doesn't mean actors have to schmooze industry insiders at cheesy parties, make eyes at lecherous producers, or accost strangers with our headshots. It just means we must consistently *build relationships* with others in the industry. Networking can be as simple as following an admired colleague on Twitter, taking a class, or attending a gathering of fellow professionals.

Many inexperienced actors think of "promotion" and "networking" as dirty words, vowing to get to the top on talent alone. They believe the "cultivation of productive relationships" is beneath them, far from the art they pledged to serve. But this mentality is victim to a false narrative that separates our craft from our work. The truth is the two are inescapably linked.

Throughout your career, you will self-promote and network in your own way and develop your own personal style. As we keep repeating, one size does not fit all. The most important considerations are 1) what is most effective *for you*, and 2) what best aligns with your own personality and ethics. Neglecting either of these considerations can make for an uncomfortable imbalance.

Questions and Answers

Dear Jackie,

I'm a nonunion actor who has lived in NY for two years. It's been hard trying to get work by myself and I feel I should get an agent. I go to networking parties and try to talk with other actors and industry people, but I'm not sure how to act, what to say, or how to get noticed. I have a hard time going up to people. I know I need to market myself but how exactly can I do that? Is there anything I can do to stand out?

—Lost in the Crowd

Dear Lost,

Marketing and self-promotion are important parts of an actor's business, but in order to be effective, they must come from an organic place. No one is going to spend much time on a stranger at a party, no matter how forward they may be. And the kind of thing you describe, going up to random people in an effort to get ahead, is annoying, obtrusive, and all too obvious. An agent I know told me, ruefully, that he always knows the moment at a party when his friends have told the group he's an agent. It's the moment people stop ignoring him.

Happily, networking (in the best sense) has everything to do with working and living a real life and almost nothing to do with parties. You should be working with a theatre company, auditioning for everything you can, and taking a great scene study class as well as other classes—such as improv, commercials, and cold reading—as you can afford them. With so much time devoted to your classes, auditions, and theatre work you're bound to meet some great actors and directors. Some of them will have tips for you, introduce you to others in the industry, and even invite you to—you guessed it—parties. This is actual networking—meeting people through work and mutual connections.

It might seem for now like you don't know anyone who can help you get a leg up in this industry, but as long as you keep working you'll find that your actual circle of friends and colleagues will grow and grow. Those are the people who will help you—and you them. It's not a matter of getting in with a group of successful people, it's a matter of getting to know your colleagues—all of whom are aiming for success.

Forget networking and pitching yourself to strangers over drinks. Focus on the nuts and bolts of your career and soon you'll be at a party and realize you're networking, casually, alongside your friends. JA

Reader Response

Dear Jackie,

I appreciated your comments about networking in your last column. Here are some other ideas.

For the NY actor, my method of networking (and it works!) is to get on the web sites of the A-list theatres and start going to their readings of new plays. Participate in talk-backs, volunteer to read stage directions. You'll meet really serious actors, many of whom have agents (as well as directors, writers, artistic directors, etc.).

And, as you know, most plays that get a reading won't end up getting done on the mainstage of the important theatre where it got that reading, which does *not* mean the play won't have a life elsewhere. So I say to the actor who has been to a good reading, put in a Google alert for the play's title and author and when information comes up in any media about where/when the play will be done, track down the playwright. Write and tell them how much you loved the play and say, if it's going forward with a different cast, how much you'd love the opportunity to meet and audition for that playwright (obviously you'd know there is a part you'd be right for—and the character's name—-since you went to the reading).

You'd be amazed at how often the playwright gets back to the actor and says they would love to have the actor read and the sides[1] are attached! This is especially the case when the playwright is up-and-coming and not yet a major player (which is sometimes why the play didn't get picked up by the A-list theatre in the first place).

—Brian O'Neil

Author of *Acting as a Business*

Dear Jackie,

Can I email my headshot and résumé directly to casting directors? To agents?

—Why Buy Postage?

Dear Why,

Of course, if they give you their email address or their website, it indicates an openness to receiving such submissions. Send them a link to your materials on your personal acting or public casting website. For obvious reasons, they won't open attachments (some have their inboxes set so that any emails with attachments are automatically deleted). Many casting sites, like actorsaccess.com, offer free registration, including the uploading of your résumé and at least a couple of pictures, so you can easily get your materials on the web at no cost (these sites do charge for additional photos and other extras).

And it's still not a bad idea to use snail mail, especially for first contact with a prospective representative or casting person. Emails are easy to delete. JA

Dear Jackie,

I don't get the purpose of doing a drop off to an agency or casting office. Why does it matter if I hand my headshot to a receptionist rather than her getting it in an email? Plus, a lot of the time you can't get into the office anyway after having driven across town—which takes forever, of course—so you have to stick it in a box on the office's doorstep. Why bother?

—Rather Email It

Dear Rather,

A drop-off is often, as you surmise, a waste of time. People do them because, once in a great while, they are not. Yes, actors are usually stuck leaving their headshots in an overflowing bin or with an uninterested receptionist, but sometimes—especially with smaller offices—they get to hand their résumés directly to the person who might audition or represent them. Sometimes, they get the chance to make a wonderful first impression.

If you decide you want to give drop-offs a try, I suggest you schedule just a few a week, and do them when you are in the area for another audition or meeting. Limit your list of stops to offices small enough that you might luck into meeting the person in charge. In other words, skip any office that represents stars, casts major motion pictures, or is located in a building with security or valet. As you compile your list, ask around for recommendations and check online to make sure they don't say "No drop-offs!" on their website.

Finally, you mentioned a mythical receptionist reading your email or receiving your materials in person. Keep in mind that you want to do everything you can to avoid your submission being opened by receptionists or interns, whether emailed or hand-delivered. Make sure to address every submission to a particular person—the one you want to see it—not just a general company name or address. JA

Dear Michael,

I have good credits but currently lack representation. If I want to write a letter to "Famous Film Director"—a business letter, complimentary and congratulatory, including a headshot and résumé—to what address should I mail the letter, especially if I want it to arrive with some expediency in the face of upcoming projects for which I feel I would be right? The FFD's agent? His publicist? His manager? His Facebook page?

—Pen Poised

Dear Poised,

Any established film director will have representation. Find out who that is by contacting the Directors Guild of America and send your dazzling letter through the rep. At the same time, I'd reach out via social media if you're able to find him or her and if you're *sure* you're *specifically* right for the project.

I'd send the letter with the compliments and leave out the photo and résumé. That way it won't seem quite so much like a sales pitch. If you want to include, along with your letter, a postcard or business card with your website address, or if you want to suggest to Famous Film Director that he or she might want to take a look at your website or IMDb page, that's great. I've learned over the years that there's something to be said for the patience of the fisherman, who dangles the bait and waits for the bite. If FFD takes the time to look you up online, he or she will already be a little bit invested. MK

Dear Jackie,

I have read that some agents respond better to a headshot accompanied by a cover letter. I've always thought that the résumé says it all, but apparently that's not enough. What exactly is said in a cover letter?

—Am I Covered?

Dear Covered,

Imagine you own a company and are looking to hire a new employee. Which would you respond better to: a fabulous résumé sent without context or a fabulous résumé accompanied by a friendly, relevant note?

Think about your letter, or email, from the recipient's perspective. What, specifically, are they looking for? Agents want to represent good actors, but they also want clients who are conscientious and easy to work with. Casting directors hope for talent who are well-qualified and cognizant of how they fit into the industry.

Find out all you can about the person you are submitting to. Is the agency seeking a specific type? Is the project shooting in your hometown, or does it need someone with a skill at which you excel? Keep it professional. If you're sending a submission via snail mail and include a letter, go for a standard business layout. Be sure to spell-check and proofread. (I can't tell you how many cover letters and applications I have received that have misspelled my name.) Include recent career highlights, but don't ramble on—half a page is plenty. Stay away from demands such as, "I'm looking for a top agent that can get me in front of Steven Spielberg," or arrogance such as, "If you pass me by for this role, it will be your loss." And avoid exclamation points!!!

You may also want to rethink your submission strategy and employ some not-so-typical tactics. The 8 × 10 with cover letter is certainly industry standard—meaning that there are stacks of them, gathering dust, in every office all over town. Why not print your headshot and a "highlight" version of your résumé in 4 × 6 size and enclose it in a greeting-card envelope? You can omit the card or use it as a cover letter. How about sending it on letter-paper, tri-folded in a business envelope? What about a business card with a link to your website? Why not ask friends to hand deliver your headshots to their own reps? Don't be afraid to think outside the inbox. JA

Dear Michael,

I'm looking for a reliable list of casting directors. I know people move around, but how do I find out who's where? I'm doing an Equity waiver show and want to invite all the major casting people in town so I can make the most of the opportunity and maximize my exposure. My fellow cast members don't seem to be doing anything on this front, so I'm taking it on myself. Can you point me in the right direction?
—Seat Filler

Dear Seat Filler,

You're right: casting folk do tend to move around. The two most reliable resources I've found for up-to-date listings are 1) the CSA (Casting Society of America) website, where you can type in a city and see all the CSA members in the area (keep in mind, not all casting directors belong to CSA), and 2) Casting About (castingabout.com).

When inviting casting people to your show, don't neglect the associates and assistants. Not only can they report back to their bosses, they sometimes go on to run their own casting offices, so it's good for them to know you. But I'll add this admonition: don't invite *anyone* unless the show is great. Asking people to sit through an evening of mediocre theatre just so you can get seen tends to foster resentment. When actors invited her to their shows, the late, great, legendary casting director Joy Todd always had a great response: "Honey, is it *fantastic*? If you can promise me it's *fantastic*, I will be there. Otherwise I'll have to miss it." MK

Dear Jackie,

I have been at this a while and I am good at it. I want to stay in touch with CDs and have always heard that post-carding is a great way to do it, but what do you say when you don't have anything new going on?

—Writer's Block

Dear Writer's,

There are tons of excuses to send postcards, but the truth is that CDs know the real reason you are sending a mini-headshot to them: to remind them that you exist. While it's nice to have something positive to report, there's nothing wrong with keeping your note simple and straightforward. "I would love to have an opportunity to read for you"—or something to that effect—is just fine. At least it's honest!

Instead of (or in addition to) mass post-carding, why not narrow the field and really target a couple dozen CDs? Look up twenty or thirty recent projects that you think you would have been well suited for. Don't rely simply on prime time, network shows, or box-office smashes—really think about your type, your acting style, and your experience level. After you've made your picks, look up the projects' casting directors on IMDb. You may be surprised to find that many of the projects you admire were cast by the same people. From there, create your shortlist of CDs and find out everything you can about them. Google them, look for their names in the trades,[2] and read their old interviews or press mentions. Use what you learn to better target and refine your submissions. The more you know about someone, the more you'll have to say. JA

Dear Michael,

I've been thinking of ways to promote myself that I haven't tried. What do you think of the idea of doing a one-person show? I've heard of actors writing and producing their own solo pieces, but I don't know if it does any good. I'm not even sure what to write about, or how to put it on. And what about finding a director and so on?

—Me, Myself & I

Dear M, M & I,

It's time for some tough love. A one-person show? Oh, my dear friend, what can I do to dissuade you from inflicting such agony on yourself and others? Why on earth would you want to deliberately perpetuate—or, one could say, perpetrate—one of the most hated theatre conventions of all time? The one-person show holds its place among such notoriously groan-evoking categories of live performance as mime, bagpipe concerts, and *Lord of the Dance*.

It's not that they're always bad. Noooo, it's just that most people shouldn't do them. One-person shows by wizened and withered theatre veterans with great war stories from a lifetime in show business—like *Elaine Stritch at Liberty* or Ian McKellen's *Acting Shakespeare*—can be terrific. One-person shows about fascinating individuals, like *Mark Twain Tonight*, *Give 'Em Hell Harry* or *The Belle of Amherst* can also be quite engaging, if you go in for that sort of thing. I saw a brilliant one-man show that was all about drinking. But when less-established actors present one-person shows, it's often for the wrong reasons: as a means of increasing exposure, as an experiment in artistic expression, or—heaven forfend—to confront their personal demons—in other words, therapy. And that usually makes for a painful evening.

Remember, it's not enough just to want to be seen. You must also present something worth seeing. Not all actors are good writers. Sadly, many who *aren't* believe they *are*, and the results of that delusion can be hard to sit through. And not everyone has something to say. Just because a story is true, or personally important, doesn't mean it's interesting to others. I found myself one night, sitting through a young woman's solo show, all about how hard it was to be an actor in LA. Help me.

If I've yet to make my case for resisting this vile format, consider this: putting on your own one-person show involves some expense. You'll probably be hiring a director, renting a space, buying some advertising, hiring someone to do lighting, and so forth. Friends may help out for free as ushers and ticket takers, but some positions will require expertise. In commercial theatre, these expenses might be defrayed by ticket revenues, but it will be difficult to sell enough tickets to fund your solo piece. And agents and casting directors— unless they're personal friends or fans of your work—avoid these things like the plague.

Some may find my answer harsh. And it's possible that you will create a solo piece that is the theatrical sensation of the year. If you believe you have such a work in you, then I say go to it. But it's my greater hope that I've guided you away from the indulgent, dull, fruitless, expensive, resentment-inducing, disappointing endeavor a one-person show can be. MK

Reader Response:

Dear Michael,

Where does one begin? Your sarcastic, self-righteous, and dismissive reasons for telling "Me, Myself & I" not to do a one-person show are so judgmental, as if you speak for the entire acting community and for industry members who attend theatre. Tell that to the casting and industry people (of whom there are many) who have enjoyed them. Theatre is theatre. If it's bad or poorly written or not relevant, it doesn't matter if it has one person or 100. It's still bad. I have seen many more multi-person shows that never should have gone on than one-person

shows. To call yourself an actor but dismiss a real, sometimes very good, and ambitious art form is offensive.
—Ticked Off

Dear Ticked,

Point taken: I may have been a bit cavalier in my response. Yes, bad theatre is bad theatre, regardless of how many are in the cast—though for me it's like the difference between an awful two-hour dinner party and an awful two-hour date. I'll take the dinner party anytime. And when an actor without writing ability, a story to tell, or the chops to hold forth alone on stage presents a one-person play as a means of self-promotion, those pieces tend to be pretty awful and poorly received. It's not an art form for amateurs. MK

Dear Jackie,

I work as an event coordinator at an upscale Manhattan bar and lounge. I organize private parties and corporate events, and many of our clients work in the entertainment business, mostly on the production end of things. I work very closely with them when coordinating their parties and always have the urge to mention that I'm an actor and give them my card. However, I never quite know how to broach the subject without feeling like it's an imposition. My job provides me with a great opportunity to network, but I've yet to find an elegant and graceful way to let these producers and directors know that I only event coordinate to pay the bills.
—Kinda Connected

Dear Kinda,

There may not be a good way to bring this up. Those production professionals are not coming to your bar to find actors, so well-intentioned pronouncements of your "real" career may be met with disinterest or even displeasure. They see you, after all, as the person that's going to help them escape from the rigors of the entertainment business, not remind them that there are 400 emails in their inbox from people who want things from them. Telling them you're an actor may make you seem like number 401.

If, however, you find an opening and want to make your pitch, be frank about your discomfort, saying something like: "I don't have any idea how to do this gracefully, but I feel like it would be a shame if I didn't tell you that I was an actor. I would love to work with you in my actual profession, instead of just on wine lists. Would you be open to my giving you my résumé?"

In most cases, it's doubtful that the people you interface with are in a position to help you, even if they wanted to. Party planning is not something most producers or directors tackle themselves, so you're probably dealing with the production coordinator or production manager, neither of whom have much to do with casting. Still, you're right to seize opportunities should they arise. You just never know. JA

Dear Jackie,

A short film I am in is premiering at the Santa Barbara International Film Festival. I know that a lot of theatre actors send postcards out to agents when their shows go up. Would it be wise for me to contact agents about the film?

—Festival Fishing

Dear Fishing,

It can't hurt. Understand that it's very unlikely that prospective agents will make the hour-plus drive up the coast to see a short film, but it's always nice to have something to contact them about other than repeatedly asking for representation. Just inviting them to your film reminds them, a) that you exist and, b) that you are working—two things they need to hear with frequency.

If you can afford it, make a professional postcard with a film frame or a publicity shot of the film on front. I regularly see postcards advertising plays, films, or television appearances with no picture other than an actor's headshot. Even if you are playing a supporting character, the image and text should be all about you. This may seem like false advertising, but remember you aren't advertising the film—you're promoting yourself.

Who knows? Santa Barbara is such a popular tourist destination, you might get an agent to take you up on your invitation as an excuse to simply get away. JA

Dear Jackie,

I got the chance to appear on *America's Next Top Model*. While I didn't make it past the initial round, I know my episode will air on Tuesday of next week. I told my friend, who is a director, and he recommended I notify all my industry contacts, but I'm having second thoughts! Since I'm modeling and not acting, I'm afraid my contacts won't take me seriously. Then when I have something to tell them about, say a TV show or web series that is acting-related, maybe they won't check it out (or take me seriously) because of what I last told them about. Is it appropriate to email people in the acting industry about reality TV?

—Model Question

Dear Model,

While there's nothing inappropriate about emailing industry contacts about your television appearance, I don't think it makes a whole lot of sense. If you are pitching yourself as a serious actor, a reality show probably isn't a good selling point. If you want to parlay this appearance into contacts, you could reach out to modeling agencies and casting folks who work with commercial and print.

But remember, with reality television you won't know how you come across until you see the episode. Reality producers do all they can to incite drama and amp up excitement in their shows—even if that means using comments out of context or making someone look bad. Have you heard the expression "Franken-byte?" That's a soundbyte pieced together by editors in post-production. In other words, by using hours of recorded material, editors can put together words or even full sentences you never spoke. If it were me, I'd want to check the show out before telling *anyone* about it—even my friends! JA

Dear Jackie,

I recently got a background job for *Law & Order: Criminal Intent*. It was hard work but a good learning experience. What I was really hoping to get out of it, however, was a chance to make some contacts, so I could get a speaking role on the show. I miserably failed. I couldn't find the right moment in an extremely busy shooting day to slip my postcard to anyone. I also didn't know if I'd be ridiculed and thrown out on the street. Could you please tell me if it's okay to introduce yourself to the director, cast, or producers during a shooting day in order to give them your card and tell them that you are a trained actor? And if it is acceptable, will it do any good?

—Boost from the Background

Dear Boost,

You said it yourself. Your day on the set of *Law & Order* was "a good learning experience." There is nothing resembling failure in that.

Background work is a great way to learn the ropes of film and television sets, see the process first hand, make friends (aka network), eat excellent food, and pay your bills. And background actors are occasionally upgraded and given lines on set, but that is the rare exception, and requires a good dose of luck.

Frankly, it's not a good idea to try to hustle principal performer work through back-ground jobs. If you approach the director, producers, or cast with your postcard—even with the most well-rehearsed and inspiring litany of your talents—you'll likely be brushed aside. You won't be thrown out, but you'll quickly be passed off to whomever is coordinating the background actors, and it will be made very clear to you that you aren't there to get jobs. As far as production sees it, you already have a job—one you're not doing while you look for producers to schmooze.

How about this? Next time you have a job on set, take your postcards with you but keep them in your bag. If you end up chatting with someone who asks for one, you'll have it handy. JA

Dear Michael,

I'm wrapping up my training at an acting conservatory and getting ready to venture out into the "real world." I know that no matter how much training or talent you might have, it doesn't mean diddly-squat unless you know people. Recently, I've been going about making connections by emailing or "Facebook-ing" directors and other actors who I don't know personally just to forge connections. This doesn't amount to anything except a forced, awkward communication that probably repels them and disappoints me. I've been noticing that the best connections to be had are the ones that involve friendship, and, in some cases, even sexual interest, yet how does a person in my position develop these connections naturally and productively? What avenues are there for me to pursue to ease my way into having a personal connection without appearing as an overly ambitious opportunist?

—Looking for the Ladder

Dear Looking,

Now, I'm hoping I'm misreading you here, but it sounds like, among other things, you're asking my advice on how to sleep your way to an acting career. I've never known anyone who was involved in such a tryst, so I wouldn't know how to tell you to go about finding the influential partners you seek. But also, it isn't a wise path to pursue. I think the cost to one's self-esteem is too high. And—perhaps more to your point—I don't think it's effective as a method of career advancement. You might find that promised results aren't delivered, or that allegedly "connected" individuals who are interested in bedding you aren't quite as connected as they claimed to be. Even if they are, they're probably not going to put themselves in the vulnerable position of handing you a juicy acting job unless they sincerely like your acting.

Van Badham, a former university lecturer in theatre and current associate at the Malthouse Theatre in Melbourne, says she often finds herself advising students on this very subject. "Consider what giving yourself away sexually does to your brand," Badham tells them:

> Where you see someone as a person of influence who can get you ahead, if you sleep with them they see you as desperate, powerless, and manipulable . . . Remember: the best way of getting ahead is to hone your talent and work your ass off. Reliable, professional, and talented will always win the job ahead of sexually opportunistic.

I know your question was also about seeking out non-sexual industry friendships but, as you said—and you're absolutely right—whenever connections are "manufactured," rather than occurring organically, they feel awkward. If you're making friends with people solely because of what they can do for you, there's a good chance they'll be savvy enough to know they're being schmoozed. And again, here's the problem: it doesn't work. I don't think the person with whom you've created a forced friendship will think, "Wow, what a fine actor. I want to mentor him and support his career." He or she may do you a favor or two, but I think you'd be disappointed overall.

I have some good friends who are in positions to assist me in my career. They include producers, directors, casting people, and even a celebrity or two. But the reason we're able to be friends is that I genuinely like them, and I'm not asking for anything. I'm really not. On those rare occasions when one of these people connects me with an opportunity, it's always a surprise. Once—and only once— my sister, who's a producer, set up an audition for me. That was the only time that relationship provided a career advantage. Mostly, my influential friends and I all go out of our way *not* to cross those lines.

So here's the puzzle—and I think you already see this: how do you make influential friends without doing it for the benefits of their influence?

Well, one answer is to just be friendly to everyone, and socialize whenever the opportunities arise. You don't know who leads to whom, so just be a good friend. Be a giver, not a taker. When you meet people, don't look for your earliest chance to hand them your résumé or ask for help finding an agent. Instead, ask them about themselves. Take an interest. Do nice things, and don't ask anything in return. Remember, these people are probably asked for favors a lot. You want to stand out? Behave differently by *not* asking for anything. People can smell hunger, so put the potential benefits of these friendships completely out of your mind. Focus on the friendship, and benefits may come.

Be a joiner. If there's a cause you believe in, get involved. Do a walk for charity. Volunteer your time. Join clubs and groups—anything that reflects who you are. It makes you more well-rounded, and may connect you with business contacts who share your pet causes and interests. Joining actor groups is also a good idea, as it broadens your circle.

Maybe you can get a job at a casting office, talent agency, or management company. Seeing people every day gives you the opportunity to get to know each other personally and establish true rapport. Or, work as an assistant to a writer or producer. You'll meet and interact with their contacts in the course of your duties, so you won't need to create reasons to approach them.

Finally: I disagree with your assertion that talent and training are worthless. And I think you're far too young to be that cynical. Sure, these things aren't guarantees of success, but then again, what is? If I were you, I wouldn't give up so quickly on the idea of plying your trade honestly and seeing what happens. Most solid careers developed that way. Wouldn't moving forward in your career by virtue of your talent feel a hell of a lot better than getting a role because you wormed your way into a false friendship? MK

Dear Jackie,

I'm an unrepresented actor who recently self-submitted and was called back for the lead on a new series on a well-known cable network. I didn't get it, but the experience was exciting. I have mostly been doing experimental/indie-type work so to be considered for something mainstream was very nice. I sent a thank-you note to the CD via email and let her know I was interested in other roles on the series if she was casting any in the near future, but now I am sitting here wondering: Should others be made aware of this—like some of the agents I've met in the past at seminars and workshops? What do you suggest I do to get the most mileage out of this callback?

—Close But No

Dear Close,

I wouldn't announce a callback because it opens the door to the question, "Did you book it?" or, worse, "Why didn't you book it?" Instead, congratulate yourself on how far you got in the process and continue submitting. Your opportunity to get mileage out of that success was in doing good work at that callback. Hopefully, you'll be back in front of that CD again soon. JA

Dear Jackie,

I have always been very motivated to achieve my goal to be a professional actor. I have worked very hard, harder than most of my peers, and have sacrificed a lot. I work on my career at least six hours a day, whether I have any auditions or classes or not, and I started a networking group. We meet once a month and share experiences and advice with each other—everything from "Casting director X hates it when people wear perfume in his office," to passing on tips about upcoming projects. It's been a great group, but I have a real problem with one member.

Most people come to each meeting with at least one thing to share—I usually have four or five—but there is one girl who never brings anything of value to the discussion. She just sits there writing down everyone else's tips and ideas. The whole point of this group is that everyone is supposed to help each other, and I feel like she is only there for herself. It's not fair. I'd like to kick her out of the group but someone else invited her in to begin with, so I don't know if that would seem too rude. I don't mind helping other people, that's why I started this group—so we could help each other—but I don't really want to be this girl's career coach.

—Unfair

Dear Unfair,

You're wrong. This clueless girl has already given you valuable practice in one of the most underrated skills required of anyone working in the entertainment industry: tolerating injustice.

No, it's not fair that this actor uses your cooperative group as her personal information piggy bank, but here's my question to you: What does it hurt? Is she disruptive at meetings? Does she ask annoying questions, forcing the rest of you to wait as someone explains to her what a "side" is? If not, and her only infraction is her lack of helpful input, it might be time to set some rules for your meetings. Formalizing the process may make it clear to her that she is not contributing, or, if she's shy, give her the boost she needs to speak up.

Remember, you're not directly competing with this girl—the field is far too crowded for you to worry over one person or another—so, contrary to how it might feel, helping her is not harming you. Maybe you should just enjoy all the good karma you're earning. JA

Dear Michael,

I am a newcomer to Los Angeles and have auditioned for and joined one of the casting workshop companies where you sign up to meet agents and casting directors. I have gotten called in for a couple of co-star roles from one of the meetings, so I'm pleased with the results.

However, I wondered how these workshops were perceived in the business. Since I'm new, I felt it was an expedient way to get myself out there quickly. Some actors I know have said they would never do it because they don't think it's right to pay for auditions. I don't agree, because you're actually paying for three hours of this casting director or agent's time, expertise, and advice. What's your take on this?

—A New York Transplant in the Valley

Dear Transplant,

You've hit a hot-button issue, one that always seems to stir up debate. There is no question that actors sometimes get work from these workshops. But should we do them? That's another question entirely.

After years of pondering this complex issue, my answer to whether or not actors should attend casting director workshops is this: it depends. The dividing line between yes and no has to do with several things: who's teaching, your reasons for attending, and your personal sense of (now don't be shocked) ethics.

If you're interested in educating yourself and learning more about auditioning, and you want to take a class to improve that skill, then some of the very best people you could study with would be seasoned, established casting directors—people who've spent years watching actors come in and out of the office to audition and have a lot to impart on that subject. For the class to be worthwhile, however, the casting director must also understand acting . . . and be a good teacher.

Let's look at those qualifications carefully before we move on. For the workshop to be an educational experience, the person teaching must have expertise on the subject and a talent for teaching it, and the students must be there to learn. Under those circumstances, paying to attend a casting director workshop is perfectly legal and ethical, and it's money well-spent.

But many of the guest "teachers" at these places aren't really there to teach. Some are there for the supplemental income you're providing. And if there's no instruction, then it's not a class and it's not a workshop. You're paying to meet someone who might someday be able to give you work, and that's where things get a bit shady.

Casting directors are paid to find talent. That's the job description. So it's not ethical for them to turn around and charge talent to be seen. That's called "double dipping"—getting paid twice for the same job. Some claim they don't have enough time to meet new actors, so after-hours workshops are a necessity. Hold on a second. Let's think about that: they only have time to meet new actors if the actors are paying them?

On our side of the transaction, if nothing is being taught or learned, then we are in essence paying to be interviewed for possible future work. Charging for a job interview is an illegal practice, which is why these paid meetings have to be called "workshops," even if they're not. Some actors will protest, "But I've gotten work from these things." I know. And young starlets in the old days of Hollywood sometimes got work from having sex with film producers. *Effectiveness doesn't prove that something is right.* Do the ends justify the means at any cost?

As for how actors who take workshops are perceived in the business, I'm sure there are many opinions. I think actors who pay purely to meet contacts are viewed as young in their careers and perhaps a bit needier, though I doubt anyone's reputation is permanently besmirched. Early in my career, I was at one of the very few "workshops" I ever took. The casting director, recognizing an actor in the class, asked him, "What are you doing here? You're a good actor." Another actor I know attended a workshop in which she and fellow students were kept waiting for an hour while the guest casting associate went to the gym. That doesn't indicate much respect, does it?

Yes, there are certainly other viewpoints. One friend of mine sees it this way: "To me, it's always worth going to these things. Even if the teacher sucks, I'm getting practice. It's like my audition gym." Another friend says, "I can't afford to be ethical. With no agent, this is the only way I can get seen." Many have called "workshops" a "necessary evil." And yet plenty of professional actors—me included—have built solid careers virtually workshop-free.

Personally, I'm angry and frustrated to see actors routinely bilked out of their hard-earned funds by people taking advantage of their need to be seen—only to learn nothing more than the contact preferences of a particular casting office—something that could easily be added to the company's website.

So . . . what should you do? Well, what makes this such a compelling issue (albeit challenging and hotly debated) is that it requires us, as actors, to weigh things like dignity and ethics—topics that aren't considered nearly often enough in our business—and make our individual decisions accordingly. I know I've made mine. MK

Reader Response:
Dear Michael,
I am so surprised at you! I found it utterly offensive to read your comments regarding workshops. Let's look at the facts: we already pay for headshots, transportation, postage, etc. Paying to attend CD workshops is part of the game now. I've been in New York for thirteen months, and these things have definitely bolstered my career. I got my manager through a showcase, a one-shot deal I gladly paid about $200 for. My manager introduced me to an agent from a top-tier New York agency, and I now freelance[3] with that agency. I was also cast in my first feature film because a CD was looking through the workshop company's files and brought me in to read. It was the best money I ever spent in my life.

At the end of the day, it's all about networking. It's untrue that those industry types have a low opinion of actors who pay to be seen. If that were the case, I wouldn't be signed exclusively with my manager. It is not a racket. If you get signed, these same people work for you for free until you book a job. That's the poetic justice.
—Get With the Program

Dear Get With the Program,
I'm always shocked by the enthusiasm and passion with which actors defend their right to pay for meetings and interviews, but I recognize that yours is a popular view and I'm glad for all your exciting success.

But again—and this seems to need frequent repetition—the question is not whether these pay-to-meet situations can lead to positive results. It's whether they're legal and/or ethical and, if not, whether we ought to participate. As long as actors are comfortable paying agents and casting directors for interviews, the practice will continue to thrive. So, not to worry. You'll be able to continue bolstering your career this way, at least for the time being. MK

Dear Jackie,

I find myself disillusioned by the industry of "meeting the industry." A handful of times, I've paid $50–$150 for a seminar/meeting with a casting person or agent and I am now on the email list of a few of these "leading" actor/industry places. I receive emails on an almost daily basis about the latest seminars, workshops, and short classes with so-and-so unattainable casting director that seem to promise work and cost $300.

Sometimes I wonder if I should be more open to participating in these things. A large part of me, however, thinks it makes me feel bad, and it's unjust to perpetuate the process of paying $50 for seven minutes of face time. I want to hold onto my cash, but is that even possible?

—Slow-cooked

Dear Slow,

It is entirely unethical and illegal for a prospective employee in any industry to be expected to pay to be considered for a job. Sure, an employer might require a certain level of education or experience, and it doesn't hurt when the boss is also your uncle (nepotism isn't just a Hollywood thing), but I don't know of any other industry where paying to get in front of human resources personnel is an accepted practice. Yes, *some* of the workshops are well-taught classes worth attending, but many are just thinly veiled pay-to-audition schemes at which a casting assistant or associate sees actors read scenes, gives little-to-no feedback, and takes headshots and résumés out in the parking lot (since they can no longer legally take them in the classroom). And the idea that actors with money to spare are able to buy opportunities less affluent actors can't afford is unsettling.

California's 2010 Krekorian Act makes it a misdemeanor for casting director workshops to charge for auditions, even under the guise of an "educational opportunity." In 2017, several prominent workshop companies closed their doors due to crackdowns on the practice. The days of the pay-to-play workshop may be coming to an end.

In the meantime, don't lose hope. It sounds like you are doing good work on your own behalf, and I encourage you to keep up with your self-representation. When things are slow, I understand that getting in front of an agent or casting director can be tempting at any price, and there are occasional success stories from such arrangements. I can't tell you what to do, but I encourage you to use your head and keep your principles intact. JA

Dear Jackie,

I have an agent who pushes me to do casting director workshops. She says that since CDs don't know me they won't call me in, but that through the workshops I would get in with them. She has four specific workshops on her list. Maybe I should go because she has only sent me out to four auditions in six months. Should I stay with this agent or find another one?

—Stay or Go

Dear Stay or Go,

Your agent is not breaking any laws or union rules by suggesting you do casting director workshops. She can and should suggest that you do things that will help your career, such as take acting classes, get new photos, and look for a manager. However, if she *requires* you to do the workshops—or just about anything—as a condition of representation, that crosses the line.

Billy DaMota, casting director, former member of the board of directors of the Casting Society of America (CSA) and longtime actors' advocate, discusses the matter in depth in his book, *An Actor Grovels—Exposing the Casting Director Payola Scheme in Hollywood.* Here's an excerpt:

> Sadly, many talent agents have allowed the workshops to run the way they do their business and these agents encourage their actors to enroll in workshops in order to create and maintain relationships with casting directors that the agent has been unable to facilitate. This is a lazy and exceptionally selfish game plan, and speaks to the extent that workshops have infiltrated the business of access.
>
> The workshop scheme has become such an acceptable part of doing business in Hollywood that casting directors, actors, and talent agents have been brainwashed—or bullied—into believing that workshops are the way to cast, and to be cast. Much of the casting profession and a large segment of Hollywood actors have accepted workshops as a viable shortcut to success, and have allowed them to replace a genuine work ethic with special favor. And some talent agents, instead of fighting the workshop system, and complaining about the fact that they cannot get their clients in to read for casting directors without first having them go through the toll booth, have simply acquiesced to the pay-for-access racket.

While not officially requiring you to do the workshops, it sounds as if your agent is unwilling to do much work for you without your participation in them.

This leaves you in the undesirable position of choosing to: a) leave your agent, b) acquiesce to her implicit demands, c) report the agent and attempt to prove that she is coercing you into doing workshops, or d) maintain the status quo of .66 auditions per month.

Fear is a powerful obstacle. Many actors hang onto unsatisfactory representation because they worry they will never find anyone better. Only you know whether you have given this relationship a fighting chance. JA

Dear Jackie,

If not CD workshops, what are the options for unrepresented talent? How do we get agents to look at us without a referral? How do we get CDs to look at us without a representative? How can we meet and get in front of people without having to pay them?
—Tired of Dishing Out

Dear Tired,

This is a small industry, and while you can't ask a new acquaintance to cast you in his next film, or a fellow screening attendee for her agent's unlisted phone number, the more people you get to know, the smaller it will become. Every event you attend, every actor you take the time to get to know, will pay off in your future—often in unexpected ways. This industry is a community. Get out and meet your neighbors.

- —The SAG-AFTRA Foundation offers the Casting Access Project (CAP), which provides free workshops sessions with casting professionals to Guild members in New York and Los Angeles. Complete the CAP orientation process to become eligible. They also offer an industry speaker series, "Conversations," and an acting business series dubbed "LifeRaft," as well as occasional screenings and Q and As. You can also network while doing a good deed by volunteering for their children's literacy program, Book-PALS (see Chapter 12, "Financial Matters", p. 244).
- —Actors' Equity Association also hosts member auditions and workshops. Upcoming events are listed on the main page of the AEA website. The Member Workshops and Seminars link lists additional offerings, while the Area Liaison News link will take you to events in your region.
- —Actors Fund, a nonprofit organization dedicated to protecting the welfare of entertainment professionals, hosts numerous offerings. Eligibility requirements may apply, although union membership is not required, and orientations are required for some events. Check their website for more information.
- —Los Angeles and New York actors should check out theatre company "Naked Angels" writers' program, Tuesdays at 9, or T@9. Writers bring

in work to be cold read, and actors are cast on the spot. Hang out, make friends, and see exciting new work come to life.

—Kindred spirits might also be found at an actors' "tweetup"—a free networking event for actors, writers, directors, producers and other artists in the social media sphere. The New York and Los Angeles events provide opportunities for online friends to get to know each other in person.

—In Los Angeles, actors can rub elbows with filmmakers at Film Independent, a non-profit arts organization for independent filmmakers. "If you're an actor in LA hoping to meet indie filmmakers, you should definitely consider joining," says president Josh Welsh. "We produce the Los Angeles Film Festival and the Independent Spirit Awards, as well as many, many educational events and film screenings for our members throughout the year."

—Some casting directors and legitimate teachers offer free workshops and demo classes. While their end goal may be to sign more students, there's no reason not to take advantage of the freebies.

The list I just gave was pulled together in a week—through asking around and searching the web. I can only imagine what you can find when you reach out to your own connections, in your own region. Remember, networking isn't hanging out with the famous and powerful. Networking is meeting your peers. JA

What Do You Think?

1   Name five ways that actors can create new connections.
2   List five promotion or networking techniques you will use in the next year.
3   Define networking. Why is it sometimes considered a dirty word in our industry?
4   What are some promotion techniques you would consider inappropriate?
5   Is it fair for people to hire others based on their personal relationship? Why or why not? Can you think of professional settings where you have seen this happen?
6   Can introverts have successful acting careers? How might they navigate promotion and networking?
7   Describe the controversy over "workshops" taught by casting directors and agents. What are the two sides of the issue? Which side is right and why?
8   Is it ever appropriate to pay for an interview for a job in another industry? How does your answer change your perspective on the workshop dilemma?
9   What makes something a legitimate class or workshop?
10 How does networking change as an actor gains success? Is there a time when an actor can stop networking altogether? If so, when?

Notes

1 Sides—script pages provided to actors for auditioning purposes, as opposed to a full script.
2 The "trades" are major industry news sources such as *The Hollywood Reporter, Variety*, deadline.com, and *American Theatre*.
3 Freelance—in actor jargon, "freelancing" means working with an agency under a non-binding, non-exclusive agreement. This practice is common in New York, but rare in other markets. An actor may freelance with several agencies at once, but will not receive the priority treatment given to signed clients.

7

AUDITIONS AND THE CASTING PROCESS

Auditioning and casting are two sides of the same event: casting is the process by which actors are chosen for acting jobs; auditions are the way actors apply for those jobs. There are so many variables to this event (stage vs. television, union vs. nonunion, and so forth) that coming to a working understanding of the process can be a daunting, if necessary, pursuit. To make the most of these opportunities, we must understand not only the various types of auditions and their distinguishing characteristics, but also the professional guidelines and protocols, how to find out whether an audition is legitimate or a scam, how to choose a monologue or audition song, how to prepare sides, how to approach callbacks, and how to deal with nerves.

Many actors ascribe unlimited power in this process to the casting director. In reality, casting directors operate like a human resource department. They place job notices, review submissions (headshots, résumés, and talent rep pitches), and select candidates for the employer to interview (audition). They do not normally make the final selection as to which candidate gets the job, but use their contacts, knowledge, and skill to cull the list of possible employees (actors) into a reasonable number of high-quality applicants. They run auditions, further refining the final list of candidates, and help guide the production company, studio, or director towards a choice. Some producers and directors rely heavily on CDs' opinions to help them make decisions. Others utilize a CD's organizational talents, but prefer to make artistic choices without input.

Those who hate auditioning need to think carefully about whether to pursue the acting profession, since it's probably what we'll do the most of throughout our careers—it is a regular, consistent part of an actor's life.

About the Casting Process

While there are many variations, the most common audition/casting scenario works this way:

1 Director needs an actor for a role in a project.
2 Director (or producer) hires casting director.
3 Casting director puts out a job listing, or "breakdown" (see next section, "About the Breakdowns"), to agents and managers.
4 Agents and managers look through their talent lists and select actors to submit for the project.
5 Casting director selects talent from agent and manager submissions.
6 Agents and managers contact the talent selected by the casting director for auditions.
7 Actors audition.
8 Casting directors (and possibly directors) cut down talent pool to a smaller pool.
9 Actors in that smaller pool attend callbacks.
10 Director (with possible guidance from casting director) casts project.
11 Casting director alerts agent or manager to actor's booking.
12 Agent or manager contacts actor to alert them of booking, providing initial details of the offer.
13 Agent or manager negotiates with casting director, conveying offer updates to the actor.
14 Once the actor and reps agree to accept the terms, the booking is "closed," or finalized, and all parties are committed.
15 Actor works job . . . and starts looking for the next one.

Notice that in this typical process, the casting notice goes out exclusively to agents and managers, and *not* to unrepresented actors. So as you can see, agents and managers serve as something like gatekeepers to the industry. Generally speaking (we'll explain the exceptions further on), you don't get access to legitimate professional projects without a representative who is in a position to know about the "job openings." It's an elitist system, designed to filter out amateurs, beginners, and—theoretically—the unworthy. But it can get even more exclusive than that. Some casting directors select only a few agents and managers to share casting notices with, and do so privately. So even having representation does not guarantee that an actor who fits a role will be considered or have the opportunity to audition.

About The Breakdowns

The Breakdowns are an organized job list that comes out every business day, detailing roles for which casting people are seeking actors. It is only *legally* available to legitimate agents and managers. (Many actors seem to find them through secret sources, a questionable practice of questionable value.)

While the term has become generalized, and might be applied to any casting call job listing, professional breakdowns are most commonly generated by the company Breakdown Services, owned and operated by founder Gary Marsh. Before this system was in place, casting personnel had to call each agent and manager individually, repeating their needs again and again. In 1971, Marsh founded Breakdown Services to compile casting notices and get them out to talent reps quickly and consistently. Talent agents and eligible managers subscribe to the service and pay a fee to receive the information. Breakdown Services—in essence a middleman—does not decide who gets the information; it only streamlines and transfers it.

This may all seem unfair to the unrepresented actor looking for opportunities, but with an overabundance of qualified applicants for every role, casting directors use their discretion to limit the casting pool to a manageable size. Employers (with the exception of government agencies) are not required to publicize job listings—each has a prerogative to choose its own hiring process—and casting directors are free to consider as many or as few applicants as they like.

About Casting Websites

While the official Breakdowns aren't available to individuals, actors can find and submit themselves for opportunities on various casting websites, usually for a subscription fee. Some of the most popular and legitimate of these are the regional sites run by Casting Networks (which include lacasting.com, nycasting.com, sfcasting.com), backstage.com, Casting Frontier (castingfrontier.com), and Actors Access (actorsaccess.com), a subsidiary of Breakdown Services. Casting directors who list roles in The Breakdowns have the option of also posting them on Actors Access, inviting direct submissions from actors. These listings will be mostly for the smallest of roles, which is a fine place to start for those without representation.

Additionally, opportunities for low-budget, low-paying projects are often available to unrepresented actors via these same types of sites. Hiring a casting director costs money. It's an expense that's often beyond the scope of low-budget productions like student films, webisodes, indie films, and some nonunion theatre, TV, film, and digital projects. Producers of these projects usually opt to announce their auditions via public online postings.

While casting sites can yield opportunity, they come with their share of risk. Unlike the official casting notices that come from Breakdown Services, audition information that's available to the public via paid sites is often un-vetted. On some sites, anyone who wants to place a notice may do so, with no background checking or proof of legitimacy. It falls to actors to protect themselves. A good general rule: auditions that seem sketchy aren't worth pursuing, as they can be a waste of time at best and dangerous at worst. Always, always, always err on the side of skepticism.

About Open Calls

"Open call" is shorthand for an audition that is open to the general acting public. It is also referred to as a "general call" or "cattle call" and is typically done when producers or casting personnel want to cast a wide net in their talent search. The term "cattle call" resulted from the fact that these auditions are often swamped by hordes of performers, many of them non-professionals, who are "herded" through the process.

While auditors usually try and see only a handful of qualified and prescreened applicants, open calls are useful when they need to find numerous new actors, such as a theatre company casting an entire season of work or a musical theatre production seeking a chorus full of performers. And some union productions are required to hold open calls for union members. Agents and casting people once did "generals" (open call auditions or interviews) to seek out new talent on a regular basis. Unfortunately, those opportunities have mostly gone the way of the dodo in favor of paid casting director or agency workshops. The massive auditions reality shows hold throughout the country are a repurposed, hyped-up form of the open call. These, like most "talent searches," aren't usually auditions at all, but publicity campaigns or talent scams.

Questions and Answers

Dear Jackie,

My college acting teacher said that you should always memorize the material ahead of time for any audition you go to so you can be totally prepared. Then I was in a workshop and the teacher said not to memorize stuff for auditions. This doesn't make sense. Why wouldn't you want to be prepared? Which advice is right?

—Memory

Dear Memory,

They are both right. Your college teacher was right to encourage you to prepare fully for audition opportunities, your workshop teacher was right to suggest you don't overdo it. You wouldn't audition in full make-up and costume, would you? In a way, going in "off book" indicates the same thing to the auditors—that they are watching you "perform" the scene. Better to show them you are still discovering the material—that, while you are quite prepared, you are still flexible and unrehearsed. So: do both.

Memorize the material, but hold onto the sides. Glance at them a couple times during your reading, whether you need to or not. (This also avoids the nightmare situation of telling them you don't need the script and then calling for line.) If things go well, they'll be left saying, "Wow! Such a great interpretation! We can't wait to see what she does after she gets off book!" JA

Dear Michael,

I've had my agent send me in for a few co-star roles on network shows. I usually get the sides around 5 or 6pm, and the audition is usually the next day. I've spoken to a few casting directors, and some are adamant about memorizing before going into the room. I've screwed up my last couple of auditions because I've let this information really freak me out. If I could just look down once or twice, I wouldn't have the fear of forgetting them at all! Am I shooting myself in the foot by occasionally glancing at the lines during an audition? Do casting people immediately dismiss you if you haven't fully memorized?

—No Time for Lines

Dear No Time,

I'll tell you what *never* works well for auditions: anxiety.

Honestly, expecting actors to memorize overnight betrays a poor grasp of what actors do. And adding that kind of stress all but guarantees a less-than-best presentation of the actor's skills. If I were you, I'd graciously refuse to take on the pressure of that utterly unreasonable expectation. I have to believe that, however adamant some casting folks may be, if you're a good actor who's right for the part, they won't let non-memorization stop them from considering you.

We actors need to take firmer hold of our own artistic authority, and approach our work in the way that we know works best for us. If using the page helps you perform the scene without the distraction of wondering whether you'll remember the lines, then for heaven's sake, do it. If the casting director balks, be gracious, friendly, and firm: "I just got the scenes last night. I haven't had an opportunity to memorize them." Don't apologize. Don't shrink into a ball. Just state the facts, and do your work. I believe that generates more respect than allowing yourself to get freaked out or apologetic.

However—and get out your neck brace, because I'm about to make a sharp left—you really should memorize if at all possible; not because someone demands it, and not out of anxiety to please, but because it will substantially enhance your work at the audition. It frees you to play the role, and makes it easier to interact with the reader, allowing the casting director to see your face. Embrace the challenge of getting off book, even in a short amount of time. Our brains have the capacity to do that. More importantly, in studying those words, poring over them again and again, grooving them in, and getting them solidly learned, you'll have a much better understanding of what the writer intended, who the character is, and what's going on in the scene.

Now that I've guided you in two opposite directions at once (both empowering, I hope), I'm going to share my favorite memorization techniques (besides the obvious one: lots and lots of repetition), honed over years of hastily staged readings, last-minute rewrites, and understudying huge roles:

—Write your lines out in longhand. Here's what happens: when you're writing, you're moving through the lines more slowly, in a more concentrated way. It makes you really think about what you're saying, and the exact word choices. By writing the words out, they become your words; you commit to them. Instead of just reading them, you're interacting with them, spelling them with your own hand. This also means you're looking at each line, then looking away from the script to write it on the new page. So you're already calling on your memory.

—Record each line several times in a row, leaving pauses in between. Break longer speeches into short, repeatable sections. Then listen to the recording and repeat each line out loud.

—If you have the technology to play recordings on a repeating loop, play the lines at a very low level while you sleep. Weird but true: they'll go into your subconscious that way.

—Have a friend help; it's one of the best things you can do. It gets the script out of your hand and allows you to drill.

—If you still don't know the lines, it might mean that you don't fully understand them. Carefully consider why the writer chose these specific words. Once you understand that, they'll be the *only* words you could possibly say.

But never let an audition become a test—or even a demonstration—of your memorization skills. Always hold the script, even if you have the lines down cold. (If you don't hold the script, the casting director's attention might focus on the fact that you're off book, rather than on your work.) And during the scene, look at the lines, as needed, without hesitation or regret. Otherwise, you've stopped acting and started proving you can remember words. And that's not what you're there for.

By doing your work in the way you know produces the best results, using the tools of your trade, you help casting directors by delivering what they *really* want: a poised professional who knows what he's doing. MK

Dear Jackie,

I've been called in to audition for a movie. They've given me the circumstances—pretty well defined—but no dialogue. I have a rough idea of the script and the character, but they want me to improvise. Any tips for how to prepare? Obviously they're looking for fresh, un-robotic, un-pre-planned performances, which is good, I'm just not sure what I should be doing between now and the audition.

—Trying to Prepare

Dear Trying,

Don't *over*-prepare. Directors who ask for improvised auditions are often quite open to ideas or just plain unsure about what they want. You don't want to lock yourself into any particular characterization. Ready your "take" on the role, but be equally prepared to toss it out the window.

I asked actor, comedian, and podcaster Matt Gourley what he does for improvised auditions. "I like to come up with a few ideas and not plan how I'll string one to the next," he says,

> It allows me to deliver something substantive but in a way that still seems spontaneous and alive. The nature of an improvised audition implies that they want to see what you do with the character and circumstances. This means whatever you decide, based on a full understanding of the character, you should commit to 100 percent. If they ask you for something different after that, you can adjust accordingly.

JA

Dear Michael,

In an audition yesterday, the casting director had me do the scene again and said, "Go ahead and improv the first part a little." I am trained, but I haven't taken improv classes yet, so I was taken aback. I'm looking into improv classes; but what if this comes up at an audition between now and then?

—Caught Off-Guard

Dear Caught,

Okay, give yourself a break. You can't possibly be ready for everything. Improv classes are a great idea for any actor, so good for you for signing up. One day, you'll be a master at this. But meanwhile, I can give you the bare-bones basics:

The golden rule of improv is "Never deny." That means that if another actor says, "Well, here we are at the beach," you should never respond, "No, we're not. This is the mall." It stops a scene cold, and it's the ultimate improv no-no. We use the basic principle of "Yes, and": you take what's given and add to it. For example, "Isn't that a beautiful flower, Gustav?" "Yes, Friedrich, it's probably the most beautiful flower I've ever seen." "You're right, Gustav. This flower should be in Guinness Book of World Flowers."

Those without training often seem to think improvisation is a contest to see who can talk the most or the loudest, and who can win control over the scene. That is wrong on both counts. Good improv is a lot like basketball. It requires intense collaboration, keen awareness and support of your fellow players, and a willingness to pass the ball. MK

Dear Jackie,

I've never, ever had this happen before. Have you ever been asked to bring a bathing suit to change into at a first audition since the role calls for it? Is this a scam?
—Cautious

Dear Cautious,

I can imagine instances where this would be creepy and others that make perfect sense. Here are a couple examples:

I used to produce and do casting for low-budget commercials and infomercials for weight loss products and fitness equipment. (Yes, I know. I am sorry. It was my day job.) Anyway, we were always having people (mostly models) audition in bathing suits. At some auditions, the agents had clearly sent actors who were NOT models and the actors did appear to be uncomfortable. But the roles I was casting were for people in bathing suits—or other revealing getups—that looked super fabulous in skimpy clothes. Sometimes the model or actor had to talk, and sometimes they just needed to stand around a pool and show off their fabulous abs (that they had ostensibly chiseled by using the product of the day, of course). There was nothing "scammy" about the jobs, which were nonunion but paid well. Bathing suits were just what the roles required. We were selling fitness and ripped abs. It would have been a big waste of time for everyone involved for us to hold callbacks for people who didn't look like fitness models in their bathing suits as that—not acting—was the most crucial criteria for the job.

On the other hand, I once opted out of a wine cooler audition where I was supposed to wear a bathing suit. That's not me . . . it just felt too weird. This was a well-paid, union gig. It was legitimate. But so was my choice not to attend the session.

If you'd like, check further into the company or casting office in question and take your cues from what you find. Or, if the whole idea of a bathing suit audition gives you the creeps, go ahead and sit it out. It's not likely to pay off for you to show up and sweat through the session. JA

Dear Jackie,

Recently, I went to an audition for a short film. The assistant director took my headshot and walked me into the office where the director was sitting. When the director saw me, he chuckled, looked at the AD and said loudly (like I'm not standing right there), "*Twilight* much?" I awkwardly laughed, but they didn't laugh along with me. There was just silence. So, of course I was totally out of it during my audition and I'm pretty sure it's safe to say I did not get the part.

It's been hard to shake the dehumanization right in front of my face. I was very tempted to just say, "Actually, I'm sorry, I have a vampire audition I should go to. Thanks!" and walk out. But I held it in. I didn't want to possibly burn any bridges, even though he was young and probably didn't know anybody.

What should I have done? Why do people have to behave this way?
—Not on Team Edward

Dear Not,
Sitting in such obvious judgment of others seems to bring out the worst in some people. Still, this kind of nonsense is usually reserved for behind the actors' backs—after we leave the room or while they are viewing the audition tape. But take heart in knowing that most professional casting personnel don't lower themselves to this kind of commentary.

I think you showed restraint and poise in going ahead with your audition after being greeted that way. Give yourself credit for rising above the petty comment— you even attempted to laugh it off! I admire you for that. Thank goodness you didn't get the part—can you imagine working with those jerks? And although this probably isn't the best of advice, I honestly wish you had gone ahead with your vampire audition comment. They wanted to joke, why not give them one to remember? JA

Dear Michael,
I have a friend who submits her headshot for everything. I mean literally *every-thing* she can find. She says "you never know how they're going to cast a role." She also goes to every open call she can. She's an older woman, and sometimes it's a bunch of 20-somethings and her. Am I missing something? Is this a smart tactic?
—Learning the Ropes

Dear Learning,
It's a *terrible* tactic. Yes, we should go for any role we're even remotely right for rather than playing casting director and eliminating ourselves from the run-ning. Many is the time I've been cast in a role I didn't think I was right for. But coming in for a role for which you're completely unsuited—and I mean *completely*, like a petite 22-year-old Asian woman auditioning to play the role of a 300-pound, 90-year-old black man—is just dumb.

New York casting director Michael Cassara says that one of the few things that aggravates him is "when someone comes in who is truly not right for anything in the project at hand; they are taking the time away from someone who might be perfect."

So a word of caution to all you actors out there who submit for literally everything, figuring "what the hell?": don't do it. There's a big difference between your widest possible range and the realm of the ridiculous that lies beyond. Don't be the 80-year-old granny who submits herself for the role of Hamlet, or the 17-year-old guy who insists he was born to play Blanche in *Streetcar*. (Believe me, people. It happens.) Alternative casting notwithstanding, you have to be reasonable about which roles you could actually play. By all means, push the limits, but for Pete's sake, do so intelligently. MK

Dear Jackie,

This disclaimer has been increasingly prevalent in casting breakdowns as of late: "Seeking submissions from Equity members *only*." I wonder if this is legal. Is it permissible to exclude nonunion actors from auditioning?

Also, on a similar note, I get that it's at the casting director's discretion to see nonunion actors at EPAs[1] but the information about whether we can attend is not available to us non-Equity riff-raff until the EPA starts—after we've traveled to the audition and sat around for a couple hours because we've arrived early to write our names as close to the top of the list as possible. Are we—the lacking of Equity card, the wannabe union actors, the hopefuls—being discriminated against?

—EMC[2] Questions

Dear EMC,

Is it permissible, by law, for producers to deny access to Equity open calls to nonunion actors? Sure.

Equity membership has certain perks and EPAs are a prime example. According to AEA, "Equity's audition process is compliant with federal law. Among the auditions that casting directors/theatres conduct are interviews or auditions for Equity performers." In other words, although Equity requires producers working under its contract to hold an open call for its members, it doesn't preclude producers from auditioning nonunion talent.

Keep in mind that anyone can submit their materials at any time to any casting director for any job on earth and a good agent may be able to get you seen, union card or no. Anyone can apply, but casting gets to make the call about who to see. It's just like a human resources department selecting which applicants to bring in for an interview after culling through a pile of résumés. Equity members have a built-in chance to fill some of those interview slots, but nonunion performers can apply for others.

All that said, many nonunion performers do get seen at EPAs in just the manner you mentioned: they show up, sign in, and wait and see. Since the audition itself is meant to accommodate Equity members who may or may not take up all the slots—it seems like there isn't an easy way for this determination to be made ahead of time. If some casting directors choose not to see nonunion performers at all, that's within their rights and usually done simply to save time—not to exclude the "riff-raff," as you put it. The job of casting, for better or worse, is not to find the best possible actor for each role. If that were the case, they'd have to review thousands—maybe tens of thousands—of actors for each part. Instead, the job is to create a manageable pool of actors likely to fit the role, and pull out the "best" ones to pass on to the director. Union membership, or representation, fits into this scenario by, in effect, providing a sort of screening mechanism, pushing some actors into the "likely" category and removing a little of the unknown from the casting director's job.

I suggest you take the energy you've got tied up with the EPAs and put it into landing a role in a fantastic nonunion play. Sooner or later, you'll be showing up early and signing in amongst the union members, and you'll be dealing with the frustrating fact that many of the roles you are auditioning for at an EPA have already been cast.

That's right. Just because Equity can require producers to hold EPAs, doesn't mean they can enforce the validity of the audition. I still remember an agent-less roommate of mine in New York gleefully telling me that she had just attended an EPA for *The Seagull*, while I stood there silent, not knowing how to tell her I'd auditioned for the show, through my agency, months before and that it had already been cast. JA

Dear Jackie,

The last EPA I went to was being run by an older man and a young woman who was clearly an assistant. The older man was asleep and the woman was on her phone the whole time. Great, I thought, I woke up extra early to wait around and be ignored and disrespected? I find EPAs to be a bigger pain than an opportunity. I think the way they are run should be completely reorganized or the entire thing should be shut down. If they aren't actually going to cast anyone from a call, and are just having it because they are required to, what's the point?

—Forget About It

Dear Forget,

Many actors complain about the frustrating realities of EPAs. While Actors' Equity Association will only comment that the EPA rules are agreed upon by all parties at the bargaining table, I reached out to other actors for insight into the issues. Here are some of their most provocative comments:

> I have found no other equally draining, depressing experience than being on the audition line for an EPA. It's as if every morsel of joy has been barred from the space—all you can feel and smell is the desperation and negativity surging around you. It feels like a welfare line. It may have started out as a useful tool, but over time it has changed to a time-sucking, morale-damaging waste of precious time. I have seen and heard some amazing stories of both actors and casting people behaving atrociously at these auditions. And no wonder. Neither the actor nor the organizations or their reps want to have their time wasted. I believe that if it truly were a practical and useful system, part of the fruit of that would be an air, attitude, or spark of potential and excitement.

★★★

> If you think they're a waste of time, don't go! I use EPAs for more than just the projects in question by 1) Networking. It is not true that all EPAs are run by interns. I have auditioned at EPAs for at least half of the New York theatre casting directors working today. And why be snobbish about interns and "underlings" you meet in this business? Those interns have an amazing way of suddenly becoming someone you want very much to know. 2) Keeping yourself in shape. Doing EPAs is like going to the gym. If you use them correctly, you will soon have a portfolio of thoroughly prepared monologues and/or songs that you can do at the drop of a hat. 3) Preparing the ground for agent submissions. If you make a good impression at an EPA—and casting directors have amazing memories—they are more apt to see you when an agent submits you for a future project.

★★★

> EPAs are Equity's way of making the audition process less like a cattle call, but it's still a cattle call, with a little paint to make it look more dignified. It gives actors the illusion that somebody is looking at us, but the only ones they're looking at are the ones with connections.

★★★

> A few years ago I went to an EPA and, as usual, nothing came of it. But a few weeks ago, I received a call from a director who got my name from

the casting person I met at that very EPA. Let's face it, in this business your chances are slim to begin with. If you want to stay in this crazy game, you have to play to be considered.

My advice? Do EPAs only if you can let go of the dream of an immediate outcome. Nothing in our industry is fair, but if this particular flavor of injustice hits you too hard, give yourself permission not to go. JA

Dear Michael,

Lately, my auditions have mostly been requests for self-taped submissions, instead of coming in to meet with the casting director in person. It's definitely frustrating, but I know it's sort of the new trend. But I realized that I have a bunch of questions that I don't want to bother my agent with about the taping procedure. First of all, where are we supposed to look? What if we're talking to more than one other character? How many takes of a scene should we send? Do they want a close-up and a long shot? Anything else I should know? I really want to get this right.

—Camera Shy

Dear CS,

Many of us are less than comfortable with doing self-taped auditions. And rest assured: you're not the only one with these questions. So here goes.

— In real filmmaking, your off-screen scene partner is most often directly beside the camera. As a general rule, that's where you should "place" the other characters. Never look into the lens (except in a few rare instances, such as narrating or playing a newscaster).
— If you have more than one character to relate to, you can place them on different sides of the camera if that helps you. Don't make yourself crazy with this one. You don't need a different spot for each person in the scene. It's enough just to shift your focus. Remember, the casting people know the scene, so they know to whom your various lines are addressed.
— Ideally, you should only send one take (your favorite one) of each scene. If you're working with an agent, you can send them choices if you feel there's some real variety. But the general rule is: the fewer the better. While you may feel that your takes are vastly different, they probably aren't to the viewer. Your essence, your voice, your appearance, your idea of the character—these things will be more or less the same from take to take.
— Don't make the casting person's life harder by sending a variety of frame sizes. Choose one. That choice depends on the type of material. Generally, you want to be close enough so viewers can really see your

face—framed from just below your ribs to just above your head. But if it's something highly physical, or a musical theatre audition, you'll want to go for a somewhat wider shot.

— Ask scene partners to read their lines softly. They'll probably be closer to the mic, which can create a huge volume discrepancy if they speak at a normal level.

— If friends are helping you, it's ideal to recruit two of them—one to hold the camera and the other to be your reader. It's hard to do both.

— Bad lighting can kill your recording. Be sure you're not standing in front of a window or other light source, and that there's enough light on you to clearly see your face.

— Try to record someplace that's relatively quiet, and *be sure* to turn off things that make noise, particularly air conditioners and cell phones— they can easily ruin your best take.

And . . . action! MK

Dear Michael,

I really wish casting directors would stop demanding that we put ourselves on tape for roles. Isn't that their job? Suddenly, we all have to be good at filming as well as acting? Or we have to hire someone to film it for us? Also, no one I know does their best work when they have to send in a video recording. Don't CDs realize that? So what's the deal? With the few auditions I get, I'd like to at least have a real shot.

—Bitter in Burbank

Dear Bitter,

I want to appeal to your sense of reason here. I get that you don't like putting yourself on video, but if a casting director has chosen to go that route, you have only two choices: a) be bitter about it, or b) make the best of it. (You could also refuse the audition or leave the business, but I don't think you want those choices on the menu.) What you *can't* do is change the casting director's chosen method for seeing actors. So your ranting has no effect but to raise your level of aggravation. I don't want you to do that to yourself.

In all likelihood, everyone auditioning for the role is doing so via a self-taped audition, so it's a level playing field. Putting yourself on tape isn't ruining your chances; that's how they're seeing people for that role. So yes, you have a "real shot." And logic dictates that, while you may not personally know people who've booked acting jobs via taped submissions, *someone* is getting cast that way (I've been, by the way). If the practice wasn't working, it's pretty obvious that casting directors would have abandoned it by now.

Put your mind at ease about the idea that you have to be "good at filming." A few friends, someone's iPhone, a relatively quiet room with enough light, and you're good to go. It's *you* they want to see, not your cinematic techniques. Most self-taped auditions are made without professional cameras or lighting equipment and without any editing.

And finally, I promise you, all that anger and frustration is showing up on camera. The lens sees all. So it's crucial you make your peace with this type of audition and *enjoy* it. Relish the chance to play a role for a few minutes, knowing that at least one person will be watching. Remember, *many* of your fellow actors aren't getting those opportunities. MK

Dear Jackie,

I recently went to a commercial audition and all they had us do was slate.[3] Literally, all I did was go in with a group of people and stand in a line and say my name and turn from side to side to show my profiles. Then they let all of us go home.

From what I could tell, that's what they were doing with everyone. I heard some girls talking about it on the way out, and I also noticed that the groups before mine were all in there for only a couple minutes each. Why would they bother calling us in just to say our names? It seems like such a waste of time. It took me over an hour to drive across town to this audition and they didn't even bother to see me do anything!

—Frustrated

Dear Frustrated,

Au contraire! They did indeed see you say your name and do profiles. That, sometimes, is all it takes. You said this was for a commercial. I'm sure you've noticed that in many commercials, the actors simply stand around, looking swell. After your audition, the casting folks know whether that's something you can "do."

As to why they couldn't accomplish this through your headshot alone, well, we're all aware that a picture can indeed lie. Actor's headshots are not always an accurate representation of their current looks, whether due to new haircuts or facial hair, or because beauty lighting and retouching can cover flaws so effectively that they end up obscuring the actor's actual appearance. And a picture can't capture an actor's general "vibe." When there's not a lot of acting required for a role, your vibe, aura, essence—whatever you want to call it—and your mannerisms, posture, and body language become central.

Were you relaxed, confident, and open during your slate? Were you yourself? If so, chalk it up as a success. JA

Dear Jackie,

Recently I submitted for a student film at a local school. When I received the sides, it was just two lines of language that I found objectionable. I agonized over this for several days. My first thoughts were: couldn't they have found a scene that was more representative of the character? Does she just spew four-letter words? Then I thought about going in and ad-libbing a more PG-rated read. Eventually I sent what I hoped was a very polite email excusing myself from the audition because of the language of the character.

I do understand that as an actor I am expected to act like someone who is not me, but what is the professional response to audition material that is offensive to the actor for religious, language, or sexual reasons? I don't want to start building a reputation for being difficult.

—Not Into That

Dear Not Into That,

You don't need to audition for anything you aren't interested in working on. What I'm curious about is why you felt you needed to tell the students that you were passing because of the foul language. It sounds as if you may have been hoping to teach them something or get them to rethink their script. That's where you might pick up the "difficult" mantle. It's perfectly all right to decline an audition for whatever reason—actors do it all the time. You don't owe auditors an explanation—just a polite note stating you won't be able to make it. Do not offer anything sounding like criticism, even if the script is the worst thing you've ever read. Contrary to your intentions, it's not likely to be helpful and will only spur resentment. And you were right not to ad-lib a "better" version of the material—that too could lead to unflattering impressions.

Look, a lot of student filmmakers love to use profanity. I once taught a class in which students made black-and-white, silent, one-minute films. Even without sound at their disposal, their actors were passionately mouthing "f . . k!" at every turn. Hilarious. JA

Dear Michael,

Sometimes after an audition the casting director, or whoever is in the room, will say, "Great job!" It always leaves me feeling happy about my audition, whether I get a callback or not. But I was wondering if they sincerely think that I did a great job, or if it's just what they say to thank you for coming out and auditioning for them. I don't want to be stuck with a false hope.

—Just Wondering

Dear Wondering,

And what's wrong with false hope? Who cares if they mean it or not? Probably some do and some don't, but it's a moot point, really. You can't read people's minds; you'll only drive yourself crazy if you try, and most of us are crazy enough as it is. If hearing "great job" is making you feel happy, then why analyze? Listen to the voice of experience on this one: those good feelings are in short enough supply for actors. Why shoot them down? Besides, feeling good about an audition builds your confidence, and that means you'll do even better on the next one, and the next. So relish any encouragement that comes along. Take the compliments, assume they're meant sincerely, and go on your happy way. This is one instance in which, as the saying goes, ignorance is bliss. MK

Dear Jackie,

Over the last six months, I have been really lucky to get about nine auditions. I was thrilled and pumped and felt great about all of them—until I got no callbacks and no work. After the fifth one, I started to lose my confidence more and more each time. At my last audition, a national commercial that could have been my big break, I was exhausted from working my two jobs. My gut told me not to, but I forced myself to go.

I have never been so humiliated. I dropped lines, paused, my hands wouldn't stop shaking, and I broke character at the end. I kept apologizing, which made it worse. Then, as I was holding back tears and walking out of the room, everyone just stared at me. Everyone in the waiting room could hear everything I was saying, so not only did I embarrass myself in front of the casting director—who never casts me for anything—I humiliated myself in front of the girls that I have to compete with at every audition. I walked out and left the room crying. How do I recover from that? How will I be able to work with that casting director again?

—Humiliated

Dear Humiliated,

Don't give this audition another thought. Casting people see all sorts of strange things in a day's work. Someone forgetting lines or turning red isn't anything out of the ordinary. Apologizing and breaking into tears? I'd bet that this casting director, who has called you in before, thought something along the lines of "Aww, she must be having a bad day," and proceeded to forget all about it. Let it go.

Let's go back to what led up to this unfortunate moment, apart from standard work fatigue. You say you've had nine auditions in six months and characterize that as "lucky." With so few auditions, you've let each of them take on monumental significance, which is an unhealthy place to begin. It's downright debilitating to look at any single audition as your "big break." Most successful actors didn't have one single "break" at all—they benefited from a series of events that slowly led to greater and greater success. And most—maybe all—actors must continue to prove themselves throughout their careers.

When you audition, try to enjoy it as an opportunity to act, however briefly. To better process your experiences, buy a journal—a great place to keep track of your mileage and acting expenses as well as your audition progress. After you leave an audition, sit for a few moments in your car or on the subway and write down anything you learned or felt great about or would like to do differently next time. This should take you about five minutes, max. When you're done, close the journal, and put your focus on whatever comes next. Reflection's usefulness will have run its course. When you start your car or arrive at your stop, that's your cue to come back to the present and move on. JA

Dear Michael,

I had an audition today for a commercial. I did fine, but for some reason, I just didn't have the "me" energy that I usually have. It might be because I haven't slept well the last few nights, and boy, if I don't get my sleep it can really affect my performance, especially on a wordy spot like this one was. The casting director seemed fine with my performance, but I feel terrible because I work so hard and haven't had a bad audition in a long time. It's hard to let it go. Should I send the casting director an email apologizing?

—I Need a Nap

Dear I Need a Nap,

Whatever you do, *do not* send the casting director a note apologizing. You will only be calling attention to something that by now is long forgotten on his or her end. I know what it's like to think you've completely blown it at an audition. From the actor's point of view, it feels like we've made an enormous, unforgivable screw-up, so bad that the casting director is going to immediately add our name to some universal list of people who should never be invited to audition for anything ever again, and we'll be banished from show business. That sound about right? And in the moment, those concerns seem almost rational.

But rest assured, that isn't the case. Having an off day doesn't ruin your reputation or your career. Casting directors are focused on finding the right actors. So, if they don't think you're it, they'll just move on to the next candidate. It's important to understand this: you not being right for a role isn't a failure in their eyes. It's simply the math. Most of the actors who audition won't be the right choice. That doesn't mean the casting person hates their work, or never wants to audition them again. It only means those actors aren't getting hired this time around.

Here's my analogy: you're shopping for a new shirt, going down the rack, seeing what's available. Some of them will work for you, some of them won't. The ones that aren't quite right, you pass on. But at no point are you thinking, "My God, what horrible, terrible, stupid shirts! Who would design such things?" Right?

Your focus is on hunting down the right choice, and you're not giving the discards a second thought. They're just not for you.

And the fact is, we actors are, frankly, not the best evaluators of our own work. I can't tell you how many times I've done what I considered a terrible audition, and gotten a call from my agent saying I had a callback or a job. I've also had what I considered terrific auditions that led exactly nowhere. An actor I know once did so badly at an audition that she took it as the final sign that she'd gone into the wrong profession. Tearfully, she drove straight to her agent's office and reported her decision, explaining that this audition had opened her eyes; she'd been kidding herself all along. She could see now that she had no talent, and that it was time to quit. Mid-rant, the agent's phone rang. He briefly took the call, then returned to the conversation. "Go on," he said, adding, "By the way, that was the casting director calling to book you. So, you were saying . . . ?"

Consider the possibility that your audition didn't go as badly as you thought. You said it yourself: the casting director seemed to feel fine about what you did. And the only way he or she will have any residual negative thoughts about your work is if you call attention to your perceived shortcomings by sending an apology note. You have nothing to apologize for. And the next time you're in for this casting director, you have no reason not to come in friendly, upbeat, and ready to do your thing. The casting director has moved on. So should you. MK

Dear Jackie,

When you are reviewing monologues for a film audition, do you prefer those that are more internal? I ask this because most of the theatre monologues I use are directed towards the audience, so when I deliver my lines I break down the fourth wall.[4] I guess my question is: when auditioning for films, should actors keep that fourth wall up or break it down?

—Wall to Wall

Dear Wall,

You will (almost) never be asked to do a monologue for a film or television audition. You'll prep sides, which you'll read directly with a reader, another actor, or the casting director.

Your comments about the fourth wall, however, need addressing. In just about every circumstance, apart from your initial slate and on those rare occasions when you are specifically asked, you should avoid looking directly into the camera or at your auditors. When doing a monologue or reading with a character made out of thin air, place your imaginary scene partner just off to the side of the camera or over the heads of your auditors. Don't turn sideways, talk to a chair or other inanimate object, or use the auditor as your scene partner. Focus on the imagined person you rehearsed with, a person who should feed your imagination and intention. Casting people will look away while you audition—they need to think, take notes, and maybe even eat. They aren't your fellow actors, and some resent being utilized as such. They are there to do their own job, which isn't nodding along as you go. JA

Dear Jackie,

Do you have any suggestions or ideas on where to find very short new monologues? I'm looking for something contemporary, but trying to avoid a movie or something that everyone has seen.

—Looking

Dear Looking,

Let's start with the obvious: you should be consistently reading plays and screenplays. This is the primary way you'll find interesting material and stay informed.

The complete texts of many scripts are available, for free, at the library or online at sites such as Simply Scripts (simplyscripts.com), which links you to tons of plays, screenplays, television, radio, musical, and yet-to-be-produced scripts. The works of many of the better-known writers, with work in the public domain, have entire websites devoted to them. The Virtual Library for Theatre and Drama (vl-theatre.com) lists several, containing the complete works of writers such as Shakespeare, O'Neill, and Moliere, as well as some new material. For screenplays, check in at Drew's Scriptorama (script-o-rama.com).

Beyond traditional scripts, you might try going off the beaten path. First-person fiction, essays, and published journals or letters can be great sources for interesting material. If you really want to go nuts you might try searching for first person stories on Reddit or personal blogs. One of the best monologues I have seen recently was a hilarious rant (about the intense, mind-bending energy you can get from drinking double-brewed coffee) stolen directly from Reddit. Just be sure the selection you choose is active—in other words, go for material in which your character has a clear objective. And whatever you do, stay away from those horribly generic monologue books. JA

Dear Jackie,

Is it not hard enough for an actor to wait tables and bartend, without having to prepare "a brief contemporary monologue" for every audition? Sure, you can have some already prepared, but many auditors ask for pieces specific to the play or the time period. While casting people would probably think me lazy for not wanting to prepare a monologue for each audition, I think they're lazy for not wanting to put together sides. Since they are often just looking for types, aren't cold readings a better way for them to find what they are looking for?

—Pained by Prep

Dear Pained,

I find it curious that your letter didn't begin: "Is it not hard enough for actors to have to prepare 'a brief contemporary monologue' for every audition they go to, without having to wait tables and bartend?" You seem to have it backwards.

I get that the necessities of making a living can sometimes get the better of even the most motivated actor—it's easy to lose touch with what we want through sheer fatigue. But preparing your audition should not be a chore. It's the meat of the labor you love. It's acting. Yes, someone else asked you to do it. Yes, you had to match your work to the genre and requirements at hand. And yes, you may only present this piece once to an audience of one, who may eat throughout the performance. But it's still acting.

It's hard to say whether cold readings are a better audition tool than prepared monologues. Some actors give great cold reads and fade out in rehearsal, while others can blow you away with something they've been rehearsing for two years but can't create spontaneously. Either way, it's not your call. JA

Dear Michael,

What is it directors and casting directors think they're looking for when they request that an actor come to an audition prepared to do a monologue? I have no problem delivering monologues in a production but in an audition situation, I feel phony and unenthusiastic, like I'm being asked to entertain them or be showy. I'm trying to see things from their point of view, but the monologue isn't a reliable indicator of an actor's potential.

—Baffled in New York

Dear Baffled,

I won't lie to you. Most actors I know hate auditioning with monologues. They feel artificial, forced, and hopelessly uninteresting. In the context of a play, a monologue is usually justified by the character's journey. But at an audition, all you've done is walk in and introduce yourself.

I quizzed my favorite theatre casting person and, surprisingly, she loves monologues. According to her, here's what's in it for those behind the table:

> Monologues show more of how actors speak and handle language, how they present themselves, their style, personality, acting ability, and the

types of characters and material to which they respond. And it gives auditors a few uninterrupted minutes to look at you and consider you for the job.

You can help yourself by selecting pieces that suit you and the style of the play (don't audition for Shakespeare with a piece by Simon[5]). Pick one that's relatively short; they'll love you for that. Resist the urge to go for the "big guns" (screaming, wailing, crying, deliberate shock value) unless the role demands it; auditors have to listen to these things all day long, and all that emoting can be draining. Never do a long preparation in the room. And don't worry about the response, or lack thereof. Often, they'll be reading your résumé and making notes while you act. Trust me, it's a good sign. Just be as honest and connected as you can under the circumstances. "Most important," says my CD friend, "pick pieces that speak to you. If it resonates for you, it will resonate for us." MK

Dear Jackie,

I have always been told to engage in a conversation with casting people while in an audition. This is because it will let them see your personality and can help you to stand out as different from everyone else. However, I was recently told to keep the small talk to a minimum. Any ideas on what I should do? I have an audition for a guest star role[6] and was wondering if I should try and talk to them or just smile and perform the sides?
—Talker

Dear Talker,

Auditioning, even with prepared sides, is an improvisatory art. You have to be open to whatever comes your way. If you walk into a room and a very friendly casting associate strikes up a conversation, by all means, join in. Sometimes a candid moment, on or off camera, can help to personalize you and make you stand out. Some auditions are set up to maximize this personal aspect, with casting directors asking seemingly random questions after your slate and before you read the sides. If that's the case, relax and enjoy the friendly chat.

If, however, you are greeted by silence—or a quick and formal hello—from the person behind the casting desk, get to the point. Say hello, introduce yourself, and read the sides as directed. It never hurts to greet someone in a friendly manner, but trying to force someone into a conversation so they can "see your personality" may do more harm than good. JA

Dear Jackie,

Do you need to try to sell yourself at the callback? Aside from your performance, are there things you should be saying or discussing? For example, would it help to say something like, "Do you have any reservations in terms of casting me for this role?" or maybe, "Is there anything else that you would like to see from me that you haven't seen?" How about, "I can give you anything you need. I am the right person for this part."

—Sell Well

Dear Sell,

Selling yourself, as you describe it, sounds more desperate than professional. None of the comments you asked about are likely to help, and they could actually hurt.

It's the casting director's job to run the audition session, and saying something like, "I am the right person for this part" implies that you know better than the CD what the producers and director are looking for. If a CD wants to see something else from you, they will ask. If you say something like, "I can do anything!" well, that just isn't true, and the casting people know it. We all have our limitations. Sometimes it may be our current skill level, but other times it could be that we're shorter than the (pre-cast) co-star or that we look like the producer's ex. Numerous actors audition for each role and many times—most of the time—there is another actor who strikes the CD or director or producer as more "right," for whatever reason. No amount of swagger or sweet talk is going to change their minds.

Let your confidence shine through in your overall demeanor, not in a pitch. The truth is that you have a lot to be confident about. You got called back, didn't you? You beat out most of the actors who submitted for that opportunity. JA

Dear Michael,

I was recently visiting LA, just to check it out, and while I was there, I was lucky enough to get a few auditions through my manager. At one, the casting director asked me if I was a "local hire." I replied, "I live in New York," which probably was a dumb answer. What's "local hire," and how should I respond?

—Where am I?

Dear WAI,

When a casting director asks whether you're a "local hire," they're asking whether, if they cast you, the producers for whom they're casting would have to pay to fly you in and put you up in a hotel.

Here's why they ask the question the way they do: according to SAG-AFTRA rules, if producers cast an actor who lives in another city (for example, the production is Los Angeles-based and the actor lives in New York), they're automatically required to provide housing and first-class transportation for that actor. They can't ask the actor to pay for those things, and the actor can't offer, as both of those discussions would be union violations. So, "Are you a local hire?" has become code for "Can we say you live here, so we can cast you without having to pay for travel and lodging?"

Your answer, "I live in New York," will be taken to indicate that you're *not* willing to be a local hire, and that they would indeed need to pay for your transportation and housing, making it less likely they'll cast you, since you'd cost them more money than a local actor. Some actors make themselves available as local hires in cities other than their own to increase their chances of work, particularly if they have friends they can stay with and/or frequent flyer points they can use for transportation, or if, like you, they're already visiting the "local" city.

So here's the real question: if offered a role on an LA show, are you willing to fly yourself out and put yourself up? To assess that, you first have to figure out whether it's worth it financially. I've been in the position of being a "local hire" away from home and in one instance, while doing a recurring role on a TV series, found I was spending more money on transportation and hotels than I was making on the job! I had to have my agent take a hard-line position to get the producers to pay for my travel and accommodations. But if your net, after expenses and commissions, lands on the plus side, that's another story.

So if you're still in LA—or if you can easily and affordably get back—I'd consider contacting the casting person and correcting your answer. MK

Dear Jackie,

 I have been going out on a lot of commercial auditions as of late, which I am thrilled about, but I have a couple questions about how to dress for them. The wardrobe requests always seem so generic. What's the difference between "casual," "upscale casual," and "casual mom?" And what about hair? I have been feeling like I always have to wear my long hair down, so I look like my picture. I know you can't give me specifics, but some general rules of thumb would be nice.

 —Clothing Curious

Dear Clothing Curious,

 You're right that there are no hard-and-fast rules, but let me try and helpfully generalize the categories you mentioned. "Casual," as you probably suspect, is not the same to commercial casting people as it is to you and me. For me, casual is old jeans and a t-shirt. When I dress for commercials, I go for a Gap, LOFT, or H&M vibe. Skew your outfit to the advertiser and the product. A cleaning product commercial probably demands a "less hip" look than an ad for computers or coffeehouses. Casting director Tom Logan says in his very helpful book *Acting in the Million Dollar Minute*, "If we want sloppy, we will tell you so."

Follow these same basic rules for "casual mom." Some products go for a "traditional" look, sometimes referred to as the P&G[7] mom. If you want tips on the P&G mom, check out your supermarket mailers or grocery store ads. The basic uniform seems to be khakis, a blue button-down over a t-shirt, and tennis shoes. "Upscale casual" is just a nicer version of casual. Instead of Gap, think Banana Republic or name brands at Nordstroms: a more "expensive" version of the same idea.

As for hair, wear it however it best suits the particular spot in question. Logan suggests bringing alternate wardrobe selections to commercial calls, and this could certainly be expanded to ponytail holders and hairspray.

Once you see the spot's storyboards,[8] you may have a very specific look you want to create. Casual and sexy is quite different than casual but frazzled— and sometimes there's no way to know which way the spot is going until you sign in. Logan advises:

> No matter what type of clothing you wear to a particular audition, always pack a few extra styles in the trunk of your car. If you're in New York City, then have extra clothes stuffed in a briefcase or tote bag.

> Many times you will show up totally wrong in the style department. By the time your agent obtains the information about the commercial, it has been passed down from the client to the director, to the producer, to the casting director, to your agent, and then to you.

Sounds like a sick game of telephone, doesn't it? With all those players between you and the advertiser, your best bet may be to make a choice and own it. You may not be exactly what the execs thought they wanted, but your confidence will give you an edge over anyone still waffling between the looks. JA

Dear Michael,

Why is it that you always hear the same story of last-minute success among actors? A despondent actor is ready to hang up his gloves and leave the business, but he auditions for just one more project, which ends up being the game changer, and it snowballs into a prosperous career. How true are these wide-spread stories? Are they, dare I say, dramatized? Don't most failed careers just kind of fizzle out?

—Flummoxed in Florida

Dear Flummoxed,

I'm not sure about the fact-to-fiction ratio. We actors tend to superstitiously seek out signs and patterns, trying to decipher what it is exactly that leads to getting work. I'm of the opinion that the whole thing is far more random than we'd like to admit. Nevertheless, I've observed the same pattern you have. It seems like actors who've decided to give up on their careers often book work that keeps them in the profession, or book jobs they don't want, or for which they're unavailable. So . . . what gives?

Well, here's my thought. We're actors. That's what we do. Unfortunately, when we audition, we sometimes take our attention away from acting and instead focus on trying to get cast. Instead of simply going in and playing a character, which we know how to do, we go in and try to get a job, which we do *not* know how to do—getting cast is a mysterious, illogical, uncontrollable thing. As a result, we don't do our best work. But when we have an audition for a gig we don't care about, or when we're ready to quit the business, we're not trying to get the job. We just go in and play the role. These discouraged or indifferent artists have accidentally gotten out of their own way, allowing the casting people to really see what they can do.

Say . . . wait a minute. What if we attended all our auditions with the goal of just acting, and made that the only task we ever assign ourselves? What if we stopped trying to break the code of how to get cast, and just shared our work? That's the approach I recommend to my coaching clients, and I'm constantly getting reports of great results—not just bookings, but better enjoyment of the whole process. It's worth a try, right? If nothing else, it's a lot easier than having to be constantly on the verge of quitting! MK

Dear Jackie,

I resent directors and other auditors who make you audition in front of, or even with, other actors auditioning for a production. The competitiveness and judgment in the air is unbearable, yet you can't complain for obvious reasons. What can I do to protest this growing trend in audition settings?

—One Man Show

Dear One Man Show,

In my experience, a professional auditor only asks actors to audition in front of one another when there is some sort of extenuating circumstance making the ideal, private situation impossible—a problematic space, a severe time crunch, etc. When, however, you are auditioning for inexperienced (or just plain unprofessional) directors and producers, all bets are off.

Group auditions can be a pain, but I don't know that they are worth protesting. If the production in question is union, you could file a complaint—even anonymously—about the environment. But consider that some auditions actually benefit from a group setting. Group improvisational and commercial auditions can save time and give the actor someone to "play" with outside the distracted casting assistant. In some cases, say for a nonspeaking commercial role, the casting director just needs to see what you look like interacting with others—in that case, a group can be helpful.

If you encounter this situation again, see if you can take the judgment you perceive from other actors and channel it into positive energy for your audition. See if you can turn, "All those people want me to fail," into "All those people are just as nervous as I am." Better yet, try: "I'm going to do my best to help all those nervous people feel more comfortable. We're actually a team, even if they don't know it." This takes your focus off yourself and puts it on your fellow actors, just like it should be. JA

Dear Michael,

I can usually control my nerves in the audition. I feel like it's such a long shot that I don't really care walking in, and I do well. But not caring is a lot harder for me in the callback.

Come callback time, my nerves are at full throttle. This is mostly because I'm so afraid of disappointing and humiliating the casting director in front of the producers if I screw up. After all, I'm representing the casting director as well as myself. How do I combat these nerves?

—Callback Catastrophe

Dear CC,

If you're attending the initial round of auditions with a sense of ease, you're ahead of the game. And as for callbacks, the answer to your dilemma lies in a simple change of perspective.

Think of it this way: A callback is, essentially, a meeting, attended by a group of people. At this particular meeting, the biggest responsibility isn't on your shoulders, nor on the casting person's, but on those of the producers, who must now choose from among several worthy actors. They're the ones with a task ahead of them, who might understandably be nervous. After all, it's their production, and casting is a big decision.

Your most important assignment is to change *nothing*. Resist any new-and-improved "insights" at all costs. Help the casting director by showing the producers roughly what you did the first time. As long as you do that, you're not going to embarrass or humiliate anyone, so let that fear go; it's irrational.

Your work is already done. You've been given the gold star that says "approved for this role." So for you, the pressure is off. Put your focus on those who have even greater stakes, and go into the room with a sense of collaboration and helpfulness. The results are in the hands of fate, luck, chance, producers' taste, and many other factors—all of them completely out of your control. Given how subjective casting is, you may as well relish the moment; don't miss out on the joy of these opportunities by letting nerves take over. Remember: we're not brain surgeons, nuclear scientists, cops, lawyers, or bankers. We're actors. We put on funny clothes and play "make pretend" for a living. This stuff is supposed to be fun. How's that for a change in perspective? MK

Dear Jackie,

Are there rules as to how many callbacks an actor can be asked to return for? If we are Equity, are we paid for these additional callbacks? If we are put on hold, what does that mean in terms of taking other work or compensation?

—Callback Overload

Dear Callback,

As grueling as it can get to do read after read, there don't seem to be any rules restricting the number of callbacks a producer can hold. Fortunately, when working under an AEA contract, producers must compensate talent after a certain number of callbacks, but there's no easy rule to go by as to when such funds start accruing.

According to AEA, it varies from contract to contract:

> Under the Production Contract, auditions and/or readings, excluding initial interviews/auditions, shall be limited to four in number for an Equity performer and said performer shall be compensated at the rate of 1/8th minimum salary for each reading and/or audition over four to which the performer is called. In some instances, an hourly rate kicks in if you are kept at a callback for more than three hours. Chorus receives compensation starting with the fourth callback. LORT requires payments starting with the fourth callback; and TYA[9] requires payments starting with the third callback.

Whew! I'm exhausted just reading that list, let alone auditioning that many times. As you can see, there's no one-size-fits-all answer to your question—even just within AEA's jurisdiction. SAG-AFTRA talent have other rules to sort through. So, the most accurate answer to the first part of your question will keep you on your toes: when in doubt, check with your union. As for passing up other jobs or being compensated while you stand by, there's no specific provision governing actors' "on hold" status under the AEA collective bargaining agreement. Generally, being "on hold" or "on avail" just means you are in serious consideration for the role and producers are asking you to keep the production dates clear or "available," as a courtesy. In other words, they aren't paying you and you should keep auditioning for other jobs. Usually, you will be cast or released from a hold within a week or so. If you get another offer in the meantime, you or your representative should call the producers who have you on hold and—assuming you prefer that first job—give them a chance to hire you before you accept the other gig. If you prefer gig number two, you should still call the holding producers to gracefully back out of your standby position. JA

Dear Michael,

Is it unprofessional to ask the people auditioning me if they have any constructive criticism about my work? Or, what about if I find out I didn't get the part? Can I contact the casting director to ask for input on what I could have done better? I'm nonunion, and I don't have an agent I can turn to, so it would be helpful to know how I'm coming across.

—A Beginner in Brooklyn

Dear Brooklyn,

You should never ask for feedback at an audition. First, it marks you as a beginner who needs reassurance. Professionals come in, do their thing, and leave the rest to the casting people. Beginners are often hoping for audition experiences that make them feel more confident about their work. But the *savvy* beginner knows not to ask for that reassurance. It's never too early to look for ways to exude confidence and professionalism. If you ask for feedback, they're less inclined to cast you, because—fair or not—they may perceive you as needy.

Secondly, discussion of your work isn't appropriate to the situation. The purpose of an audition is for casting directors, directors, and producers to find actors for roles, not for them to assist with actors' education or improve actors' self-esteem. It's not really fair to ask them to teach you how to audition better. They're there to cast, not to coach.

Third, asking for feedback puts casting directors on the spot, and they may feel inclined to say something positive, even if it isn't their true opinion. Most people aren't comfortable offering honest negative criticism in person. So you're putting them in kind of an awkward position, and not necessarily getting any real information. And they could, potentially, resent you for making them uncomfortable, which is certainly not something you want. It's different when you have an agent. Casting people feel more comfortable being honest with an actor's representative than with an actor.

Finally, feedback may not be as valuable as you think. You either get a role or you don't—feedback doesn't change that. And it's only one person's opinion, so it really doesn't represent anything concrete, unless you're getting identical responses again and again. If you think about it that way . . . what's it really worth? The best place for feedback is a good acting class.

When auditioning, I say we should conduct ourselves like carpet salesmen. Come in, show the carpet samples to the potential client, then leave, and go on to your next appointment. No one wants to buy carpet from the insecure salesperson who asks, before leaving, "What did you think of the way I presented those carpet samples? Was that OK?" "Can you tell me how I can improve my pitch?" See what I mean? MK

What Do You Think?

1 How does the casting process work? Explain as many of the steps as you can remember. You can make a list or draw a chart to show details.
2 Explain The Breakdowns.
3 Why do casting directors usually share job information only with talent representatives?
4 Explain the difference between an open call and an audition by appointment.
5 What are some ways an unrepresented actor might get an audition?
6 What is an Equity Principal Audition (EPA)?
7 What are sides and how do you prepare them?
8 What are some ways to deal with audition nerves?
9 Should you attend auditions for plays that don't contain roles for you, just for the opportunity to be seen?
10 Can you expect feedback from your auditions? Is it appropriate to ask? Why or why not?

Notes

1 EPAs—Equity Principal Auditions are auditions for principal (leading) roles, for which all AEA members can sign up to be seen by auditors. At EPA Open Calls, nonunion performers may also be seen, time permitting.
2 EMC stands for Equity Membership Candidacy. See Chapter 9, "Unions" for more information.
3 "Slating" is stating your name (and sometimes your height, agent, or other requested information) into camera. The slate serves as a simple introduction that links your name to your image.

4 "Fourth wall"—a common theatre term for the imaginary "wall" separating the actors from the audience.
5 Neil Simon is a prolific playwright best known for his comedies, which include *The Odd Couple*, *Barefoot in the Park*, and *The Sunshine Boys*.
6 Guest star is an official designation in TV casting that indicates role size and pay rates.
7 P&G—Procter & Gamble, a consumer goods corporation founded in the 1830s and known for its "wholesome" advertising and "all-American" branding.
8 Storyboards are visual scripts drawn by an artist to convey the director's idea for the major shots in a film/digital project. For commercials, they are often posted in the audition waiting room and can give you an idea of what the director might have planned.
9 TYA—Theatre for Young Audiences—another type of Equity contract.

8

AGENTS AND MANAGERS

The two primary types of actor representatives are agents and managers. (Others, such as publicists[1] and entertainment lawyers, may join the team much further down the road, if at all.) As explained in the previous chapter on the casting process, agents and managers get much of their information from The Breakdowns, a daily list of casting opportunities that—*officially*—is only available to professional talent representatives. Talent representatives use Breakdowns to match and submit selected actors to casting directors for consideration on these projects. Actors without representation are, unfortunately, cut out of this particular casting loop. So clearly, finding a good talent rep is an important career step that vastly increases potential audition opportunities.

Agents are the most common type of actor representative. Talent agencies must be licensed and bonded to practice in their state, and must be SAG-AFTRA franchised (sagaftra.org), or belong to either the Association of Talent Agencies (agentassocation.com) or the National Association of Talent Representatives (natragents.com). Current members are listed on each organization's website, along with contact and submission information. Many talent agencies focus exclusively on one area of the business: commercial agents represent clients for acting gigs in commercials, theatrical agents—also known as "legit" agents— cover theatre, television, film, and digital media. Some agencies are "full service," covering all areas and signing their clients "across the board," which means they work with their actors in every market. However, most specialize, which is why many actors work with more than one type of agent.

An agent's job is, first and foremost, to procure work for their clients. They must be aware of upcoming projects, select actors from amongst their client list who fit the available roles, secure audition appointments from the casting director for those clients, and communicate with their actor clients, informing them of audition appointments, callbacks, and bookings. They can also act as advisors, suggesting which jobs are worth doing, what kinds of headshots are needed, and so forth. When an actor books a gig, the agent negotiates the contract. In exchange for these services, the agent receives a percentage—usually 10%—of what the actor makes on all acting jobs.

The job description for a manager is slightly more nebulous. Talent managers tend to have fewer clients, allowing them to offer more attention and individualized support. A manager might help build an actor's career by cultivating contacts, advising on career decisions, connecting their clients with appropriate talent agencies, or helping an actor hone his or her image. Though managers are not technically permitted to negotiate contracts, many do. Typically, managers collect 15% commissions on their clients' gross acting income, but there are many possible variations on that arrangement. While some managers belong to trade organizations which loosely regulate their practices, such as the Talent Managers Association (talentmanagers.org) or the National Conference of Personal Managers (ncopm.com), they, unlike agents, are unregulated and unlicensed. This creates a freer working relationship and, unfortunately, increases the likelihood of fraud, foul-play, and scams. Many actors choose not to work with managers, but some—particularly early on before an agent will sign them, or late in their careers when more focus and care is needed—find them helpful.

When an actor has both an agent and a manager, the representatives should, ideally, be in close contact. A manager might "stay on top" of an agent, keeping their mutual clients on the agent's radar, suggesting projects that should be pursued, following up after auditions, or weighing in on negotiations.

Legitimate talent representatives won't ask for funds up front for themselves or for another party (licensed agents can be disciplined for requiring actors to pay for, for example, headshots from a specific photographer or acting classes from a particular teacher, often in return for kickbacks). An agent or manager should be paid by commission only—that is to say, they don't get paid until you do.

Some organizations with the word "agency" in their names do ask for up-front fees, but they are restricted by state law from procuring work for their clients.[2] In other words, they cannot submit actors for paying jobs or promise to connect them to those who will. Many of these outfits sell themselves as "counseling," "networking," or "training" companies, but few are worth your time. Better to avoid them altogether and stick to this simple rule: if they ask for money up front, they are not allowed to get you auditions. If they get you auditions, they are not allowed to ask for money up front.[3]

As for the way actors and representatives find one another, as with just about everything in the industry, there is no formula, very little pattern, and hardly anything consistent about that. Terrific actors sometimes struggle to land an agent, while those of questionable ability might be signed right out of the gate. Although it can be hard to accept, agents and managers aren't focused on rescuing actors from anonymity or day jobs. They aren't even committed to getting the "best" actor into the public eye. They're in business to make money. When they sign a contract with an actor it's for one reason alone: they believe the actor is marketable. While it may sound unfair, wonderful actors with limited experience or a scarcity of credits are rarely of value to agents and managers. A talent representative might sometimes take a chance and sign a young or inexperienced actor, usually someone fresh out of school, but they make that decision based on marketability; the vast majority of available roles are for attractive 20-somethings.

Getting an agent or a manager is hard. Getting a good one (they're not all good) is nearly impossible. But thousands upon thousands of actors have accomplished this seemingly impossible goal.

Many young actors mistakenly believe that getting an agent—any agent—is a panacea. They bank on the myth that if they can just get an agent's name on their résumés they'll be on their way, with auditions flowing in and bookings around every corner. The truth is that not every agent is established enough to secure audition appointments for their clients; and some are so busy they may neglect those not booking regularly. Even a good agent at a great agency has to convince a bevy of casting people to see their clients and, unfortunately, casting people can be reticent to take a chance on someone unknown. With limited time, they may prefer actors with proven track records.

Once representation is secured, it does not necessarily remain in place. Agents and managers regularly drop clients. Though it's a harsh experience for the suddenly unrepresented actor, it's a practice that makes sound business sense for the representatives. Their bottom line demands that they focus on clients who produce results— bookings and a paycheck—so they'll periodically eliminate the "dead wood." These relationships can end in other ways as well: agencies go out of business; managers move on to other jobs; agents move to new agencies and are unable to bring their clients with them, and sometimes, actors decide to change their representation. Far from permanent, these collaborations generally evolve along with an actor's career.

Questions and Answers

Dear Michael,

I'm a fresh-out-of-college actress and I've recently done my first blind mailing[4] to agents. I haven't heard anything from anyone yet. I've been researching other ways to find representation, as I know random mailings aren't always the most effective. I've heard other actors mention acting workshops offered by agents, and how continuing to attend these may help toward getting an agent interested in you. However, in trying to find these workshops, I've mostly come across what seem to be scams. I'm clueless as to what to look for and where. Are there reliable sources? And can you suggest any other ways to find an agent?

—Lost in La-La Land

Dear Lost,

It's said there are three great philosophical questions that haunt the soul of man: "Who am I?" "Why am I here?" and "Where am I going?" For actors in the early stages of their careers, there's a different trio of mysteries, no less haunting. They are, "How do I get casting people to notice me?" "How do I get into the unions?" and, inevitably, "How do I get an agent?"

Finding representation is among the most difficult tasks a professional actor faces, and unfortunately, getting no response to a mass mailing is the norm. Agents look for clients who'll make them money. So they'll rarely call in a newcomer from a mailing, unless there's something about that newcomer (superhuman beauty, an unusual-but-marketable look, etc.) that makes them see dollar signs. But generally, it leads to exactly zip, zilch, and zero.

Now, your workshop/scam question has many answers.[5] Yes, there are lots of outright scams out there, and you're smart to steer clear of them. But workshops set up for actors to meet agents (and casting directors) are another matter. While ethically questionable, they aren't scams, exactly. Some actors have secured representation by attending them, but that seems to be far more the exception than the rule.

If you're not able to meet agents without having to pay them, it may be that you're not yet there in your career journey. If that's the case, go for plays, student films, classes, theatre companies, reading groups, anything you can get into. Develop your "chops." Get around others who are in the business. Along the way, if colleagues express admiration for your work, ask for introductions to their agents. That's one way to have an agent take you seriously; they're far more inclined to trust their clients' personal recommendations than to respond to cold mailings.

I'd love to tell you there's some secret method. There really aren't any shortcuts (though they're often advertised). Generally, diligence, professionalism, assertiveness, and patience are the only tools you've got. MK

Dear Jackie,

I got a great referral to an agent and sent in my materials. Unfortunately, the agent didn't respond. I asked the person who referred me to please make contact on my behalf again, which she did. The agent then called me and left a message that I should call her for a "meet" at the end of the first week of January. She said if I got her voicemail to remind her about the referral. When I called, her assistant put me through to voicemail again and, as instructed, I mentioned the referral.

Well, I never heard back from her! Tomorrow it will be ten days since I left the message. Do you think it's a good idea to leave a second message tomorrow? Or is that unprofessional?
—Calling the Abyss

Dear Calling,

Pretend, for a moment, that you are not an actor. Let's say the call you are asking about is a business call between two professionals from the same industry. Imagine you have been playing phone tag with a colleague, but she failed to respond to your most recent call. What would you do? There's your answer.

Once we realize that we are part of the industry, and not beggars at the doorstep, we can relax and take things in stride. So she forgot to call you back—so what? If she has decided she isn't interested in meeting with you, let her tell you that herself, like any other professional would do. Don't try and second-guess the situation, just behave like a member of the club. For better or worse, you are one. JA

Dear Michael,

A few weeks ago, at the end of an audition, the casting director looked at me and said, "Wow. You need to be on *SNL*. You are hysterical." He asked me if I had a manager. I told him I didn't, and he gave me the number of a guy he said I needed to call. He told me he would call the manager later that day to tell him about me. I was ecstatic, blown away that this type of thing happened to me at an audition. I called the manager, told him what the CD said and he asked me to send my stuff. I emailed him my headshot, résumé, and some links to some of my work online.

A few days went by and I heard nothing. I called him to confirm that he got the email. When I reached him, he said he had got the email, but was going to "pass" on me, because he already had another guy who was my "type." I was baffled. I was simply trying to get him to agree to a meeting, but he wouldn't budge. He said, "Postcard me, keep me in the loop, let me know when you are doing something . . . blah, blah, blah." If a referral from a legit casting director isn't enough to get me in the door, what the heck is?
—Flattered and Flattened!

Dear F and F,

It is indeed unusual to have someone gush like that at an audition. But, in terms of dry facts, the casting director's reaction only tells you one thing: that this one particular casting director liked your work enough to recommend you to a manager. And that's great; it's no small compliment. But the manager is a different person. He has his own taste, his own client list, and he might not have the same reaction as the casting director. When you think about it that way, what happened is really not such an outrage.

Here's the hard truth: the manager saw your materials, and wasn't interested. It happens, even when someone is highly recommended. In our profession, there are all kinds of potentially misleading signs (like the casting director who exclaimed, after my audition, "My God! It's as if this part was written for you!" and then didn't call me back). Nothing is anything until it's something. Until there's ink on a page or a paycheck in your hand, just smile, and enjoy the compliment. MK

Dear Jackie,

I'm a native New Yorker who has been in the business for a good ten years and has been pursuing a legitimate agent for eight of them. I'm Equity, but chose not to join SAG-AFTRA yet, as I planned to build up my film credits with nonunion work and join SAG-AFTRA after landing an agent. I'm dependent on public listings and websites for auditions and the majority are nonunion. I do work with a manager, but he doesn't have the clout to get me interviews with agents or solid film and theatre auditions—he only gets me print go-sees.[6] I would appreciate your advice on some strategies for landing a legit agent.

I've already done tons of off-off Broadway—always inviting industry (and can count on one hand how many times they've shown up. I've even offered car services!). I've asked peers in my classes or shows for referrals to their agents. I read K. Callan's *The New York Agent Book* and applied her strategies (targeted mailings, drop-offs) consistently. I've paid to perform for agents at workshops and interned for an agency to learn about the business. My husband is a semi-famous actor who has numerous television credits and I have met with his agent. Finally, I have always created opportunities for myself in order to be seen. I co-produced and starred in two indie films, wrote and performed my own one-woman show, and organized other shows and showcases. What's left?

   —Decade-Long Search

Dear Decade,

Reading over your long list of proactive steps gave me a chill because, well, if someone as hard-working as you has had this much trouble netting an agent, what can I possibly say to help? I turned to Tony Martinez, agent and author of *An Agent Tells All*, for an insider's opinion. What he said made that chill even colder.

"There is only one honest answer to this question," he said:

> The actor is not going to like hearing this, but it's time to walk away. You cannot spend over ten years of your life chasing a dream and not have something to show for it. At this point, she's competing with established actors who have been working for a long time and have substantial résumés. She needs to refocus her energy towards some new goals. She gave it a good shot but now it's time to move on. And from what I hear, there are some very happy people in this world who are not working actors.

Wow. Martinez knows of what he speaks, but *I know* that if we asked ten industry pros we might get ten different answers. Here's mine: Go ahead and join SAG-AFTRA via the 4As clause.[7] While taking full advantage of nonunion projects as you built your reel and résumé was a logical choice, it's time to try the alternative. It's possible that some agents have been reluctant to bring you in because of your union status, so you may as well knock down that possible hurdle.

Update your goal from "to get a legit agent" to "to get in front of agents." Without the pressure of jumping straight to the outcome, you may find the process less intimidating. You already, smartly, tried interning for an agent—working at an agency, casting office, or production company can provide valuable contacts. Most agencies don't sign their own interns, but occasionally an assistant branches out and begins his own company, bringing along contacts he has made along the way. If you do good work for a casting office, you may find a CD willing to recommend you to her favorite agents. And production companies are great places to come in contact with both agents and casting directors. The more familiar agents are with you and your name, the longer they will pause over your submission as they hurry through the pile. Maybe it's time to try this one again.

Continue doing plays. Beyond embracing your most consistent avenue to act, connecting with other professionals, and staying involved in the acting scene, such performances will get you in front of at least a few industry folks. While many agents avoid unsolicited invitations, most make efforts to see their own clients perform. If they see another actor of interest in the cast, they will send inquiries. At the least, you can send a follow-up submission to any rep or CD who attends your shows. Additionally, if you continue to improve your theatre résumé and book work at respected theatres *that pay*, you will become more desirable to an agent's bottom line.

I like your practice of targeted mailings, but it looks like you might be aiming in the wrong direction. Throw out your old lists and begin again. You don't need updated information on, say, Rick Rosen at WME[8] at this stage of the game.

Your focus should be on boutique and commercial agencies that will take a chance on an unrepresented, less commercially successful actor.

Keep track of your submission history and any interaction you have with an agent on your list. Make notes when you read news about those agents, hear things—good or bad—from other actors about them, and track any referrals you are able to land. This list, kept up to date, will be far more helpful than any general list could ever be.

Consider other representation possibilities. Commercial agents are usually easier to land, and if you begin to book jobs, a meeting with theatrical reps in the same office will be easier to finagle. Try finding a manager, or develop relationships with casting people themselves. One actor I spoke to told me, "The way I got work in New York was that the casting directors called me in directly . . . Instead of complaining about not getting an agent, I'm going directly to the person who has the jobs." And don't be afraid to ask for help. Does getting a referral from your husband qualify as nepotism? Yes, and amen!

Finally, and this may be hard to hear: you have been barking up this agent tree for years without success. Maybe it's time to throw caution to the wind and sally forth, agent-free. You've got a track record of producing your own work and booking jobs on your own. As Nancy Rainford says in her excellent book, *How to Agent Your Agent*, "You didn't become an actor to get an agent." JA

Dear Jackie,

I had an interview with an agency today. I was told I was cute and perfect for what they are looking for, but too commercial. What does this mean? I wasn't even able to defend myself, which left me confused and angry.

—Cute But Commercial

Dear Cute,

When a representative makes a vague statement like this, it usually means a) They are having a hard time pinpointing why they don't want to represent you, b) They know why they don't want to represent you but don't want to have to explain, or c) They don't want to represent you and are trying to let you down easy. Notice that none of these options indicate that they *want* to represent you.

An agent's decision to sign a new client is based on all kinds of factors. Yes, there are some givens—the client should be talented and marketable—but the rest is as varied as agents themselves. The same thing that can work against you with some reps—you look a little like, say, Elvis[9]—can help you seal the deal with others. There's not much separating, "He's too Elvis! Let's pass." from "He's so Elvis! Let's sign him!"

"Too commercial" may mean that you are too P&G—or "Procter and Gamble"— as in too clean cut, wholesome, and typical of an outdated commercial archetype. Or it might mean nothing. Even if reps know why they'd like to pass on an actor, they aren't always eager to share. "We have too many brunettes in their early 30s" might elicit the response, "I could dye my hair!" and "You're just not good enough" might conjure tears. From an agent's perspective, why not offer a vague but agent-y sounding excuse? Your desire to "defend" yourself is precisely the urge the agent is trying to deflect.

Don't let this—or anything else an agent says as they usher you out of the office— get you riled up. The simple truth is that there are far too many actors soliciting representation for them to take more than a minute with those they pass on. If you think there might be something helpful in the feedback, speak to a mentor about what you might change. If not, brush it off and move on. JA

Dear Michael,
    Do you have any tips for agency meetings?
    —First Timer

Dear First,
    I do. Actors who are relatively new to agency meetings often make the mistake of thinking they've been summoned to see The Wizard of Oz. They approach these meetings with great trepidation, as if they might be permanently booted out of show business if they were to say or do the wrong thing in the interview. Good news: that's a completely warped interpretation of the circumstances. Here are some tips to make the meeting go more smoothly:

    —Agency meetings are hard to get. Agents are busy people. So own the fact that these people want to meet you. You're not starting at zero. You're already walking in as a potential client. You and the agent are both there just to see whether it's a good match.
    —Don't overdress, and don't underdress. You don't need to dress up as if you're interviewing for a corporate position. The best thing to wear is something that reflects the kinds of characters you play, without being costumey. If you play business types, wear a suit. If you're often cast as the female love interest, wear make-up and something pretty. If you're an interesting character type who plays psychos and homeless guys, dress casually and don't shave. Don't try too hard and again, *don't wear a costume!* Wear a version of normal attire that suits your type. Now, regarding the second wardrobe danger, underdressing: sexy women, it's great to know your category, but wearing something distractingly skimpy is more likely to get you an indecent proposal than to get you an agent. There are ways to demonstrate your type and still leave something to the imagination.

—No matter how desperate you may feel about getting an agent, remember, you might not click with this person. Whether you realize it or not, you don't want just any agent. You want to find the *right* agent, one who is reputable, understands what roles you play, and has the clout to get you auditions. So don't just answer questions as if taking a test; ask some as well. Find out what shows they're watching, or what they do when they're not agenting. It's not an interrogation, it's a conversation.

—When discussing your career, in addition to sharing what you've done, talk also about what you'd *like* to do. Agents like knowing you have a healthy combination of realism and ambition. They want to know that you understand your type and your place in the business, and also that you have a sense about the kind of work you'd like to do as your career grows.

—Don't feel that you have to list your credits. Part of what you're there to do is get a sense of each other's personalities. You can achieve that by discussing any number of things, from how you spent a recent holiday to the show you're bingeing on Netflix. Be open to wherever the conversation leads.

—Keep answers simple and pleasant. That's more important than accuracy. Too many details make answers hard to follow, and therefore less interesting. It almost doesn't matter what you say, as long as you relax and present yourself well.

—Be prepared to perform a monologue (you should always have several ready) or a scene (which may be provided by the agent you're meeting with) if asked, so you'll never be thrown by that request.

—You want to do something that will impress an agent? Decide when to end the meeting, rather than waiting for the agent to end it. No actor ever does this. I think it shows strength and a sense of your own value.

—Finally—and some will find this strange or controversial—don't be too nice. I don't mean you should be a jerk. But the groveling, self-deprecating, worshipping approach reads as needy and creepy. Most people don't respond well to that, whereas a sense of equal status suggests you're worthy of notice.

The worst thing to do at an interview is panic. And there's no need. Think about the actual circumstances—just two people, in a room, conversing. That's all it is. I promise, that hidden lever that opens the trapdoor under your chair, sending you careening into a pool full of sharks as soon as you give the wrong answer only exists in the movies (. . . and OK, maybe at CAA, but that's never been confirmed). MK

Dear Jackie,

Another actor and I may decide to team up and be each other's manager. What do you think?

—Ready to Go

Dear Ready,

I may be wrong, but I'm guessing that what you and the other actor are really considering is teaming up to get acting audition notices, or breakdowns, illegally so you can submit each other for jobs. I think that is a big mistake.

If casting professionals and studios wanted to receive submissions from the general acting public, they could put casting notices out for all to see—and some do. Many, however, want their notices kept private, sent only to agents, or just some agents, or even just one person! However much we dislike it, however unfair it seems, casting folks have the right to control their casting information and see only talent they choose to see.

The success rate for actors who self-submit (or submit a friend) using pirated breakdowns is extremely low. Casting professionals aren't blindly clicking on headshots or opening emails—they recognize senders. Most will smell a fake manager submission from a mile away. Sure, there are those one-in-a-million stories of auditions booked through pirated breakdowns, but there are just as many stories about actors being discovered at banks or restaurants.

As far as setting up a management company to legally access The Breakdowns, your chances aren't much better. Since there are not state licensing boards for managers, Breakdown Services requires managers to meet other criteria—done on a case-by-case basis—before they can purchase subscriptions. Since you and your friend would not have a group of working clients, history in the industry, or other concrete experience to draw on, your chances of approval would be slim.

I asked two well-respected managers what they thought of your idea.

"It's a huge mistake for many, many, many reasons," says Paulo Andrés, a manager at Rothman/Andrés Entertainment:

> No casting director will take them seriously. It takes time to develop relationships with casting so that our phone calls are answered and that casting will see our clients. In part, that relationship is built because of an excellent roster. A roster of one won't work.

Manager Brad Lemack, of Lemack & Company, was so fired up by your question he offered to send you a copy of his book, *The New Business of Acting*. "I think teaming with a friend, or rather *scheming* with a friend, to manage each other is a ridiculous idea," he says:

> Of course it is done all the time by actors who think they know better than the person they hired to represent them—or by actors who either don't

want to do the work necessary to find representation or who are not yet ready to be represented. Instead of becoming each other's manager, put this effort, this energy, and this money into becoming better actors who are ready to be represented.

While trying to literally manage each other is a bad idea, working with another actor, or group of actors, to encourage, promote, and otherwise help each other handle the business aspects of your collective careers is a great idea. Here's what I mean: you and your friend could start an actors' support group and schedule weekly meetings at which you could share information, respond to each other's marketing materials, and check in on what you have each done to further your careers. You could attend plays, screenings, and free workshops and seminars as a group. You might share the costs of subscribing to the trades and decipher industry news together. You could do play readings, or rent a low-cost studio space and present scenes or monologues that you are preparing to use in auditions—not to "teach" one another anything, but to get more comfortable auditioning in front of an audience. Or you might sit down together and chat while you organize your mailings.

Perhaps most importantly, you could set your goals aloud in front of the group and then hold each other accountable for sticking to them. They say that when people are trying to get into an exercise routine, it works wonders to set up exercise "dates" with other people—it keeps you from flaking out. Why wouldn't the same principle work here? You and your friend both want to work on your careers— why not set up weekly meetings to make specific progress in that direction? JA

Dear Michael,

I recently interviewed with a new agent. While the office impressed me, I encountered some red flags. First, I felt he was too touchy-feely. He has a thick Italian accent and told me he is from Italy. He kissed me hello, then, when I got up to leave he touched the side of my body and said "Ooh, nice body," kissed me again, and mentioned something about "getting coffee together." Since his English is broken and I could tell he didn't understand some of the things I said, I chalked it up to a cultural thing. During the interview he promised the world and talked a good game, but of course I took it with a grain of salt.

I tried digging up as much info on him as possible. Some said he talks a big game but doesn't deliver, while one girl said she booked two major speaking roles on TV from him, plus was sent out on other legit auditions for principal roles. One nonunion actor said he demanded 20% from her on a job! Another guy posted that he has not gotten him any auditions. Of course, I want to see how everything pans out. Even with my red flags, I was willing to audition and possibly work with him.

The agent asked me to audition for a producer at a different office at 6pm on a Wednesday. I also thought this odd, but agreed. As the gods would have it, that Wednesday, my husband didn't get home until 5:45. We have two kids, so I couldn't just take off. Not having the producer's number (I also tried digging up information on him but found nothing), I called the agent and said I was running late. He told me I had to be there at 6pm, because he sends "no more than seven people at a time" to this producer. I asked if I could reschedule for the following Wednesday. He told me the producer was booked next Wednesday, but possibly Friday at his office or a later date, and he would email me. I called him the next day and left a brief message. I didn't hear back. I emailed him. It's only been three business days, but I think I screwed myself. How do you think I should proceed from here?

—Trying

Dear Trying,

Wow. To say that this man's conduct is unorthodox is an understatement. If it were not for the few positive reports, I'd dismiss him as a complete charlatan.

But let's look at what we know:

> —During your first meeting, he touched you inappropriately and commented lewdly about your body. Italian or not, that behavior is off-the-charts unacceptable. And it's unacceptable in a way that doesn't call for a second chance.
> —He wants you to meet some guy, after business hours. And the guy—about whom you know *nothing*—can only see you at a specific time. Please listen: you should not go to this meeting, whatever it's for, under any circumstances, unless someone is with you. What is this man casting, exactly? Did the agent say? And have you ever heard of an audition that only took place at 6pm sharp? And note that when you needed to reschedule, your agent knew the producer's schedule off the top of his head. Something is shady here. I know of no legitimate casting sessions that fit this description. Drug drops fit this description; plans for sinister capers in gangster films fit this description, but not casting sessions. If I were you, I wouldn't go at all.
> —You're now worried that you've botched things with this agent, whose behavior has been questionable at best (and you've only just started working together).

Rather than trying to fix things, you should pay attention to your suspicions. You could track down more clients and ask them what the deal is. You could speak with casting people who've dealt with the agency, or call SAG-AFTRA and see if they have any more info. But here's my question, regardless: is this really someone you want to work with? Why would you enter a business relationship with someone who makes your warning bells go off? Don't you deserve an agent to whom you can relate with ease and comfort? Remember, your direct collaboration isn't the only issue. He would also be representing you to others. That means, first of all, making appointments, and negotiating on your behalf, in an accent which, according to your email, seems to cause misunderstandings. What's more, he could be just as inappropriate and unprofessional with casting people and producers, and that would reflect on you. I'd be very concerned. My advice: move on, rather than giving the benefit of the doubt. Don't be like those people who wait by the phone, hoping their abusive lover will call. Dump him. MK

Dear Jackie,

I met with an agent yesterday, and although she offered to sign me, I feel strangely unhappy. I had gotten the interview from a mailing I did last month— this was the only interview I got from that, actually—and I was excited because she works at a legit agency that has a decent reputation, even though it's pretty small. I wasn't expecting it to be super fancy, and I wasn't even put off by the tiny, smelly office. I did, however, have a really hard time with how this woman behaved. She acted the whole time like I was annoying her and she just wanted to get me out of there, even though she was the one who had called me in and given me the appointment. We talked for like eight minutes total. I did a monologue—which she cut off after about one minute—and then she said she'd be willing to work with me for a while and "see what she could do with me." I thanked her and stood to shake her hand, but she was already taking a call that was coming in and just sort of waved me away.

I know I should be happy about having an agent, but I just feel kind of resistant. Should I suck it up and move forward with her? I don't have anyone else offering to rep me and I feel foolish not jumping on this, but maybe I need to hold out for someone better? Are all agents this mean?
—Uneasy

Dear Uneasy,

I was recently reminded of just how unusual a good actor-agent relationship can be when I met a New York transplant who had, coincidentally, once worked with my first agency. Not only were we both with the same agency, we were there at the exact same time. But that's where the similarities ended. While I gushed over my experience with the agents there, he told me some depressing stories of mistreatment and lack of effort. We had both been with the same agents at the same time, and I had walked away totally satisfied while he'd left angry and disappointed. Why the difference? Relationships—all kinds of relationships—are tricky.

While you and this agent got off on the wrong foot, there's no saying you won't end up having a solid partnership. A kind, chatty agent isn't necessarily better than a standoffish but hardworking one. Perhaps she makes up in dogged advocacy for her clients what she lacks in social acumen.

Can you encourage a more productive collaboration? Start by making an appointment to show her your current headshots—she needs to see them. In person, explain that you are eager to create a great working relationship and ask for clarity on the following: Does she mind if you self-submit? Does she want you to notify her if you do so? Should you use your own phone number for those? How would she like to communicate in the future—email, text, calls, meetings? What kinds of things does she want you to contact her about? And finally, what can you do to help?

Hopefully, a straightforward and polite approach will yield you the respect you felt was missing at your last meeting. If your questions are met with resistance, or sighs and moans, you'll have a clearer idea of what to do.

If you do sign with her—or anyone else—don't make the common mistake of thinking that landing an agent means you can let up on your own personal career management. If you continue to find your own auditions, take classes, and make contacts—in other words if you continue to work for yourself as if you don't have a representative—and the agent ends up being unhelpful, you'll still be in good shape. You may have even met your new representative in the interim— after all, you're in demand! If, however, you spend the next few months sitting back and waiting for her to get you auditions, worrying in the meantime over her lack of professionalism, you'll end up having wasted a lot of time.

Finally, your self-respect is paramount to your success. It's more than alright to say no to situations that make you uneasy or unhappy. Everyone has a bad day now and then, but if this agent is consistently rude or dismissive, you'd likely be better off without her on your team. You are the only representative who will stick with you throughout your entire career. Treat yourself with respect, even when others don't. JA

Dear Michael,

Recently, I submitted my headshot, résumé, and cover letter to several agents and managers. One agent got back to me right away and said he wanted me to audition for him, and that I could either attend his "seminar" or reserve studio space and bring an accompanist on another day if I could not attend. I'm very confused now. The "seminar" sounds like a scam. But if I reserve studio space and bring an accompanist, I'll end up spending about three times the cost of the "seminar." So, I don't know. I don't want to waste my money, and I'm unsure of how to proceed.

—Skeptical of "Seminars"

Dear Skeptical,

If this were strictly a TV, film, or commercial agent offering a "seminar," I'd tell you to avoid them. But agents who handle musical theatre actors face a unique challenge: they need to be able to hear potential clients sing. And since they don't typically have facilities in their offices for that, unless they've seen your work on stage, meetings must take place at venues that can accommodate this need.

I polled some experienced New York musical theatre actors to see what they thought of the practice you've described. We all agree that, though it's more expensive, between the two options you mentioned, you're much better off renting studio space. Let's compare. At a "seminar," you'll have about five minutes to present yourself, and you're mixed in among performers at who-knows-what level of talent or professional achievement—they're just people who decided to spend their money to meet an agent. If their work puts the guest in a sour mood, you might suffer by association. And the pianist is sight-reading your music for the first time. Conversely, when you rent studio space, you get an appointment that's all about you, during which you have time to sing several songs that you've rehearsed with your accompanist and talk one-on-one with the agents. And they're making the time, and the trip to the studio, to see you, which indicates sincere interest. And though you're still spending money on a meeting, that money goes to the facility and the accompanist, rather than into the pockets of the people you're meeting, which makes the whole thing a lot "cleaner." You're not paying agents to consider working with you, and you don't have to worry that their interest extends no further than your money.

There are other alternatives. One actor told me he simply went to a pianist and recorded accompaniment for several songs, then sung live in an agent's office. He said it was a little weird at first, but everyone relaxed when they saw how comfortable he was and heard he could sing. They now represent him. While any number of paths could lead to finding representation, you've got a better shot at making a real connection if you go classy . . . and skip the "class." MK

Dear Jackie,

If a so-called freelance agent I am working with is not SAG-AFTRA franchised, does that mean he doesn't have access to SAG-AFTRA auditions or quality stuff? Lately, I have been freelancing with a guy who lives in New Jersey, and is interested in me because I'm a "good looking guy."

I have not gone on any auditions, but he says he "knows people." He is trying to put together a portfolio for me with ten photos that I have emailed to him, but I do not hear from him. When I call, I am lectured about relaxing and told to be patient. I know it's not easy to get signed with a reputable agent—that it takes hard work, discipline, perseverance, and luck. But I don't want people wasting my time if they are unable to help me advance my career. I am tired of meeting people who cannot help me.

—Exasperated

Dear Exasperated,

A legitimate agency might be SAG-AFTRA franchised or a member of the Association of Talent Agencies (ATA) or National Association of Talent Representatives (NATR), and each organization lists current members on its website. If your agent is not on any of those lists, proceed with caution.

The real deal-breaker, however, is the lack of a license. Talent agencies should always be licensed by the state in which they practice. Licensed agents are regulated and bonded—giving them an incentive to keep on the up and up. Only licensed agents can legally submit you for work. To find out if your agent is licensed, contact the New York Department of Consumer Affairs at 212-487-4444. In California, contact the Department of Industrial Relations Division of Labor Standards Enforcement at 415-703-4810 or check its online database at dir.ca.gov/databases/dlselr/talag.html. Since your agent is in New Jersey, you may have to contact the New Jersey Division of Consumer Affairs. In other states, check the state-by-state licensing rules listed on ATA's website at agentassociation.com.

There are many unlicensed, unregulated talent reps—including managers, who are not required to hold licenses—who do try to land jobs for actors. Some are legitimate business people, others, frauds. What's important for you, I gather, is results. A rep's effectiveness will depend on her contacts and persuasiveness. If your agent really has the connections he's claiming, he may prove helpful. Of course, it's just as likely that he doesn't.

I suggest you clarify your freelance status with him. Common in New York, such arrangements are extremely unusual in Los Angeles and most other markets. If your agent is on board for freelancing, you can continue to pursue other representation. If he does come through with something, great! In the meantime, you'll keep your options open.

Your letter included some possible red flags. I'm not sure, for example, how he plans to use the ten-photo "portfolio" he's assembling. Before going any farther, find out everything you can about him via the state, SAG-AFTRA, the ATA/NATR, the Better Business Bureau, your instructors, and your fellow actors. Check message boards like the one at actorsaccess.com. Do a simple Google search.

Finally, you may want to dial back some of the "I am tired of meeting people who cannot help me" rhetoric. I understand your frustration, but it's going to get extremely hard for you to pursue an acting career if you don't stay open to the wonderful experiences you can have that don't lead to a paying gig. Many people you cross paths with won't directly help you, just as you won't help many of them. That isn't—and can't be—the point. JA

Dear Jackie,

Like the majority of actors in NYC, I do not have an agent, but freelance with a couple of them which, overall, has been a good arrangement for me. I contacted a manager more than a year ago and we agreed on a freelance arrangement as well. At that time, I didn't know exactly the fees involved. It turns out that she is doing what an agent does: she calls me and sends me for auditions. There have not been any traditional management duties involved in our relationship. In other words, she does not do more than an agent. Don't get me wrong: I am fine with it and I think that agents do an exhausting and good job.

A couple of months ago, I booked a nonunion voiceover with her and, to my surprise, she took 25% out of my fee. Now, while I feel that 75% of something is better than 100% of nothing, I feel that she is doing an agent's job and taking a manager's pay. My other reps take between 10% and 15% of the fee.

I understand that agents need to be licensed and somehow need to adhere to a very strict set of rules, as opposed to managers, who, basically, can do what they want. But when a manager does the job of an agent without doing a manager's job, I feel that is wrong. Am I right? Or am I just being a complainer?
—75% Left

Dear 75% Left,

As you now realize, the time to discuss commission fees is in the initial meeting when you are agreeing to work with a representative. Had you brought up the issue at that time, you and the manager may have been able to come to a compromise about her rate. At the least, you could have known what to expect.

According to the New York Department of Consumer Affairs, theatrical agents are licensed as employment agencies. Their commissions are capped at 10%, except in orchestra and concert engagements, for which the cap is 20%. However, talent managers are not licensed by the state, and are, according to the DCA,

> . . . exempt from the definition of employment agencies if their placement of their clients in employment is 'incidental to' their management services. The Arts and Cultural Affairs Law limits payments to 'agreed commissions, royalties, or similar compensation based upon payments received by the client as a result of his employment in the field of show business.'

"Agreed commissions" means that you and your manager could set any commission rate you want, as long as you both agreed to it—10%, 25%, 99%—whatever. Legally, a manager isn't supposed to be working simply as an unlicensed agent—solely procuring work for you—but it sounds as if you are okay with that aspect, and only object to the commission.

My suggestion is that you let this 25% be water under the bridge, but go in and speak to the manager about the future. Don't complain, just let her know that while you love that she's sending you out, you would like to use the agency commission model if she's not working with you in a management capacity. You can present this in a simple and respectful manner, and it might help cushion the point if you take responsibility for your part in not clarifying the issue earlier. She may go for your plan, or present you with compelling reasons to pay her a higher commission. She may step up her managerial duties. You may decide to part ways. Whatever happens, you'll have the conversation you needed to have back at the beginning.

Finally, New York actors who feel a manager or agent is acting outside the law can call 311 to speak to a DCA representative with questions or complaints. JA

Dear Jackie,

My new agent—at a well known, established, SAG-AFTRA-franchised agency—recently sent me on an audition for a big pay, nonunion commercial, which I subsequently booked. Although my agent was paid 20% from the production company on top of my fee, she took another 20% commission from my pay. Therefore, she made 40% total on the job. When I asked her about it, she said that is standard in the industry for nonunion jobs and it is an incentive for agents to handle nonunion actors and to submit them for nonunion jobs. Does this all sound correct to you?

—Clueless

Dear Clueless,

Nope. Your agent should not have taken more than a 10% total commission. SAG-AFTRA-franchised agencies are prohibited from taking more than a 10% commission on any project in any medium under the Guild's jurisdiction (such as commercials, films, internet, etc.). That rule applies to nonunion projects and actors as well as Guild signatory shows and performers. For areas in which the Guild has no jurisdiction, such as print or live theatre, franchised agencies are held to a commission rate determined by the state Labor Commissioner's office. New York law caps all commissions at 10%, while California pushes the cap up to 20% (a standard print commission). Franchised agencies are also prohibited from "double-dipping"—that is, taking the commission from the production company once and again from you.

Those represented by non-franchised agencies, however, should know their agents don't have to adhere to the same standards. While Association of Talent Agencies (ATA) agencies do follow the commission caps set by the state, those in California have the flexibility to take the 20% commission in any medium. Non-franchised agencies can also heed the letter of the law while violating its spirit by double-dipping, since the Labor Commission's caps apply only to monies commissioned from a performer, and don't mention extra payments made by a production company to the agency.

So, while a 40% payday may be "legal" under certain circumstances, your agent is violating the regulations of its *franchise* agreement in taking that much for your gig.

What now? You are entitled to file a complaint with SAG-AFTRA reporting your agent's actions, or you could handle this directly with your agent. If you want to go that route, tell her you've researched the rules and, while you love working with her, you'd feel more comfortable following the rules and paying her the standard 10% commission in the SAG-AFTRA-regulated arenas. Or just ask the nice folks in production on your next gig to send the check directly to your home address—then promptly send your agent a copy of your pay stub with a check for 10% and a thank-you note. She can always call you and argue for more. If both of these suggestions sound unappealing, you may not have long to wait before they are also unnecessary. Once you join the Guild, you won't have to navigate nonunion waters. While they can be full of wonderful opportunity, they are also rife with this kind of frustration. JA

Dear Michael,

I took a commercial class and got called in by a very big, well-respected agency. I met with them, and they seemed to like me. They signed me as a client. The next day, I got sent out on an audition, and the next day, another. I haven't booked or been called back for either of the auditions they sent me on. It's been three weeks since then, and I haven't heard from them at all. Have they given up on me?

—What to Do Now

Dear What to Do Now,

Commercials are a volume business, and no one expects you to book every one you audition for. Any established commercial agent knows that, rather than evaluating clients based on their first appointments, they have to just keep getting them out. They're also in the business of remembering who's who on their client list. You shouldn't worry that, after two auditions, they've forgotten you altogether. There probably just hasn't been anything you were right for. That happens.

I ran your question by my own commercial agent, the wonderful Tracey Gold-blum of Abrams Artists. Here's her response:

> The fact that this person hasn't been sent out in three weeks does not mean the agents are not submitting him/her—the casting directors might not be selecting this talent . . . probably because they aren't familiar with his/her work yet. But a good agent will keep pushing. We certainly don't give up on talent, old or new, because they have not booked or been called back.

So there you have it, straight from the source. MK

Dear Michael,

How do I know whether I'm calling my agents too much? I don't want to get on their nerves, but I don't want to be invisible. It's been pretty quiet for the past couple of months; when I call to check in, they sound annoyed. I'm trying to have a partnership, not be a nuisance. Any advice?

—Call Waiting

Dear Call Waiting,

Agents, like actors, are individuals, so they'll each respond differently to different approaches. But these guidelines I can offer with confidence:

—The general consensus seems to be that if three weeks have gone by, you need to check in.
—Never call your agency before noon. They're busy going over the breakdowns, trying to score appointments for you and other clients. Later in the day is best.
—Unless it's urgent, most talent representatives strongly prefer hearing from clients by email, rather than by phone, so they can address your issue when they have time to give it their full attention.
—Calling to ask if there's "anything going on" suggests that you think your agent was just sitting around doing nothing and needed your reminder to look for appointments. Better to ask about her weekend, or tell him a joke, then say goodbye. That's enough to keep you on the radar.
—By all means, call if you have a new contact or job lead.

Next time you're in the area, call and ask if it's a good time for a visit. Then stop by and chat with your agent. But here's the thing: don't talk business. Talk about what's happening in your life, or a great movie you just saw. Or the latest juicy Hollywood rumor. Ask your agent what she thinks of the crazy weather. Then go. I've been told directly by my own agents that this helps them keep me in mind. A friend of mine swears that every time he drops in like this, he gets an audition the next day.

But don't feel like you have to sit there, wondering if you've been forgotten, or worse, whether you need new representation. When an agency signs you, you're no longer an outsider, hoping for attention. You're on the roster, and presumably, considered a valuable addition. By keeping yourself on their front burner, you're doing them a favor; the more they send you out, the greater their chances of making money. So by all means, help them by reminding them you're there, but do it without putting them on the spot. No agent likes being nagged, but most appreciate an *occasional*, indirect nudge. MK

Dear Jackie,

I have been signed with my agent for four or five months now. I had one audition for a commercial about three months ago. He has sent me notices for other auditions I'm not interested in doing, such as hair shows and hand modeling (I want to act!) and also for things I have already seen on either sfcasting.com or craigslist (I know!). I almost think he doesn't have access to the bigger auditions. Granted, I'm in Northern California and I know there's not a big market here, but I'm hoping to gain experience before moving to LA. I have not booked any roles yet, but I've gotten several auditions on my own. Should I stay with the agency to see if they can get me any auditions? Should I just go it alone here doing indies, shorts, student films, and training, and then wait to get an agent in LA?

By the way, this agent also sent me to a headshot photographer (I wasn't required to go to him, just encouraged), and the pictures turned out horrible. They are so bad that I don't want to print any of them. When I go to auditions I print one at a time. Is this a total red flag?
—Out Here in Oakland

Dear Out Here,

Yes, that's a red flag, as are the craigslist auditions and the hair shows. But in a smaller market some of those practices *might* be less suspicious than they would in a bigger city. Your first step is to check the California state agency license database. All you need is the agency's name. If it isn't licensed, do not work with this agent. Period. (Just to be clear, managers are not agents and work unlicensed.)

If he is licensed, I don't see you needing to drop him at this point. He isn't keeping you from seeking work on your own, and it sounds like you have been able to skip the auditions you weren't interested in. Since you clearly realize you aren't working with a stellar rep, and will of course take any advice he gives you with a grain of salt, can it be harmful to stay with him for a while and see if anything good comes of it?

When I first got to LA, I did some mailings and eventually ended up working with a manager I knew nothing about. Yes, it seemed suspect that she had no office and when we met, she'd expect me to pick her up in my car and take her to lunch (I paid!). However, she did have other clients, one of whom booked pretty regularly, so I figured she must be doing something right. She soon introduced me to the people who would become my first Los Angeles agents. Eventually, I became more concerned about her strange ideas and *finally* checked around about her reputation. I quickly learned she had been investigated for all kinds of awful things. I dropped her that day . . . but kept the agents. So, was that manager worth working with? In my case, yes.

As for looking for another representative: why not? Since your current rep has no issue with you seeking work on your own, you may be able to build up your reel and résumé and make the jump to a better agency. Or maybe you'll have saved enough to head down to LA and leave this conundrum behind. JA

Dear Michael,

I've discovered that my agent has a terrible reputation and is thought to have questionable business practices and possibly anger issues. How do I extricate myself from this person and not destroy my future job prospects, or legitimate representation in the industry? Do I just let the contract lapse or do I send him notice that I want to end the contract immediately? Could he retaliate somehow?

—Regretful Client

Dear Regretful,

If you've done your homework and found that the accusations have merit, then leaving an agent like this isn't going to hurt your career—*staying* with an agent like this may hurt your career. Even if this guy wanted to deliberately undermine you as revenge for leaving him, I'd hazard a guess that he doesn't have the kind of industry clout to have much effect. Who is he going to tell? Who'll listen to him? Besides, *no one* can "fix it so you'll never work in this town again." Also, I doubt you're the first client to leave, and I'm sure he has better things to do than spend his time trying to destroy former clients' careers.

So, if I've successfully dispensed with that fear, then it boils down to this: Plan A—start looking for a new agent, and make the switch once you find one. If you go this route, you may find it opens more doors being able to say you're looking to *change* agencies, rather than just looking, like everyone else. Plan B—just leave the agency. Normally, I suggest waiting until you've found new representation. But if being with your current agent is worse than being unrepped, you should pull the plug and move on.

Whenever you decide to sever the relationship, do it simply, and with as little emotion as possible. Send a nice, lightly worded letter, thanking him and telling him you've decided to work with someone else. Don't make it a big deal. It's just business.

Now, having dealt with a lot of crazy people in my life, I know there's a possibility he won't react well. Here's my advice: don't get drawn into the craziness. Stay cordial, professional, businesslike, and dead calm. If he yells, say "I can tell you're upset. Would you prefer to talk later?" If he says "You'll never work again," just say "Well, I certainly hope that's not true." Stay neutral, no matter what. Thank him for his help. Wish him well. It's not your job to teach him what he's doing wrong. Even if it's a rough departure, you'll be so relieved when it's done. MK

Dear Jackie,

I signed with my first agent about two months ago and needless to say, I was ecstatic. He called me off a blind submission and I went in for an interview, during which I found him warm and intuitive. He seemed to understand actors' struggles—I liked him right away. He offered to represent me for both commercial and theatrical, and I signed a week later.

Because he is from a newer, smaller agency based in Torrance, California and I lack a reel and have résumé constraints, I knew there would be some limitations. But after two months I have not gone out once. I certainly wasn't expecting to be going on high-profile auditions for major motion pictures, but I thought I would be going out for commercials and occasional under-fives. Several people have mentioned that this is due to his lack of clout or position in the agent hierarchy. Can you elaborate on this? Is there a way to make the most out of this relationship since I like his attitude and perspective?

—Feeling Undervalued

Dear Feeling,

One of my first agents upon relocating to California was based in Orange County—an hour-plus drive from the LA industry hub—and similarly, I got almost no auditions through her connections. Eventually, I believe, her agency folded. I say, "I believe" because we had so little contact that I don't really know what happened. While I think she meant well, she just didn't have the clout or resources to get her clients into auditions. I know my experience with her was not unusual as I had a friend who worked in her office—which was how I connected with her in the first place.

Some agencies don't have the ability to do much on behalf of their clients—even if they're warm and receptive. Agents, like actors, rely on their contacts, and a new agent, especially one so far away from the major action, is going to have a very hard time competing. That said, your agent might have connections with small, nonunion producers or casting people in Orange County. The one or two auditions I did while with my OC agent were in OC—and they weren't bad jobs, either.

That said, there is very little any agency can do for you without your hustle. In other words, you must create your own opportunities with or without an agent. I know it can be a hard pill to swallow, but agents are only as effective as you give them ammunition to be. Of course a more prestigious agency will have an easier time selling you, but all agents will rely on you to get the ball rolling.

I failed my OC agent just as badly as she failed me. We had almost no contact and I did very little to maximize what connections she may have had. She once paid for me to take a casting director workshop (I was against paying—and, honestly, pretty poor at the time). Did I follow up with some cordial schmoozing or a thank-you postcard to the CD? Nope. I just did my time and left. Only later did I recognize that I had dropped the ball.

So, while your agent might not be well-known or well-placed, I'd suggest you stay with him for the time being as you go about the business of building your fledgling career. Instead of waiting for him to call you, meet with him and be sure you're doing all you can to maximize what he *can* give. JA

Dear Michael,

I signed with a new agent a while ago. It's a start-up agency but I liked her passion and decided to give her a chance. It's been about five months and so far she has gotten me out on one audition, whereas I go out sometimes multiple times per week on auditions I find myself, and have given the agency a percentage from things I submitted myself on and booked. How much longer should I stay before looking for a new agent?
—Tick-Tick-Tick

Dear 3Ts,

You described this as a start-up agency. That means they probably have limited clout with casting people; it takes time to grow those relationships. If you're early in your career, a start-up agency can be a great place to be, because you can grow with them. But it's important to be realistic in your expectations (they can't be ICM[10]). It's also important to think like a team, and not resent generating your own opportunities as well. It's all good for the partnership. You bring in your contacts, they bring in theirs. Everybody benefits.

And you should feel good about paying those commissions on work you've generated. Each booking enhances your value as a client, connects your agent with new contacts to whom she can pitch you in the future, and helps her keep the doors open so she can continue seeking out opportunities for you. Remember, *most of the work agents do to promote you goes uncompensated.*

You could talk with your agent about the shortage of auditions, but I can almost predict what she'll say: you need new headshots. They love saying that, because no agent wants to admit he isn't getting responses because casting people don't know him yet.

So, how long do you stay? It depends. The managing of a professional acting career requires constantly monitoring one's own place in the scheme of things. In the early phases, when credits and experience are light, it's unrealistic to expect any agency to find you frequent auditions, or for a high-status agency to sign you. But you also need to know when it's time to move up. And that can be hard. We actors are sometimes freakishly loyal to our representatives, to the point of ignoring signs we've outgrown them.

If you're feeling you could do better elsewhere, there's a very simple way to test that theory. Try shopping. If you find a more established agent who wants to sign you, and you feel the rapport is good, you should make the move without hesitation. If not, you should stay where you are, grateful for your agent's belief in you. MK

Dear Jackie,

I submitted myself for this commercial that I thought really fit me. They called me up today letting me know they might use me for it, but it's nothing for sure. What do you think I should do? Should I let my agency know ASAP about this? I don't want them getting mad at me and then I end up not booking the job. Maybe I should wait until I know I actually booked it and let them know about it.

—Maybe Baby

Dear Maybe,

Did your agency specifically tell you not to self-submit? If so, why? Agents don't often have the time or inclination to focus on non-or low-paying gigs, and understand that many of their clients self-promote and submit themselves for "under-the-agency-radar" jobs on their own. In fact, most representatives consider that kind of proactive work ethic desirable.

The exception to the "self-submissions are okay" rule is if you are sending yourself out for the same things your agent submits you for, without their permission. Sometimes an unsolicited self-submission landing in the very same casting office your agent is trying to get you into could be seen as complicating their work. They rep you in the field and probably don't want you "going rogue" in their territory. What if they're pitching other clients for the role, for example, and end up having to explain to the casting director how your lone submission arrived the same day as their package? Unless you get pirated Breakdowns, however, you're not seeing casting information for these bigger projects. Anything you see on Actors Access, *Backstage*, or a Casting Networks site is there for the explicit purpose of soliciting actor self-submissions. There's very rarely going to be any agent interest in these posts, especially in the commercial realm.

Instead of worrying about upsetting your agency, call them up and check in about the overall situation. Tell them you have been self-submitting for small, low-paying projects and ask whether they'd like to handle any possible upcoming bookings or if they'd prefer you to take care of those details. Let them know, too, that you plan to pay them commission on any work you book on your own, as required by the standard agency contract. If they express any hesitation about you submitting yourself, ask if you can meet with them to find out how they'd like to handle such situations in the future.

Instead of angry, I'm going to guess they'll be happy that you're working on your own behalf. JA

Dear Michael,

I'm on tour with a major show, and it looks like it'll run for a long time to come. My agents, who I was with when I booked it, are just kind of so-so. They don't do a lot, I hardly ever hear from them, and they don't return my calls. What makes it worse is, a couple of months ago, my agent there moved on to another agency, so I feel even less loyal now. Obviously, I'm thinking about looking for new reps.

I'm not sure how to go about this. I want to start looking now, but I'm not ready to leave this job. And do I offer the new agent a commission on the show I'm currently in? Do I just fire my agent and go without one? Or do I keep things the way they are and wait before I even do anything at all?
—Lost in America

Dear Lost,

I've known several actors who offered potential new agents commissions on existing jobs, sort of as an incentive, to get agents excited about working with them as a new client. Many of these actors found that, while the new reps were happy to collect commissions they didn't earn, the relationship fizzled after that. It seems that, once it's established you'll be bringing in money from work you book without them, agents can sometimes take a back seat and expect you to do all the driving. I don't mean this as a slight to agents in general. I'm just saying that I've known several actors in your position who've found that to be the case. Coming in with a commission is one of those things that sounds good, but doesn't always create the excitement you thought it would.

Instead, let the new agent's incentive be this: your current employment in a hit show can be used as a selling point when they pitch you. They can parlay that prestige into your next job, which will, ideally, be more prestigious and more lucrative. And that's when their commissions will kick in, so everyone wins.

However, no agency wants to sign an unavailable actor. So until you're at a point where, if the right opportunity presented itself, you'd be ready to leave your tour, I suggest sitting tight with your current reps until you're ready to be available for new projects. That's the time to go shopping. MK

Dear Michael,

I'm a fairly successful New York actor who performs mostly in regional theatre. I've been in the business for about fifteen years, and I've had an agent for about ten. I feel that my career is at a plateau, and I want to branch out into other areas of the business, like TV and film, as well as into roles at better theatres. I'm considering signing with a manager whom I feel might open doors for me and help casting people see me in a new light. How do you know when it's time to add a manager? What should I look out for? And should I be concerned about my agent's reaction?

—Growing Pains

Dear Growing,

Generally, the timing is right when you find the right manager. If you've met one whom you sense has the clout, drive, connections, and interest in you to make a difference, I wouldn't worry about the timing, or about your agent's feelings. You're trying to run a business, and you have a right to do that as you see fit. Most agents understand that. True, they don't always *like* working with managers, but if everyone ends up making more money as a result of the addition, you'll be surprised by how quickly that tension can dissipate. Just assure your agent that the decision doesn't indicate a lack of faith on your part.

A good manager brings a new set of contacts into the picture and will work hard for you to justify the added expense of his or her commission. Also, managers and agents sometimes get competitive with each other, and that's very much to your benefit. Each wants to claim credit for getting you more auditions. Let them duke it out while you watch your job opportunities become more frequent and more prestigious. And good managers—note that I keep using the word "good"—will think in terms of shaping your overall career. They're big-picture people, and at your point in the game, that could be a great asset.

That, of course, is the best-case scenario. But there are a few things to be wary of with managers. The field of talent management attracts all kinds of questionable characters, from poseurs with absolutely no showbiz clout to outright swindlers and even casting-couch Casanovas. As with any business arrangement, use caution and be smart. Never sign a management contract without first reading it through very carefully. And be sure to have a detailed talk with your potential new partner to learn what his or her plans for your career are. Just because someone hangs out a "manager" shingle doesn't mean that person knows what he or she is doing.

And keep in mind that a manager, like an agent, represents you. So his or her behavior affects how you're perceived. I once had a manager who used to come visit me on the set and hit on young actresses. It was embarrassing. That wasn't how I wanted to be represented, so I had to fire him, even though he was an asset to my career.

Another caveat: you'll need to monitor things closely to make sure the manager isn't just passing along appointments from the agent, letting the agent negotiate, and taking a commission. That does happen. Don't be afraid to have discussions with her about what she's doing on your behalf.

Look for this magic combination: good chemistry with someone who has both ethics and clout. If the manager you're considering passes the test, it may be well worth it to work together. You might find yourself on the threshold of a whole new level of your career. MK

Dear Jackie,

   I'm a recent conservatory graduate and have very extensive training. I was signed with a reputable agency for a short time and I was their only non-SAG-AFTRA client, but I didn't work once while I was with them. So, I recently decided to take my career into my own hands and forget about working with a rep. Not only have I landed a guest starring role on a Fox show, I was Taft-Hartleyed[11]—all without an agent. When I got the letter inviting me to join SAG-AFTRA the other day I almost fell to the floor.

I'm not the only one who is dropping the idea of an agency to better my career. Recently, a lot of my schoolmates were becoming extremely upset and negative about the future. That all changed when we stopped making excuses and started doing things for ourselves. With no agent I have no one to blame for not working but myself.

Now, when someone makes an excuse about why they aren't working, I just walk away. I don't surround myself with people who complain because it's contagious. I think you might be surprised at how many people feel held back by their representation. I feel really strongly about taking accountability for my failures along with my successes and it seems to be working. Actors are not animals and should never feel the need to beg. That kind of fear overshadows what makes us so unique and amazing. This self-reliant mentality could make us stronger as performers and as a community.

—Agent-Free

Dear Agent-Free,

Much of the frustration you are referencing comes from a misperception of what an agent or manager actually does. While representation can make a huge difference, it can't create a career. And while some agents and managers are kind and supportive, others can be standoffish or demeaning. Unfortunately, many actors—afraid they won't be able to find a better alternative—stick with bad representation, growing more frustrated with each passing season.

Stories like yours remind us that we are each responsible for our own path, which is not a bad thing. It can be, as you've discovered, downright empowering to throw off standardized expectations and make your own way. Far better to hustle up our own luck than to blame others. No rep, no matter how wonderful, can give you a job. They are just one facet of what must be a multi-layered approach towards cultivating a career. Every actor, as you've so eloquently expressed, is her own first and best agent. While I believe there are many hard-working, talented agents out there, Shakespeare had a point when he wrote, "Let every eye negotiate for itself and trust no agent." JA

What Do You Think?

1 How do you get an agent?
2 What is the difference between an agent and a manager?
3 What is a commission? How do agents and managers differ in regards to commissions?
4 What is an agent's primary job? What is a manager's primary job?
5 Why do agencies have to be licensed? Who grants them a license? Does a legitimate agent have to be SAG-AFTRA franchised?
6 What is "freelancing" with an agent or manager?
7 What are some ways to improve your relationship with an agent or manager?
8 What are some advantages to having both an agent and a manager? Disadvantages?
9 How do you end a working relationship with an agent or manager?
10 What are some ways to build an acting career without an agent or manager?

Notes

1 Publicists are tasked with increasing an actor's public visibility. They do this by seeking out interviews, public appearances, and other opportunities for exposure.
2 In California, such organizations are referred to as "advance fee talent organizations," and must be licensed and bonded.
3 There is only *one* exception to this general rule. Some SAG-AFTRA franchised agents in smaller markets (outside New York and Los Angeles) can apply for a waiver to charge clients a yearly $100 website fee. Check with SAG-AFTRA to see whether a particular agency has received the waiver before paying the fee.
4 Blind mailing—mailing promotional materials without a contact or introduction to the recipient.
5 See Chapter 6, "Marketing: Promotion and Networking," as well as Chapter 10, "Scams, Shams, and Ripoffs."
6 "Go-see" is the term used in place of "audition" in the print world, because there's no performance of material involved.
7 Performers may join any member of the Associated Actors and Artistes of America (4As) if the applicant is a paid-up member of one of its unions (SAG-AFTRA, AEA, AGMA, AGVA, GIAA) for at least one year and has worked and been paid as a principal performer in that union's jurisdiction during the previous year.
8 WME—Founded in 1898, William Morris Endeavor is the oldest talent agency in America and one of the most powerful in the world.
9 Elvis Presley. Look him up.
10 ICM—International Creative Management, a talent agency that occupies the very top echelon in terms of clout, prestige, and celebrity clientele.
11 Taft-Hartley (a.k.a. The Labor–Management Relations Act of 1947) was designed to level the unfair playing field formerly tipped in favor of labor unions. For actors, the provision means that if a producer wants to cast a nonunion actor in a union project, he can do so by requesting a Taft-Hartley waiver.

9

UNIONS

There are two major labor unions representing actors: The Actors' Equity Association (AEA)—commonly referred to as simply "Equity," which has jurisdiction over union stage productions, and The Screen Actors Guild-American Federation of Television and Radio Artists (SAG-AFTRA), which covers union film, television, and internet projects.

Membership in actors' unions has many advantages, including wage minimums, safety regulations, and the potential to qualify for health insurance. More importantly, membership renders an actor eligible to work on union projects.

However, union membership comes with an important restriction: once actors join, they can no longer work on nonunion projects. In SAG-AFTRA, this is known as Global Rule One, which states,

> No member shall render any services or make an agreement to perform services for any employer who has not executed a basic minimum agreement with the Union, which is in full force and effect, in any jurisdiction in which there is a SAG-AFTRA national collective bargaining agreement in place. This provision applies worldwide.

Equity has a similar rule. Violators are penalized, up to and including the loss of their membership. For this reason, it's advisable to weigh carefully the decision to join an actors' union. There are many nonunion projects that are perfectly suited to those early in their careers. Joining a union too soon puts a beginning actor in competition with seasoned professionals, making it all the more difficult to get hired. For most, this isn't an issue, because actors' unions have qualification requirements for joining that are hard to meet. There's also a substantial fee for initiation, followed by dues.

Actors can qualify for union membership in a number of ways. Here are the basics:

SAG-AFTRA

Eligibility to join SAG-AFTRA can be earned in one of three ways:

1   Booking a SAG-AFTRA job.
      The Taft-Hartley Act, otherwise known as the Labor-Management Relations Act, created a path for nonunion workers in all fields to land union jobs, therefore qualifying them for membership. Essentially, the law stipulates that all union jobs must be available to nonunion applicants, and employment must provide a path to joining the union. In popular vernacular, earning entry in this way is referred to as being "Taft-Hartleyed."
2   Earning membership in a sister union and joining through the 4As clause.
      The 4 in 4As refers not to the number of unions encompassed in the sisterhood, but to the unions' umbrella organization, the Associated Actors and Artistes of America (AAAA) which operates, in turn, under the national trade union federation, the AFL-CIO. It includes Actors' Equity Association (AEA), Screen Actors Guild-American Federation of Television and Radio Artists (SAG-AFTRA), American Guild of Variety Artists (AGVA), and American Guild of Musical Artists (AGMA). These trade unions hold reciprocal agreements with one another, including those on membership. Actors can join SAG-AFTRA if they have been a paid-up member of another 4As union for a period of one year and have worked (and been paid) at least once as a principal performer in that union's jurisdiction in the previous year. In other words, working members of AEA can join SAG-AFTRA by just paying the fee, and vice versa.
3   Earning three vouchers (also called waivers).
      Actors working as a background talent (or extras) who earn three SAG-AFTRA vouchers are eligible to join. Earning vouchers is not, however, as simple as doing a day of union background work—more about that in this chapter.

Equity

Equity eligibility can be earned in two of the same ways: by booking an AEA job and being Taft-Hartleyed, or via the 4As clause.

In addition, Equity offers an apprenticeship program called the Equity Membership Candidate (or EMC) Program. This program provides nonunion actors with a path to achieve Equity membership through work at participating Equity theatres. Each week of work counts as a point, and once a candidate completes

25 weeks/points, they may join the union or elect to enter Phase II of the EMC, which affords them 25 more weeks before they must join. To register, an actor must first book an EMC-eligible job at a participating theatre and pay a $100 registration fee—which will be credited towards their later Equity initiation fee. More information and a list of participating theatres can be found at actorsequity.org.

Questions and Answers

Dear Jackie,

I have a problem with the fact that every time I hear or read a lecture about being patient to join the unions, it always comes from someone blessed enough to have their SAG-AFTRA or AEA card. I simply do not have the patience or humility to do any more background work. I view myself as better than that.
   —Not Buying It

Dear Not Buying It,

I am not sure who suggested you get your union cards through background work, but it certainly wasn't me. Not to say such a route is invalid, but it's riddled with problems. Most notably, actors end up gaining union status before they are ready to compete for union jobs. Don't be patient, but shift your focus from the unions to your craft. Patience implies waiting around, refocusing requires effort. With consistent acting growth and auditions, union membership should fall in line with improved opportunities and representation.

You say you view yourself as "better" than background work. It sounds as if you've tired yourself out doing it—not for experience, pay, or fun—but for an elusive payout that has escaped you. It's frustrating, I'm sure. But the answer isn't to knock the work itself. Background is a legitimate job and none of us is too good for it. Your problem comes from believing it's a magic ticket into SAG-AFTRA instead of seeing it for the job it is.

All the time you're putting into striving for vouchers would be better spent auditioning, learning, and growing as an actor. Have you spent as much time in class as on background jobs? Do you self-submit on a consistent basis? Are you doing projects within your reach? In short: are you acting? You didn't become an actor to join a union. JA

Dear Jackie,

I just did a day of stand-in for a lead actor in a huge movie. Shouldn't that be good for one of the three vouchers I need to join SAG-AFTRA? As I understand it, stand-ins are automatically given a SAG-AFTRA voucher, but I was not.
   —Stand-In

Dear Stand-In,

SAG-AFTRA's rules pertaining to vouchers are somewhat mysterious in that there are so many variables, from the location of the shoot to the exact specifications of your work on set. I asked the Guild for some general guidelines on this issue:

> Depending on the location of the shoot and the terms of initial hire, it is possible that this actor should have been on a SAG-AFTRA voucher. It would be best if the actor called the Background Department so that we can gather the necessary information and provide a full response. We are happy to talk to anyone working on a SAG-AFTRA production whether they are union or nonunion and often we can help them with issues like these. If they should have been on a SAG-AFTRA voucher, there is a very narrow time-frame within which we can take action, so we encourage this actor to call us as soon as possible.

Many actors are hesitant to call performers' unions directly, especially if they are nonunion, but in this case it looks as if that's your best and only option. Theoretically, the three-voucher system, often called corrupt and flawed by members and nonmembers alike, is on its way out. SAG-AFTRA has been promising reform for years. The plan has been to switch to a point system that would take education and nonunion work experience into account. While the changes sound promising, I don't advise you hold your breath waiting for them. I have been writing about this "forthcoming" point system since 2005. JA

Dear Michael,

I am a nonunion New York actor. I recently joined Central Casting, a background-casting agency, and worked a one-day gig. During Central's nonunion initiation session, one of the casting directors said, "I never want to hear you ask me if you can earn a SAG-AFTRA waiver from a job. If you bring up SAG-AFTRA waivers, you won't work for us again." Later, we got the same message from the second assistant director, "Folks, I understand your plight and respect your needs as actors, but please stop asking me about getting a waiver."

If my asking for the thing that I need to get into the union is viewed as annoying by the people who are my only shot at becoming part of the union, then how am I supposed to get into the union? It seems it's either keeping quiet, making my $75 for thirteen hours of work and being last in the picked-over union lunch line, or speaking out and running the risk of blackballing myself in my chosen career. What in the world should we nonunion actors do?

—Damned If I Do

Dear DIID,

Oh, you're *really* not going to like my answer on this one. You find yourself in a situation that calls for a large dose of perspective, and putting yourself in someone else's shoes.

As you've no doubt observed, a film set is a huge operation. The main task, of course, is getting the day's scenes shot, which involves unimaginable feats of coordination. Having worked briefly in production (never again) I can tell you that ADs have a *lot* of details to wrangle: schedules, catering, transportation, script changes, locations, getting actors in and out of make-up and wardrobe, avoiding overtime. Sometimes they have to run around putting out fires—the weather changes, throwing the whole schedule into chaos; there's an equipment failure; sunset is approaching, and they're losing the light. Production folks have to deal with this stuff in order to keep things on track and achieve the main goal: getting the scenes "in the can."[1]

Accommodating your need to join SAG-AFTRA, on the other hand, is *not* something that helps achieve the day's goal. It's not why they rented equipment, found a location, or even why they hired you. Like it or not, part of a background actor's job is to be unobtrusive. That's the gig. I understand that you have career goals. What *you* need to understand is that when you're on set as a nonunion background player, it's simply not about you. MK

Dear Jackie,

I recently was Taft-Hartleyed and I am now SAG-AFTRA eligible, which has been a goal of mine for about five years. I wanted to start putting SAG-AFTRA-E (E for eligible) on my résumé but I've heard lately that casting directors don't like that and frown upon it. I've heard they see eligible actors as a "hassle." It might be some extra paperwork for them or something. I'm not planning on joining the union for another few months, until I've saved up money for the initiation fee. In the meantime, should I list my status or hide it?

—Proudly SAG-AFTRA Eligible

Dear Proudly,

Why would casting directors see SAG-AFTRA eligibility as a hassle? Since you have already done a Guild job and been Taft-Hartleyed, the CD paperwork is done and you can work SAG-AFTRA gigs for thirty days before you become a "must join." If you plan to join in a couple months, you're almost certainly not going to encounter any problems.

If you do book another union job after the grace period, the only hassle is for *you* to get down to SAG-AFTRA, fill out the paperwork, choose your name—provided it's available[2]—and pay the initiation fee (currently $3000) in a timely fashion, all of which might be actually fun if you've been looking forward to it.

"Most casting directors understand that if a union-eligible actor is hired for a union job, all they have to do is go down and pay the initiation fee," says one well-known casting director. "CDs are more concerned with finding exceptional talent than fretting about your union status."

The casting director paperwork you mention is filled out when you are originally Taft-Hartleyed, and is far less daunting than you may imagine. Bonnie Gillespie, author of *Self-Management for Actors*, says,

> Two of the biggest myths in Hollywood are that doing a Taft–Hartley report on an actor is a lot of work and that the fine for Taft–Hartley-ing an actor is steep. Wrong and wrong. The T-H Report is a single page and it takes ten minutes to fill out, if you are seriously verbose. Two minutes if you are concise. Fines are low—and that's if the production is fined for casting and Taft–Hartley-ing the actor at all.

As Gillespie alludes, the fine is not a foregone conclusion. Casting directors and producers can argue for your necessity to the project. Although a fine may be assessed if such arguments are rejected, it's less than a grand—chump change for big-budget projects. I'm not suggesting Taft–Hartley-ing an actor is fun or desirable, but it's nothing like filing your taxes.

"Whenever I hear actors talk about gigs they didn't get because they're non-union," Gillespie continues,

> I know that the producers, directors, or casting directors are using a very easy excuse that simply isn't true. Certainly, there are TV casting directors who get told, after a certain number of Taft-Hartleys over a season, 'Hey! No more!' And feature film casting directors aren't out looking for ways to Taft-Hartley more actors either. But if they have to do a couple on each project, it's really no big deal.

There are a lot of rumors out there about what CDs like and dislike, and while some may be sitting around trashing actors for attaching their photos to their résumés with staples instead of glue or for writing SAG-AFTRA-E on their résumés, most are reasonable and very busy people without time for such triviality. JA

Dear Michael,

   Last summer I booked a co-star role on a network episodic through my San Diego agent (I don't have representation in Los Angeles). As a result of that job, I am now SAG-AFTRA eligible. My agent has advised me to wait to join the union, I'm sure in no small part because most of the auditions she gets me are for nonunion work. However, I've read articles in which LA casting directors emphasized the importance of being in the union, especially for actors without representation.

I don't want to lose out on work by joining SAG-AFTRA too soon, but I also don't want to miss out on opportunities by not being a member. I have been developing my career for several years, and I have a BFA from a prestigious drama program, so of course I want to be able to access the best caliber of jobs and opportunities possible. I am a professional actor and want to be seen as such. Should I join SAG-AFTRA now?
    —To Join or Not to Join

Dear TJNTJ,
    In typical Gemini fashion, I'm going to argue both sides. On the one hand, joining SAG-AFTRA will not magically create audition appointments for you. There are plenty of Guild members who dutifully submit to casting directors every week, with no better than meager results. Since you're without an LA agent, most legitimate projects will pass you by. Meanwhile, the agent you have, in San Diego, suggests remaining nonunion, because she feels she can get you more auditions that way, and there's no reason to doubt her assessment. Though casting directors may advocate SAG-AFTRA membership, that membership won't give you access to those same casting directors. For that, you need a good LA agent. Until you have one, it may be a good idea to hold off on joining.

On the other hand, your stated goal is to be viewed as a professional actor, and professional television and film actors are members of SAG-AFTRA. Sooner or later you'll need to join. Joining now moves you closer to your goal. Though you'll almost certainly go through a transitional period during which auditions are scarce, it may be well worth it in the long run. After all, doing nonunion TV work in San Diego isn't your greatest aspiration, is it?

Whatever you do, you're going to miss out on something else. If you get married, you forfeit dating other people. Go to a party, and you sacrifice an evening at home. Sign on for a tour, you'll miss auditions. Without a crystal ball, no one can predict your career path. But this we know for sure: If you remain nonunion, you will miss out on SAG-AFTRA opportunities, and if you join SAG-AFTRA, you'll miss out on nonunion opportunities. Until cloning is perfected, you can't be union and nonunion, so obviously you have to make a choice. But now that you're eligible, you have the luxury of time, and I think that rather than rushing to a decision, waiting until the choice becomes a bit clearer is probably the best plan. MK

Dear Jackie,
    I am a young actor who just finished his first summer stock experience. I had an incredible time, and even gained about a dozen EMC points. How can I make

these points work for me now that they are accruing? Do they give me any perks or clout at Equity auditions? How should I make mention of these points on my résumé? I am a serious theatre actor and don't want to waste time reaching my goal.

—Future AEA Member

Dear Future,

While an eventual membership in Actors' Equity sounds imperative to your long-term plan, be sure you don't hurry to the end of that race. Enjoy and exhaust nonunion theatre opportunities as you go. While some theatres employ 99-Seat or Equity Waiver contracts, allowing Equity members to work in an essentially nonunion environment, the majority of opportunities available to Equity members are highly competitive regional theatre jobs. Join Equity only when you are ready to compete at that level.

"At this point in your career, you need to hone your craft and get experience for your résumé," explains the company manager of a small regional theatre:

> As a young actor, the quickest roadblock to this is joining Equity! Right now, you can be hired as a non-Equity actor by virtually every theatre in America, both Equity and non-Equity. Once you join Equity, you can only work at Equity theatres, and only on Equity contract there, and thus immediately, most of your opportunities will be gone. I can't tell you how many times we have to turn down promising young actors, because they pushed to get their Equity cards prematurely.

In the meantime, you can add "EMC" under your name on your résumé and skip over nonunion actors at EPAs.

"In NYC, EMC members are seen at EPAs, time permitting, before nonunion members, as long as they sign up prior to the scheduled lunch break," explains one go-getting New York actor:

> This may not seem like a big deal, but I know from first-hand experience that it can be a sanity saver. We all know actors who get out of bed and are at the audition site to be number one on the nonunion list at 6am. Since I am not a morning person and find that I am much happier and perform better with those extra hours of 'zzzs,' it is wonderful that—armed with my EMC card—I can arrive at 8am for a 10am call and be seen before the tired, cold, and unhappy actor who has already been sitting in a room for four hours before anyone has even shown up. Not to mention that when nonunion members get told they will not be seen, that does not rule out EMC members. This is only at EPA auditions, but it's something.

This actor also brought up another perk that I think deserves mention: "Your EMC card can get you into the Equity Lounge to use the coveted bathroom, unlike nonunion members." Perk indeed. JA

Dear Michael,

I've been in New York for five years, working consistently from gig to gig as a nonunion actor (major national tours, off-Broadway, readings, etc.). About two years ago, I booked a great off-Broadway show and got my Equity card. And I haven't had an Equity contract since—*two years*! I did book a national tour, but then it was forced to go nonunion, so I couldn't do it. I've talked with AEA, and the answer I got was that they can't force producers to work with the union. What is an Equity card if you can't get a job? I've already been forced to get health care elsewhere.[3] And I used to have steady work before I joined.

I'm trying not to become bitter. I want so badly to believe that Equity is good and right for me. I went in with that notion, and I want to believe it's my ignorance that's made me so disillusioned. But I've worked for a number of non-Equity companies, *all* of which treated me wonderfully, and paid me better than my union gigs! It seems to me Equity only benefits major Broadway performers, and I'm sick of it. Any suggestions?

—Disillusioned Actor

Dear Disillusioned,

Now that you're on the other side of the Equity fence, you can see why we union members have found it so disappointing to see Broadway tours go non-Equity. There was a time, really not that long ago, when such a thing was completely unheard of. That's no longer the case.

Some choose to vilify the union; that's their prerogative. I believe those who think conditions are terrible under Equity don't know their history well enough to know how terrible conditions were *before* Equity. Besides access to auditions and potential access to health care, membership offers protection of work conditions and hours, free workshops, professional status, information, and support. And, Equity is already succeeding in efforts to bring more tours under the union umbrella.

But let's talk in practical terms, OK? Here's an interesting scientific fact: bitching about Equity doesn't produce any actual results. Some actors spend their entire lives doing that (they're those crazy people you see at auditions with the homemade pamphlets and conspiracy theories). Not much benefit in that. But here's what's in your immediate control: remaining vs. resigning. And that's a big decision. Think of how long it took to earn your card. Regardless of your current frustrations, having that card is an achievement. It's also an adjustment; just as it took time to earn membership, it may take time to establish yourself at this new level. You've moved to the lower rungs of a more prestigious ladder. And you've already been offered a national tour. That the tour went nonunion is certainly no reflection on you. In vying for a big Equity contract role, you *succeeded*.

But all that said, it's you, ultimately, who must take charge of your career and your life. You're telling me that being nonunion was better for you in every way. So what stops you from relinquishing your card? If you believe returning to your nonunion status would make your life better, you should do that, rather than bemoaning the state of things and making yourself miserable. Honestly, life's too short. MK

Dear Michael,

I know that, as union actors, we're not supposed to do nonunion work. But, hypothetically, what happens if we do? I'm not saying I would. But what are the penalties? Do you get kicked out? Fined? Blacklisted?

—Curious about Consequences

Dear Curious,

You're referencing what SAG-AFTRA calls Global Rule One, which says that SAG-AFTRA members don't work on nonunion projects—period. That title, "Global Rule One," is an indication of how important it is. Discovered violations are viewed with considerable gravity, both by union employees and by union members.

In fact, for generations, the undermining of one's own union has been considered among the lowest acts a person can commit, so much so that those rare union members who do so are called "scabs"—a derogatory slang term meaning "a low or despicable person" that dates back to the 1500s. According to word-detective. com, this usage "most likely stems from the implication that such a scoundrel might well be afflicted with syphilis, which in its advanced stages causes a 'scabby' skin condition." Wow. That's some pretty serious condemnation. Word-detective continues:

> Since 'scab' already was being used to mean 'lowlife creep,' it's not surprising that by the late 1700s it was being applied to any worker who refused to join an organized trade union movement. As one source explained in 1792, 'What is a scab? He is to his trade what a traitor is to his country . . . He first sells the journeymen, and is himself afterwards sold in his turn by the masters, till at last he is despised by both and deserted by all.'

According to Webster's, the definition of "scab" now includes, among others, "one who works for less than union wages or on nonunion terms."

But your question wasn't about ethics, or etymology; it was about consequences. I asked representatives from our two largest unions to weigh in. SAG-AFTRA's CEO and General Counsel Duncan Crabtree-Ireland responded, in part,

> Our members understand that a union contract is essential for SAG-AFTRA to be able to provide union standards and protections. Members who are charged with a violation of Global Rule One are required to appear before the Guild's Disciplinary Review Committee or a Trial Board conducted by a group of their peers. A Trial Board has the authority to impose penalties including reprimands, fines, suspension, or expulsion from membership in the Guild.

At Actors' Equity, the matter is taken very seriously as well, and the union makes every effort to educate its membership about the ramifications of scabbing. If a member ignores those admonishments, dealing with the infraction. Equity spokesperson Maria Somma explains:

> When a situation is brought to the attention of Equity, a business rep is assigned to investigate. If it is demonstrated. The business rep will determine, based on all the findings, whether or not to go to charges. If that happens, the case is brought before a Charges Committee, which examines all the evidence, including any and all material submitted by the member. It is at the discretion of the Committee as to what action to take—from taking no action, to fines and/or expulsion.

So there you have it. That's what can happen to you if you're caught. But I also want to tell you about another kind of penalty—one that can happen even if you're *not* caught. This penalty falls on your colleagues, your fellow members, the people in your union family. If a union actor does nonunion work, the whole membership suffers. Here's why:

—If producers can get union actors without signing union contracts, they have far less incentive for coming under the union umbrella. They're getting full-fledged professionals without having to pay into pension and welfare. As a result, more jobs could go nonunion, and employment for dues-paying union members who refuse to scab could decrease.

—Violating our most important rule suggests to producers that we don't take our rules seriously. If they can circumvent this fundamental policy, why should they adhere to others? Suddenly, your colleagues may find productions neglecting to break them on time for meals, pushing them to do dangerous stunts, misreporting overtime, and who knows what else?

—Working nonunion puts pressure on your fellow union members to do the same, making it look like those who won't scab are being difficult.
—Lack of solidarity makes a union appear weak and vulnerable, which compromises our position when it comes time to negotiate for fair pay and decent working conditions.

In researching your question, I looked for union actors who'd been caught violating Rule One. I wanted to interview them about the consequences imposed on them. Even using my best resources, I wasn't able to find a single interview subject. That may mean that very few have been guilty of this violation, or that those who have were too ashamed to discuss it, even anonymously. Maybe both things are true. In either event, even if you're not bothered by the ethics, it would seem that violating Rule One isn't worth the trouble or embarrassment it can cause. Glad to know you're not planning to do that. MK

Dear Jackie,

If someone in SAG-AFTRA doesn't pay dues for a long time, what happens? Are they kicked out of the union, do they have to pay all the back dues to become current, or what? I haven't acted in years and somewhere along the line I stopped paying my dues. There's no way I could pay off what I must owe right now, but I wonder what would happen if I were to suddenly land a union job. Does SAG-AFTRA have a policy in place for a slacker like me who wants to get right with the union? I suspect this must happen a lot—I mean, most SAG-AFTRA members don't work, and I bet lots of people let their dues fall behind.
    —Slacker

Dear Slacker,

You are right that a lot of SAG-AFTRA actors don't work regularly, but many keep their memberships paid up nonetheless. I've heard this referred to as holding a "vanity membership," meaning the actor likes the feeling of belonging to the Guild, although their professional aspirations may have dimmed.

SAG-AFTRA does indeed have protocols for members who want to take a break from acting work. Members who are paid up on dues can ask to be put on "Honorable Withdrawal," and members who owe the Guild back-dues can opt for a status called, "Suspended Pay." In either case, the actor agrees to abstain from all union-covered acting work, including auditions, during their inactivity with the Guild. This isn't a break from SAG-AFTRA as much as a break from acting, and needs to be cleared with the Guild up front. (AEA has similar policies.)

SAG-AFTRA's National Director of Membership Services clarifies the consequences of ceasing to pay dues without contacting SAG-AFTRA directly: "An active member delinquent in the payment of dues for three dues periods shall be terminated from membership."

Don't worry—it gets better:

> If a terminated former member reinstates their SAG-AFTRA membership within five years of their termination date, rather than paying a new full initiation fee, on a one-time basis, the performer will pay 20% of the applicable rate, plus current dues, dues leading up to termination, and a $100.00 application fee. If the performer reinstates after five years, the full initiation fee is assessed, plus the current dues, dues leading up to termination, and a $100.00 application fee. Please contact the Guild's Membership Services Department for further information. JA

Dear Jackie,

I'm pursuing a career as a stage actor in New York, and have a reasonable number of good nonunion NYC and regional credits on my résumé, plus training and a degree.

Recently I submitted for a featured extra role in a major feature film with an A-list celebrity and, although I have zero film credits, I was cast immediately at my audition. During the shoot, I was upgraded to a small principal role, and now I find myself a member of SAG-AFTRA with no clue what to do next. Can I still pursue nonunion stage? I'm not a member of AEA yet, and I don't want to have effectively cut my possibilities down that much. There is a confusing clause in the SAG-AFTRA rules where it states that a member will not accept any nonunion work within the other unions' jurisdictions.

    —Stuck with SAG-AFTRA

Dear Stuck,

As you may know, you didn't actually have to join SAG-AFTRA and be "stuck" as you call it, as this was your first booking. Performers are given a one-time freebie. Once you were Taft-Hartleyed (the process of being invited into the union after being cast in a role) you could have postponed joining and held on to your nonunion status, even continued to work on union projects for thirty days. Only after that grace period, upon your booking of another Guild job, would you be a "must join," meaning you'd have to join SAG-AFTRA in order to take the job.

I bring this up (too late I realize) because—to answer the second part of your question first—your joining SAG-AFTRA will put a damper on your nonunion theatre career. You have technically agreed not to take nonunion acting jobs, except in very rare circumstances.

Here's a response to your question from Actors' Equity:

> Both AEA and SAG-AFTRA are members of the 4As, and under that umbrella organization, as well as stipulated in each Union's constitution, there is language that prohibits a member from taking nonunion work in a sister Union's jurisdiction without first contacting that union. The reason for the call is to determine if there is an organizing drive going on, or if a producer is on an unfair or banned list, or if other restrictions exist. There are a few instances—like a showcase—where a union member would be able to take nonunion work. But ultimately, when a union member takes a job nonunion, such a decision weakens and ultimately erodes the strides a union has made for its membership.

Since AEA is the union with jurisdiction over the theatre world, it's the organization from which you—a member of its sister union SAG-AFTRA—would need permission to work nonunion. Frankly, your chances don't look good.

AEA continues:

> Actors' Equity will not give an okay for a union member to take nonunion work in New York regardless of the situation because we consider New York to always be in an organizing drive. Again, the only exception to this in New York would be showcases.

I know this is not what you wanted to hear. And the truth is that many, many actors do not follow—or even know about—this guideline. It's common for SAG-AFTRA actors who are not in Equity to do nonunion theatre, and AEA members who aren't in SAG-AFTRA to do nonunion film, and it's rare that they are reprimanded. Many actors don't understand the 4A collaboration nor do they realize that all 4A union members working in any of their jurisdictions are entitled to the same perks and protections. While this rule limits nonunion opportunities, its intention is to strengthen rights and protections for all union members. As utopian as this may sound, if 4A union members stuck together, we'd all be in much stronger positions. JA

Dear Jackie,

I am SAG-AFTRA, but am not working as much as I want. A friend of mine suggested I go "Fi-Core." I am not really sure what that is, but he said if I went "Fi-Core" I could do both union and nonunion work. I can't believe that's true. When I tried to look it up online, most of the comments were really negative and insulting, but I can't understand why. There isn't enough union work to go around so why doesn't everyone do it?

—Confused

Dear Confused,

There isn't enough acting work to go around, period. Whether you are union, nonunion, or Fi-Core, you are likely to be disappointed in the number of opportunities out there.

Financial core, or Fi-Core, is not a SAG-AFTRA thing. It's a status a worker in any union can elect to take, rendering them, basically, a dues-paying non-member. (And yes, you must become eligible to join the union before you can opt out of it in this way.) Some states, such as Texas and Florida, are "right-to-work" states, meaning that union membership is not required as a prerequisite for work of any kind. In a right-to-work state, a nonunion actor can be cast in local SAG-AFTRA productions and never need join the Guild. Membership is completely voluntary. Other states, such as California and New York, are "union states," in which union membership is the norm. But employees of union jobs cannot actually be required to join a union. Because labor unions actively engage in democracy, endorsing candidates and donating millions of dollars to political campaigns, they cannot legally require membership. Doing so, the Supreme Court has said, would interfere with a person's right to political freedom.

Two Supreme Court cases are relevant here, *Labor Board v. General Motors*[4] and *Communications Workers of America v. Beck*[5]. In brief, the Supreme Court has ruled that unions must offer workers the option to refuse union membership while retaining the right to work on union-regulated jobs. However, the union can require a nonunion worker to pay an amount equal to the membership initiation fee and all dues related to collective bargaining. This financial requirement is referred to as financial core.

For actors, this means that—after getting into SAG-AFTRA or AEA—they are legally permitted to decline membership and take financial core status. This allows the actor to work on union projects without adhering to union rules. The actor will still be required to pay initiation fees and all dues related to collective bargaining, and although they will receive any pension and health benefits they earn on union work, they relinquish full membership—possibly forever. There are some selective cases in which Fi-Core actors are permitted to go back and join SAG-AFTRA or AEA, but each is looked at on an individual basis. You can't "go financial core" for a project or two and then just switch back when it suits you. Fi-Core actors also give up their right to participate in any union programs, such as screenings, casting director workshops, and seminars for SAG-AFTRA and the right to attend Equity Principal Auditions (EPAs) and Equity Chorus

Calls (ECCs) for AEA. They are also ineligible for any member services or elections and, of course, forego all union protections when working nonunion.

In other words, Fi-Core actors get the union's protections on SAG-AFTRA jobs, while remaining free to compete for work that fails to meet those requirements. They benefit from collective bargaining agreements without making the parallel sacrifices. They can do this because most union members continue to uphold their agreements to the union and each other, thereby keeping protections and minimums intact.

Still interested in exploiting this loophole? Consider this: If actors begin going Fi-Core en masse—if "everyone" does it, as you suggest—the protections our unions now provide will become null and void. Collective bargaining power rests on the shoulders of the collection of people doing the bargaining. If too many actors shrug off their responsibility to the group, we will lose the ground we, as a collection of artists, have made.

The strength of any union comes from the agreement of its members to uphold its basic tenets. In SAG-AFTRA, declining nonunion acting work (Global Rule One) is a paramount parameter. Union actors benefit from basic minimums on pay and safety in exchange for giving up work that won't meet those minimums. Because many of the most qualified performers have agreed not to work for less than union minimums, producers are pressured to offer compensation and protections at those levels. Collectively, we have power.

It's no shock that you found online reports of disdain for Fi-Core—many in Hollywood are strongly opposed to its use and abuse. SAG-AFTRA actually classifies it as a "hostile act." The decent working environments and wages actors benefit from are due, not to the good will of producers, but to the dedication of our forebears who were willing to make sacrifices and stand up for artists' rights. Why should some actors be exempt from the rules, while others uphold them in order to better all of our chances at earning a decent wage or being fed or getting extra pay for overtime? Why should some actors get those benefits without paying the same costs?

I can think of maybe one good reason to go Fi-Core. Namely, you're not an actor. Dave Thomas, the owner of Wendy's who used to star in all of its commercials, was Fi-Core—and that made perfect sense. The man wasn't an actor—he just wanted to sell hamburgers for his family business in any medium available.

For someone on a serious path to an acting career, joining SAG-AFTRA and AEA is a rite of passage, a pivotal hurdle in the climb to financial and professional success. Many actors are anxious to give up nonunion work as soon as they can, but some do so too soon. They have yet to learn the ropes, get anything on tape, or land representation. Still, they think simple union membership will be a ticket into the "good auditions," the big time. How disappointed they must feel when they learn the truth: jobs are scarce, on every level. This is why I continuously encourage actors to hold off on joining the unions until they are ready. Non-union work is a great testing ground. You need to pay your dues before you . . . pay your dues.

To me, Fi-Core actors are a lot like those guys who drive on the shoulder of the freeway during rush hour—the ones who think they are too important or too busy to face the traffic the rest of us are sitting in. Don't you just hate those guys? JA

Dear Jackie,

As a nonunion actor, how would a union strike affect me? If I were to accept work while the strike was going on, would that look bad for my career? Would I be blacklisted? I wouldn't want to damage my chances for a career as a working actor. I would hate to cross the picket lines and have it be held against me.
—Not a Scab

Dear Not a Scab,

Should there be a strike, nonunion actors wouldn't be expected to refrain from taking all work, just jobs that would traditionally go to striking union actors. Nonunion jobs would remain fair game.

If you do cross the picket line and take a normally union job during a strike, there's no certainty as to what will happen. Both SAG and AFTRA (then sepa-rate unions) penalized nonunion actors who crossed picket lines during the com-mercial strike of 2000 when they later wanted to join the unions. Of course not all "scabs" were discovered or penalized, but SAG took measures to identify strikebreaking actors, going as far as photographing them as they crossed picket lines and posting their photos on a "Wall of Shame" at strike headquarters. Some were publicly named and many were ridiculed and harassed by union actors as they reported for struck jobs.

In 2002, SAG banned 187 actors known to have crossed picket lines from joining the Guild. While an angry strike committee suggested such actors be banned for life, the actual prohibitions on membership were from six months to five years. Some big names such as Tiger Woods and Elizabeth Hurley were also penalized with fines, probation, and ridicule.

I could go into a long and probably boring tirade about why you should honor picket lines and how performing struck work helps the AMPTP[6] and hurts your fellow actors—not to mention you, since you eventually hope to join their card-carrying ranks—but instead I'll just encourage you to educate yourself about the issues. If SAG-AFTRA or AEA does strike, union and nonunion actors alike will need as much knowledge, patience, and energy as they can get. JA

Dear Jackie,

I am a producer in Coeur d'Alene, Idaho—a right-to-work state—and am working on several nonunion commercials. We would like to fly some SAG-AFTRA actors out from Los Angeles to work with us. What does a right-to-work state mean for them?

—Talent Importer

Dear Talent Importer,

You've got the meaning of the right-to-work laws a bit backwards. Such laws are meant to give nonunion and union workers equal access to available jobs. They do not release union members from union rules and regulations. Under the laws of right-to-work states, which include Alabama, Arizona, Arkansas, Florida, Georgia, Idaho, Iowa, Kansas, Louisiana, Mississippi, Nebraska, Nevada, North Carolina, North Dakota, Oklahoma, South Carolina, South Dakota, Tennessee, Texas, Utah, Virginia, and Wyoming, actors cannot be required to obtain union membership or pay any portion of union dues as a condition of employment. Nonunion actors in right-to-work states don't need to join SAG-AFTRA to work on SAG-AFTRA jobs—they are free to join unions or to decline at their discretion, and have the "right" to work regardless.

SAG-AFTRA members, however, agree upon joining the union to adhere to Global Rule One—it's right on the back of the card. "This provision applies worldwide." There are ongoing disputes over right-to-work laws and union regulations, and I encourage anyone interested to Google "right-to-work states" for a taste of the issues, but the upshot is: SAG-AFTRA members are not permitted to work on your nonunion project.

SAG-AFTRA's National Organizing Director, responded to your question as follows:

> Union membership follows the member regardless of whether the member is working in a union security state or a right-to-work state. So a SAG-AFTRA actor working nonunion in Idaho would be in violation of Global Rule One and would face disciplinary action. A member may resign their membership and work nonunion. As a reminder, SAG-AFTRA considers a member's resignation to be permanent. The interesting thing about this producer's question is that it clearly acknowledges that real professionals carry a SAG-AFTRA card and that they are unable to produce a quality project without using union talent. They want the quality without paying for it.

So, it looks like you'll either have to become a SAG-AFTRA signatory or use non-union talent on this one. Either choice has its perks. If you simply do not have the budget for a union contract, rest assured that there are plenty of talented nonunion actors out there waiting for a job like this one. Years ago, before I was a SAG-AFTRA member, I was flown out to Arizona to shoot a nonunion commercial. It was a great learning experience on a very professional project. I hope you're able to give some deserving nonunion actors the same treatment. JA

What Do You Think?

1 What are some advantages of joining an actors' union? Are there disadvantages?
2 What do SAG-AFTRA and AEA stand for?
3 What are the 4As and how do they work together?
4 Can nonunion actors audition for union projects? Explain.
5 How do you join SAG-AFTRA? (Hint: there are three methods.)
6 How do you join AEA? (Hint: there are three methods.)
7 What should you do if you are a union member who cannot afford to pay your dues?
8 What is Global Rule One and how might it affect your career?
9 What is a Taft-Hartley waiver? How does it work?
10 Explain financial core or "Fi-Core." Would you consider taking this status? Why or why not?

Notes

1 "In the can"—finished filming (from the days when film was stored on reels in metal canisters).
2 Actors' unions do not accept new members with the same name as existing members. When joining, if someone with your name is already in the union, you will need to use a different name. (This is why some actors add their middle initials or middle names, or create a different professional name.)
3 In order to qualify for health care, Equity members must work a certain number of weeks. See the union's website for details.
4 [1950] 179 F.2d 221, Second Circuit.
5 [1988] 487 U.S. 735.
6 AMPTP, the Alliance of Motion Picture and Television Producers, is the trade association responsible for negotiating the majority of industry union contracts.

10

SCAMS, SHAMS, AND RIPOFFS

Show business has always been plagued by con artists, forever inventing ways to dupe those with dreams of performing and preying on those too naive to spot their scams. Predators may offer major roles, business contacts, representation, little-known secrets to success, access to the big time, introductions to famous directors, or union memberships in exchange for money or other favors. While many swindlers are full-fledged snake-oil salesmen, some are merely misguided individuals with an inflated sense of their own influence. In either case, it's important for actors to be fully aware of the presence of this opportunistic element, and savvy enough to steer clear. Falling for a scam can be costly, career damaging, and even dangerous.

There are more actors than acting gigs. Even job interviews—auditions—can be almost impossible to access. With such scarcity facing all but the most in-demand of performers, it's no wonder our industry is crowded with charlatans, offering shortcuts at a price. As the old adage says, "If it seems too good to be true, it probably is."

Spotting cons can sometimes be as simple as taking time to work through the logic, or lack thereof, of a given "opportunity." For example, say you're out shopping and you're approached by someone claiming to be an agent. The entertainment industry is bursting with talented, qualified actors. Any decent agent has no shortage of potential clients requesting representation. So why would this one be looking for actors at the mall? Or what if you see an online ad seeking actors for a major film role? Directors, producers, and casting directors need do no more than post a casting notice through Breakdown Services for instant access to thousands of worthy applicants for their projects. So why would this one post a public ad, inviting those with no acting experience to apply?

Show business never has been, and never will be, easy. There are no secret shortcuts. No fast tracks. Be skeptical of any unusual opportunities, and never allow your ambition to override your common sense.

Questions and Answers

Dear Michael,

Yesterday I went to an audition for a Will Smith movie that I found on craigslist (which I know is not exactly the most reliable resource, but I thought I might as well give it a shot). When I called for details, the man told me to bring a head-shot if I had one and come "camera ready," prepared to do a monologue. When I was called into the audition room, the woman took one look at my headshot and told me that in order to do anything I need a better headshot. She then looked over my résumé and asked if I am currently taking classes, so I explained that I'm moving to Ireland in the fall to study drama and film. When I asked if she could recommend some places for headshots, she said she couldn't unless I gave her a deposit. Then she started talking about acting classes at her studio that end with a Broadway showcase and told me I could take them for free if I pay $395 for the headshots, and some extra fees, so that it would come out to about $500. She said that she has never offered this to anyone before, but I "might be the next Kirsten Dunst," and then I can thank her for helping me make it. She made an appointment for me to meet her again Monday with a deposit for the headshots so that I can jump into the middle of a session of acting classes and do the showcase. (The woman looked at her calendar to make sure I was available Tuesday nights for the classes and that I'd be in town for the showcase.) I asked about auditioning for the Will Smith movie, but she said I couldn't because I "seemed too nervous." Should I return on Monday with the deposit or cancel the appointment? I cannot decide if this is a great opportunity to gain more experience and training before I leave for school or a complete scam.
—Amateur's Dilemma

Dear AD,

I'm very careful, in answering these letters, not to jump to conclusions. I weigh both sides before forming opinions. But in this case, it's so clear, and I'm so sure, that there is no other side to consider. It's really simple: it's a scam. There's no Will Smith movie, no Broadway opportunity. It's just the *classic* set-up to rip off aspiring actors like you. I urge you in the strongest possible terms to stay far away from these people. Give them neither a dime of your money nor a second of your time.

In case you're not convinced, allow me to point out a few bright red flags:

> —I know of no legitimate operations that do film casting, headshot pho-tography, and Broadway showcases, all under one roof. Those are three completely different arenas.
> —These people require a deposit in order to give you headshot advice?
> —99.99% of the time, film auditions involve reading from the script, not monologues. Certainly, no one wants to hear a monologue for a small film role.

—With some possible low-end exceptions, casting isn't done through craigslist. I can promise you, there are no speaking roles in major films there.

—This may be harsh, but I'm afraid it's true: actors fresh out of high school with no credits don't easily encounter opportunities to audition for major motion pictures. Those opportunities are hard to come by even when you're established.

—Only a con artist says "I've never offered this to anyone before."

—And if you *still* need convincing, just research this company via Google and IMDb and see whether they have any legitimate casting credits. I'm betting they don't.

Now listen: these kinds of people are very good at being persuasive. If I were you, I wouldn't even call to cancel. They don't deserve that courtesy. I would just not show, then ignore any communication from them. But if you feel obligated to contact them to cancel, promise yourself that no matter what they say, you won't be swayed, and stick to your guns, even if they yell, act hurt, tell you you'll never work in this town—whatever. If they persist, tell them not to contact you again, and that you've related your experience to your parents and the Better Business Bureau.

Heed this advice, and you will have spared yourself the grief and disappointment of losing $500 to these vultures. MK

Dear Jackie,

I got this in an email the other day:

Want to be famous? Are you a model or an actor? Or do you simply hope to become one? Aspiring models and performers of any age or gender are welcome here! Create your own, personal account profile with up to 20 pictures and loads of space for your résumé and personal information! Plus, you'll be able to exchange messages with other actors, talent agents, casting directors, and fans! Search our private casting callboard, for links to the job of your dreams! Sign up so talent scouts and agents can discover you!

I know it sounds fishy but how can I know for sure? I'm tempted to sign up and see if it's legitimate. It's really cheap.

—Should I Try It?

Dear Should I,

Over the years, I've received my share of solicitations from online talent databases using similar pitches. I went ahead and signed up for a few, including the one you shared, so I could report my findings.

One site, which claimed to be the place to "go for fame," boasted 1017 members currently visiting when I signed on. Aspiring types from all over the world were registered—their sexed up, hopeful pictures looked desperate, competing for space on the busy black page. Casting notices were posted for things like a beer promo and lingerie modeling. One specified the respondents should have a "rockin'" face, body, and attitude. Another was for a state-sponsored "bikini team" that does car washes and boat shows.

An ad on another site for "gorgeous models" interested in "a once-in-a-lifetime opportunity" caught my eye. According to the post, "soft-core webcam porn is the new hardcore" and were I deemed hot enough I could make "10K a month with no physical interaction required!" Did I mention the $1,000 signing bonus? Oh, wait a minute . . . I just noticed they want women who look under 18. Gulp.

Your impulse to "sign up and see" because it's "cheap" is dead wrong. You'll do nothing but waste time and money, and you may end up in an embarrassing or even dangerous situation. I imagine you've heard that anything "too good to be true probably is." Take that to heart and add: solicitations are just sales-jobs.

I'm sorry, but you aren't the exception. No one is waiting to discover you. There are thousands of candidates for each paid acting job and often hundreds for unpaid gigs. Producers can put out audition notices or breakdowns through any number of services—it's easier than it's ever been, takes just minutes, and is often free. Those with legitimate gigs don't have to troll internet profiles or search the mall for potential talent. They don't have to hold talent searches or ask the general public to show up to galas or seminars at hotel ballrooms around the country. Unless they're looking for something truly unusual, they'll go through the usual channels, time and again. It's a nice fantasy, to believe our talent and hard work will be noticed and we'll catch a magical break somehow, somewhere. But no one you want to work for will take your half-naked picture on a website seriously.

You don't have to follow the rules or work within the "system" at every moment of your career, and I encourage you to be aggressive and original in your pursuits. Just use your head. And for heaven's sake, stay away from anyone or anything that promises you fame. Don't register for a big, cruel, awful, waste of time—no matter how cheap it may seem. JA

Dear Michael,

I recently submitted for a commercial job through one of the many online resources. I wasn't invited to audition, but I did receive an email from the casting director's assistant inviting me to "participate in a very special opportunity." It was the chance to pay $49—cash only, at the door—to meet with said casting director. So I went. The assistant was sort of condescending, and I heard her giving bad business advice to a teenage girl there with her mom. I met with the CD for about four minutes and read copy, and left $49 poorer and with a not-so-great feeling in my gut. A close friend said he and his castmates got similar emails after inviting the same casting director to their show. "So-and-so couldn't make it, but sent an assistant who saw some great work. We'd like to invite you to participate in a very special opportunity . . ." You know the rest. Is it just me or do I have a right to feel this office is preying on actors who submit to them? How fair is this? Aren't they giving the actor a false sense that the CD is specifically interested in them?

—Feeling Swindled

Dear Swindled,

Yes, you have every right to feel preyed-upon. You were. This shockingly transparent money-making racket is particularly shameful because, by contacting individual actors directly, this CD is obviously dangling the casting carrot. But as I've said again and again, we should never pay just to meet someone, especially, as you note, when they solicit us, offering "very special opportunities" to part with our hard-earned cash in exchange for a tease.

I urge you to report this unethical tactic to SAG-AFTRA, Equity, CSA, the New York State Division of Consumer Protection, and the Better Business Bureau. And spread the word among colleagues. Maybe in time, people will catch on, and keep their forty-nine bucks in their pockets.

Here's a good rule of thumb: if they ask for money, they're just not that into you. MK

Dear Michael,

I'm tired of seeing other actors getting ripped off. I copied an ad below from craigslist (I know that CL is not the best place to look for any type of entertainment job); but this does not appear to even be legal. Is it? It's a script-reading job for no pay, with the vague promise of possible future work from two "production companies":

We're looking for script readers! Earn yourself a place on our crew by getting involved now. The Movie Deal! Screenplay Contest needs readers, then CREW in SPRING in LA.

Yes you can be first in line as an associate producer or for a crew position. Of course ALL experience levels will be considered, but please keep in mind, you won't be our 1st AD if you've never AD'd. This is merely an opportunity to help us out by reading scripts while earning a place on our production. We want to be honest with you and fair. So again, we are looking for people to put some time in now, for an opportunity in Spring.

We've done many films in Chicago and are legitimate companies. If you have little experience but want to be there to help out and get involved, we'd love to bring you on! Again, no

pay, but you can get involved with the production in SPRING! Thanks so much, Squid Brothers, Inc. & American Stonehenge Films, THE MOVIE DEAL!

Is there any regulation or limit to what these companies can expect people to do for free? Is there a legal line they can cross? Other than steering clear of them, do we have any protection?
—Perpetual Intern

Dear P.I.,

Outrageous? Yes. Illegal? No. I share your umbrage; these folks have a lot of nerve. But more shocking than this invitation to work for free is the probability that the ad will get plenty of responses from people willing to do just that. The internet—a Petri dish where such things breed and multiply—easily connects the unwitting—particularly those who dream of shortcuts to success—with end-less opportunities to be misled, ripped off, scammed, duped, conned, bilked, and bamboozled.

But this ad, you'll notice, isn't a scam at all. These folks are completely up front about the fact that they're offering no payment and no guarantees of payment, only the opportunity to work as a script reader now, and a crew member on a production in the spring. As I read it, the crew positions are also non-paying. Not much of a deal, that, but the ad seems to spell it out without any deceit or intent to mislead.

Shockingly, even after all my years as a TV attorney (I always seem to get cast as those), I am by no means an expert on the law. But I can tell you this: false advertising is illegal. Breach of contract is illegal. Asking people to work for free—no matter how outrageous the request—is not. There's no law against taking advantage of people's ambitions, as long as you don't lie about it.

You ask what kind of protection we have. One word: savvy. Everyone in show business needs it, big time. And if they don't have it, they'd better develop it, quickly. We're in a business that requires us to be more investigative, more skeptical and better informed than others. We have to ask questions, do research, and learn who's who. We have to be smart about how we spend our time and money as we pursue our careers. There will always be offers inviting us to pay to become an instant working actor, to attend late-night casting calls at producers' apartments, to work for free to gain "valuable crew experience." We have to know better, and that's that. MK

Dear Michael,

I was recently called up by a man who apparently wanted to connect me with tons of auditions, such as for a supporting role in an upcoming Disney film. It was hard to understand him because of his thick accent, and the moment he said I needed to make a small investment of $120, I began to say goodbye. I asked my acting teacher, and she disdainfully answered that anyone who asks for money in exchange for connections is not legitimate. Was it really a scam?

—Disappointed

Dear Disappointed,

I can answer you in one word. Absolutely. MK

Dear Jackie,

I wish that student filmmakers would stop trying to disguise their little projects as something other than what they are . . . student film projects. Some are listed on casting sites as short films, some as pilots, or better yet, trailers. I have nothing against student filmmakers—everyone starts somewhere, and being a student is how we all learn. However, I am personally at the point in my career where I no longer want to audition for student films. Been there, done that. Why can't they call it what it is . . . a student film? That way, I could stop wasting my time submitting for these things and driving out to audition for something that I want no part of. I feel like they are being sneaky and slimy.

—Done That

Dear Done,

I see your point. I also taught filmmaking at a University.

Here's something to consider: students think of themselves as making Films, with a capital F. They see themselves as artists, just like actors do. Student filmmakers don't imagine their films will die on campus, but that they'll get into festivals and even earn distribution. I'm not saying they should omit the student aspect from their breakdowns—of course they should be honest about what they are doing. But consider that they probably aren't mislabeling their posts to sucker actors— they just don't see their work the same way you do. That being said, reputable casting sites make an effort to ensure notices are posted accurately by providing specific project categories, including "Student Film." Bob Brody, Actors Access General Manager, says:

> If someone does misrepresent their project and the breakdown is published, we pull the breakdown and cancel their account. We're on that 24/7. What's important is that if an actor discovers genuine misrepresentation (they discover nudity is required but the breakdown said no nudity, they are subsequently told they have to pay to be in the project but this was not up front on the breakdown, and so forth) that they let us know.

"Any time we're talking to student filmmakers we always encourage them to be up front about the fact that they're making student films," *Backstage*'s National Casting Editor Luke Crowe explains:

> A lot of actors actually prefer student films over other 'no pay' indie projects because they provide a lot of benefits: student filmmakers often have access to great camera, lights, and sound equipment through their school that low-budget indie filmmakers might not be able to afford; they're usually well-trained by film-school faculty that have professional experience; student films are often submitted to film festivals across the world, getting the actors extra exposure; and if something goes wrong, then the actors can report the problem directly to the college (a safety net that non-student projects can't provide). Because of how popular student projects are among a lot of actors, we've actually seen non-students pretending that they're making a film as part of a university program that they're not really attending.

Didn't see that coming, did you? JA

Dear Michael,

A friend of mine, not in the industry, is aware that I have an interest in finding work as a background actor while I take classes and look for other acting work and sent me a link to this Hollywood background jobs website. I looked it up, and it shows a bunch of major film and TV networks and asks for credit card information in order to get set up with the company. Even though it's asking for a small amount, I just don't trust them. I'm holding off because I'm afraid it is a scam. What do you think?

—Skeptical in Sherman Oaks

Dear Skeptical,

I think your instincts are correct. I know the website you're referring to, so I called and spoke to a representative in their sales department who, after insisting several times that the total cost was $1.95, period, finally admitted that after a fourteen-day trial it was $49.95 a month. Further research turned up a number of complaints about them on various message boards. There were posts on sites such as complaintsboard.com and ripoffreport.com, saying there were buried charges and that those who tried to immediately cancel their memberships have been unable to get their money back, even after being promised a refund by the company. So it sounds like people have had some less-than-satisfactory encounters there. So follow your hunch and stay away.

But this brings me to a wider point. This business attracts all manner of scam artists because so many people are looking for easy ways to get into acting. And generally speaking, there are no easy ways to get into acting. It's unlikely you'll be the one who discovers the first legitimate "pay us money and we'll get you work in television" offer, or the first "actors needed" ad that leads to a juicy, lucrative, high-profile film role. These types of cons have been around for ages, preying on people's fantasies of instant success.

Unfortunately, the internet provides these predators with the perfect cloak for their activities, one that allows them to appear professional, remain anonymous, and then disappear without a trace. On the upside, the internet also allows us to research companies to get a better sense of whether they're legitimate, which is always a wise thing to do. It's also wise to take a moment, put the excitement aside, and consider how realistic the offer is. A website cannot guarantee paid acting work, for any price. And if it could, why would the site owners put the offer out to actors whose work they'd never seen? Doesn't smell right, does it? MK

Dear Jackie,

I recently auditioned for what I thought was a low-budget independent SAG-AFTRA film. I drove all the way to the director's house—which was about an hour from Los Angeles—to read for a small role. After I did the sides, the director told me he thought I'd be great for another, bigger part in the film but that the role—a stripper—required nudity. There was another actor reading for the role too, and the director asked us to dance to this techno music and strip. Obviously the actor who plays the part would have to be naked in the film, so the director suggested we needed to show him we were comfortable with that. He acted like it was no big deal. The other actor did it, but I felt really funny about it so I ended up just sort of pretending to strip by taking off my coat.

After the dancing, the director told me he wanted to consider photographing me for a book of nude portraits he was working on. He showed me his pictures, and they were really good and very artistic, so I told him I'd think about it. He seemed pleased and then invited me to stick around and join him and some of the other actors who had auditioned for a beer. The actor who had stripped decided to stay, and there were a few other actors still hanging around, but I left, even though it probably would have been better to stay and network. When I got home, I called SAG-AFTRA and found out that the project's contract had expired a few years ago. A few days later, I got a call from the director offering me a callback, but when I asked about the film's SAG-AFTRA status, he got sort of irritated and told me it was nonunion. I checked the original casting notice and saw it requested submissions from SAG-AFTRA talent only, but didn't say it was a SAG-AFTRA film. Should I go to my callback or just say I can't because I got another job?

—Not Really Comfortable With This

Dear NRCWT,

Wow. The director's house, the nudity, the photo book, the falsely advertised contract, the beer—there are just so many things to address here, I don't know where to start.

Let's begin at the beginning. Never, ever, ever audition for a project at a stranger's house. A director who asks talent to drive an hour outside of the city to read in his home, whether in the living room or "home office" or whatever he wants to call it, is not someone you should waste your time dealing with. It would have cost this guy less than a hundred bucks to rent a theatre or rehearsal studio for a day. You need to ask yourself why he wouldn't take that small, easy step. Auditioning at someone's home is dangerous, foolhardy, and at best a waste of time because anyone who can't manage to rent a rehearsal studio for an audition is not likely to be capable of producing a film. I can think of about two exceptions to this rule: 1) the director is a close friend of yours, or 2) a reclusive A-list director invites you, your agent, your publicist, your manager, and your lawyer over for tea.

Reputable casting sites require producers and casting directors to indicate on the casting notice whether a role requires nudity. Calling an actor in for a non-nudity role and then suggesting they read for a role that requires nudity reeks of bait-and-switch. Yes, I know there are times when casting personnel realize that an actor would be good for a role they weren't originally called in for, but suggesting an actor strip on the spur of the moment is unprofessional and wrong. SAG-AFTRA rules stipulate that actors can never be required to remove their clothing at auditions, although they are permitted to undress to a G-string and pasties. But why would such a reveal be necessary in the beginning of the casting process? Such a delicate issue should at the very least be explained and agreed upon before a callback. It is *always* a "big deal."

What would you do if some guy on the street approached you and asked you to strip? Slap him? Run? Just because the request comes from a "director" doesn't mean you should violate your personal boundaries. If he is working on a photography book of nudes, he should do a specific casting call for models for that project. He should not try to recruit actors angling for roles in a live-action project. I am truly sorry the other actor at your audition took her clothes off and danced for this creep.

Good for you for following up with SAG-AFTRA. It's not a shock that the project is nonunion, and it's even less surprising that the director was irked that you asked. SAG-AFTRA was created partly to keep you from doing projects like this one, in which your craft and possibly your person could be misused. While it's sometimes hard to know where to draw our own professional lines, the Guild's mission is to standardize otherwise messy situations for our benefit. Sometimes, ironically, we need protection from ourselves.

Don't think for one more minute about attending a callback for this director's project. And when you reject the offer, don't make excuses about another job. Just decline. If he presses you for a reason or tries to convince you to come back out to his place, take that as proof of his lack of merit. How many legitimate casting people beg actors to return?

As for "sticking around for a beer"? I can hardly bear how obvious, cheesy, and frightening that suggestion was. Casting calls are not social events. No matter how nice the director or producer seems, no matter how comfy they make you feel, or how much you could use a drink, keep your priorities straight. Your safety should outweigh flimsy excuses for creepy parties every time. Don't think it's about safety? Google "Kristine Johnson murder victim" to read about the aspiring Los Angeles actor who was killed after being lured to a fake audition. JA

Dear Michael,

I was recently asked to sign by an agent of questionable reputation. Among the things he suggested I do was to call a woman who he said would help me with becoming SAG-AFTRA. Although I decided not to sign with him, I called the woman out of curiosity. She told me that her husband owned a production company and that for a fee (about $1,200 if I remember correctly) they would secure me three days of background work on a SAG-AFTRA voucher.[1] How legit is this? It seems like a shady way to go if you ask me, but I'd like a second opinion.

    —Voucher-less in LA

Dear Voucher-less,

Wow. That pretty much takes the cake. I don't know if I've ever heard of anything more clearly, boldly, and shamelessly illegitimate. Mind you, shady methods like this may actually work; people might be able to get their SAG-AFTRA cards this way. But how disgusting of this woman and her husband to take such opportunistic advantage of nonunion actors. And yes, it's beyond illegal. Me, I'd turn them in without a moment's hesitation. Then again, I tend to get a little hot-headed about stuff like this.

Good for you for spotting a sleazy situation and avoiding it.

You know, one of our best defenses against getting swindled is being willing to embrace where we are in our careers. That can be a tough one; it's tempting to want to jump to the next level, whether we're ready for it or not. We talk about "breaking in" which, if you think about it, means entering where we aren't supposed to be.

Any actor who's contemplating something as desperate as *paying* to *illegally* obtain a SAG-AFTRA card should take a step back and think about what he's doing. If that's the only way to get in, maybe it's too soon. Sure, an actor might sneak in or break in, but then what? You've got your card, but how will you get seen for SAG-AFTRA projects? And what if you do get seen? You'll be auditioning against actors who've earned their cards legitimately. Suddenly, beating the system isn't such a bargain. I'm not saying actors shouldn't be ambitious or assertive, but there's a lot to be said for honoring the process. MK

Dear Jackie,

My daughter auditioned for an acting academy in New Jersey last year. She saw the ad on a kids' television channel and I called and got her an appointment. I was surprised to see so many children and parents lining up for the audition, which was held at a hotel ballroom. We were asked to bring head and body shots of the children. The kids were interviewed to see how badly they wanted to be on TV and were given lines to read for a sample commercial in front of the camera.

I called at the designated date and time to find out if my daughter got a callback, and she did. To confirm her participation, she is supposed to take one of the acting workshops (which costs a minimum of $1,950 and goes up to $7,500 for ten weeks of one- or two-hour classes). The fee must be paid up front and I was told that the classes would not start for months. I asked if there was a payment installment plan but they said no.

I love my daughter. She's only eleven but she has been taking musical theatre classes and has a fantastic voice. I want to support her and help her follow her dreams. Could you please tell me if you know anything about this acting school for kids and teens? Is it legitimate? I desperately need advice.

—New Jersey Mom

Dear Mom,

Is this school "legitimate?" Hell no.

How do I know? The money! Acting classes just don't cost that much. As far as I could tell from this academy's website, we're talking about a weekly class—so your daughter would get a whopping ten sessions for her $1,950–$7,500. That's $97.50 per hour for the bargain, cut-rate class at two hours per session. On the other end of the spectrum, we get to $750 per hour. For that kind of money, they better transport you back in time to study with Stanislavski himself. Of course I'm taking your word for the class prices, since the website itself didn't disclose any prices and from my research the company only reveals the price tag after you've "auditioned" and gotten the hard sell.

If you want to support your daughter and her burgeoning talent, research established private singing instructors, licensed children's talent agencies, and respected children's acting classes—all in your nearby New York City. You have the cream of the acting world crop in your neighboring state. Use your money for train fare and take your daughter to classes that have earned their reputations over many years. Investigate anything that sparks your interest—go over the details with a fine-toothed comb—before you commit your resources, and your daughter's time, to anything.

As an aspiring stage mom, I recommend you check out the BizParentz Foundation (bizparentz.org), a resource for parents of child performers. The site, run by honest and hardworking parents like you, has tons of information and tips on how to support your child the right way.

I understand that you love your daughter and want to provide her with any advantage you can, but never let anyone prey on those feelings. Far better for her to watch you say no to suspicious offerings than for her to learn to take these kinds of risks. JA

Dear Michael,

This past summer, through a background casting company, I landed a gig that was a promo for a new television game show. Unlike any other background gig I've had, I was filmed saying several different lines. A few weeks later I discovered that I appear in the promo, saying one of my lines! Even more to my surprise, after the game show premiered last week, I discovered I appear at the very beginning of each episode, and can be heard speaking. I contacted the company that cast me and they're going to follow up with the production company. Since I signed no release, what can I expect, if anything, for the use of my image and voice, beyond the $60 I was paid as nonunion background actor? If additional compensation is due to me, how is that determined, and who determines it?
—Anonymously Famous

Dear Anonymously,

Unfortunately, when you're working as a nonunion performer, there's not much you can do in a situation like this. It sounds like, although the company specialized in casting background players, there was nothing in the job offer that indicated you'd be doing strictly background work. And without a signed contract or agreement, it would be difficult to prove that the terms were changed from the original offer without your knowledge or approval. The time for that discussion would have been when the producer first proposed putting you on camera delivering lines. It might have been a bit messy—they would have had to stop filming while the producer phoned the casting agency and set new terms—but that would have clarified what you were earning for the gig. Unfortunately, it's unlikely you'll be able to negotiate for more money after the fact. Chalk this one up to experience, and don't be too hard on yourself. Though it's small consolation, at least you were the one they picked. MK

Dear Jackie,

I'm a young LA actor looking for a way in. I use an industry website for blogging and chatting with friends. Someone I met there told me about a manager who has an online profile on the site and might be interested in me. Should I contact him? Do you think he would meet with me if I contacted him through this site or would I seem too unprofessional? His page seems to be kind of personal, but there are a lot of actors posting comments there so maybe he uses it that way too. I don't want to miss out on an opportunity.

—Aspiring

Dear Aspiring,

I looked at the manager's profile on this website and I will tell you in no uncertain terms, STAY AWAY. His profile and posts, while they do make mention of his career, are clearly personal in nature. I'd bet the farm that he's using the title of "talent manager" to attract actors and models to his page and enhance his . . . social opportunities.

Bear in mind that talent managers are not regulated in California—they are unlicensed and self-appointed. You must do your due diligence before contacting or responding to anyone you find online, and industry people—or those that *claim* to be such—are no different.

First, find out whether this manager is a member of the Talent Managers Association (talentmanagers.org) or the National Conference of Personal Managers (ncopm.com). Both trade organizations strive to hold their members to baseline professional standards. While every legitimate manager does not belong to one of these organizations, and every manager that does belong is not legitimate, it's a good place to begin. Search for the manager on IMDb and see what kinds of clients he represents. How long has he been in the business? If his name doesn't come up, that's a sign he's either very, very new or not what he claims to be. Google him. Are there articles about his company or complaints on various message boards? Ask around. Speak to your acting teacher and actor friends. Research requires some time, but will save you much more.

Did you notice that all his online companions were very young women? That is more than a red flag—it's a fiery banner. I understand that—at this point in your career—the temptation is high to seize upon any opportunity you believe you have found—even one riddled with warnings. But don't waste your energy or, worse, put yourself in a compromising or dangerous position. Spend less time worrying about whether you'll seem unprofessional and more time verifying the professionalism of those with whom you seek to do business. Don't let your ambition get in the way of your common sense. JA

Dear Michael,

I'm currently doing a show. We were hired to do six performances—without a contract, mind you. But the playwright/director, who has no directing experience whatsoever, canceled two of them, so we weren't paid for either of those days, and then another time, he paid us only partially for another show because he had to pay the venue what he owed them. Now he wants us to tour out of state, and we still haven't seen a contract. So basically, he's booking dates without asking any of us if we are available to do these dates! I refuse to leave the state to do this play with this man only to get screwed over and possibly not get paid all my money for my performances. I'm a very good actor, I'm dedicated to my craft, but I refuse to get taken advantage of. I'm not feeling this at all. What would you do in this situation?

—Fed Up

Dear Fed Up,

I could give you some long, detailed, pithy answer about pros and cons, but I think I can just cut to the chase on this one. Not only should you quit, but you should do so immediately, and not think twice about it. There's no need to weigh options, give anyone the benefit of the doubt, exercise patience, or anything of the sort. Just quit.

Contract or not, it is an undeniable fact, according to your account, that this guy isn't someone who keeps his word. He committed to a certain rate of pay, and then simply changed his mind and didn't pay what he'd promised. That alone confirms beyond a shadow of a doubt that he is not running a legitimate production. If you continue to work with him, you'll never be able to trust anything he says. You're not on solid ground. He could leave you stranded somewhere, refuse to pay your salary, change your schedule without notice, or make the whole cast share a room. Even if you *had* a contract, he might do these things anyway. Sure, a contract would give you the ability to sue him, but that isn't of much comfort when you're stuck somewhere without a plane ticket. Besides, do you really want the ordeal of a lawsuit?

I can't imagine you'd have any regrets if you walked away. Believe me, you don't need this kind of headache. Just inform your producer that you're quitting, and move on. You'll be glad you did. MK

What Do You Think?

1 Why are actors common targets for scam artists? What is it about our industry that attracts such abuse?
2 List five warning signs of talent scams.
3 Name three ways to evaluate the legitimacy of an opportunity.
4 Are nonunion projects more likely to be scams? Why or why not?
5 Are actors obligated to report scams and/or dangerous situations? If so, to whom should these be reported?
6 What are the risks of reporting scams? What would you do and why?
7 How do legitimate agents and casting professionals search for talent?
8 When is it appropriate for a casting professional to ask an actor to disrobe? Is nudity ever appropriate at an audition?
9 Should you ever quit an acting job? Why or why not? If so, what are some circumstances where quitting would be justified?
10 When is it worthwhile for you to take a risk on something that might be a scam?

Note

1 See Chapter 9, "Unions."

11

ON THE JOB

So much energy goes into booking a gig that it's no wonder actors are sometimes less than prepared for the realities of the job itself. After you (understandably) celebrate landing a role, there is still the matter of going to your new place of business and *doing* it.

As actors, we have to navigate an ever-changing work environment. Each project introduces a new boss, new venue, and in many ways, a new job description. (Are you learning legal terms? Taking on white-river rafting? Psychoanalyzing a killer? Mastering the dialect and mannerisms of another culture?) Actors at work encounter circumstances and puzzles one would never face in other professions, and each job presents a whole new set of co-workers, which can be the most challenging thing of all.

There are certain steadfast protocols (like no autograph requests on set, no talking back during note sessions, never be late, etc.) that are easily and quickly learned, either through experience, study, or the great show business tradition of mentorship. But no matter how diligently you prepare, unusual, unforeseeable questions unique to your journey are sure to arise. You will need to develop well-tuned instincts and perspicacity to manage those inevitable bumps in the road. Learning to handle the unexpected and sometimes frustrating realities of your day-to-day work environment with grace, class, and kindness is better for your reputation and, therefore, the health of your career.

Questions and Answers

Dear Michael,

I'm a working TV actor and I do mostly hour-long dramas. My problem is that whenever I'm on a show as a guest star or as a co-star, it seems like it's hard to get on board with the dynamics of the cast and crew. They have been working together for a while, and already have their relationships established. I don't know whether to go around saying hello and introducing myself, or just hang back and do my work . . . or what? I was recently on a long-running TV show as a guest, and it felt sort of like a factory. Not that it was a bad vibe or anything. Just that they seemed to want to get my stuff "in the can" and move on.

—Guest Guy

Dear GG,

Those of us who work mostly at the guest star level rarely get a chance to get completely comfortable, unless we're lucky enough to be on a set where the full-timers are dedicated to making their guests feel welcome and honored (I've been on several like that). The extent to which you blend or don't blend with an established cast and crew is mostly a matter of personal style, but here are some things to think about:

While shyness is understandable, believe it or not, sometimes the full-time cast, crew, and production team are shy too. It's hard to imagine, particularly on a hit show, but not everyone is comfortable making conversation with strangers. You might need to be the one to break the ice. Remember, you're the actor who was selected, not some unwelcome infiltrator of the inner sanctum. So, unless they're real jerks (I've been on those sets too), they're probably going to be receptive to a warm, professional introduction. Years ago, as a guest star on a popular sitcom, I was introduced to the whole cast as a group. "Hi," I said sheepishly, "It's nice to be on your show." Without missing a beat, one of the stars responded, "This week, it's your show too." Classy.

A good place to test the waters is in the make-up and hair trailer. Those folks tend to be the friendlier, more nurturing members of the crew, and you can often get a sense of the show's atmosphere from chatting with them. Or talk with the caterers, the PAs, the background actors. They're sometimes taken for granted, and may appreciate your interest. Then, you walk on the set having already made some friendly acquaintances.

Alternatively, you could just keep to yourself until they're ready to rehearse your scenes. It's OK to lay back, as long as you can come to the set with confidence and dignity. There's no rule that says you have to be outgoing.

What you describe as a factory atmosphere is just people busy doing their usual gig, a bit less excited than you might be. Sometimes, they have inside jokes or established rituals. And while it's much nicer when people extend themselves, you don't want to impose your need for acceptance. Instead, focus on making their jobs easier with your comfortable professionalism. Whether you bond or not, your temporary family will appreciate that more than anything. And if, down the road, you find yourself on a series as a regular, remember what it was like to be the guest actor, and always go out of your way to make yours feel welcome. MK

Dear Jackie,

I am in a play with a director I really can't stand. He's not abusive; he just doesn't really do . . . anything. He doesn't take notes or give almost any direction. He just has the cast run the show again and again and again. He always seems quite pleased with what we're doing, but I can tell there are many scenes that need more real work. I want to quit the play because I am not getting anything out of the process, but I don't want to be unprofessional. What should I do?
—Run-Out

Dear Run-Out,

It can be frustrating working with someone who doesn't appeal to your personal methodology, and certainly running a show day in and day out isn't the most creative, successful, or even quickest way to get a good performance from an actor, but the onus is on you to do the best with what you've got. While running a play incessantly would tick me off, I'd also prefer not to be told to, "Take two steps forward, do a triple take, wait one second, and then fall onto the couch" either. (And yes, I once got that exact direction.) Too much direction can be just as annoying and debilitating as too little. Many directors aren't, as they say, "actor-friendly," and some are just plain bad. Certainly you'll run into a variety along your journey in film, theatre, and television.

Hopefully, this experience will give you a chance to bond with new cast members, perform in a new space, and continue developing your craft. You have a job to do. Don't let someone else's ineptitude keep you from doing it. JA

Dear Michael,

I recently landed a role as a swing[1] at the only Equity theatre in town. I was super excited, because it meant I would become an Equity Membership Candidate.[2] Unfortunately, I overlooked the fine print about the swings also doing stage crew work. Once tech week started, I saw how much of that we'd be doing and got a bit overwhelmed. We move sets, operate special effects, and spend two hours after each show cleaning up (the show gets really messy).

Aren't swings supposed to be watching and taking notes? When the director gives notes to the cast, we don't even get that information. When I asked if we could leave the cleaning up to another crew member so we could have some vocal rehearsal, I was told absolutely not. I've tried to sneak around and watch the show to make sure I'm prepared, but every time I try I get bitched at by the stage manager.

I feel a bit taken advantage of here. Are swings normally stage crew as well? Is it worth the stress just to get EMC points? I keep going back and forth. I really want to perform, and I know I can, but this experience is so demoralizing, I'm about ready to drop out.
  —Conscientious Objector

Dear Conscientious Objector,
  If you were to quit, I'm concerned that you could be walking away from a far more valuable opportunity than you realize. At this early stage of your career, there's so much to be learned from gigs that are less than ideal—perhaps more than from those which run smoothly. At times, the professional actor must have acrobatic social skills, navigating challenging interactions with grace, restraint, and a nuanced sense of diplomacy that can only be learned in circumstances that require those skills.

So . . . do swings normally do tech work? No, not normally, and if they're Equity members, never. Tom Miller, Coordinator of the Equity Membership Candidate Program, says the only Equity members who can do tech work are Stage Managers and Assistant Stage Managers, and only when it's part of their contractual duties. For EMCs, however, the rules are a little different. "An EMC may be asked to do tech work," says Miller, "but they must be fully prepared to perform and sufficiently unencumbered by other duties." That means that, according to the rules, your tech duties can't interfere with your primary job as a performer.

But it's important to understand this: production teams usually don't want to think much about swings and understudies until a show is up and running. Only then do they turn their focus to preparing for the possibility that a cast member may miss a performance. And it is absolutely up to them to decide when and how to do that. So don't assume you'll be in on note sessions, or even get on stage, until you're needed, and you might never get to work with the director, even though all those things would help you do your job.

Here's the big lesson—it's a hard one, but now is as good a time as any to learn it, because it'll serve you throughout your career: it's not your decision. What's more, no one's asking for your input on how to run things. So unless something's illegal, immoral, a violation of your contract, or a threat to your safety, do yourself this enormous favor: butt out. It doesn't matter if your plan is better. Even if those in charge are dead wrong, operating in the dumbest possible way, they're still in charge. Trust me, you'll encounter that throughout your career. Most actors could tell you lots of stories about poor decisions made by producers and directors, and describe their much-more-sensible approaches, and you'd agree with them. It doesn't matter. The folks you're working with get to run their theatre any way they want, even if it's stupid. Learn to keep your ideas to yourself.

This is a situation in which your dedication could really piss people off. Helpful suggestions and self-created opportunities to observe can come across like you're questioning the expertise of your superiors, and that's never going to be popular. So follow the schedule you're given, stop sneaking in to watch the show, and do the best job you can within the given parameters. Otherwise, you'll be miserable, and they'll be annoyed. Embrace the experience. Do your tech work with gusto. And if they're not giving you the chance to learn your tracks, let that be their problem. If an actor misses a show, and they've neglected to properly rehearse the swings, they'll pay the consequences at that time. But I think what's more likely to happen is this: no one will be out. The theatre will get a free crew member; you'll get EMC points and some very valuable education. And really, that's what internships are all about. Is it worth it? You bet. MK

Dear Jackie,

I was recently cast in an Equity Guest Artist[3] contract in a fantastic role in a play that I love that performs in a very cool venue. I know this all sounds like a dream come true, but here's the problem. Last night, the cast met for the first time for the read-through and I met my co-star. She is a well-trained actor, and was fine in the reading, except that she and I have no chemistry whatsoever. The success of the play, I think, hinges on our characters having a really obvious attraction to each other. We are supposed to be soulmates and the play really depends on the audience seeing us generate some "heat." I'm afraid that even if I try really hard, I won't be able to act enough to fill the dead space between us. She just seems so cold. What should I do?

—Partner Pains

Dear Partner Pains,

You should hold off on the judgments. It could be that she was a) having a bad night, b) sick, c) withholding the "heat" until you guys got to know each other a little bit, d) nervous about the reading, or e) nervous about you. It sounds like you didn't meet before the read-through, so you didn't get the benefit of bonding during the audition process, but this doesn't mean you have to jump to full performance level at your first meeting. It's a process, remember?

Trust that the director realizes how important the match between you and your co-star is and cast appropriately. For your part, feel free to try and get to know her a bit offstage, but don't push it. Stay open and be ready to meet her attempts at camaraderie with warmth. Look for things about her that you find interesting or appealing. Not to say you should cultivate a romantic interest in her, just that the more positively you view her, the easier it will be to cozy up onstage.

More important than your real-world relationship, use the script to build a strong history between your characters. Decide on facts that inspire passion. Private facts and personal character history are just for you; no one else needs to know anything about them. Their sole purpose is to get you where you want to be as you begin a scene. The more specific you can be in the fictional back-story you build, the more realistic your onstage relationship will become.

I guess I'm just saying you'll need to act. JA

Dear Michael,

I've been a professional actor for several decades, but this was a new one on me. Recently I was working as a guest star on a TV show. On my third day of shooting, the first assistant director came up to me privately and said, "Listen, they're telling me we have a budget problem, and they'd like you to stand in[4] for yourself tomorrow. Are you cool with that?"

I'd never been asked to do that before, and I've been acting for a while. I wanted to be a team player, and I guess I was too surprised to fully process, so I said yes. But afterwards I felt a bit taken advantage of. I mean, honestly, they couldn't afford the small cost of a stand-in? I also felt like I'd taken a job away from someone who could have used it. And I have to say, it felt strange to be standing in for myself, when all the series regulars had stand-ins, and then to go immediately from that to shooting the scene.

I didn't want to call the union and make it a big thing, but for future reference, I wanted to know what to do in a situation like this. Is this kind of thing kosher?
    —My Achin' Feet

Dear Achin',

Absolutely not. The television contract stipulates that no SAG-AFTRA member can be hired in more than one capacity simultaneously. In fact, technically, having violated that rule, the production company now owes you additional salary as a stand-in. And what's more, if the folks at the union happen to discover the violation—and, somehow or another, it seems they always do—it can turn into a big thing.

If this happens again, there's a very easy solution. As a union member, you don't have the option of deciding whether or not to follow union rules. It's like deciding whether or not to drive through a red light. It's simply not allowed, period. There's this myth that says if the actors get together and take a vote, they can waive rights that are contractually guaranteed, or if someone asks you very nicely, it's okay to agree to do something that's prohibited by the union. Not so. Agreeing to a violation is a huge no-no. And it also sets a bad precedent: it guts the union's ability to protect its members by suggesting that the rules don't have to be followed.

You may feel awkward about declining a request, but that discussion will go more smoothly if you let the requester know you don't have a choice in the matter. "I wish I could" is a magical phrase. It lets the other person know that you honor his or her need; you regret your inability to help, but that it's absolutely impossible for you to comply. This way, there's no emotion, no negotiating, no sense that you aren't a team player. Simply say, "I wish I could, but as a union member, I'm not allowed to [insert inappropriate request here]." If they suggest doing it without telling the union, you can still keep it simple, "You mean break the rules? Oh, I'm sorry. I don't do that." Be friendly and gracious but firm, and let the other person know there's nothing to discuss. MK

Dear Jackie,

I am currently in a play and we opened a week ago. I think the show is going well, but I do have one problem. I very specifically asked that people not show me the reviews. I really hate to see them while I am in a show, even if the reviewer says I am good. I find that it really throws me. After my request, the stage manager announced that no one should bring copies backstage, but people are doing it anyway. And I often overhear people talking about specific comments the reviewers made. I want to remind them to not do it around me, but I don't know them very well and I don't want to seem like a pain. I even had someone say, "Congratulations on your review!" to me. Ugh! Any suggestions?

—Shhh!

Dear Shhh!,

Your request to avoid seeing press until after the show closes is perfectly valid. Of course, other actors' desire to debate and discuss every comma and period in a given review is also natural. Start by speaking to the stage manager about copies of reviews that are making their way backstage despite clear requests to the contrary. A reminder announcement is probably in order.

But while the stage manager can prohibit hard copies, they can't police backstage conversations or what people look at on their iPhones—so you're going to have to deal with that situation on your own. Stay away from group announcements or condemnations. Instead, speak to the two or three worst offenders, saying something along the lines of, "I just wanted to remind you not to tell me about reviews until we close. I know most actors are fine with it, but it really throws off my performance." If you are genuine, as opposed to accusatory, your request should go a long way.

And if you do overhear a snippet about yourself, or someone rushes up quoting a reviewer's commentary before you have a chance to shove cotton in your ears, try and let it slide. Reviewers are just people, and while many are knowledgeable and perceptive, all they can offer are their opinions about a show on one particular night. Whether a rave or a slam, you can't take it too seriously.

A friend of mine once explained to me why she doesn't look at reviews until after a show closes: "It's not worth it for me to try and make sense of the reviews while I'm in a show. Reviewers always use the same, vague words; like 'aplomb.' What does 'She performed with aplomb' even mean?" JA

Dear Jackie,

I've gotten my first bad review. It stung a little, but the pain has subsided because I know that I'm a good actor and my director, fellow actors, the playwright, and the audience were happy. Audience members even singled me out after the show to compliment me.

One of the comments from the critic was about the choices I made. Well, a lot of those were not my ideas. Critics are often unaware that what they see onstage (or on film for that matter) is not 100% the actor's choice. The director massively influences an actor's take on the character. Why didn't he put the blame where it belonged?

—Not My Fault

Dear Not,

It can be hard to distinguish between actor and director choices in the final product. I have seen brilliant actors seem terrible and bad actors come off pretty damn good—all based on the quality of direction. Of course a director can't take all the blame or credit. There are actors who are virtually "director-proof,"[5] as they say, and the script itself greatly affects an actor's work, but I want to affirm your assertion that critics don't always diagnose the real situation. And honestly, that's not their job. Sure, you're right, they're being unfair in chalking up problems to the wrong party. But they aren't there to accurately assign blame for every blemish, only to offer their subjective reaction to that night's performance.

Am I absolving critics of responsibility? Of course not. But since the root of their work is their personal opinion, it's hard to take any of what they say too seriously—raves or slams. Try not to give negative reviews more power than positive. You are probably only as "terrible" and "stilted" this week as you were "luminous" and "remarkable" the last. As basketball great Charles Barkley put it, "I know I'm never as good or bad as one single performance. I've never believed my critics or my worshippers, and I've always been able to leave the game at the arena." JA

Dear Michael,

I'm in a show with a rather significant number of cast members. I've been having a lot of fun, but there's a lot of chit-chatting during rehearsals, people goofing off in the wings while other actors are doing scenes on stage, and one cast member will even point out what we're doing wrong while we're in the middle of rehearsing a musical number (which pulls me completely out of character!). I understand they're just having fun, but it's kind of affecting my work. Do you have any tips on how to still do my job in an ensemble that likes to mess around? Or am I being too much of a hard-ass and need to take a chill-pill?

—Driven to Distraction

Dear Driven,

I can't stand it when fellow cast members don't show basic professional decorum, respect for the work, and respect for time-honored protocols. But the question of how to react is much trickier than you might think. Pointing out unprofessional behavior doesn't usually yield best results. No one likes being shamed. Also, few things will exclude you from intra-cast socializing faster than being labeled a kill-joy. And let's be honest; it's nice to be liked.

Ignore the offenses whenever you can. Work hard to cultivate a light, agreeable attitude toward these jokers. Getting riled up is only going to hurt your performance. Try to be gracious, accepting, friendly, and complimentary . . . if possible.

However . . . if cast behavior is really making it hard to do your work, I suggest using very sneaky, passive/aggressive means to point it out. Getting notes in the middle of rehearsing a musical number? Stop cold and give the person your full attention. Ask for clarification so you can get it just right. If the director asks why you're stopping, "Oh, I'm sorry. Ralph was just helping me with the step." Director: "Ralph, please don't give notes during rehearsal." Later, tell Ralph, "So sorry! I was just trying to hear what you were saying." Manipulative? Sure. But it gets the job done. And none of it falls on you. People talking or goofing off? Cup your ear and strain to hear your fellow actors' lines. Or say with your friendliest voice and nicest smile, "I'm sorry, can you repeat that? I didn't hear you." The stage manager or director will usually see what's happening and shush the talkers. You just smile like an angel.

Finally, if you do need to address something one-on-one, approach your colleague as a respected collaborator with whom you share similar goals. Presuming disrespect or nefarious motives makes for a tense conversation. Instead of complaining, try asking advice, or solving the puzzle together. It's not as satisfying as telling someone off, but it works a damn sight better. MK

Dear Jackie,

I'm acting in a nonunion short film and I am having a problem with the director. He is really dismissive of me, and makes weird, sexist comments, right in front of my face. For example, I only have two scenes, but at the read-through he made a joke about me being too "hot" to be expected to act well and yesterday he told someone, jokingly, that I only got this job because of my "rack" (that's not the word he used). I have no idea what to do. Should I just go along with this guy? Or should I tell him where to shove it? I only have one more day on the project.

—"Hot"

Dear "Hot,"

This director's comments are sexist, disgusting, and ridiculous. I'd like to advise you to punch him in the face. Unfortunately, his behavior, while entirely wrong, happens (and not infrequently) on film sets and backstage—and probably more often there than in many other workplaces. And, unfortunately, it may not rise to the standards needed to pursue a sexual harassment case, depending on the exact circumstance. Your nonunion employer may not even be equipped to handle such claims, meaning you'd need outside counsel to pursue any legal recourse. If this was a union job, your next step would be clear (go straight to the SAG-AFTRA helpline or your AEA deputy). But in the nonunion world, you, like many before, need to decide for yourself how to handle the situation.

You have every right to tell him directly, firmly, and in front of a witness, to knock it off. My guess (from personal experience) is that if you do, he will say he was just joking and you should lighten up. And he *might* stop. If he does it again (after your straightforward request), your next step would be to go over his head and file an official complaint with production. This is more likely to get him to stop, but may also put you in an uncomfortable position, depending on who's in charge and how professional this production is.

Or you could go another way: deflect his idiocy and wrap up this job without comment. Avoid him when you can, finish your last day on set with your head held high, and leave it behind. To be honest, that's what I'd do.

Is that politically correct? No. Does it command the respect you and I both deserve? Nope. But is deflection the least stressful choice *in my experience*? Yes. I think I have been mildly or majorly hassled or sexually "joked with" on every job I've ever had—acting and otherwise. Did I lose promotions because of it? No. Was I asked to perform sex acts? Not directly . . . they were "jokes!" Was my appearance a topic of general discussion? Of course. Was I touched and propositioned in the name of "fun?" What do you think? In my experience, speaking up has led to disappointing results and, yes, even retaliation. Deflection and reverse-joke-engineering ("Oooh! Sexual harassment! How 90s!") has kept me sane.

Is it right that we have to deal with this? No. Is it fair? No. Is this industry sexist? Yes. I'm sorry I don't have a better answer for you. JA

Dear Jackie,

Until recently, I was under contract with a nonunion professional theatre company. One of the roles I performed had a few graphic simulated sexual scenes with a male actor. Unfortunately, I found myself being sexually harassed by this actor during rehearsals and even during the run. I expressed my concern to the director who moved this actor into another role so that we were no longer on stage together. However, we still shared a small, co-ed dressing room backstage with a few other actors.

Before a performance about a week after the role was re-cast, this actor verbally accosted me and physically intimidated me in the dressing room. It was approximately three minutes to places. He even went so far as to follow me on-stage to places while the curtains were still closed. He had to be physically restrained by another actor and my assistant stage manager. We had a heated argument and I became distressed to the point that I couldn't perform. I walked out that night and gave notice of my resignation.

Later that same evening I received a voicemail from my director reminding me that I was under contract and saying that I could not quit the show. He said he could "guarantee" I would be sued by his board for lost ticket sales and "ruined" in town. He clearly stated in his voicemail that he didn't care what the other actor did or said to me that evening, but assured me that he would "police" the situation backstage to make sure nothing else happened.

I expressed my emotional distress at being forced to return. I went up the chain of command and appealed to the managing director and board president to release me from my contract without the threat of a lawsuit and damage to my reputation, all to no avail. I returned to the theatre and performed two more evenings, but all I could focus on was the fact that I was in the vicinity of that other actor.

During the final evening I performed, this actor spontaneously changed his blocking and planted himself next to me and held my hand during curtain call. This upset me greatly: he wasn't supposed to speak to me, much less touch me. I presented the director with the ultimatum that either he got rid of the other actor or I would leave the show. The director replied that he intended to fix the curtain call situation and refused to get rid of the other actor. I quit the production.

I am concerned that the theatre will not only sue me for breach of contract and lost ticket sales but that they will ruin me in town as the director threatened.
   —Violated and Vexed

Dear Violated,
   Congratulations on quitting that ridiculous, and possibly dangerous, fiasco before you got seriously hurt. And don't worry: "You'll never work in this town again!" is a clichéd, empty threat.

I spoke to a lawyer on the generalities of your case. "If someone is being sued," she says,

> They shouldn't worry about whether the other party *can* sue, they should hire a lawyer. If you have been threatened with a lawsuit, it may just be that, a threat, but it makes sense to spend a little money and consult an attorney, or use whatever resources are available, such as California Lawyers for the Arts at calawyersforthearts.org. East Coasters might contact Volunteer Lawyers for the Arts at vlany.org. If the actor did sign a contract then she is bound by the terms of that contract. Whatever the contract says about how and why and when she can leave the show governs. If she breached a term of the contract, then she is liable.

>   That being said, no valid contract can allow for someone to commit a crime or engage in improper, unethical conduct that is not tolerated by society, e.g., sexual harassment. If the contract purports to allow it, then either the offending provision or the entire contract is unenforceable. Chances are her contract does not contain a paragraph that says, 'I agree to perform even if I am being sexually harassed and abused.' And, even if it did, it would not be enforceable.

In all likelihood, the producers will realize such a lawsuit won't fly. If you do hear from them, a strongly worded letter from your own attorney regarding the willful allowance of sexual harassment on their watch should stop them in their tracks.

Actors badly want to act, so badly that sometimes we let ourselves be bullied and mistreated in the process. I'm glad you followed your instincts. Your desire to perform or "show must go on" mentality should not override your safety or common sense. JA

Dear Michael,

I recently went through a rough experience involving my first professional tour. During rehearsals, while we were working with puppets that were created for the show, the muscles in my left arm became inflamed. The use of my arm became limited, and I was laid off until after the Christmas break. I was sort of puzzled, because I hadn't even gone to a doctor to get a diagnosis and see how long it would take me to recover.

About a month later, they flew me to the tour's next venue to watch and get worked in. Upon arriving, I encountered lots of drama. Cast members had been starting gossip. The manager had been favoring certain people, buying them gifts and having them report any rumors. I learned there'd been a quarrel and that the director would not be returning after Christmas break. One cast member said, "If this is how show business is run, I don't want to be part of it."

My one official "rehearsal" lasted for ten minutes after a matinee and focused on the puppets. The producer happened to be there, and complained that I wasn't handling them well enough. Then I was thrown into the show. I missed one cue. The next day, the choreographer came to my room and scolded me for not knowing the choreography (which was never taught to me), telling me I should ask more questions and that shy people don't get anywhere in this business. One night, the tour manager had a party in a suite at the hotel. Older crew members and some of the cast (her favorites) became so intoxicated and out of control that police were called, and everyone was asked to leave the hotel. I didn't know about this until I was called to a meeting, where the manager chastised everyone.

A week after the leg ended, the tour manager called to say I was no longer needed for the production. She gave no reason. I called the choreographer, who claimed the show was making budget cuts and that I wasn't the only one being let go, none of which was true. I've gotten no explanation, and was thoroughly confused by the behavior of the tour manager.

Is this how normal shows are run? Do I have to get used to this sort of behavior? Was it my own fault I got fired? The only rationalization I've had for being fired was that while laid off, I got a haircut which may not have been to the producer's liking, but I wasn't under contract when I did. Or it might have been for missing that cue the first time I went on? I keep going over it in my head, and it's driving me nuts.
    —Really Confused

Dear Really Confused,

No, this is not how professional shows are run, and no, it wasn't your fault you got fired. Most of the confusing, outrageous stuff you experienced has to do with the production's nonunion status. Equity has strict protocols dictating the handling of company member injuries, the circumstances under which someone can be fired (missing a cue or getting a haircut isn't adequate grounds), and so forth. These rules can protect us from at least some of the insanity and abuse.

But even in an Equity show, people who join an existing cast have no guarantee they'll get rehearsals before being thrown into a performance in front of hundreds, or thousands. It's one of those things that keep showbiz exciting, and it makes for a good story later on. But, just going by your description, what happened to you was unprofessional, unfair, and a bit cuckoo.

As for the gossip, rumors, and the way show people sometimes treat each other—well, I'm afraid there is no union protection against that. We're a crazy, emotional bunch, and drama isn't unusual. Producers and directors sometimes scream and rant and say terrible things to their actors. Choreographers can be monsters and make their dancers cry. Fellow performers can be downright sinister. And the road can bring out our worst if we're not careful. As the months and the cities rack up, we can get restless, or sick of each other. And that's when the rumors and feuds and politics and cliques can start. And if the show is bad, or the housing is uncomfortable, it's even worse. Some people learn to skate over all the muck and mire and keep a sense of humor, but it's easier to get drawn in.

Now, please know that it's not always like that—not by any means. With younger or less experienced show folk, it's not uncommon for things to get vicious, but rest assured that much happier experiences lie ahead. (For an encouraging comparison, you might enjoy the tales from the road featured in my book, *Letters from Backstage*.) You'll find each job has its own vibe, and future ones will seem like a skip through the tulips compared to this one, especially once you get your Equity card. Just don't expect all the craziness to disappear. Instead, embrace it as part of the profession we've chosen, and a characteristic of the colorful people with whom we work. Hey, it beats the hell out of an office job, right? MK

Dear Jackie,

I'm currently in a non-Equity show. We rehearsed long nights, seven times a week for over a month. However, the piece is good and being in a showcase of a published play is a great experience. My question is in regards to the director.

We have been exposed to a lot of hard criticism but I am slowly realizing that his criticism could be deemed abusive. We are at the halfway point in performances and still—after receiving much positive feedback from the audience and ovations every night—he is constantly, after each show, finding fault at every turn. So, instead of feeling proud of our work, by the time we leave the theatre our enthusiasm has been watered down to, "Uggh . . . I'm sorry I messed up!"

How do you know when a director's criticism has gotten out of control?
   —Dread my Director

Dear Dread,
   Time-honored custom, professional courtesy, and even many contracts dictate that a director's notes stop after the final rehearsal or preview, and the show is "given" to the actors and stage manager on opening night. And for good reason.

I don't suggest the director is intentionally trying to hurt you or your castmates. It's likely he is simply unpracticed in the subtleties of leading a play. Criticism must always be in service, not only to the production, but to the collaboration that is necessary to any performance's success. The director is not a puppeteer—only in working with the cast and accepting all their strengths and weaknesses can they create a truly unique and layered production. There's no "director's cut"[6] in the theatre.

Directors use all sorts of methods to get a good performance from an actor, and certainly some tactics are harsher than others. It's possible your director is trying to influence the production for the best—maybe by bonding you and your castmates against an outside enemy—but more likely he's just unskilled and unwilling to let go. While the rehearsal process and some early adjustments (during previews) fall within his scope, at some point he must release the play to the cast. In the best cases, this happens on opening night. In the worst, the director hangs around nit-picking deliveries and blocking until the sad, beaten horse of a play limps back into its stall—defeated.

At this point, you and your castmates should approach the stage manager for assistance. Express your frustration and ask her to run interference and keep the director at bay. If this is not a realistic option, your cast would be best to get together and agree on a plan of action. Present a calm and united front. You can have a meeting with the director, or give him your comments in writing—choose the tactic you think will best serve the process—and result in the least yelling. The message you want to convey is not, "Leave us alone! We hate you!" but simply,

> The message you want to convey is not, "Leave us alone! We hate you!" but simply, "Thank you for all your help, but we have opened the show

and now need a chance to play it. We have all agreed that, in keeping with theatrical custom, we won't be accepting any more notes at this time. If you are compelled to continue to give notes, please do so through the stage manager or, barring that, in writing." No one says you have to read them.

If you can't get the cast to agree on a solution, or the initial attempt to hold the director back results in more abuse, you'll have to decide whether the "great experience" onstage is worth the trouble off. JA

Dear Michael,

I'm an actor from the United Kingdom. I recently finished a leading role in a Shakespeare play, for which I got rave reviews. There was one problem: my cast-mates. I'm a normal actor in most ways, focused, driven, and as neurotic as the best of us, but I care about my work and want to do my best. Some cast members were untrained and would mock my pre-show warm-ups and even the fact that I hate being in a tour bus pissed as a newt[7] like them, and opted to ride with other (sober) actors so I was not surrounded by drunks. I mentioned I felt it was wrong to drink excessively before a matinee as it's a paying audience. I was criticised by the director (also in the cast) as being elitist and arrogant and not being willing to fit in and he said he wouldn't cast me in the next show, mainly because I hate drunkenness and would rather withdraw when it gets too much.

My coach says, "He's right. They are not the company for you. You need to work with higher-level people who care about the work." But the rejection hurts like hell, despite me bringing in great reviews and being thoroughly consistent.
  —Pissed Off

Dear Pissed,

Years ago, I was on tour with some people who didn't want to do their jobs on stage. We were in a beautiful show—a huge hit that, on a nightly basis, deeply affected audience members, some of whom came back to see the show again and again. But many of my castmates didn't care to invest in the story. They fooled around on stage and tried to make each other laugh. They talked sports scores and gossiped when their mics were off. It was immensely disheartening. I was so thrilled to have such a great job, and felt a responsibility to this much-loved piece of theatre, so I tried to give it my all. Many of the actors seemed to resent me for that. And because I found the on-stage chatter distracting, I asked the stage manager if he could give a note. He did. That didn't do much to improve those relationships. Some decided I was a diva who wanted silence around me and wanted to be the star. It was lonely, being in a cast that didn't like me. And I'm sorry to say, I eventually gave in and started playing around on stage, just to fit in. I hated how that felt, but people were friendlier to me once I joined in the jiggery-pokery. If I had it to do again, I'd do things differently. Instead, I'd follow the advice I'm about to give you:

As you mature in your career, you may find ways to do your work in the lovely, professional way you've learned *without* commenting on the unprofessional behavior around you. Remember, it's not our job to teach, correct, or scold, and we don't get points for being right. You'll get along better with less disciplined colleagues if you just do your thing without making it a statement. Be friendly, and never show your disapproval, but faithfully maintain your professional ethics. You never have to convince them that your way is right. In fact, I don't believe you can. If they mock your warm-ups, you can say something like, "Oh, I know. They're silly. It just makes me feel more prepared," or "I don't know how you guys do it. I can't jump into the show cold the way you do. You're so lucky." Or you can give it right back to them in a funny, kidding way with something like, "Ugh! Amateurs!" (Just don't say it seriously.)

Still, if they dislike you because you don't want to be on a bus full of drunkards, to hell with them. Your coach is right: they aren't worthy of you. And if such unprofessional animals reject you, rather than feeling hurt, I suggest you count yourself very lucky. By not hiring you back, they're only sparing you further aggravation. Stop throwing pearls before swine. Shake the dust from your feet and move on to greener (and more professional) pastures. MK

Dear Jackie,

For a five-year period I ran around LA doing everything I could to further my acting career, from getting a huge, national commercial (that Taft-Hartleyed me into SAG-AFTRA) to buying my own equipment and producing my own films. I went through three agents and a manager during that span and met numerous acting people in class, on acting message boards, and on set.

Then I finally got my feature film break. I was on set, mic'd up in my period costume and ready to take direction for my scene from a major Hollywood director. After one take the 1st AD asked that I step down. He stated that they had a different scene in mind for me later that day. One hour later the director called wrap and the day was done. The 1st AD came up to me afterwards, took down my information personally and said he had something else in mind for me later in the month for another scene.

For a full month I was awake at night punishing myself on whether I did the scene wrong and wishing I had one more chance to do it over again. I was also excited because I truly believed the 1st AD when he said he would contact me. The weeks went by but the call never came. I tried to contact him at the studio, but had to leave a message.

Soon after that, I split away from the acting world. I worked so hard to get those few lines in a feature film and when it disappeared I felt defeated. To make matters worse, when I saw the film two years later there was another guy in my place, saying my exact lines. On and off for the past two years I have had the itch to come back—but I remember how hard I worked just to get where I was and it's tough to go through the journey of acting classes, auditions, and networking all over again. It's like going back to college as a freshman years after you graduate.

I have done well for myself in other ways the past few years, including going to Europe, Asia, and Africa on photography trips and saving up a boatload of money. I also have my two kids who I look after all the time since I work from home. But something keeps pulling me back to the acting world and it scares me to even think about jumping in again.

By the way, I took a big risk on my ego relaying this story. If you have some helpful words or suggestions please let me know. I really need that right now.
  —Dismissed

Dear Dismissed,
  Don't beat yourself up about this one more second. Here's my guess: They saw you on camera and someone said something along the lines of "Hey he looks kind of like (some other actor in the film or someone famous)" and they decided to pull you from that role to avoid confusing the audience. Or someone said "Hey, he seems too young/old/white/black/tall/short to be a (whatever)." Or they said, "Hey, the executive producer's cousin is on set today and we told him we'd give him a line—can he have that one?" And just like that they removed you from the scene with no real plan on where to put you. I'm sure the 1st AD did have some vague notion of giving you another role, but film sets are notoriously hectic and you got lost in the proverbial shuffle.

There's absolutely no way that you doing the line *one time* could have made them decide to cut you for acting reasons. No competent director would do that. Sure, if you tried the line twelve times and were *then* cut, it might be another story. But once? Directors direct actors. Even bad directors at least think they direct actors. I would wager they had some goofy but "real" reason, like the ones I described, that had to do with story or the broader casting of the film. I once lost a job because the guy who booked the male lead had similar hair to mine—a dark bob. What can you do?

As far as I can see you're in a perfect place to start again. You've saved money, spent time with your family, traveled, and grown as a person. What's stopping you? Oh, right. Fear.

In many ways your letter reminds me of someone getting over a bad breakup. You fell in love with acting, gave it your all, and were dumped. You've been getting over it. The trouble is that you've been heartbroken over nothing. Acting didn't dump you—some random situation did. You might benefit from talking over your fear with a therapist—someone who can help identify why the very idea of returning to a job you love is giving you so much trouble. You'll naturally be faced with these types of scenarios again, so you may as well prepare for the inanity, rejection, and chaos. You might want to ease back in with a class or a play before going full steam ahead, the way you so admirably did before.

And if you decide that the arbitrary, chaotic, and sometimes cruel nature of our profession means it's not for you? There's absolutely nothing wrong with that. You don't have to be a professional actor to carry on a love affair with acting itself. JA

What Do You Think?

1 What are some of the most common on-the-job challenges of working as a freelance artist? How can acting jobs be uniquely challenging?
2 What are some tactics you might employ in working with a difficult director or colleague? A difficult cast member?
3 What kind of immature or rude behavior crosses your line? What might you be able to laugh off or ignore?
4 What tactics can you employ to do your best work when castmates behave unprofessionally?
5 Can an actor be sued for breach of contract for quitting a truly terrible job?
6 What are some possible benefits of sticking with a less-than-perfect job?
7 Do you read reviews during the run of a show you're in? After it closes? Never? Why?
8 Would you like to work as a touring actor? If so, how might you prepare for the inherent challenges of life on the road?
9 What are two ways to say no to inappropriate requests on stage or set?
10 Who is responsible for your on-the-job safety? Who can you go to for help if you feel you may be in danger?

Notes

1 A "swing" is an off-stage understudy who "covers" several ensemble "tracks" in a show. (A "track" is a series of appearances by an ensemble performer within a single performance.) Swings are prepared to step into any of the tracks they cover when the usual performer is out.
2 See Chapter 9, "Unions."
3 Equity Guest Artist—Equity Guest Artist contracts are usually used in small or mid-sized theatres with majority nonunion casts. Descriptions of the various contracts can be found on the AEA website.

4 "Standing in"—Once a TV or film scene has been blocked and rehearsed, stand-ins replace the actors while the crew does the technical set-up, which includes lighting and rehearsing camera moves. This frees the actors to change wardrobe, visit the hair and make-up departments, and review lines.

5 "Director-proof"—immune to bad direction.

6 Director's cut—Many people influence the editing of a film. The director's cut is the version signed off on by the director, over which she has full artistic control. Often, however, it's not the final edit that's publicly released.

7 "Pissed as a newt"—a UK expression meaning extremely drunk.

12

FINANCIAL MATTERS

All freelance workers can expect to face some degree of financial uncertainty, simply because freelancing, by its very nature, offers no long-term guarantees of employment. For actors, this uncertainty and unpredictability can be especially acute.

Actors are particularly vulnerable workers for numerous reasons. First, there's the well-known supply-to-demand imbalance in the acting profession—way too many actors for way too few jobs. Clients seeking an office manager may sort through five or six candidates; clients seeking an actor may sort through twenty, thirty, or even hundreds. There's also a discrepancy in the reasonable expectation of repeat clientele. Most freelancers who are good at their jobs can safely predict repeat business—once homeowners find a good contractor, they'll hire that person again and again. Not so for actors; a successful performance is not a reliable predictor of future work. Actors have ever-changing job descriptions and shifting clientele, so good work on a children's theatre production doesn't automatically translate into preferred consideration for an HBO original series; a rave review in the role of a drug addict doesn't mean people will think of you for the role of an accountant. Finally, because an actor's product—him or herself—is always changing, we can age out of or move past opportunities that were previously within our reach.

For all these reasons, actors need to be highly circumspect regarding their finances. They must be conservative spenders, even when incomes are high. Far too many an actor has landed a lucrative job and mistaken that one gig as a reliable indicator of things to come. Shrewd actors keep overhead low, save whenever possible, eschew frivolous spending, and have plans in place to face inevitable periods of unemployment.

This also means (with the rare exception) that all actors need "day jobs"— employment that pays the bills while providing enough flexibility for them to pursue acting work. In other words, your source of survival income shouldn't be at odds with the demands of your career.

Questions and Answers

Dear Jackie,

Is it just me or do other newbies find it hard to justify taking off work or quitting a survival job to audition for and/or shoot non-paying films? I know they will add to your résumé and you could make contacts, but here in LA where cost of living is sky-high, even losing one day of pay can be devastating! How are you supposed to make this work? Someone in a workshop once said, "Trust that the business will take care of you." I am sorry, but that scares me. What if it doesn't? Maybe I am not cut out for this.

—Scared

Dear Scared,

What you need is a flexible survival job in which auditions and shoots aren't prohibitive to making a living. Waiting tables and bartending are popular actor gigs primarily because they are group-based jobs. In other words, restaurants don't employ just one waiter, and their group of servers are relatively interchangeable. Schedules can be made to accommodate workers' needs and there's usually a sub when a shift needs covering. A few other service industry jobs also offer decent flexibility: overnight hotel front-desk clerks, substitute teachers, taxi drivers, caterers, baristas, massage therapists, hair stylists, and nannies can all avoid the 9-to-5 grind. Entertainment industry jobs like writing script coverage, production assisting, or even occasional background acting work also have their benefits.

After waiting tables, the most popular actor's day job is temp work. Temping can be a wonderful way to pay the bills without being tied down, and many companies let their registrants come in and take computer tutorials whenever they'd like, thereby increasing their skill and pay levels. Temping does require comfort with the unknown. Jobs come and go, and while your agency might contact you every day one month, you might not receive a single call the next. Additionally, temping and managing to sneak out to auditions is a lot harder in LA than in New York.

When I lived in New York, my temp employers were never bothered by me running out during my lunch hour—which I took at whatever time my audition was. They didn't care about me getting back a little late, changing clothes in the bathroom, or talking to my agent while I typed their memos. I worked at huge accounting and finance firms in midtown skyscrapers, usually as an assistant to some VP or another, but without exception, these folks were okay with my acting/temping mesh, as long as I behaved professionally and did a full day's work.

I was eager to temp again when I got to LA, but after I had gotten over the shocking reduction in pay, I ended up at much smaller, less financially confident companies. Not only were my superiors themselves less "cool" to temps in every way by constantly piling on busy work and dragging out ridiculous, often dirty old projects the entire staff had managed to avoid for years—one company had me crawl onto their roof to clean their skylights—they were not open to the flexible audition lunch. Even had they been, there's just no way to navigate the sprawling LA freeways fast enough to make such a situation work. In NYC, I could get from midtown to uptown, audition, and be back at my desk in an hour. Most days in LA, it takes longer than that to go one way from the Westside to the Valley.

In spite of the challenges, your sanity requires that you come up with a creative way to focus on what you love while paying your rent. Fight against getting bogged down in the drudgery or succumbing to endless Netflix binges, fueled by self-doubt. If you are cut out for hard work, long days, and lean months, mixed with excitement and endless possibility, you are cut out to join the LA actor ranks.

I think you're right to be scared of the claim that, "The business will take care of you"—that sounds like a bad inspirational GIF. Try turning that statement on its head and remembering that you can take care of yourself. JA

Dear Michael,

I'm in New York City, fresh out of acting school. I have yet to land an acting job, I am out of health insurance, and I am broke. It's kind of ridiculous at this point. This is not how I pictured my career going. Besides giving up and getting some crappy day job, what are my options?

—Broadway Baby

Dear Baby,

I'm really sorry that no one explained this to you. Unfortunately, I have the unenviable task of breaking the news: hardly any of us can count on acting as a means of maintaining financial equilibrium, and most beginning actors can't afford to sit around and wait for acting offers to come rolling in—especially not in New York City, where it costs forty bucks just to walk to the corner.

No, that doesn't mean you have to give up. It just means you have to stop feeling entitled and do what generations of actors before you have done: get a job. This is what we in the profession call "paying your dues." It's part of our tradition, and it builds character. Before he made it as an actor, Harrison Ford was a carpenter. Charles Durning drove a truck. Marla Gibbs was a phone operator, who, understanding the fickle nature of our business, hung onto that job long after landing her role on *The Jeffersons*.

This is how it is. Show business is hard. Maybe, with luck, training, talent, contacts, and determination, you'll eventually be able to "quit your day job," as they say. Until then, welcome to your chosen profession. Better start memorizing the nightly specials. MK

Dear Jackie,

I want to make a living as an actor, but am not at that point yet. I have a job, but the hours are too long and I can't focus on auditions with all of the work I am doing. I need to find something else to do—a job that lets me put my acting career first.

My problem is that I don't want to do menial labor. I don't want to be stuck doing something I hate or that makes me feel bad about myself. I want to know that I am not wasting my life while I wait for my acting career to pick up. But it seems like none of the good jobs are flexible enough for someone like me, who has to go to last-minute auditions and take time off for shoots.

—No Menial for Me

Dear No Menial,

You don't have to love making coffee to be content working at Starbucks. Remember: you aren't looking for a dream job—we already know what that is.

Instead of searching for something "good," look for a job you can find the good in. You might substitute teach, tutor, assist the elderly, or work at an animal rescue organization—all noble and rewarding positions. Maybe you'll wait tables, work at a spa, sell clothes, or bartend—helping to provide creature comforts to others. How about babysitting, personal assisting, or gardening—helping overworked people create more balanced lives. If you try, you can find the good in almost any job. If that's not enough, look up Idealist.org, a website that lists numerous non-profit and socially responsible jobs that may be up your alley.

Look beyond obvious "support jobs," for careers you might pursue alongside your acting journey. I have actor friends who are: university professors and adjuncts, casting directors, writers, film-festival organizers, personal trainers, dance instructors, film editors, realtors, photographers, webmasters, wedding planners, production coordinators, producers, therapists, headhunters, hotel staff, box-office managers, and singing waiters. Many employers are willing to provide flexibility to keep great employees. You may have to prove you are worth the extra effort on their part, but with hard work and creativity you should be able to make a lot of jobs work with your schedule.

If you end up in a job you hate, consider volunteerism as a way to fill the meaning gap. An added plus: if you choose carefully, you'll meet other industry types in the process. Opportunities are plentiful: do a simple Google search for "volunteer+arts" plus the name of your city, and you'll be amazed at what's out there. If you're SAG-AFTRA, you might begin with BookPALS. This program's all-volunteer team of professional actors reads aloud to children at places like public elementary schools, museums, and fairs, helping them find pleasure in the world of books. BookPALS estimates that its volunteers read to more than 100,000 children each week—wow. JA

Dear Michael,

I am a senior musical theatre major at SUNY Fredonia in New York. I was wondering if you could give me examples of jobs for actors and singers that use our skills—like being a reader,[1] teaching, etc.—and the best ways of finding these jobs.

—Gettin' Started

Dear Gettin',

I must say, I like your approach. Since most actors need support jobs, why not find one that uses your skills? Let's start with the two you've listed:

Working as a reader for auditions is a brilliant job for an actor. Not only are you using your skills, but it's also highly educational. I always tell actors: if you ever have a chance to observe a casting session, do not miss that opportunity. Those jobs can be hard to snag, but try reaching out to casting offices. They may tell you they already have a full list of readers, but that's the only way I know to get in, so give it a shot.

Teaching is a great gig, and actors seem to excel at it. You could teach privately, sharing your expertise in your field, in which case the best way to build a clientele is to start with your own social media network and offer free or low-cost lessons to people and ask them to spread the word. If you get certified, you can also work as a substitute teacher or on-set tutor for child actors. Every state has its own requirements, so your first step should be to visit the Board of Education website.

Here are some more possibilities to consider:

—Educational theatre programs, murder mystery weekends, special events, or party entertainment. Just do a search and see how such companies do their hiring.
—Singing waiter (the tips are better, because your customers are seeing you do your thing).
—Teaching traffic school or SAT prep (actors are often hired for these jobs).
—Mock trials or medical consultations: law schools occasionally bring in actors so students can practice their courtroom skills, and medical schools sometimes have actors play patients for their students to interview.
—Trade shows and product demonstration: these jobs pay well, particularly New York's annual Toy Fair.
—Hosting karaoke or trivia evenings at bars and restaurants: in many ways, it's the perfect support job for a singer, if you don't mind listening to lots of bad, drunken singing.
—Tour guide: actors are great at this, and many companies prefer hiring performers for their outgoing personalities and good storytelling skills.

Performers often have natural skills that are more marketable than we realize, and there are many jobs where those skills will be highly valued. Happy hunting! MK

Dear Jackie,

I came to LA ten years ago, but didn't have the courage to just live hand-to-mouth waiting for an acting part. I did get inside the movie industry, but in an office. I work for (get this) one of the major movie studios, in the accounting department. My dream is still to become an actor. Problem is, I have no one to depend on but me. If I don't pay the rent and the bills, nobody will. Is there a way to act part-time, or gradually move into it? I'm willing to try anything. I just want to act before I get too old to pursue my dream.
—Accountant Actor

Dear Accountant Actor,

The answer to your question is as varied as the acting population. Don't discount the possibility that you might pursue your dream from within your current setup. Speak to your boss about working a more flexible schedule. Often, employers don't care what time work gets done—as long as it does. And, of course, for the first few months of your acting pursuits, you probably won't be called in for daily auditions, so any inconvenience to the accounting department should be minor.

If that won't work, assess your risk tolerance before making a move. Salary requirements depend on lifestyle choices and circumstances. Your ability to stomach lean
months will depend on your obligations. Do you have family to support? Can you
move to a cheaper apartment or do you have a mortgage? Are you in debt? Draw
up a budget for the minimum amount you need to earn to get by—whatever that
means to you. With that, you should be able to determine whether the move to
more flexible but possibly less-well-paying work is something you want to do.
And if it's not, don't lose hope. Act part-time and enter the field gradually.

No more waiting. Get your headshot and résumé in shape and begin submitting
to student and indie films, local plays, and theatre companies. Most nonunion
plays rehearse and perform outside of standard business hours—why not start
there? Get into an acting class one night a week. Take action, even if it's not on
the scale you imagined when you began your journey. JA

Dear Jackie,
    I earn my SAG-AFTRA health insurance each year by doing stand-in and
photo double work. I have to make a certain amount of money or work a certain
amount of hours in four consecutive quarters each year to stay covered. But lately,
work has been scarce. If I'm not able to work regularly and I don't qualify for my
insurance, what happens?
    —A Concerned Member

Dear Concerned,
    SAG-AFTRA's Pension and Health plan was created under federal law and is
mandated only to provide benefits exactly as outlined in the plan, which requires
members to meet earnings minimums to qualify. You can find the details on
their site. That doesn't mean, however, that even an extended work stoppage
will cause you to lose your health coverage. The Consolidated Omnibus Budget
Reconciliation Act (COBRA) requires employer-provided group health plans to
offer continued coverage for a limited time if a participant loses eligibility due to
circumstances such as a decrease in work. SAG-AFTRA's plan offers this option
through its self-pay program. Performers who have earned eligibility for fewer
than seventeen years qualify for a maximum of eighteen months additional coverage, and those whose eligibility stretches back longer can extend coverage for
three years. Unfortunately, self-pay means what it says—you will have to pay to
retain your coverage. The exact premium for your plan is set in accordance with
federal COBRA law and may change yearly. You may also elect a less compre-
hensive but cheaper plan within the system. See the SAG-AFTRA P&H website
at sagaftraplans.org for more information.

If you receive the dreaded letter announcing your imminent booting out of
the program and explaining your rights, know that self-pay COBRA coverage

can be pricey. If you are in need, take a look at the SAG-AFTRA Foundation, a philanthropic 501c3 organization devoted to bettering the lives of actors, and SAG-AFTRA members in particular. When it comes to healthcare, the Foundation offers several valuable assistance programs to carry actors through hard times.

I lost coverage after the commercial strike in 2000, and was shocked at the price tag for self-pay. It was somewhere in the vicinity of $500 per month for a single, healthy, young woman. Too bad I didn't call (what was then) the SAG Foundation, but I glossed over the information on where to go for help, assuming such programs were only for the truly destitute or the once famous. Wrong. Most SAG-AFTRA Foundation assistance programs are open to any actor who has been a member of the Guild for at least five years, although even that rule is not hard-and-fast. "We're more focused on compassion than criteria," says Stacey Jackson, Foundation Emergency Assistance Administrator, explaining that any performer in trouble should not hesitate to call for help. "If we're not able to help you, we will try and help you find another organization that can."

The SAG-AFTRA Foundation Self-Pay Premium Program does just what the name implies—it pays your self-pay premium for three months while you figure out another arrangement. There are income caps, but Jackson is clear that the Foundation always considers each case individually and is understanding of special circumstances. The Foundation also grants funds to actors in need via its Catastrophic Health Fund—for members in dire health straits—and its Emergency Assistance Program. The latter can help pay for basic living expenses such as rent and utilities in times of trouble. For more information on all that's offered by the SAG-AFTRA Foundation go to sagaftrafoundation.org.

The Actors' Fund (actorsfund.org) and The Motion Picture and Television Fund (mptf.com) are two other resources for performers in need. See their websites for eligibility requirements.

In brief, don't do what I did and assume assistance programs aren't for you. Get informed, and if you need help, don't be afraid to ask. JA

Dear Michael,

I guess the holidays are tough for a lot of people. But our business seems to shut down almost entirely from Thanksgiving through New Year, and this year, I'm really struggling. I'm way too embarrassed to ask anyone for help, but the truth is, my bills are falling seriously behind. I've been looking for support jobs, but so far, nothing. And New York's not a good city to be poor in. It's getting kind of frightening at this point. I swear I'm not a flake. I've always been responsible. But I have to ask, are there any resources for loans or anything I should know about?

—S.O.S.

Dear S.O.S.,

Take heart. Though struggle has always been part of the artist's life, somehow, we get through it. Lord knows, I spent many of the early years of my career on a financial tightrope, living hand-to-mouth on a diet of Top Ramen and tuna, worrying every month about the rent. For years, I never saw a movie, ate in a restaurant or bought new clothes. Things worked out. Just hang in there.

I want to strongly suggest that you contact the Actors Fund of America (actors fund.org). Since 1882, this great organization has been providing assistance to professional performers. Now, if you're like most people, you'll feel awkward asking them for help. Don't. This is what the Actors Fund is for. Put your pride aside, contact them, and set up an appointment. They'll assess your situation and see what, if anything, can be done. They may be able to temporarily pay your bills, help you find a job, or provide other solutions. Still hesitant? Then do what a friend of mine did. She made a deal with herself. She promised herself that when she got back on her feet, she'd become a donor. She now gives regularly, and has repaid the Actors Fund many times over for its help.

Finally, whether you call it karma or just plain therapeutic, when you're feeling low or needy, finding a way to help someone else is always a great boost. MK

Dear Jackie,

I started taking acting classes when I was about 16 years old but I always get distracted from it one way or another. For a while it was my day job as a manager. Then for eight months it was college, but I realized I hated it so I dropped out. Besides, I don't want anything to fall back on. I want to act 100%.

Basically I get distracted by trying to find other ways of making money. I'm always trying to find the perfect job or situation that will allow me to fully commit to my acting work—and in the meantime I don't do the actual acting.

I have spent a lot of time thinking about what a good day job would be, but it seems like everything I can think of takes so much energy away from what I really want to do. I would probably be much happier living as a starving artist than some people with money are while doing something they don't love.

—100%

Dear 100%,

Perhaps you need to rethink your entire situation. Sit down with last month's bills and a calculator—or an online tool like Budget Tracker or Quicken if you're so inclined—and create a realistic budget for yourself. You say you would be happy being a starving artist, but your ongoing focus on making money indicates you actually do care quite a bit about keeping your finances in order. There's nothing wrong with that—put your practical side to work for you. Figure out exactly how much you need to work to meet your goals. Then, work just enough to make that amount and no more. If you find your needed work hours are more extensive than you'd like, investigate ways to lower your cost of living. Can you take on a roommate? Move to another part of town? Disconnect cable TV? Quit a Starbucks habit? The less you spend, the less you need.

Forget about arranging the perfect life—I assure you, it will never happen. Instead, invest your newly budgeted time wisely. Take a class, read plays, screen-plays, craft and business books, join a theatre company, see plays and screenings, begin submitting for projects and representation and audition regularly. Once your body spends most of its energy acting, your mind will follow and distractions should lessen.

On a final note: it may sound noble to skip college and avoid jobs you could "fall back on," but be careful you aren't talking yourself into making unnecessary and unwise sacrifices. "Act or Die" is a bumper sticker—not an advisable life motto. JA

Dear Michael,

It feels like it's time for me to submit my two-week notice at my "survival" job. The number one reason is that it leaves me out of energy when I am done at 5:30. It's a lot of running around and putting up with an angry, stuck-up boss.

I've been going to auditions and getting some small-time but very important (for me) gigs. However, my ability to submit and prepare is quite limited, because lately my job has been making me feel depressed to the point of constant head-aches and sometimes nausea. It's ironic that I'm using my health benefits for issues that arose because it makes me sick to be in an office from 9 to 5.

I feel I have what it takes, and that I'm wasting precious time. However, I am scared to submit my notice because of the economy. Should I try and stick it out until I get a steady paying performing gig, or is it time to quit?
—Exhausted

Dear Exhausted,

There's a third option you're overlooking: find a job that doesn't make you sick, depressed, and wiped out. Life is too short for the kind of misery you've described, but struggling sucks too, and you'd likely find that the anxiety of being without a reliable income can make you just as tired and depressed.

You might just be one of those people (like me) who can't function long in fluorescent lighting without feeling zapped; working someplace that has incandescents may be just the fix you need. Or maybe it's just that angry, stuck-up boss of yours. Whatever it is, there are always other options. Here's the bottom line: you're not ready to pay your bills with acting until you're paying your bills with acting. So focus on getting a job you can really live with, and you'll be better empowered to pursue that goal. MK

Dear Jackie,

When doing my taxes, may I deduct the cost of haircuts and the hair dye that I must purchase in order to maintain the look I have on my headshots?

—Locked into Locks

Dear Locked,

According to accountant Chuck Sloan of Sloan and Associates, "The cost of maintaining your appearance, even to match your headshots, is not deductible."

Sloan makes the point that office workers can't write off items needed to maintain a professional appearance, even when such clothing or haircuts would benefit their careers. That goes for clothes, personal trainers, yoga classes, eyebrow waxing, Botox, and so on.

"Here is the IRS' argument," writes Sloan in an email:

> If a producer wants you to look a certain way, the producer will usually pay the cost of having you look that way. On the other hand, if a certain look is incumbent on getting the job, and keeping the job, then arguably maintaining that look would be deductible, but only when the employer (not an agent, casting director, etc.) demands it.

As for the argument that you need to pay for haircuts and dye so you can look like your picture? Sloan points out that "a smart-ass IRS agent will tell you, 'Then go get a headshot that looks like you.'" JA

Dear Michael,

After all my years in the business it would be nice if I could achieve some financial stability, but that's show biz, right? I know I need a second income source, but I don't know how to figure out what I'm qualified to do. I have no objection to getting a job, but I need help figuring out what it's going to be. At the moment, I'm baffled.

—Somebody Pay Me

Dear Pay Me,

You may have heard about the Actors Fund as a resource for actors in financial crisis, but you may not know about their Career Center (formerly the Actors Fund Work Program), which offers "career counseling, job training, and job placement to help clients find work that can be done while continuing in the entertainment industry or while developing a new professional direction."

Now, you want to do something really, really smart? Like "I can't believe I was this smart" smart? Take advantage of the Career Center long before you need to. "We encourage entertainment industry professionals to become active in our program while their careers are going WELL!," says the Actors Fund's Patch Schwadron,

> Since it can take time to identify and develop meaningful sideline/parallel/ new careers that will complement the pursuit of industry work, why not invest some of the time you have when you are less stressed about finding paying work, so that when you need to generate additional income, you will have a plan of action?

She's right. Instead of waiting for a crisis (like couples who start marriage counseling too late), consider attending an orientation, meeting with an Actors Fund counselor, and cultivating new sources of income now to avoid a potential emergency later. I did it last week, and I'm a "working actor." I'm going to learn to write grants, just in case. MK

Dear Jackie,

Once again I have scoured online listings and found several roles that are absolutely right for me. The problem is that these roles are out of town. I realize that in many cases I would get housing and per diem, but even so, the amount of money an actor gets paid can be absolutely ridiculous.

Obviously I'm not in this business for the money—that would be *really* ridiculous—but I do expect my union to have some vague notion that if one is a character actor in late middle age, one has a life and apartment in New York with little things like electricity bills, and one needs some sort of living wage, for heaven's sake. There is a call listed this week with a ton of parts I'd love to do, but I can't afford to go out of town for $324 per week.

I never mind doing showcases in New York, stipend or not, since I can keep my survival job and rehearse at night, but to ask someone to leave town for $324 per week? How are you supposed to live?

—Realist

Dear Realist,

While your frustration makes perfect sense, I think you're disregarding one of the main issues at play here: the budgetary constraints of small theatres. In many cases, it's just not possible for a company to pay an actor, no matter how talented, more than a few hundred dollars per week. A small but wonderful Shakespeare company I used to work with gave out two Equity Guest Artist contracts per show, and repeatedly struggled to find trained, nonunion actors to fill the rest. The artistic director wanted to hire more Equity actors (and pay everyone more money) but it was impossible. She could barely cover the show's expenses with all corners cut to the quick.

"Actors' Equity has established developing theatre contracts for the purposes of both assisting theatres in their growth towards a standard contract and creating job opportunities for our members," agrees Equity spokesperson Maria Somma.

> This type of contract provides a salary, albeit a sometimes low salary, as well as contributions to the health and the pension funds, and the opportunity for an Equity actor to do a role they might not otherwise have the opportunity to play. While recognizing that not every Equity member can afford to take these jobs, especially when they are out of town, other Equity members are eager for the opportunities. It becomes a business choice for each individual actor.

For more specific information about Equity contracts, go to actorsequity.org, click on About Equity and then Contracts and Codes.

It sounds as if you are not in a position to take such a job, and I'm sure you're in good company. Without such contract options, however, many of these jobs would simply vanish altogether into the nonunion chasm. In many cases, if producers could pay for more Equity actors, they would. JA

Dear Michael,

I just booked a lead in a SAG-AFTRA ultra-low-budget film. I am super happy and blessed. The script is really good and the part is perfect for me. It will boost my career, I'm sure. The people working on this are professionals with many more credits than I have. I really want to do this film. But the pay offered is nearly non-existent, and I may end up on the street if I take this many days off from my day job in order to do this film. I can't afford to lose this opportunity, but I also can't afford to starve to death. How do I handle this situation?

—A Starving "Star"

Dear Starving,

Often, actors operate under the mistaken belief that we have no options, no value, and no power, particularly when it comes to negotiating for ourselves.

We're not usually business-minded, and we feel so lucky to have a gig, we fear it may be yanked away if we ask for anything beyond that opportunity. That's all just actor mythology.

In most cases, people are expecting and prepared for negotiation. It's neither an insult, nor viewed as ungrateful, as long as both parties are reasonable. When negotiating for yourself, the key word is "collaboration." Reject the adversarial "us against them" attitude and work together with the people hiring you. In this case, I'd give it to them straight:

"Here's the situation. I love this script and this role, and I really want to accept. But here's the problem. I haven't figured out how to do it without going broke. I just need to know whether you're able to come up in salary so we can make this work. I'm not looking to get rich, just keep the roof over my head and my bills paid."

They may ask what you need to make. Trust me on this: pad it a little. They may feel they've failed as negotiators if they don't land lower than the figure you quote, so give them some room to do that.

Remember, casting is hard. By the time producers and directors have chosen their actors, they don't want to make changes. You're who they want. They're not about to fire you over a friendly negotiating attempt.

Be ready for the possibility they won't be able to pay you what you need, and decide what you'll do in that case. Can you compromise (they pay a bit more, even if it's not what you're hoping for)? Do you need to decline the project? (Remember: nothing is ever your last opportunity.) Or will you do it regardless of the financial consequences? (The poverty we fear very rarely comes to pass. Chances are, you'll pull through.) None of those choices are wrong. Just be clear with yourself about what you need to do. There are always options. MK

Dear Michael,

I've been in LA for about a year. My job is actor-friendly, sort of. It's 9-to-5, but I can go to auditions during lunch or come late or leave early if I need to. I don't have to lie to my boss since she's cool with me pursuing acting. So what's the problem? For years I made my living as a theatre actor in Chicago, and this office work is driving me batty. As an Equity member, I know I can buy into SAG-AFTRA, and the word on the street is that SAG-AFTRA extras can make good money. It wouldn't be my ultimate goal, but it'd be a hell of a lot closer to it than where I am now. My friends think I'm crazy to leave a job this comfortable, but I think I'll go crazy if I don't get out of here and get around real actors again.

—Carrot or Stick

Dear Carrot,

If you were just starting out, weren't in the union, had a big family to support, or had no alternative way of paying the bills, I'd urge you to hold onto your honey of a gig at all costs. But your situation allows me to address this from another angle.

Few people outside the arts understand the soul issue—the way we artists draw on what's inside of us to dance, to sing, to paint, to play characters, to tell stories, to make music. And there are times when we can't afford to give bits of ourselves away. There are times when even a comfortable, lucrative job can bleed the art out of us, dampening our creative natures. Sometimes you have to leave a situation, regardless of what you might lose.

Does that mean we should all sit around collecting unemployment as we wait for the muse? Absolutely not. I've known artists who refused to do anything but their art; all of them were broke. Just like everyone else, artists have to be responsible, active members of society. We must pay bills and carry insurance. We must earn paychecks. But how we earn those paychecks is important; you have to have a day job you can live with.

Working as a background player, however, has its own soul-stealing potential. You'll very likely encounter disrespect from production people, long hours with nothing to do, and uncomfortable holding areas.[2] And that's when you're lucky enough to work. You may also discover, as I did when I did background work years ago, that some of the people who do this for a living can be petty and prone to complaining. Contrary to your expectation, you may not find yourself among peers—some extras don't even consider themselves actors. And although you will indeed be in the right setting, background work rarely leads to roles. I found that sitting around all day doing nothing while my brain turned to mush was far worse than any office job. Of course, your experience will be your own, and background work suits some people just fine.

Warning notwithstanding, the larger point is this: when it's time for a change, it's time for a change. The same will be true for the actor reading this who, noting the security and flexibility of your current gig, is already on his or her way to fill the vacancy. MK

Dear Jackie,

If I have a principal credited role in a major motion picture, but am nonunion, will I still get residuals?[3] Even though I had the money to pay to join when I first got this job, I was told by friends to hold off. Now, I don't. The film is due to be released in a few weeks and I want to be sure I am paid the residuals. It could be a lot of money!

—Making Sure

Dear Making Sure,

Yes, not only did you benefit from all the same protections as your union colleagues on set, you'll be paid like them as well. "With very few exceptions, it makes no difference whether an actor is a member of SAG-AFTRA or not, or what their membership status is," a Guild representative explained. "Any actor hired as a principal performer under a SAG-AFTRA contract on a SAG-AFTRA-covered project—whose performance remains in the picture—is entitled to residuals." JA

Dear Michael,

I booked a six-month gig in China. It pays great and is with a very reputable company. Everything was signed and ready to go—I had my music learned and contract signed. The only thing left to get was my Chinese work visa, which the company assured me was coming, though probably at the last minute. In the meanwhile both my agent and the company insisted that I wrap up my life here in NYC. So at their urging, I gave up my survival job, booked out,[4] and stopped auditioning for other things. And then—you guessed it—the work visa didn't come . . .

And still hasn't come. I'm now coming up on a month of unemployment that I hadn't budgeted for. The company is apologetic, but can't give me a start date for sure because it's all conditional on me getting that work visa. My agent is apologetic, but it's not his fault and he can't do anything.

The time has come for some serious decisions. I can't financially continue to wait around for something I'm afraid may never come. If I go back to my survival job, I'll probably lose out on an entire season of work (because I stopped auditioning), and it will take me a long time to make up the financial difference. If I continue to wait and the visa does come through soon, I'll be able to make up the money much faster. But I hadn't planned on this limbo, and God only knows—it could come tomorrow, in a month, or never.

I really, really, really want to go to China, not just because of the money, but because it's a once-in-a-lifetime experience. But my life has been on hold, and I can't continue that for much longer. What should I do? Give up on it? Or try to hold out a little longer?
    —Languishing in Limbo

Dear Limbo,

My suggestion would be to find temp work, and keep waiting. Your former job isn't the only one out there. If you can tread water with short-term employment that you can quit with little notice, maybe you'll be able to hold out. It sounds like this is spitting distance from happening, and it would be a shame to miss it. Meanwhile, make sure the booking company keeps you posted, especially if the delay forces them to move on to another performer.

It's wise for us to remember that in show business, "definites" aren't always defi-
nite. Productions get cancelled, scenes get edited out, companies fold . . . visas
arrive late. We really can't count on things until they become iron-clad realities.
So here's one of my many mottos: "In this business, nothing is anything until it's
something." MK

Dear Jackie,
    I graduated from a theatre program in June and I am absolutely miserable.
I have been working for a well-known insurance company for the past three
months. Well, that says it all doesn't it?

I feel extremely lost. I hate working for the devil and miss performing dearly.
I really don't know what step to take next as I want to progress and make a film
career for myself. What should I do? Is there even a point in trying?
    —Lost Soul Working for the Devil

Dear Lost,
    Three months and you still haven't booked a series regular or at least co-
starred in a Broadway musical? You're probably too old now: pack it in.

Or. Let's consider the possibility that you're right where you're supposed to be.
You've nailed down your day job and had a nice little break from acting after several
years in a training program. What should you? I'd like to invite you to take the following suggestions quite literally. Before the next three months pass you by; submit
to twenty student or independent films, enroll in and attend a weekly acting for the
camera class, read several entertainment business publications or blogs each week,
purchase and read three "how to" acting career books, do a few days of background
work to see the machinery of a professional film set first hand, get together with actor
friends once a month and strategize about your career, read ten screenplays (you can
find pdfs free online), go to five open calls, audition for three nonunion plays, see at
least three plays at small local theatre companies, attend two open mics, take at least
one improv class, refine your résumé, and locate a fantastic but affordable headshot
photographer. If you do all these things in ninety days, I bet the answer to your
second question will become quite clear. Don't try and catapult yourself to the front
of the line. Lay some groundwork for what ideally will be a long and varied career.

And don't be too hard on yourself about the day job—it's only temporary, and
I hear the devil prefers politics to insurance companies. JA

Reader Response:
Dear Jackie,
    As far as "The Devil" is concerned—and I have no doubt that this is your
reader's way of describing corporate America—I've been working for him for

quite sometime now. And what have I found out? This evil entity gives me paid vacation and sick days so that I can do occasional gigs. He provides medical insurance so that I can take proper care of myself, and a 401K so I can save for the future. He gives me a nice check every two weeks so that I can pay my bills and rent, have cable TV, and afford acting lessons, singing lessons, nice clothes and shoes to audition with. Oh, and food . . . That's very nice. I can have my hair cut and colored every couple of months because of The Devil. I can save up and create my own work with the awful money provided by The Devil, renting out a theatre to collaborate with other actors and putting on a production or renting out a cabaret space to sing. I have money for photographers, headshots, and flyers. If I want to go on an Equity open call, I can take the morning off as one of the many vacation or sick days available to me and sometimes I can even just come in a couple of hours late and still be paid.

Yes, I do need to make some very tough decisions about what auditions I have to skip and what I really must go to. Sometimes it's heartbreaking, I admit it. But guess what? If you give it a chance, you might find out that the Devil Corporation consists of really great people who actually get excited when they hear you're performing.
   —Anonymous

Dear Michael,
   The good news: I'm employed (albeit at a mom-and-popish theatre which, for now, will remain nameless)! The bad news: my check bounced! Now what? Do I walk out? Sue? Call the Better Business Bureau?
   —Utterly Unamused

Dear Un,
   First and foremost, keep a cool head at all costs. As tempting as it may be to assume that the theatre has done this on purpose, that is very, very rarely the case. Most often, it's a simple error that can be corrected quickly.

Here's the procedure: first, calmly call the person who issues your paychecks and—without accusing—let that person know what's happened. If you have reps, notify them right away as well—this is exactly what actor representatives are there for. If you've incurred any bank charges as a result of the bounced check, be sure to mention that as well.

If things aren't rectified in a week or two, report the situation. If it's a union production, report them to Equity (Equity has certain safeguards built in to protect actors in these situations). If not, contact your state's department (or division) of consumer affairs, as well as the Better Business Bureau at bbb.org. If your production is currently running, don't do anything too rash; threatening to quit or refusing to show up for your call until you're paid may sound like a good idea, but it's actually a violation of your contract. So easy there, Norma Rae.[5]

The good news: though, admittedly, it's a big drag, most of the time, these things work out. And they're best solved with gentle but persistent personal contact with the people who are the most able to get you paid. So before you start calling out the big Hollywood lawyers or staging a one-actor protest in front of the theatre, see if you can solve the problem amicably. MK

What Do You Think?

1   What are some viable support jobs for those pursuing acting careers? Name at least five and discuss their merits.
2   What are some ways of finding non-acting work?
3   What does it mean to "live beneath your means"? What are some methods for keeping your monthly expenses low?
4   Is the purchase of a new outfit or make-up for an audition tax-deductible? Why or why not?
5   Should you ever attempt to negotiate for more money on an acting job? If so, how?
6   What are some good reasons for quitting a support job? What are some benefits, besides salary, to keeping a steady day job?
7   What are some available resources for actors who are struggling financially?
8   What happens if you lose your SAG-AFTRA or AEA health insurance?
9   How can you find balance between a day job and an acting career?
10   At what point should you "quit your day job" and rely on acting income alone?

Notes

1   Reader—an actor hired by a casting director to read opposite auditioning actors.
2   Holding area—Since background actors don't get dressing rooms, production establishes a designated place for them to hang out while they're waiting to work. That's the holding area.
3   Residuals are fees paid to an actor for each showing or sale of an on-camera project. These are in addition to the actor's "session fee," which is his payment for actual days of filming.
4   Booking out is the practice of informing your representatives of dates during which you'll be unavailable for auditions and/or work.
5   *Norma Rae* (1979) is a film starring Sally Field as a factory worker who rallies her coworkers to join a union.

13

ETHICS AND ETIQUETTE

Because of the wide variety of their professional interactions, career actors must develop an expert knowledge of the protocols of the business—what is and is not considered appropriate—as well as their own personal policies—the ways they choose to conduct themselves and the codes to which they subscribe.

Having clarity about these ideas is particularly important, because challenging situations arise quickly; decisions need to be made on the spot. You're committed to a play and get offered a lucrative television gig; what do you do? You are asked to do something that violates union regulations; how do you respond? What do you say if someone asks your opinion of a script you hated? Know your ethics and etiquette in advance, and these circumstances are far more easily navigated.

For union members, some of the protocols are set down in writing in the form of official regulations, and a union rep can be a powerful ally. But union rules can't cover every eventuality—or even most of them—so it falls to each individual to become well acquainted with both the time-honored traditions and one's own ethical barometer.

While show business has a reputation for loose morals and dirty dealings, there's a healthy dose of fiction in that stereotype. In truth, our industry is chock full of truly ethical people who are dedicated to being their very best selves. And while the artistic universe might be indulgent in certain areas, it has its own set of unpardonable sins: a reputation for promiscuity, though not ideal, might not be nearly as damaging as a reputation for showing up late to the set. As actors, we sometimes worry far more than we need to about the danger of committing some *faux pas* or other, but an understanding of professional protocols and conduct is a necessity in cultivating a long and healthy acting career.

Questions and Answers

Dear Michael,

As you know, auditions are hard to get, whether they're for commercials, theatre, whatever. So what do you do if you finally get one, but it conflicts with something you've already committed to? When my agent finally calls with an appointment, it always seems like I'm booked for a temp job or a shift at my restaurant job, and the audition always comes in at the last minute—like, 5 or 6pm the night before. Do I try to get out of work on short notice? Just not show up? Or (gulp) turn down the audition? And if I do, will they ever call me in again, or will they figure I'm not serious about my career?

—I Need a Clone

Dear Clone,

Even at the last minute, you may find that your coworkers are willing to switch shifts with you, or that your work is able to accommodate your absence while you attend an audition. If you're in a major city, believe me, the people you work for are used to actors and their unpredictable schedules. As long as you're respectful and not demanding, it's worth asking.

But there's another—perhaps even better—alternative you may not have thought of, which is to try to switch your audition appointment to a day or time that works better for you. You're not the first actor to face this dilemma. It goes on constantly. Casting assistants will tell you that when they're setting up audition appointments, much of their time is spent juggling appointment times to accommodate actors' availability to come in. Neither your agent nor the casting director will be thrown by this. They're both interested in making it work.

Finally, if neither your coworkers nor your boss nor your agent nor the casting person is able to make it work, you may have to miss an audition. I promise, it will not be your last opportunity. And your fears of being added to some "naughty" list for having to turn down an audition are thoroughly unfounded. Casting people are way too busy to keep track of which actors were unavailable for auditions so they can make them pay for it later. So take a deep breath, and reach out to the various parties. I can tell you from experience that 99.99% of the time, it all works out. MK

Dear Jackie,

I never know how to deal with thank-you gifts for my agent and manager. What should I buy and how much do I need to spend? What about the holidays?

I don't want to miss a chance to network, but I'm not rich and I don't want to send the wrong thing.

—Gift Giver

Dear Gift,

Presents are lovely, but don't feel pressure to spend money you don't have: cards are plenty. If you do want to splurge on a few gifts for those you work with regularly or someone who went above and beyond, flowers, a gift certificate to a specialty shop or coffeehouse, or movie passes are all kind-yet-unassuming tokens of appreciation. Once a year, you might want to splurge on something nicer for an agent who's proved loyal and hardworking (take them to lunch so you can do some relationship-building in the process!) or a CD who calls you in without fail. Keep in mind you might be able to write off at least a small portion of the cost of industry-related gifts, so be sure to save your receipts. JA

Dear Michael,

This past weekend I attended a show that one of my friends was in. I always try to find the good in any performance, but this show was *so bad*! I tried to like it, I really did, but it was honestly awful! I always want to support my friends when they're in shows. But what do you say if they ask what you thought, and you hated it? I don't want to lie, but I also don't want to hurt their feelings.

—Say What?

Dear Say What,

I'm going to make a case for some controversial advice that's gotten me into many debates. When asked your opinion of a play you hated . . . *say you loved it*. That's right: *lie*. For some reason, actors who have no qualms about calling in sick when they're not, fudging on their résumés, or lying to their bosses so they can skip work for an audition have a sudden burst of militant morality when it comes to their assessments of a show's flaws. Rather than commit the ultimate sin of giving a false compliment, they'll just mention an aspect of the show they liked or say "congratulations." But here's the thing: they're not fooling anyone. When you gush about the set, praise the sound design, or stop at "congratulations," your actor friend knows you didn't like the show. And sharing your truthful negative "insights" has zero value; the show is already up and running. At this point, people just want to hear nice things about the work they're involved in.

If someone asks, "So, what did you think of my cousin?", even if she's a raving shrew, you're likely to say, "Oh, she's very nice," just out of courtesy. Similarly, when you see a show, gushing over it—sincere or not—is just good manners.

One actor I know practices this policy: "If someone insists three times that they really want my honest opinion, I'll share my less-favorable observations." But even that can backfire. One colleague who positively harangued me for my absolute honest opinion of his performance lost his mind when, at long last, I gently shared my only negative observation. "Are you kidding?!" he screamed, "I worked on that specifically!" And he sulked the rest of the night. What good did it do either of us?

I think maybe the Southerners have it right, with their lovely manners that can completely obscure negative feelings. There, in the South, I've been told by several natives, "Well, bless your heart" is sometimes code for "F★%@ you." It's false, but ever so much more pleasant . . . don't you think? MK

Dear Jackie,

The other day I had an audition for a new play (nonunion, non-paying). It went well, and they called me back for the next day. When I arrived, I was told I wouldn't need to audition again. The production team just started telling me about the role and asking about my conflicts, since rehearsals were scheduled to start in a week. "Before saying yes," I told them, "I need to read the script."

Had I asked them to sacrifice their firstborn, I would have gotten a less hostile reaction. One woman started to leave but the person next to her calmed her down and asked her to send me the script via email. Up to now, nothing has arrived, and, honestly, I don't think it ever will. Was it too much to ask for the script before committing to a project? Or are starving actors supposed to take anything without asking questions?

—Committed but Careful

Dear Committed,

My guess is that there was a misunderstanding along the way. Remember that small, unpaid (or low-paying) theatre gigs are usually run on a shoestring budget. We all know what this means to actors' salaries and benefits—but keep in mind how this permeates the rest of the production. Without a real casting pro in the mix, the person communicating with actors is probably unpaid and doing the work "as a favor." Even if the producer or director handles auditions, they are probably juggling a dozen other duties. The result is a less-than-stellar system under which everyone suffers.

There are instances, generally with new plays, in which the script is not made available to performers before they are booked because a playwright needs to keep her work private—at least until all the cast members are committed and can be asked to keep the text in confidence before a premiere.

I asked Emmy-winning writer and actor Kevin Del Aguila for his input:

If actors are being called back for lead roles, they should have a chance to read the whole script. It behooves the production for an actor being considered to have a more specific understanding of the role at that point. For smaller roles? Maybe not. It's definitely not out of the question for someone who is cast in any role to request to see a script before they commit.

Tim Wright, Artistic Director of Circle X, a Los Angeles-based theatre company dedicated to new works, had this to say:

> We encourage anyone auditioning for us to read the entire script—not just so they can see what they are getting into, but so they have a better idea of the story and the context for the sides they are auditioning with. Typically we make a read-only copy available so they can't print or keep it, but if a playwright or theatre is really protective they can make a hard copy available and have the actor sit and read it at the theatre or office. I always prefer an actor who wants to read the whole script—that shows me that they have a passion for the craft and want to invest in the process.

JA

Dear Michael,

I keep encountering auditions for readings of new musicals where neither the music nor the script is available in advance. Several times I've auditioned for a project (written, produced, and directed by the same person) only to find out, after being cast, that the script and/or the music is laughable, or worse. I've thought, "There is no way I can spend six weeks rehearsing for this project, and suffer the embarrassment of performing this mess on stage." And so I've quit. I came in with good intentions, and left feeling like I'd burned bridges and let people down. There have also been established musicals I've been cast in, only to learn at the first rehearsal that the director had a "brilliant vision" (like the local production of *Hair* whose director wanted to split the role of Claude into three distinct characters, to "represent the Holy Trinity." Oy vey!)

Why can't I get these materials and know about "concepts" in advance without being seen as demanding, unprofessional, or difficult?
—Too Many Turkeys[1]

Dear TMT,

I think you have every right to request a script—particularly when you're being asked to work for little or no money. Your time is valuable; you get to be selective. Writers of new pieces sometimes hesitate to release copies for fear of theft (which is, in most cases, *completely* unjustified). And if that's the case, you have every right to drop out once the materials *are* available to you.

268 Ethics and Etiquette

One way to avoid the situation you've described, though, is to be very wary of projects that are written, directed, and starring the same person. No good can come from that. It's said that every project should pass this time-honored test: they must either pay great money, advance your career, or offer artistic satisfaction. If a project does none of these things, why do it?

Now, *how* you quit is key. If you're quitting because you think the show stinks, feel free to lie. Tell the director and/or writer you've been offered a highly lucrative project (be prepared to describe it), that you desperately need the money, or that you have a health problem, far too personal to discuss, and how heartbroken you are that you won't be able to be a part of this brilliant musical. Then quit, quickly, giving them time to replace you. Trust me. This advice comes from years of experience with these exact circumstances. There's nothing to be gained by "enlightening" anyone about their work.

And if they're angry, gently deflect with something like, "I don't blame you for being angry. I'm angry too. I hate having to miss this." But whatever it takes to extricate yourself, do it. Life's too short for bad musicals. MK

Dear Michael,

I've been doing a lot of extra work to support myself while I wait for my big break. It's also somewhat educational as far as how TV and film actors work. Sometimes, I see my fellow extras getting upgraded to featured[2] or even getting a line or two of dialogue, and I wonder, "Why him? Why her?" Is there a secret to getting noticed? I try to project a professional image when I'm on the set and stay near the camera as much as possible, but so far, nothing. Any tips?

—Back to One

Dear Back,

How to get upgraded? One word: unexpectedly. The job of an extra is to unobtrusively serve the needs of the production. Aggressive background actors who campaign for upgrades are the banes of the 2nd assistant director's existence. In fact, far from being your ticket to stardom, muscling your way into the lens is a sure way not to be asked back. The same goes for schmoozing the stars, director, or crew. A movie set is a busy place, and as much as you may want to parlay the opportunity into something bigger, this just isn't the time. It sounds like you're already doing the right thing, being professional. So just sit tight, and cultivate your career when you're *not* on set. MK

Dear Jackie,

Are there any guidelines for etiquette while waiting for an audition? The other day I was at an audition for a pretty big role in a feature when all of a sudden this dude whips out his cell phone and starts having a loud, obnoxious conversation. Everyone in the room started looking at each other in disbelief. It didn't take long for him to get even louder, so I finally went over to him and told him that some of us were trying to concentrate and would he please take his conversation elsewhere. He replied that I must not have been in Hollywood very long if I let something like that rattle me. Is there a code of conduct while waiting for an audition?

—Rattled

Dear Rattled,

You can't really apply a set of hard-and-fast rules to the matter because waiting rooms, like projects, vary. I asked a few working actors for their views on a waiting room code of conduct. "For a theatrical audition, I just like to focus," said one:

> If I happen to know someone there I may catch up for a minute but then it's back to work. When it comes to a commercial audition I think it's a little more lenient—especially if there is no copy to worry about. In those cases I think a talkative waiting room can actually be helpful because you start to get to know people and feel even more loose and relaxed.

Another had this to say:

> I've seen some pretty horrendous behavior. Sometimes people are just posturing. Others are attempting to 'psych out' the competition. And in some cases it's because they're just idiots. And the boorish behavior seems to be inversely proportional to the quality and status of the project. You're far more likely to see it at auditions for commercials or student films. By the time people are testing for series[3] or reading for feature directors, they've usually learned the ropes.

"I don't think this is all that rare," another actor weighed in:

> My favorite is the bragging actor who sits in the waiting room and nonchalantly boasts to anyone who'll listen about how many commercials and TV spots he's booked recently and how swamped he is with auditions. I hate that guy. In New York there are several rehearsal and audition spaces where the monitors do their best to tell people to stop warming up at the top of their lungs, screaming into their cell phones, or tap dancing in the middle of a busy hallway. Unfortunately, rude is rude.

It's understandable that actors—operating in a heightened state of nerves as they await auditions—might be oblivious to those around them. But this is directly contrary to the state they should be in. Acting requires deep empathy, awareness, and full investment in the present moment. Blabbing on a cell phone or bragging about past success doesn't promote openness and immediacy. Your frustration, however, can lend itself to dynamic work. Any emotions jerks like your cell phone guy stir up can be used to strengthen your acting. Turn, "He won't stop talking—I can't concentrate!" into "Why won't you listen to me—I need you to help me!" or whatever your scene calls for.

And you can always bring headphones. JA

Dear Michael,

Lately I've been working more and more on television, doing mostly guest star roles. It's great, but I get so shy when I'm on the set, especially when dealing with the series regulars. I just clam up, maybe because they're all successful and I'm still early in my career. How do I get out of my shell?

—Too Quiet on the Set

Dear Too,

Coming onto the set as a guest star can be intimidating, especially for actors who, like you (and me), have a shy side. But believe it or not, some of those big, successful series regulars are shy too. So be bold but not needy. If you're a guest star, it's perfectly appropriate—even almost expected—to greet your fellow actors with, "Hi, I'm so-and-so; I'm playing such-and-such. Nice to meet you." In several years of doing this, I've only once gotten a cold response. Most actors will be relieved that you've broken the ice, and it'll make for a more enjoyable shoot. Follow my favorite rule—one that applies to meetings, auditions, performing, and almost anything else we do—"Take care of them. Don't ask them to take care of you." MK

Dear Michael,

I'm about to do my first Broadway show and I recently found out that the actors typically tip their dressers on a weekly or monthly basis. But how much should you tip your dresser? Is it based on your salary or the size of your role?

—Cash on the Dresser

Dear COD,

It depends on several things. First, salary. If you're in the ensemble, making minimum, less is expected than if you're playing a lead, making considerably more. Second, the number of costume changes. If your dresser has to track, wash, press, and re-hang thirty-two costumes a night for you, she or he is working a lot harder than if you just wear one dress for the whole show. Next, how many of your changes require help? Are they fast changes, or do you have enough time to change yourself?

For an expert opinion, I went to Kendall Louis, a career dresser who's worked all over the country. "You can't go wrong in giving a dresser cash," says Kendall,

> If they are working on Broadway, yes, their weekly paycheck is good, but it's just the little courtesy that can help pay for a MetroCard. My most recent experience was as an ensemble dresser for a tour stop of *Mamma Mia*. We each had assigned actors but also did whatever for whoever needed help. Before they left, each actor chipped in an equal amount and it was split between us—a very fair system. I don't know if it's the economy or people just don't know to do it any longer, but we've had situations where nothing was offered. I've only had it happen once. Adult actors should know better than to stiff people. Twenty a week is righteous (if you are working in NY you are getting paid real money). If the dressing track is especially hard, thirty.

Of course, you should remember to adjust that for inflation. If in doubt, ask one of the dressers you're *not* working with. They'll know what's appropriate. MK

Dear Jackie,

I'm trying to get into the musical theatre scene but I have a visual disability. Even with my glasses on—and yes, I need them to read—I have to hold things very close to my face. For a typical audition this is no big deal but occasionally, a cold reading is required. I don't want to look like a total dork when I do the cold reading but I can't think of a good way to explain the issue. It would be a lot of help to me if I could arrange to have an enlarged copy of the script at the audition. Do you think they would work with me if I made that request ahead of time?

—Bigger is Better

Dear BiB,

Equity's agreement with producers states that sides will be made available at least two days in advance, for the benefit of the visually impaired. And according to AEA, "For Equity Principal Auditions in New York City, the producer sends sides to the Equity Auditions Department. Visually impaired performers may request a copy on the business day before the EPA." That means you have the right to get the sides in advance and enlarge them—or memorize them—to your liking.

If the audition is nonunion, however, no such formalities exist and you will have to confront the situation on a case-by-case basis. While you would almost certainly have to make your own enlarged copies, I doubt many producers or casting people would have any problem allowing you early access to do so. For an open call, show up as early as possible and sign up for a later time slot. Take the sides to a nearby copy shop for alteration. Many actors make a habit of getting sides at the top of the audition time just to prepare, so your request won't seem out of the ordinary. If it does, just explain your needs.

I spoke to an optometrist and low-vision specialist—okay, my dad—about your condition to see whether he had any other ideas for you. Here's what he said:

> It sounds as if she has a vision condition that reduces her visual acuity despite her prescription. There are 'low-vision' glasses she could get, but they look a little funny. If she sees a 'low-vision optometrist' they might be able to help her but, as she says, enlarged print works, so the best solution would probably be for her to photocopy the print at 150 or even 200%.

What can you do if the producers won't let you take the sides off the premises? I'd suggest you pass on the audition since your request is reasonable and their refusal denotes a lack of sensitivity you'd be better off avoiding. My dad, however, has this advice:

> If she is a little brash (and sneaky) she could ask to be excused to the bathroom, go out to a nearby office, request a quick use of the copy machine from the secretary and do an enlargement herself—or trick the secretary into doing it—and go back and audition.

I don't know if that's a strategy to count on, but in desperate times . . . JA

Dear Jackie,

I recently emailed a group of my contacts with an invitation to a new play I was in and got this response from one of the recipients: "No no no! I don't share my email with people I don't know!" Well, this person had given me her email address so I don't know what she was talking about. How do I respond?

    —Oopsie

Dear Oopsie,

Send a brief apology, of course.

As for what she was talking about? I bet you sent a mass email without using BCC. This means everyone got a giant list of all your recipients' email addresses—perfect for spamming! You know how frustrating it is when you're added to a group text or Facebook PM and dinged again and again until you leave the discussion? Those on the receiving end of promotional emails from actors have this experience *all the time*. If you don't reach out to them individually, or at least protect them from the group barrage, you may be viewed as disrespectful, clueless, or lazy.

While personally addressing emails, messages, and notes is best, mass email announcements like "Watch me this Thursday on *This is Us*," or "Please come see my one-person *Hamlet*," should be addressed via BCC (Blind Carbon Copy). This means numerous people can be sent the same email at the same time without sharing their contact information with a bunch of strangers. It's the professional (and compassionate) method for sending mass emails, even amongst friends, and a whole lot better than lumping everyone into a giant blob. Especially when someone in that blob invariably follows up with cutesy comments as they cluelessly "reply all" again. And again. JA

Dear Michael,

Ok, now I know giving another actor a note is something that is not cool in the real world, but what if you're also the writer? My best friend and I were reading through a scene that I wrote. We recorded it several times, and then watched it after each take. After he sucked several times, I gave him a suggestion to try on his opening moment. He got very angry and said, "You're not the director." Now he's right, we were going to have another friend direct it. So was I totally out of line? FYI: we are not doing the scene anymore.

—Iceman,

Dear Iceman,

Yes, you were totally out of line. The long-standing, time-honored rule about actors not giving fellow actors notes is not only hallowed and etched in stone, it's also a really good rule. And it applies even if you're also the writer. As a cast member, you lack the necessary objectivity (even if you're watching video playback), and fellow actors will resent it, because it suggests you're at a higher status. That's also why directing something you're in is discouraged. Very few do it well, and it really upsets the balance. When I hear of someone directing, writing, and appearing in a project, I run the other way. It's usually a disaster.

Art is subjective. Your judgment that your fellow actor's work "sucked" is harsh, and not an objective truth. It's possible, as writer, that you have preconceived ideas about how the scene should be played. But don't make the mistake of thinking it's the only way. I'm sure that as an actor, you'd hate for a writer to give you acting notes.

Protocol is important. It helps things run smoothly, and reduces the opportunities for chaos. No one but the director may direct. And that rule applies even when you think another actor sucks. It applies even if you think the *director* sucks. Unless someone privately requests your input, you just have to hold your tongue.

There are a few—and only a few—exceptions. If you feel that you are in physical danger, or that your personal space is being violated in a way that has nothing to do with the work, you are entitled to speak directly to the actor or actors involved. Otherwise, *no notes*.

Now, in your particular case, there's a perfectly legit work-around. Pull your director aside privately and share your concerns as the writer. If the director agrees, he—and only he—can give the notes to your fellow actor. And them's the rules.

By the way, I have a great way of graciously dealing with suggestions from fellow actors. I emphatically thank them for the note (making sure to use the word "note"). That usually does the trick. MK

Dear Jackie,

I was recently offered a role as a principal in one of my dream shows at a well-respected, nonunion theatre nearly 100 miles from my home. The next day, my offer was retracted because they could not find housing for me. The show, I was informed by the producer, cannot afford to put me up in a budget hotel. Well, the casting announcement specifically stated that pay and housing for out-of-towners would be provided. The weekly pay won't cover the costs of gas and my personal time driving.

Should I try to find my own housing? Should I fight for the part and housing (since it was promised to me in writing)? Should I offer to stay at home and try for a gas stipend on top of my weekly pay?

—Homeless

Dear Homeless,

Unless I was willing to burn the bridge, I wouldn't try to force them into housing me or giving me a stipend on the strength of a nonunion audition notice. If, as you said, this were my dream show, I'd have to think seriously about whether the sacrifice of money and time was worth making. It's *slightly* possible I'd agree to do a show 100 miles from home without housing—if, say, the rehearsal period was only a week long or I was given permission to come in only three times a week. In either case, I'd also ask for a gas stipend.

This is a situation that will require you to be very clear with your boundaries. If you do negotiate a deal with the producer, be sure you're truly happy with the arrangement before moving forward. Don't compromise more than you're really willing to give up. It may become clear upon reflection that the original offer was the minimum you're willing to accept. JA

Dear Jackie,

Oftentimes, when looking at my résumé, casting directors will point out someone and ask me, "Oh, you know so-and-so?" This can be a very good thing when we have a mutual connection, but I am about to add two acting programs to my résumé and, as every student knows, some teachers tend to like certain students more than others. There is one teacher in particular who doesn't seem to like my work, but can't seem to answer me when I ask her what it is that she dislikes.

What should I do if a casting director happens to ask me if I have worked with this teacher? Is it better to tell the truth and risk having this teacher speak lowly of me, or should I bend the truth and risk having my dishonesty revealed if I should come up in conversation between the two? I am usually a very honest person, but I am really not sure what to do in this situation.
—Not Teacher's Pet

Dear Not Teacher's Pet,

I'd err on the side of brevity. Be positive and don't dwell. Instead of lying about your experience with this teacher, try responding to, "Have you worked with so-and-so?" with an upbeat, "Yes, she's great." Period. Or you could divert the conversation into friendlier territory, as in, "Yes, a little bit. I mostly worked with (fill in the name of your favorite teacher at the school). She was incredible!" Or try a turnaround with a jolly, "Yes! Where do you know her from?" Keep in mind that nine times out of ten, folks just want to chat and find common ground—they don't actually call the person in question. What you *don't* want to do is get into a discussion revealing your frustrations with the instructor. Don't turn audition small talk into a confessional. JA

Dear Michael,

Once and for all, what is the rule about mentioning "the Scottish play"? Are we not allowed to say the title at all? What if we're actually doing the play?
—Confused About the Curse

Dear Confused,

For those readers who aren't familiar with the superstition: it's considered very bad luck to mention Shakespeare's *Macbeth*—even to quote from it—within the walls of a theatre. That's because, according to legend, tragedy and disaster have followed productions of the play for generations. So it's become customary among theatricals to refer to *Macbeth* as "the Scottish play," so as to avoid invoking its curse.

Luckily, there's a remedy when someone slips up: the guilty party must go outside, turn around counterclockwise three times, spit, say the worst curse word he or she can think of, knock on the door, and ask to be re-admitted. (These requirements vary within our ranks.)

It may sound silly to some of you, but theatre superstitions are a sacred part of our tradition. It's not necessarily that we all *believe* in the curse; the tradition is to *behave* as if we do. And that's taken very seriously.

Obviously, if you're actually performing *Macbeth* (though some would say that in itself is bad luck), the rule is lifted during rehearsals and performances. Some people, misunderstanding the superstition, believe that any mention *anywhere* is bad luck. But the curse applies only inside a theatre, which is why I'm able to mention the title here . . . I hope. MK

Dear Jackie,

   I'm a nonunion actor trying to make my way in this competitive business, and a friend offered to put me in touch with someone who could get me The Breakdowns for a nominal fee. Is it worth it to pursue this avenue?
   —Looking For an In

Dear Looking,

   Is it worthwhile to pay for stolen access to casting information that casting people don't want you to see? I don't think so.

The information in casting breakdowns is proprietary and trusted to the intermediary, Breakdown Services, with the idea that it will reach only intended recipients. Although some notices are released through Actors Access (which is owned by Breakdown Services) and open to actor self-submissions, most of the "choice" roles are sent only to actor representatives, and sometimes only to a small group of those. This may sound unfair, but such restrictions are in place in other industries as well. When Fortune 500 companies search for CEOs, you can bet they don't put an ad on craigslist.

Breakdown Services founder Gary Marsh is uninterested in prosecuting actors who look at bootlegged breakdowns, but his generosity doesn't include those who sell them. Such sales violate the California Unfair Practices Act and break copyright law and Marsh is willing to press charges. And since casting directors decide where to publicize their auditions—they aren't beholden to see all comers—the more people who send unwelcome submissions, the more likely they will just skip the process in the future. Why send out a breakdown that gets pirated and leads to 1000 unwanted submissions when you can just call your favorite agents and ask for cherry-picked talent?

I know actors have to be aggressive, creative, and sometimes break rules to make their way, but stealing breakdowns isn't particularly creative—it's lazy. If you hear about a project you'd like to submit to, go for it. But don't waste time worrying about breakdowns you don't, and weren't intended to, see. Stay on top of emerging opportunities in your area through open casting notices, unions, your contacts, regional combined auditions, and local film schools and theatre companies. There are plenty casting directors who do want to hear from you. JA

Dear Michael,

Last month I had the opportunity to perform a great part in a wonderful regional production. Unfortunately, when it rains it pours. The day I was scheduled to make the trip to the theatre, a local TV show called and asked if I would be available to reprise a small role I did last season. Production didn't know when I'd be shooting, and that can always change, so I had to be available for the whole shoot, which was running at the same time as our performances. Since I committed myself to the theatrical production, I thanked the casting director and turned them down. Because I had not signed my contract yet, I know that I could have technically backed out of the show, but I just couldn't do something like that.

I know anyone would say I did the "right" thing. I am asking you, from strictly a business standpoint, did I blow it? I could have made as much money in that one day shooting as I did for my whole time doing the play. I'm worried I made a bad business decision for myself, especially considering the possible residuals. This business has been cutthroat to me at times in my young career. Should I have been cutthroat back?

—Buyer's Remorse

Dear Remorse,

Wait a minute. Let's stop and celebrate, can we? You were offered a play and a TV role at the same time. I wouldn't call getting offered two jobs at once "unfortunate." You know what that makes you? A big deal. Listen, if you're very, very lucky in this business, you'll face these kinds of scheduling conflicts again and again. Now is as good a time as any to get used to handling them.

Yes, from a strictly professional standpoint, you made a good decision. As cutthroat as others may be, it's important to decide, establish, and steadfastly adhere to your own code of ethics and professionalism. Keeping your word makes a statement about who you are. And reputations are important in this business. I doubt that anyone connected with the TV show blames you for honoring your commitment. Most casting directors understand that if they offer you a job and you're already booked, you have to turn it down. (I say "most" because we're in show business and people are crazy; early in my career, I was yelled at for forty-five minutes for turning down background work.) It's fairly safe to say you haven't burned any bridges. In fact, you may have increased your status. As a former agent of mine used to say, "'No', is a very sexy word." That casting director and the show's producers now know you're a working actor who may not always be available, that you're not sitting there waiting for them to call. You may have missed this particular opportunity, but you've upped your image as a busy professional.

Conversely, had you dropped out of the show on such short notice, you would have created a problem for the theatre company. They might have understood that you had to take the TV job, and of course, they would have rallied—"the show must go on" and all of that. But at the very least, it would have left a bad taste in their mouths, and I don't think you would have liked how it felt. I have twice dropped out of theatre commitments to accept TV offers. The money I made on those gigs was spent long ago. What remained was the feeling that I hadn't conducted myself in a way that was consistent with my principles.

Another reason it was a good decision is that, until specific dates are booked, TV jobs can go away. Characters get written out or redefined. Producers change their minds. Had you quit the play, you might have found yourself without either job.

Incidentally, my answer would have been different if you were leaving a non-paying engagement for a paying one. In that case, you should quit without qualms.

There is one thing I would have advised you to do differently: you could have tried to work things out so you were able do *both* jobs. The theatre folks might have agreed to release you for your shooting days; the TV folks might have been able to schedule your filming around your theatre schedule. This is done *all the time*. When I was on tour, I was simultaneously recurring on a TV show. They'd fly me from whatever city we were playing to film on my days off, then get me back in time for the next performance. Things can often be worked out. At least give casting the opportunity to find a creative solution.

Bottom line: Did you wind up making less money? Probably. Are there other considerations that are more important to your career? Absolutely.

We actors seem to spend a lot of energy worrying that we've offended someone. It's as if we're playing that old board game, Operation, in which you have to remove plastic bones from the "patient." If you touch the sides of the cutout while extracting a bone, a harsh buzzer sounds, making you leap five feet in the air. We seem to feel that we're in constant danger of inadvertently saying or doing the wrong thing and, as a result, getting banished from show business forever. I find the opposite to be true. When you conduct yourself with dignity, grace, strength, and a sense of your own value, people tend to respond in kind.

Drop the TV casting person a nice note, expressing thanks for the request and mentioning that you're back in town and available should the show want to bring back your character in the future. Then pray to the showbiz gods that you'll always have to decide which acting job to take. MK

Dear Michael,

Lately I've been finding auditions on this website I visit. But I notice about half of the projects require nudity. When the question first popped up whether I would do nudity or a sex scene, I said no because I believed it was in most cases not needed, though that may have been my own insecurity talking. Recently I've been studying more into it. It seems like a lot of actors do it, so I'm reconsidering. But I've been noticing, especially in indie films and on HBO, that the sex scenes are becoming more graphic, and a lot of it is borderline soft-core pornish.

As a male aspiring actor, if I were faced with an opportunity to do a nude or sex scene, should I do it? Or would doing sex and nude scenes hurt me later on? I know sometimes actors are forced to make choices based on furthering their careers. I just would like to know the best way to deal.
　—Bodily Business

Dear Bodily Business,

When you're first starting out, with no agent and no union to vet projects for legitimacy, you're vulnerable to all kinds of less-than-reputable situations. I must caution you that nonunion, non-paying and/or amateur projects that involve sex scenes and/or nudity may be worse than unprofessional; they may be no more than scams by opportunistic pervs looking for cheap thrills. Or they could be videos for porn sites. There are so many stories of young people who've found themselves compromised (or worse, endangered) by such rackets.

You talked about sometimes being "forced" to do things for your career. I disagree; we're never forced. You always get to choose how you want to present yourself. You're the CEO of your own company. Don't give your power away. The decision whether or not to work nude is a personal one. Actors should never think of nudity as an inherent requirement of our profession. It should never be assumed that just because you're an actor, the world gets to see your naked body. Many actors have successful, busy careers without shedding their clothes.

On the other hand, nudity doesn't have the stigma it once had. As long as the project is legitimate, it's doubtful that it would hurt your reputation, unless you're planning to work primarily in religious or family-oriented projects. But even if nudity and sex scenes are compatible with your career plans, you need to decide what your policies are on the subject. Here are some I strongly recommend:

　—Never do nudity at an audition.
　—Never do nudity in someone's home.
　—Never video or photograph yourself nude for an audition, or allow someone else to (you can't control where the recordings or photos will end up).

—Unless you really don't care, don't do nudity for student, amateur, or "experimental" projects. Wait for the professional, high-level production, the one you know is 100% legitimate, safe, and worthy of such intimate exposure, like an HBO project or a first-class feature film with a known director.

—Look for signs of legitimacy, like a professional contract, an accomplished director, writer and/or producer, or a name actor.

—Never let anyone pressure you into doing nudity, regardless of what kind of clout they claim to have.

—Trust your gut. If it feels shifty, it is.

You have to be savvy—particularly if you're young and attractive—and approach any so-called "opportunity" that involves nudity with a heaping dose of skepticism. You have to be fully aware that people are going to want to see you naked, and some of those people will use unscrupulous methods to achieve that goal. You cannot afford to be naive about that. And if anyone tells you you'll be washed up in show business unless you strip, find the nearest door. MK

Dear Michael,

This year's current senior class at the conservatory where I teach has been a nightmare. The university brought in a new head for the program and the senior class in particular has been *awful* to this man. They've talked back to him, yelled at him, walked out of his class, etc. I think why this upsets me so much is that I mentored many of them. It was very disappointing to hear they've been behaving like such amateurs. I want to tell these kids that they're really damaging their reputations—and possibly their futures—but I'm not sure how to explain that. Are there any words of wisdom you could offer them about the importance of professional behavior?

—A Concerned Peer

Dear Concerned Peer,

It would be my pleasure . . .

Dear future professional actors,

I'm guessing that right now, your focus is on launching your careers—figuring out how to get hired for those first jobs. But I want to talk to you about something that's crucial to the health of your *long-term* career; I want to talk about the importance of not being a jerk.

Now, this isn't a lecture about morality, ethics, or niceness. The reason you shouldn't be a jerk is simply that it diminishes your chances of working, in a field where employment's already scarce. Now, who's a jerk?: the actor who insults people, habitually criticizes, complains unreasonably, creates drama, behaves selfishly, or undermines the work at hand. Jerks cost time, money, and morale. Producers are so determined to avoid them, they'll sometimes hire a mediocre mensch[4] over a talented jerk.

While you're in school, there's a group mentality that allows you to support each other's jerky behavior (like, for example, expressing disrespect for a new department head) and be celebrated by your peers for such conduct. But each professional actor's reputation is his alone. And no one's celebrating a pain in the ass. So now, while you're learning other important skills, it's a good time to develop a pleasant, professional demeanor that'll help you remain among the employed. You can start by daring to exclude yourself from any misbehavior that surrounds you.

Now, maybe your teachers are worthless idiots. Guess what: some directors you'll work for will be worthless idiots. And while they wear the director hat, they get to direct, even if they're lousy, whether or not they meet with your approval. So there's nothing to be gained by insulting the person in charge . . . except a bad reputation. In fact, whatever your complaint is—script, lighting, choreography, advertising—you could be 100% right in your criticism, and still be the ass no one wants to work with. That's because people prefer to work with lovely actors who make them feel great. They want to be treated with respect, spared from conflict and drama. Do yourself a favor: become that kind of actor as soon as possible . . . or you might pay a professional price.

I speak from experience. Years ago, I was in an emotionally difficult play with some production issues. I was perpetually aggravated, intolerant, and withdrawn, and I wasn't nice to people. It wasn't until a year later that I realized what a monster I'd been. In spite of consistently high praise for my performance, when the show was remounted, I was the only cast member excluded. I just wasn't worth the trouble. I've cleaned up my act since then, and now enjoy a reputation for being great to work with. But that story demonstrates two important things you should note: One: you can be the jerk and not realize it; jerks usually don't think they're being jerks. And two: for the most part, no one will tell you. If you're very, very lucky, someone will pull you aside and set you straight. But more likely, rather than deal with the confrontation, they'll make a mental note for future reference, and just not hire you again. And if anyone asks about you, they'll be sure to warn their colleagues what they're in for. That's how it works. And directors aren't the only ones who get asked. Stage managers, producers, costumers, choreographers, crew members, and of course, your fellow actors are all in positions to relate their experiences in working with you. It's remarkable how things get around.

But let's be honest: some jerks do work. Producers or directors sometimes tolerate crap from famous names, who sell tickets, bring in viewers, or attract investors.

They'll resent it, but when there are big dollars involved, they'll suffer in silence. But here's the thing: you're not famous. You're also not irreplaceable. You might be brilliant, but the industry doesn't know that yet. Anything that marks you as "difficult" this early in your career is a mistake, because it could kill your chances of even getting started—and chances are slim enough as it is. Do you want to do that to your career?

99.9% of the stars I've met are considerate, respectful, humble, accepting, and collaborative. Note that I did not say they were pushovers. Most embody the quality to which I most aspire: gracious strength. They'll make you feel like the most important person in the world, but they'll also be clear on what they need to do their jobs, and insist on it . . . and get it . . . with a smile. At the same time, most have reputations as "the nicest person you could ever hope to meet." Now's the time to start emulating their behavior, cultivating the demeanor of a star-in-training.

Here are some suggestions:

—Figure out what is and isn't your job. If it's not, stay out of it. Complaining about things that don't directly affect you is the behavior of a jerk. Gracious, established, working actors focus on their own tasks.

—There's a familiar backstage conversation that usually begins with the phrase, "Don't you think . . . ?": "Don't you think the lights should be dark if it's supposed to be a scary scene?" "Don't you think that sound cue is kind of loud?" "Don't you think she should yell that line?" Watch yourself. Even those participating might be mentally tagging you as a troublemaker. Let others damage their careers with armchair directing. Keep criticisms to yourself.

—If you have a legitimate problem to discuss, go to the person who can fix it. (Recreational bitching is a fine pastime, but it's not effective. Telling your castmate that your costume doesn't fit won't make it fit.) And when you have those conversations, watch your tone. Approach with the assumption that the other person is an intelligent collaborator, worthy of your respect, and on the same team. You'll get a better response. Jerks start with accusation, and try to make people feel stupid. No one likes that.

—Anyone can act nicely toward a person she respects. It's the super-classy actor who develops the ability to be lovely and gracious toward people who *aren't* good at their jobs. A successful actor once imparted to me some great wisdom: "I try to remember," she said, "that no one is ever trying to do a bad job. You mustn't get angry with people for being bad at something."

—Let's say you're among the many actors who have emotional problems (you wouldn't be alone; most of us are fairly nutty). Maybe you're a hothead, with a crazy temper. Maybe you're paranoid. Take care of that stuff. Get help. And in any case, don't bring it to work. Regardless of how justifiable your personal baggage may be ("I'm like this because I had a miserable childhood!"), making others pay for it can hurt your career.

—Unless you're the Equity deputy,[5] don't be a spokesperson. If everyone in the cast is grumbling about how cold the theatre is, don't be the person who goes to management with, "Everyone in the cast feels . . ." They'll throw you under the bus, claiming they never said anything of the kind. You end up with a bad rep.

—Make others feel important. When out socially, instead of pouncing on the first opportunity to talk about yourself, ask others what they've been up to. Always introduce colleagues, and promote their talent: "This is my brilliant friend so-and-so—amazing voice. You should have seen her in *such-and-such*. She was incredible."

—And when people ask what you thought of their show, regardless of how much they say they want the truth, tell them you loved it. Listing everything you thought was wrong has no value, and, on a subconscious level, registers jerk points. Praise makes people feel good, and they'll associate you with that good feeling.

—Finally . . . treat crew members with respect, learn people's names, hang up your costumes, learn to accept compliments—and to give them, fight like a tiger to avoid an "us and them" attitude between you and those in authority, and most importantly, cultivate humility; there's always someone better, and more to learn. MK

What Do You Think?

1   Is the business of acting an ethical one? Explain.

2   What do you do if you're committed to a job and get offered a better one?

3   How can you thank casting people for opportunities? Should you send cards? Gifts? When?

4   Can an actor give another actor a note? Why or why not? When, if ever, is it called for?

5   What are some reasons a project's full script may not be available to you before an audition? What would you do if, after being cast, you discovered something unacceptable about the script?

6   If you were put in charge of creating the industry's universal waiting room etiquette, what would you require? What are some behaviors you would encourage or restrict?

7   Do you think you will ever do nudity? Why or why not?

8 What are some reasons you might choose to quit a project? How would you present that decision to the folks in charge?

9 After seeing a colleague's show, do you need to offer feedback? What would you say if you didn't like the production?

10 Having a good reputation as a professional who is pleasant to work with is important. What are some ways to build that reputation? What kinds of things might hurt it?

Notes

1 "Turkey" is an old show business expression meaning a bad theatre piece.

2 "Featured" background actors are those given on-camera business that's more noticeable, like handing a prop to a principal actor, or reacting in a close-up shot.

3 Testing for series—In the final stages of casting "series regulars" (actors who appear in all or most of the episodes of a TV show), the final candidates audition for network high-ups. This is known as "testing."

4 *Mensch*—Yiddish—a kindhearted and upstanding person.

5 Each Equity cast is required by the union to elect a deputy, who may sometimes act as a liaison between cast members and management or cast members and the union.

14

STICKY SITUATIONS

Any undertaking that brings human beings together also furnishes opportunities for them to step on each other's toes and push each other's buttons. Awkwardness, miscommunication, misunderstandings, moral dilemmas, and interpersonal conflicts can arise in any environment, but there are several very logical reasons why actors encounter these workplace snags far more frequently than, say, librarians.

Actors work freelance, from job to job, and have an endless parade of employers and coworkers. The dynamics change constantly. For us, it's not just a matter of learning to work with one boss or in one environment. We constantly encounter new situations and personalities, calling on us to continually hone our abilities to analyze, assess, and manage. Like martial artists, who are trained to use different defensive techniques depending on what comes at them, actors may find themselves having to deftly move between diplomacy, assertiveness, self-preservation, restraint, quick thinking, white lies, and sometimes even graceful exits.

Our profession lacks consistency, offering instead a million variables. There are so many types of jobs, so many definitions of "professionalism," so many different contracts and budgets, so many cultural settings, our gigs might be union, nonunion, clearly legit, or ethically (even legally) questionable. On top of all that, inevitably, sooner or later, there's the real jerk or nutcase, complicating matters all the more.

While you can't avoid these situations entirely, it's important to develop methodologies for managing them as they come at you. And when you're not sure what to do, your best resources will be your colleagues. It is a time-honored tradition that each generation of actors mentors the next. As you set up your professional life, be sure to find your own mentors, and when you're a seasoned vet, it will be *your* turn to pay it forward.

Questions and Answers

Dear Jackie,

I recently landed a great role in a play with a wonderful theatre company. I was so excited when we began rehearsals, but then something big came up in my personal life that I really feel needs my full attention. I can still do the play, but it will make my personal situation harder and honestly, I won't get anything out of performing right now.

The director is being really nice about this, and said she will work around my new scheduling issues, but I don't really feel like I am going to be able to give the role my full attention. I'm not sure if it's fair to the cast and the director to stay in the project when I have this other, life-changing thing going on at the same time. Maybe I should just step down. I think it might be hard for them in the short run, but maybe they will be better off in the long run. What do you think?

—Doing My Best While Not at My Best

Dear Doing,

There's a general feeling in the acting community that you shouldn't turn anything down or quit any job you've accepted. But once in a while our principles, larger career goals, or plain old life gets in the way. Give yourself a day, or a weekend, to weigh the consequences of leaving the play with the costs of forging ahead.

Consider the remaining rehearsal weeks, number of performances, and flexibility of your schedule. Think too about possible tactics to alleviate stress while fulfilling your commitment. Do you have an understudy—or could you ask for one—so that you would know relief was available if you really needed it? Can you ask for a revised rehearsal schedule, with consideration given to your most sensitive personal time? Have you brainstormed possible replacements for yourself? (If you do feel you must quit, offering the director a list of qualified actors suited to your role will soften the blow.) Have you asked the director, straight out, what she would prefer—you at 60% or someone else at 100%?

Your director sounds understanding, so if you decide to stick with the project, take her up on any personal accommodations she is willing to make. And don't worry too much about letting the other actors down by not being at the top of your game each and every minute. We've all been there. While "the show must go on," and professionalism is paramount to your reputation as an actor, you are above all, a human being. Life is messy and sometimes we can't just put on a brave face and soldier on.

You know that actor's bumper sticker? The one that says, "Born to Act?" It's a lie. Life has to come first. JA

Dear Michael,

I'm fairly new to Los Angeles and was recently in a production where I received a great deal of attention. During the run, I was approached by several agents wanting to represent me. After meeting with each of them, I chose someone from a nice, midsize agency who seemed to represent what I thought I was looking for.

The problem is that since I selected this particular agent, he constantly wants to take me to dinner, shows, and parties. It's almost like he is trying to date me. He knows I have a girlfriend, but I don't know how to say no to someone who could hurt my career, and I don't know if I burned bridges with the agents I turned down. I'm feeling a little trapped. What do I do?
—Just Off the Bus

Dear Just,

This one is easy. You're getting a weird vibe. Don't ignore it. The only reason to stay with this agent is if he's getting you lots of auditions. I'm guessing that's not the case. But even if it is, you don't need to accept invitations that make you uncomfortable. Simply decline with my favorite catchphrase: "I wish I could." It lets you out without rejecting the person who's invited you. If this agent is legitimate, he'll work for you regardless of whether you're on his social calendar, and all will be well. However, I must admit, I'm skeptical. Good agents socialize with their clients occasionally, but not "constantly." You should probably go back to shopping.

As for agencies you rejected last time around, don't assume they've lost interest. Reach out. Tell them you made the wrong choice. They might be thrilled. But don't wait. For some reason, we actors tend to give completely ineffective agencies excessive amounts of time to prove themselves otherwise, rather than just reading the signs and moving on. Speaking from experience, that's a mistake. It's your career. Manage it assertively. MK

Dear Jackie,

I recently got cast as one of the two leads in a feature-length student film. It's a paid project, and the rest of the cast are exciting, experienced actors . . . all except for the other lead. He wrote and is planning to co-direct this film, but he has no acting experience. He is playing the role because "while the other candidates who auditioned were 'extremely talented,' they were not the right physical type." The story is fantastically thrilling and unique and all the other people involved are top-notch, established actors and technicians, and a lot of money has been invested in this project.

There are still a few weeks before shooting is scheduled to begin, and I know a phenomenal actor who wasn't in town the day of the audition but is this director's physical match. Is there any way I can gracefully suggest that he audition my friend? I never, ever would've dreamed I'd be asking a question like this because I strongly believe in giving people the benefit of the doubt and I accepted the role solely because the story is an amazing one. The only reason I'm even daring to send this question is because this already-overwhelmed student/writer/director, who has never taken on a project this size, brings no energy to the role (which is almost never off-screen) and I am afraid, on the production's behalf, that his beautiful script and their tremendous investment will be for naught.

—Bound by Professional Courtesy

Dear Bound,

What you can say in regards to the casting of the other leading role depends on your relationship with the filmmaker. If he has reached out to you for advice and input on other decisions, the door may be open for such a suggestion. If he's treated you solely as an actor, you might need to stay in your current role and serve both the script *and* the director.

Either way, don't jump into the discussion of whether the director is really "up" for playing this role. If you want to feel him out, say something like, "I was telling my actor friend about this wonderful project and he is so disappointed that he was out of town on the day of the auditions. He'd really like to meet with you for future projects or if something opens up on this one. Can I have him submit his headshot and résumé to you?"

You might even attach his materials to your email, submitting them yourself.

I spoke to a few student filmmakers to see how they'd react to such a suggestion and, across the board, they were encouraging that you should do your best to serve the film, not the director. Student film director Melissa Perez says,

> When I decide to direct a project I'm always looking for the best option in every decision I make. I know it seems scary but if someone came to me with this option I would appreciate them for showing that they really cared how well the film was made. I've made plenty of decisions that, although difficult, have made my student productions much better. Film is collaborative and that's an important lesson I have learned.

"As a director/writer I believe you always have conceptions of what kind of actors you want for particular roles," says recent film graduate Steven Ray Morris,

> But in my personal experience, trying out as many people as possible leads to more options. Often actors bring new angles to the characters. If you really care about the film, taking that brave step to voice your concern is a good thing. Sure, egos might be bruised—renaissance types who direct/write/act can be a tad inflated—but better to explore your options than settle with a mediocre product.

JA

Dear Michael,

I recently had an audition involving a romantic scene. I really wanted the role, spent lots of time preparing, and went in with confidence. During the reading, my scene partner, without warning, planted a kiss on my lips. I was thrown. Then, he did it again later in the scene. I had no idea whether this guy was a reader or another auditioning actor. I prayed he was auditioning. If he was the reader, that meant that he'd made out with possibly dozens of other women that day! Needless to say, it knocked me off my game. My character was supposed to be head-over-heels in love, a condition that's hard to portray when you're feeling like you just licked a petri dish full of viruses. What could I have done? It happened so fast I didn't have time to protest. If I complain now, I run the risk of irritating the director and not working at a well-reputed theatre. Is this behavior not as rude as I think it is?

—Sideswiped with a Kiss

Dear Sideswiped,

Whoa! WAY off base. Whether he was reading or auditioning, Mr. Hotlips should have introduced himself and asked how you wanted to handle the scene's indicated kisses. Completely rude.

I asked director and acting coach Valerie Landsburg for her take. "There are four no-nos for auditions," says Landsburg,

> Don't mime. Don't cry. Don't kiss. Don't die. In a situation like yours, there are choices. I would have gone with it and used it to have a fresh, real-time reaction. After, I would have taken the casting director aside and discussed what happened. But you can also stop the audition right on the spot and, in a professional way, explain that you weren't expecting the kiss and that it threw you, being mindful to keep it brief so you can regroup and do the work.

We're all so afraid of offending or alienating or irritating people that we some-times tolerate completely inappropriate behavior. You had every right to say, "Whoa! Hang on. I don't kiss strangers at auditions. Let's start again, and just fake the kiss. I mean, we haven't even been introduced." And with that, you could have started again. No apologies, no asking for permission.

What many actors don't realize is that, far from offending, that kind of dignity most often elicits a respectful response, because you're letting people know you require respect. Don't lose your cool, but take care of it in the moment (so it doesn't gnaw at you later) and let them know in no uncertain terms that you don't stand for that kind of thing. MK

Dear Jackie,

A commercial casting director, whom I have auditioned for on several occa-sions, has popped up in several national commercials—ones I myself auditioned for! Something doesn't seem kosher about this. It's obviously an advantage if a CD has continuous direct contact with a potential client and is allowed to pro-mote himself, more so than the regular actor who isn't fortunate enough to wear these two hats. Isn't that unfair?

—Actor Only

Dear Actor Only,

I see your point, but remember that casting directors are rarely in a position to decide who books a role. They are facilitators between clients and potential employees, working like a recruiter or human resources department. Though this CD might have the advantage of a pre-existing connection, he is not just casting himself in the role.

Jeff Gerard, former president of the Commercial Casting Directors Association, feels that whether a CD pursues acting work is a personal decision. "I think it's up to everybody's own moral judgment," he says. "I was an actor for fifteen years before I became a casting director, and personally, I don't believe I should be bringing someone in for a job and then competing with them." However, he adds, the entertainment industry is full of people with varied talents and interests, many of whom cross from one professional niche to another—and back again. "A lot of us wear many hats. In this business you should do anything you are capable of doing. You should do what makes you feel fulfilled."

Another CD puts it this way:

> Personally, I don't see a conflict. Many casting directors started as actors. If the CD/actor is qualified, why not take advantage of the situation? Yes, it's an advantage, but an 'unfair' advantage? The CD still has to go through the

audition process. If the director/producer/agency doesn't think the CD is the best actor for the role, it ain't gonna happen.

According to rule number 14 of SAG-AFTRA's Constitution,

> No member of the Guild may perform services both as a performer and as an assistant director, nor as a performer and an employee serving in any casting capacity, nor as a performer and an employee working within the jurisdiction of any theatrical teamster union in any motion picture or TV motion picture series without the consent of the Guild.

Sounds like casting directors aren't encouraged to act in projects they cast, but are free to work as actors in other projects without scrutiny. And even if a CD was to have the opportunity to take a role in a project they cast, the Guild may give its consent.

If you are deeply concerned about the issue you can contact the Guild, but I suggest—for your own sanity—you let it, and your idea that our industry should be fair, go. CD/actors may use their proximity to directors and producers to gain an edge. An "undeserving" background actor may get a voucher because the second AD thinks she's cute. Gwyneth Paltrow has famous parents. As far as I can tell, most actors use whatever advantage they can in their pursuits. They certainly use their connections, which is all this CD is really doing. If your aunt were the president of Universal Pictures, would you use that to your benefit? I would. JA

Dear Michael,

I was auditioning for a role at a small black box in Brooklyn. The play was pretty experimental, and so was the audition. We improvised a few scenes together in front of the director/playwright, occasionally changing roles. Nothing too bad. Except this went on for a good thirty to forty-five minutes (I believe the play itself was around thirty minutes long). Finally, it was down to two of us for the role of a junkie, so he asked us to take turns begging him for the part in that character, the way a junkie would beg a friend for $5 for a fix. Since that was the character, it was at least applicable. But we were literally begging. He just sat and listened to us. I did not get the part, and I do not feel bad about it. The director ended up playing it himself. Will not beg in an audition again. I guess I can be grateful the situation wasn't worse, but how do I handle this kind of thing in the future?

—Weirded Out in Williamsburg

Dear Weirded Out,

It's crucially important to know that you don't have to do everything you're asked to do as an actor. You don't have to accept every offer, jump through every hoop, or tolerate situations that are beneath your dignity or unworthy of your valuable time. It's weird out there. There are lots of folks who either don't know what they're doing, have unrealistic demands, or seek to take advantage of actors' desperation. Never presume that people will be respectful, competent, or safe. It's always *your* responsibility to vet and evaluate each opportunity for legitimacy and value, and to protect yourself. And if you miscalculate, never be afraid to graciously extricate yourself . . . and walk the hell out. MK

Dear Jackie,

A writer/director I'd worked with before was holding auditions for his new project, but I was unable to make it to the scheduled auditions. He emailed me personally and said he'd do whatever it took to have me read for one of the characters—he actually said he would come to me. He then sent me the script early (before anyone else saw it) and prodded me for feedback about the character. So I spent quite a bit of time looking over the script and writing out ideas and questions.

I didn't hear back from him, and the original audition date came and went. I emailed him again, ever so politely, to ask how things went and he wrote back, thanking me for giving him lots of ideas. He then told me that he ended up already casting the character.

What happened? This is not the first person to ask me for feedback, with the strong suggestion that I am under consideration for a role. Is it a trick? Or am I just being naive? I am also a writer by training, so are they just using me?
—Feedback Fool

Dear Feedback,

There are several possibilities of what happened here. You could have been used for your writing acumen—you had worked with this person before and he probably knew you had writing experience. Or he could have decided, because of your feedback or in spite of it, to go another way with the character and not known how to tell you that you were no longer under consideration. Or he could have simply found someone else who blew him away at the scheduled auditions—which you couldn't make. I think this last guess is the most likely. Still, since we're guessing, here's another possibility: he didn't like, or even actually want, your feedback.

Years back, one of my novel-writing friends gave me a draft of his new book and told me he wanted feedback. I figured he asked me because I was an actor and he wanted thoughts on the characters—their points of view and motivations, and all of that. I read the work diligently and took detailed notes. Then I sat down with him and my pages of feedback and went through each note, one by one.

He was nonplussed. Annoyed. Defensive. In retrospect, I can see that what he *really* wanted was, "This is wonderful! I love it!" But instead I said, "This is great, but here are some thoughts" and proceeded to go on for twenty minutes. I meant well, but I may have lacked . . . what do they call it? Tact.

In your case, perhaps this writer/director was less sure of himself than he let on, and felt threatened by your feedback. Maybe he realized it would be easier to work with someone who just said, "I love it!" I'm not saying you did anything wrong—I don't actually think I did either—but that doesn't mean our (totally logical) actions sat well with others.

Next time someone asks you for feedback on something you'd like to act in, I suggest you keep your thoughts brief and positive. And don't email anything complex. Email is notoriously rotten for subtlety and tone. If you are pressed for feedback, say something along the lines of, "Oh, this piece is just so interesting and complex! I hope I get the role so we can work through this stuff in earnest!" JA

Dear Michael,

Last week I had an audition where I was, unfortunately, paired up with a completely unprepared "partner." Apparently this girl hadn't been aware that the script was available in advance—not only in the casting office, but also via email. There were two roles, and the director stated that we'd be switching roles after the first read. This girl was rude about reading for the other role. She huffily husked an "OK," then proceeded to improvise the audition with no reference to the story or even subject matter! I worked diligently and intensively on this audition and *still* got screwed out of consideration. I know this is part of the business, but how do we handle these situations?
—Partner Problems

Dear Partner Problems,

Here's what I'd do: "This isn't going to work for me. I need to audition with someone else." Note that I didn't say, "I'm sorry." There's nothing to apologize for. You worked to be prepared and deserve to audition with someone who did the same. I also didn't ask permission. Be gracious and even-tempered about it, and don't insult the other actor, but do insist. And if the other actor's feelings are hurt, so be it. The casting director probably already sees what's happening, and may understand your stance. If not, remain graciously firm about what you need. We need to think enough of our own work not to allow it to be negated by an unprepared or unprofessional partner.

However, this advice comes with a big fat caveat, and I warn you, *do not* miss this part of my message: you don't get to play casting director and evaluate another actor's talent, choices, or suitability. You can't demand another partner because you dislike someone's interpretation or don't think the chemistry is right. You can *only* do what I've suggested when your fellow auditioner is clearly and undeniably incapable of executing the most basic audition requirements—like saying the right lines—to the extent that everyone in the room can see it. Otherwise, *you're* the one who's being unprofessional. MK

Dear Jackie,

Although I'm in my early 30s, I look as though I am in my early 20s. Every now and then I'll even get mistaken for late teens! Looking young may sound like it's a good problem to have, especially here in LA, but I'm not so sure—at least not for men. I'm pretty sure that I would never be believable as a character in his early 30s, such as a dad with kids, so I make a point to only submit for characters in their 20s.

Recently I had an audition for a film and it went really well, but then, at the end, the director asked, "How old are you?" I didn't want to lie, so I told him the truth. Somehow I think that took me out of the running.

What should I have done? On the one hand, it might benefit me to lie about my age and tell them the age that I look—mid 20s. On the other hand, if I don't tell the truth and do book the job, I have now started off the relationship on a lie and then it feels like all of the bonding amongst cast and crew that happens thereafter is insincere. Finally, if one does lie, doesn't everyone find out eventually once all of the payroll/W-4 paperwork gets completed?
—Ageless in Los Angeles

Dear Ageless,

The Age Discrimination in Employment Act of 1967 prohibits employers from awarding jobs or perks according to age criteria. While the Act doesn't specifically restrict employers from asking an applicant's age in an interview, most stay away from the question to avoid even the appearance of a violation. In the entertainment industry, the applicable question is not how old someone is, but how old they play—or look. So, while most casting pros won't ask directly, you have a couple of options when the question does arise.

The simplest response is to answer honestly, but this, as you've seen, can have negative consequences. It's no secret that ageism is a problem in our industry and facts that don't line up with an auditor's preconceived notion of a character—or specific details from the script—may throw off their perspective. You could, instead, parry the age question and follow up with the important issue at play: can you believably play this character? Try something like, "I'm about (insert the age of the character) so I get his perspective on the future." Or keep it general.

"I'm about 25." "I'm around 26." Who's to say 32 isn't "around" 25? You might also be able to joke off the question, as in, "Old enough to know better than to answer that question!" Some actors simply reply with the written or assumed age of the character, as if it's a fact. Many reply with the age range of characters they commonly play.

None of these tactics is likely to backfire when you book a gig. The person doing payroll isn't gossiping about your age with the casting director and the rest of the cast. And if they do speak about it? Well, you're in Hollywood, dahling! No one is all that worried about accuracy. JA

Dear Michael,

I prefer not to disclose my age to casting people as I believe it alters their perception of me. An actor friend who knows my real age strongly suggested that I *never* disclose it. I don't want to lie, but I'd rather not share the truth either since it really doesn't matter, as long as I look or act right for the part, no? I've thought of giving an age range, but casting directors may not like such an obvious dodge. Is there a polite way of not disclosing my age?
 —Peter Pan's Sister

Dear PPS,

"How old are you?" is a rude question that should never be asked, and if asked, should be dispatched as lightly and quickly as possible. I've heard a number of clever or creative answers over the years:

"You go first."
"What age do you want me to be?"
"Old enough."
"Somewhere between birth and death. Closer to death."
"What a coincidence! I'm exactly the same age as the character."
"I'm ageless and timeless. Next question?"
"How old do I look? . . . And answer *very* carefully."
"Don't worry; I'm legal."
Or simply, "Haven't you ever heard it isn't polite to ask a lady her age?"

But I think a simple, "Oh, I don't answer that question," accompanied by your sweetest smile closes the subject quickly and in no uncertain terms. MK

Dear Jackie,

My agent sent me on an infomercial audition for a weight loss product as a body model. When I arrived, it became clear to me that they were looking for someone to take "before" pictures of. Then they would pair my body pictures and video with someone else's—someone thinner and more toned, obviously—to create the before and after shots for the show. While my face wouldn't be shown in the shots, I still feel very weird about this. I don't know if I am comfortable being seen as the body that needs improving—the bad, before body. Then again, it pays $500 for the day and I really need the money. Do you think this is degrading? Should I just suck it up and take the job if I get it? I don't want my agent to be mad at me. Finally, is this even legal? It seems like false advertising to me.

—Not That Big

Dear Not That Big,

It doesn't matter whether I—or anyone you know—thinks this modeling gig is degrading. That's your call. And since your face won't be seen, no one besides the people on set will know that those "before" abs are yours. So, the question is not a matter of exposure, but of personal comfort level.

If you take the job, the most difficult part may be that everyone on set will be well aware that you are the "before" body. You and the other "befores" will have been cast to represent what viewers want to get away from—what they do not want to be. That could sting. Of course, you will also be representing what the viewers actually are! Your body, with all its "imperfections," will look familiar. The "after" model will be ridiculously lean and uber-cut, and look nothing like most people on earth.

It comes down to this: will you be comfortable and able to keep a sense of humor throughout a day in which everyone else sees you as out of shape? Or will you be self-conscious and embarrassed? Will you cringe every time you see yourself on TV? Or will you laugh at the easy money? You probably already know how you truly feel.

It sounds like your agent wasn't clear with you on what the job entailed and it's possible he or she didn't know. You went in to audition as a "body model," which could have meant all sorts of things. If you decide you aren't comfortable taking the job, better to let your agent know right away than to wait until the part is offered. I doubt they will be upset over losing a $50 commission.

As for legal issues, truth in advertising walks a crooked line. Do you think celebrities like Beyoncé or Jennifer Aniston really use drugstore brand hair dye? The before and after shots are simply trying to get a point across, and if there is not a graphic or voiceover stating the pictures are, in fact, of the same person, it's perfectly legal to imply. You will see plenty of disclaimers in commercials—that's the small print at the bottom of the screen that adds to or clarifies a claim the ad is making. In a commercial for a "state-of-the-art" lotion that decreases cellulite, the small print might say, "in conjunction with a healthy diet and exercise."

A wonder diet that takes thirty pounds off in a week may be partnered with a photo of a skinny model and the tiny-lettered statement, "results not typical." If you're interested, The Federal Trade Commission enforces these boundaries. You can take a look at recent FTC activities at consumer.ftc.gov. JA

Dear Michael,

I was invited to a callback for the role of a go-go dancer for a major theme park's halloween show. When I arrived, I was required to sign a waiver, acknowledging that I knew there would be filming and press at the audition and that my image could be used. I signed without giving it much thought and continued into the audition room, which was filled with reporters and cameras from every news station and newspaper in Los Angeles. The theme park was using this audition to publicize their event. As shocked as I was that they were allowed to do this, I stayed, because I really wanted the job.

Performing a go-go, stripper-like style of dance is vulnerable enough, but to expose these dancers to the entire Los Angeles public was a thoughtless move. In the actual job, the dancers are in costume, hardly recognizable, and have rehearsed. In contrast, an audition is a raw process under bright lights in which the performers are still trying out the character and dance style. It's not yet meant for outsiders' eyes.

After the audition I was so hurt and filled with such a feeling of loss that I had to rethink if the abuse is really worth the actual job. I wonder what I could have done differently. Would it have been better if I hadn't signed that waiver, or, better yet, walked away when I saw the camera crews in refusal to subject myself to such un-professional activities? Are companies allowed to require performers to sign waivers before admitting them to an audition? And if so, how can we fight for the respect and privacy that we deserve during the audition process?
—Overexposed in Burbank

Dear Overexposed,

There's no way to prevent the theme park "suits" from inviting press to auditions and asking auditioners to sign waivers allowing themselves to be filmed. AGVA, the union that governs most theme park shows, only has limitations on filming the final product—in other words, you're somewhat covered once you're in performance, but not while auditioning.

You're right. Coercing performers to sign off on letting their auditions be filmed is inappropriate and disrespectful, placing tremendously unfair added pressure on people who are just trying to get a job. Unfortunately, being right doesn't always mean getting satisfaction. No matter how many of us agree with you, the practice doesn't break any existing rules.

So, what can you do? Well, you can refuse to sign the waiver. Yes, it may decrease your chances, but we're allowed to have limits on what we're willing to do for work. You could just leave. If the experience feels demeaning, and it's going to stay with you for days or weeks to come, it's simply not worth it. In the bigger picture, you can work with the union on changing the rules.

Or, you could just make a tee shirt that reads "Didn't Sign the Press Waiver," keep it in your dance bag for such occasions, and audition wearing it. They may not hire you, but I'm pretty sure they won't use the footage. MK

Dear Jackie,

I am a non-Equity actor in New York and was recently offered a children's theatre tour. When the director called on a Friday to offer me the part he said I could take the weekend to think it over and I should call him if I had any questions.

I called Sunday and got the director's voicemail. Since I have quite a bit of experience doing children's theatre, I asked about the negotiability of the salary. I received a voicemail back from him on Tuesday saying he was sorry that "it wouldn't work out," but to call him if I would like to be notified of upcoming auditions. I returned the call within fifteen minutes and got his voicemail again. I said that I wasn't declining the part and was merely asking about the salary. He didn't return my call. When I emailed the producer she told me that, after they offered me the role, another actor—one who had done the role before—got in touch with them and expressed interest. Since I was still "thinking it over" they felt justified in going with the known quantity. I again explained that I had not turned the offer down and asked her to call me. That was a few weeks ago and I haven't heard from either of them. I know I won't be performing this part, but is there any recourse to be taken?

—Just Asking

Dear Just Asking,

Sadly, I think you're out of luck on this one. Since you didn't get the offer in writing there isn't much you can do. Even if you *had* received a written offer, what would you have done? Threatened to sue the production had they not given you the part?

So, what *could* you have done differently? I suppose you probably would have gotten the part had you immediately accepted and not taken the weekend to think it over, although—even then—the director could have pulled the plug had you not yet signed the contract. Don't beat yourself up. It's common practice to allow people a day or two to think over offers and many actors try to negotiate better salaries or conditions. You did nothing wrong.

What happened to you is not unheard of in low-budget, nonunion productions. Producers and directors, in a hurry to cast their projects and worried about finding good actors, can get nervous when an actor doesn't immediately accept. That's when the calls begin to go out to friends and actors they've worked with in the past. Discussions about "what to do if so-and-so says no" begin early. Usually "think it over" really means you can think it over, but once in a while it means, "say yes now!"

If there's anything you can take away from this, it's the lesson to be extremely clear and positive in your dealings with those on the other side of the casting table. Avoid playing it "cool" and go ahead, gush with enthusiasm. This holds true throughout the entertainment and other industries. People love working with people they think love working with them. JA

Dear Michael,

Recently I was cast in a play that's part of a short-play festival here in Gainesville, FL. I'm 100% straight with no intention of ever changing, and it's a gay/lesbian-themed play festival. I knew this from the start, and it personally doesn't bother me at all; it's a terrific play, and it's a great networking opportunity as well. I'm one of only two straight actors involved, but we're all respectful and getting along wonderfully. However, I'm extremely concerned (almost terrified) about how my "traditional" family, friends, and potential bosses/directors would react if they were to google my name and find it associated with a LGBTQ event. I am neither an advocate nor a condemner of homosexuality, and I have unwavering respect for anyone of any orientation, but is there any way to gracefully talk to my director or producer about not including me in photos or press releases come promo time?
—Mama's Straightboy

Dear Straightboy,

Patrick Stewart, when asked about his role as a flamboyant gay man in the 1995 film *Jeffrey*, marveled at the number of interviewers questioning whether he thought the role might hurt his career. He observed that, while he'd played murderers, tyrants, bullies, and thieves, no one had ever asked him about whether he thought *those* roles might cause him to be mistaken for any of *those* things. It was only the role in *Jeffrey* that worried journalists. Telling, isn't it?

I understand your situation, and don't worry, I'm not going to give you a lecture about acceptance or tolerance. But I would make a case for letting go of your near-terror, and for looking at two things: likelihoods and worst-case scenarios.

First, it's unlikely that people are spending their spare time googling you. Sorry, but it's true. If they do, I'm sure they'll come across other instances where you've played someone different from yourself. That's what actors do, yes? As for directors who might be considering you for roles: even if they were so dim as to assume that the characters you play reveal who you are, no self-respecting theatre professional would care about your sexual orientation.

If your friends and family learn about the character you're playing and they're troubled by it, let their discomfort be *their* problem. Stand firm in your pride about your work as an actor. Whatever you do, don't take the bait by defending your own self-identity; that's a crazy conversation to take on. Sometimes, people just get weird if you don't fit their stereotypes—in your case, the stereotype that says straight actors would be inept and/or uncomfortable playing gay characters. Like I said, it's *their* problem.

One of the best stage experiences I ever had (and one of the most challenging) was playing a past-his-prime, former Cuban drag queen in a heartbreaking drama. I imagine that strangers who saw the play believed I was not only gay in real life, but Cuban as well—at least, that's my hope. I enjoyed it when people made those assumptions; it meant I was doing my job. When the playwright found out I belonged to neither group, he said, "Well, you sure could have fooled us." "That's sort of the whole idea," I reminded him. Score one for the actors!

So no, you shouldn't ask the producers to leave you out of photos and press releases. It's really not fair to them to make that request. They have to be able to promote the piece in whatever way best serves that goal. If you were this concerned about it, they may say, you shouldn't have taken the role. And frankly, they'd be right. Besides, do you really want to hide work you're proud of? It's a theatre piece, and you're an actor. Be proud, be brave, do your thing, and if anyone is shocked or confused, they'll just have to deal with it! MK

Dear Jackie,

A few years ago, I was shooting a MOW[1] for one of the major networks. Early on, the small production company began taking advantage of the entire cast. As one of the leads, I took some responsibility for attempting to better our conditions. One day, while tussling with a gun on camera, an actor pulled the trigger (as directed) and three crewmembers were shot and rushed to the hospital! Fortunately, the gun contained small buckshot and no one died. The production company was simply too cheap to hire a specialist and instead allowed the prop department to handle the guns. For me, this was the last straw. I reported the incident to the union and was told my name would be kept confidential.

Well, guess what? It wasn't. As a result, I now have a reputation of being "difficult to work with," perhaps the kiss of death for actors. My advice to fledgling actors: until your name is needed by the producers to obtain financing, just wear the clothes they give you, hit your marks and deliver your lines.

—Difficult but Not Dead

Dear Difficult,

Actors should be willing to listen, take direction, and wear their costumes without complaint. But we should never keep silent when we feel we are being mistreated or are in danger. Our predecessors fought for our rights to safe and respectful working conditions. Our unions fight for fair wages and hassle-free work environments. We, as individuals, need to stand up for ourselves and for each other—just as you did. I respect your willingness to speak up, even at your own professional risk.

Many actors are terrified to do anything that might label them as "difficult." Even when those with perceived power are clearly breaking the law or ripping them off, most actors stay silent. Take, for example, the CD I saw announce to a room full of actors that—in order to audition—they all had to sign out immediately on the sign-in form,[2] to prevent her from having to pay SAG-AFTRA penalties for keeping them waiting for so long.[3] How about the manager who requires her clients to work in the office, for free, as a condition of representation? These things would not happen in a "normal" industry. The sheer number of actors vying for jobs creates a huge power imbalance—one that many are perfectly willing to exploit.

That's why our unions are so important. But unions are not enough—as you experienced first-hand. While identities are guarded, there are risks inherent in whistleblowing in this or any industry. Slip-ups occur. Staff moves around. It's a small community. Just as sadly, many complaints can never be acted upon by our unions, the police, or government authorities, because of a lack of actor cooperation. Most actors refuse to speak openly—even confidentially—for fear of retribution of the kind you suffered.

I believe that we need to stand up for ourselves on a daily basis. The less actors allow themselves to be mistreated, the less they will be mistreated. I'm not suggesting shouting a protest at an offending CD, or demanding a private appointment with an agent who's unwilling to talk. I'm saying that every actor is more than any one audition, any one representative, or—in your case—any one job. You paid a price, not only for blowing the whistle, but also for your castmates' silence. Imagine the power your cast as a whole could have wielded had you all been willing to report the company, together. JA

What Do You Think?

1   What kinds of positive approaches to difficult situations have you learned in this chapter? What are some ineffective approaches you hope to avoid?
2   What kinds of actions or behaviors might get an actor labeled as "difficult"? Are those actions or behaviors ever justified? If so, when?

3 Describe a scenario in which doing the right thing might cause you to lose an acting job. Would it still be worth doing? Why or why not?

4 Should casting directors ever ask your age? How might you respond if they do?

5 When, if ever, is it appropriate to ask for a different scene partner at an audition?

6 Should you go through with every audition you have the opportunity to do? If not, how might you handle declining an audition?

7 How realistic are threats of blackballing or blacklisting?

8 How would you handle a situation on set or stage that was clearly unsafe?

9 What kind of support system do you have in place for the inevitable difficulties you will encounter in your career? If you don't have such a system, how can you build one?

10 How have you handled your own sticky situations? In retrospect, what, if anything, would you do differently?

Notes

1 MOW—an acronym for Movie of the Week.
2 Sign-in form—SAG-AFTRA casting sessions use sign-in forms to track which actors came in and how long they were there. Finished forms are submitted to the union. When actors are required to wait over the allotted time (which differs depending on the circumstance), they're entitled to penalty fees.
3 Union auditions require auditors to keep actors waiting no longer than specific, allotted times—depending on the union or contract. See your union websites for specifics.

15

PERSONAL RELATIONSHIPS AND FAMILY MATTERS

Acting, on a fundamental level, is about human relationships. An acting career, however, can challenge *real life* relationships in myriad ways. Erratic employment, long hours, financial uncertainty, changes in location, and a uniquely emotional and intimate work environment is inherent to our freelance artist lifestyle. This can be complicated for our friends, family, and significant others to navigate. Jealousy, frustration, and uncertainty can creep into even the most stable relationship.

The decisions we make in our personal lives will have career implications and many "normal" lifestyle choices can clash with the demands of a freelance artist's career. Having a child or buying a home, for example, may mean committing to a more reliable source of income, affecting your availability for auditions and work. Moving to an industry hub may take you away from family and friends. A long-coveted audition might conflict with a friend's wedding.

What's more, our work itself is emotionally demanding, requiring much of the same energy needed to nurture our personal relationships. Connecting to scene partners and castmates can leave us eager for isolation at home. Our work "family" of other actors can take up so much space that our *real* families feel left out. "Leaving it all on the stage" sometimes means we have little energy left to give to our children or partners after a difficult performance. We may not even have anything left for ourselves. Finding balance between our home and work lives can be a maddening quest and sometimes these two worlds may be at odds.

It's well worth considering your career-versus-personal-life priorities in advance. Otherwise, the scales may tip too far in one direction.

Questions and Answers

Dear Jackie,

I'm currently in a romantic play, cast opposite someone I think is really wonderful. He's funny, sensitive, and really sweet. We're very flirtatious backstage, and have been hanging out with the cast after the performances, although he and I usually spend most of the night off to the side, talking. I would be really eager to date this guy—except for the fact that he's married.

He takes his vows seriously—we have talked about it—but he has expressed doubts that his wife is truly his soulmate. I believe that he and I may be meant to be. I don't want to help him cheat on his wife, but I also don't want to let what could be a once-in-a-lifetime chance pass me by. I won't initiate anything more, but if he does, I'm not sure how I should respond. After all, I'm not the one who's married. Shouldn't his vows be his responsibility?

—Unvowed

Dear Unvowed,

Romantic scripts, playing opposite someone you find attractive, dark and cozy backstage quarters, the free-spirited way theatre people talk to and touch each other—these things can wreak havoc on the behavior of even the best intentioned. It's possible your co-star does take his vows seriously, but enjoys flirting in what he believes to be a harmless manner. I doubt his wife would be thrilled with all of this intrigue, but even she may know her husband's tendencies.

If, on the other hand, he attempts to move your relationship out of the friendzone, you will indeed face a personal dilemma. Look, we all indulge in stories about soulmates and true love, but we also live in the real world, where betrayal has painful and serious consequences. What will it say about this guy if he's willing to betray his current wife? Why would you want to give your heart to someone who has shown he doesn't live up to his, as you put it, responsibilities? I know *you* didn't promise to love her forever, but his wife is a human being— probably one you will meet after a performance some night very soon.

If he truly feels she is not his soulmate and they divorce, your choice will be a whole lot simpler. Until then, keep the flirting to a minimum and try socializing with the other cast members you've been ignoring. And remember, even if your dreams spring to life and you and this actor pair up in heavenly fashion, even if the angels sing on the night of your nuptials, he will still be an actor. He will have other co-stars. JA

Dear Jackie,

After nine months together, my boyfriend and I are about ready to split up. The issue that is ruining our relationship is the way he behaves around the people he acts with. He gets very flirty with anyone he plays opposite and when I ask about it, he just gets defensive and tells me that, because I too am an actor, I should understand. He says he needs to develop a "charged" relationship with that person because it is then easier to play that connection in the play or film.

The truth is he doesn't seem to be doing anything exactly wrong. He's just really touchy-feely with these people—giving them little massages, hugging them and kissing them on the cheek. He even jokes with them about hooking up. We are doing a play together right now and he does all of this stuff right in front of me, which he says should make me feel less worried because if he were going to cheat on me he wouldn't do that. I overheard him tell one actor, "If you ever leave your husband, you know where I live." They both laughed at this. When I confronted him later he told me I should relax—that it was obviously a joke.

I admit I am extra nervous because of the way we got together. You guessed it: we were doing a film together.
—Worried in Westwood

Dear Worried,

I'd be worried too. And I'm curious: does your boyfriend flirt with all co-stars, regardless of looks or just the, you know, hot ones?

There are plenty of actors who flirt with their on screen/stage counterparts, and I won't pretend it can't give them chemistry onstage. If you need to appear to be in love, one way to accomplish that is to—well—fall a little bit in love, but that approach is certainly not necessary. My most successful onstage romance was with someone I absolutely hated (anger generates its own "charge"), and most actors choose to, well, *act*. For the flirtatious types, there's a difference between low-key, jovial fondness and all-out seduction. And it is a slippery slope. It's not much of a stretch to go from flirting at rehearsals to flirting backstage to flirting at cast parties to flirting your way into the guilty morning light.

But it doesn't really matter whether his flirtation will lead to cheating. What matters is that it bothers you. You've expressed that you are uncomfortable and if his response was as cold as you imply—telling you to "relax"—his fidelity is only one of your problems. While no one should coddle a partner's jealous demands, simple respect is necessary for any relationship to thrive. Telling another woman to look him up if her marriage goes under? That's not respectful. Or particularly funny. JA

Dear Michael,

I've scored a very small speaking role in one of those crime re-enactment shows. It pays reasonably well. I'm playing a 1920s bad boy who ends up killing his lover's husband. The sex scene will be done with no full nudity, but there is kissing and it has to look real.

The big problem is, I'm in a very committed relationship of five years and have a very jealous partner who forbids kissing and sex scenes. So, I'm having second thoughts . . . a *hell of a lot* of second thoughts . . . but I just can't help wondering if this type of scene is a good career move, momentum wise, especially since this will be my third paid gig in two months.

I posted this question on an actors' message board, and most of the responses said I shouldn't be with someone who's uncomfortable with me doing love scenes. It's not as simple as that. I love my partner with all my heart, and our relationship is important to me. Then again, so is my career. If I'm able to support us by playing roles that involve kissing and intimacy, isn't that a fair compromise? After all it *is* only acting. If I were to put a clause in my contract that says no to kissing and intimacy, wouldn't I be limiting my opportunities too much?
—Torn in Two Directions

Dear Torn,
While there are vastly different viewpoints on this question, I will just say that I disagree with the brash, "dump him" reactions you got from actors on the message board. Those of us with non-showbiz spouses and partners ought to be sensitive to the fact that for *most* people in *most* professions, engaging in intimate behavior with coworkers (*while working*, no less) would be outrageously abnormal. So cut your partner a break, and factor his feelings into your decision.

I recommend having a calm, rational, and—above all—collaborative conversation. Talk over the pros and cons, including the career limitations of a "no kissing" policy, and whether love scenes pose any threat to your relationship. If you decide to put your foot down, don't do it before you've tried working this out as a team.

Not long ago, I was offered an amazing role that involved some sexual carrying on. I discussed it with my wife. Instead of taking a stand, I asked her what she thought. Once we talked it over, she said, "You have to do it. It's too good a part. But I don't want to visit you on set during this one." That was our particular compromise, and I think it was more than reasonable.

Contrary to the way many actors think, there are important things besides our careers (shocking, I know). If you love this person, and he loves you, and you're good for each other, doesn't that count for something? No role is worth trashing a loving, supportive relationship. That's what addicts do. But you also have a right to your career goals. Sounds like a talk is in order. MK

Dear Jackie,

I'm a Los Angeles actor who is primarily focused on building a stage career. I am currently in a serious relationship and my boyfriend and I are talking about marriage. However, he is not a performer and we constantly fight whenever I get a part that requires me to kiss a man. I try to explain the techniques of a stage kiss and that when you are onstage, a kiss is not—for me at least—real on a romantic level. He feels like it cheapens our relationship and has gone so far as to say that the only way he will marry me is if I promise to never take a part that requires any kind of romantic scene, even if it's a comedy. I feel like this is totally unrealistic but I also know I want to start a family with this man. Can I put his fears and misconceptions to rest, or am I fighting a losing battle?

—At Wit's End

Dear Wit's End,

You want to start a family with someone who is being "totally unrealistic" about your profession? Look, your partner has given you an ultimatum. Whatever you do, don't assume you will be able to change his mind after you're married.

Realistically, you are going to have a difficult time pursuing a stage career, or any kind of performance career, with a major restriction like this bearing down on you. Never taking a part that requires "any kind of romantic scene?" Well, let's see. You can't play Rosalind or Celia in *As You Like It*, Viola or Olivia in *Twelfth Night*, Hermia or Helena or Titania in *Midsummer Night's Dream*, Juliet in *Romeo and Juliet*, Beatrice or Hero in *Much Ado About Nothing*, Elena in *Uncle Vanya*, Nina in *The Seagull*, Masha or Irina in *Three Sisters*, Hedda in *Hedda Gabler*, Nora in *A Doll's House*, Blanche or Stella in *A Streetcar Named Desire*, Laura in *The Glass Menagerie*, Ann in *All My Sons*, Emily in *Our Town* . . . and don't even get me started on contemporary plays.

I could write for days and still not list all the roles you would be giving up if you complied with your boyfriend's (absurd) rule. Sure, there is no explicit stage direction commanding Viola and Orsino in *Twelfth Night* or Laura and Jim in *The Glass Menagerie* to kiss. But what if the director decides he wants to add that? Are you planning to refuse? Will you have to risk your future husband's wrath to keep your job or ask for a break from rehearsal so you can call and ask his permission? And what if the director asks for a lingering hug or a smoldering look? Do those actions fall under the "any kind of romantic scene" jurisdiction? Where is the line? Will the rules become more and more restraining as time goes by? Unless you stick to solo work or your future husband directs all your plays himself, you'll need to be ready to do things like say your lines, do your blocking, and kiss your scene partner. As you and I both know, it's just part of the job. JA

Dear Jackie,

My boyfriend is not in the business and we are having problems because he doesn't understand how acting works. Like, he thinks women only get parts because they sleep with someone. I don't know how to fix this. It's caused fights between us and I don't know how to educate him on how things work without a long, drawn-out conversation. Do you know of a book on that specific subject? Or is there some other solution?

—Boyfriend BS

Dear Boyfriend BS,

Let's start with why you want to avoid a "long, drawn-out conversation" with your boyfriend. Isn't that what relationships are all about—talking, listening, coming to greater understandings of each other and who you are individually? If you've tried to broach the subject and been met with resistance, question your boyfriend's attitude. Does he respect your choices in other areas? Is he generally supportive of your plans? Is he willing to take the time to learn about something that's important to you? If not, you may have more than this particular BS to worry about.

If, however, he's supportive in other areas and simply ignorant to this one, you both might enjoy a mini-tour of the local acting scene. Think of it as an "acting tasting tour" where you both get a chance to see new things. Attend screenings, film festivals, plays, and panel events. You'll both learn a lot, and he'll begin to see that there's more to acting than the casting couch. You could also invite your boyfriend along with you on any upcoming auditions—to wait in the waiting room of course—where he'll get an eyeful of the mundane particulars of the trade. Or, if you're feeling a little sly, jointly audit some local acting classes, where he can see actors grappling with the craft. As for books, if you're hoping for something along the lines of *The Acting Business—An Explainer for the Actor's Significant Other*, I think you're out of luck. JA

Dear Jackie,

Recently, I began a relationship with a legitimate casting director. We have gone out a few times and I have since realized that I am not as interested in her as I had hoped.

How do I break this off without breaking up my chances of being called in to her casting house? We have not had a long history together, but I am afraid it has been long enough to cause some bitter feelings and she may possibly take me off her list of actors for projects. I know I should never mix business with pleasure, but in this biz, that's easier said than done. Do I have to just learn my lesson here the hard way or is there an easier way to save face?

—Looking for Love and a Job

Dear Looking,

If you've really only "gone out a few times" there's not too much danger that this CDs affections for you will outweigh her professionalism—at least for long. That's if, as you say, it was just a few dates. If, instead, your relationship went deeper, or to more . . . um . . . intimate places, you may be in a bit of a bind.

Dating up or down the business ladder, in ours or any industry, is likely to bring hurt feelings and frustrations when things don't go as planned. I'd like to tell you that everything will be fine: that if you end your romantic relationship in a respectful, honest fashion you'll both be able to proceed with both reputation and courtesy intact, but, unfortunately, she may feel used or misled. And if she believes you were duplicitous or exploitative, she'll be hard-pressed to recommend you to clients. But if the relationship grew out of a friendship—or built one along the way—it may eventually bring you both professional, as well as personal, perks. When I lived in LA, my ex-boyfriend, a successful commercial casting director, never failed to bring me in on everything he cast. Then again, we had broken up a decade before he became a CD.

And now for the big question, the tough question you knew I'd ask when you wrote in. Did you hope your hook-up with this CD would boost your career? Is any part of your present lack of interest in her due to her lack of action on your career's behalf? If such ideas were part of your original interest in her, you have amends to make. While CDs, producers, and others with keys to the casting kingdom are responsible for their own hearts, it's never okay to use love to get ahead—in anything.

Then again, what do I know? "All's fair in love and war" is a much more popular saying than, "You shouldn't date people who have access to things just so you can get access to those things." JA

Dear Jackie,

Tonight I had dinner with a dear friend. He knows I want to be an actor but is always pushing other ideas on me. This time it was about volunteering at some big organization because, as he explained, "Actors never make it and you know that. So when you're ready, you could turn this volunteering position into a career."

When he said that it pissed me off so much inside. I did not show it, but I was so angry. Why do people who should support me always try to convince me to do something else? They think that there is no way to make it in acting? This really disappointed me since it was from a supposed friend.

—Unsupported

Dear Unsupported,

You seem to already understand your friend's motives. If he truly believes there's no way to be successful in acting, it would be almost cruel for him not to help you find another career. Should he merely stand by as you career down into the abyss? Can he rightfully call himself your friend if he watches passively as you doom yourself to certain failure? Of course he needs to step in and help you climb out of the hellish pit of disappointment and disillusionment into which you are so obviously sinking. He's your only hope!

So, now we understand his perspective.

Instead of getting angry, try to muster some compassion for your overly worried friend. The next time he begins "helping" you, say something along the lines of, "I appreciate your concern for my future, I really do, but you should know I have thought long and hard about my decision to pursue an acting career and I am happy with my choice. I promise that the minute I have doubts about my decision, I will come to you for advice. Can we talk about something else now?"

If that's not your style, try humor, along the lines of, "I know, I know, I'm hopeless!" Followed by a quick change of subject.

Now, if he's the kind of guy who can't stop meddling, and he continues to harp on your plans, you may simply need to spend less time with him. He's entitled to his well-meant suggestions, but you don't need to be around to hear them. JA

Dear Michael,

My mom is pretty much my biggest fan. She always wants to know what I'm up to, and comes to see everything I'm in. She's the best. I just have one issue. Since she doesn't understand how auditions work (you know, like how rejection happens more or less . . . all the time), if I tell her about one, she'll keep asking if I've heard anything. I know it's because she believes in me, but it ends up depressing me because it just reminds me of things I'm not getting cast in. At the same time, I don't want to discourage her enthusiasm, since it keeps me going! What do I do?

—Smothered with Support

Dear Smothered,

Your mom sounds like an angel, and I'm so glad you have such a wonderful cheerleader. This advice is going to be challenging to take, but you need to stop sharing audition updates. When she asks, you can honestly tell your mom that nothing's going on, because until there's a booking, that's the truth. All you're withholding from her is that you went to work, as usual. That's what auditioning is: our job. (Getting hired is more like a vacation.) A student of mine makes the point this way: "I work as a bartender. I don't tell people every time I make a margarita."

Honestly, you need to be a bit more self-centered. Your need to insulate yourself from pressure and discouragement about auditioning needs to outweigh your cool mom's desire for the latest news. MK

Dear Jackie,
I'm an actor who has made a bit of a career for myself working behind the camera. It gets me on set and I get a real education watching talent work. I want to act full time, but I'm supporting a family.

My camera job allows for good chunks of time off. When I am free I try to find acting gigs and hope I don't get interrupted with work and can do the jobs I book. Lately it's been a problem. If I get an audition I seem to always get called into work on the same day. If I get an acting gig (most of these are non-paying by the way) I also book a paying camera job.

Before I was fully set up working behind the camera, I was submitting and had been called in to a few interviews with agents—but never got signed to anything. I take classes and join groups when I can, but want to do more. I'd love to make the switch to acting full time but I'm nervous about the financial hell it might put me and my family through.
    —Wanting to Switch

Dear Wanting,
    There's no easy answer here. While some might suggest you "have to follow your dreams, come what may," I—with two kids of my own—am all too familiar with the practical side of your problem. Making the choice to pursue your heart's desire risks putting your family in financial jeopardy, but choosing to stifle your dreams puts you in an unsustainable personal position. You either show your children that sacrifice is sometimes demanded in a family or you show them that dreams sacrificed can come back to haunt you.

Or maybe there's another way. Consider carefully whether you would enjoy building and maintaining an acting *career* or if you can be happy focused on acting itself? If the latter, seize the challenge to act as much as you can *in addition to* your pretty cool day job. Forget worrying about where you make your money and enjoy acting as a non-professional—with all of the freedom that brings. Many artists don't make money off their art and that doesn't denigrate the quality of their work. You can do lots of acting in class, with a theatre group, in student and indie films, and with like-minded pals. With your skills and contacts you can probably make your own film. Sure, occasionally you'll have to miss out on an acting gig because of a work commitment, but with more time in both fields under your belt, you'll soon make the juggling work to your advantage. You might even want to consider taking an annual break from freelance production to focus solely on acting. The longer you are in both worlds, the longer this "break" might become.

If, instead, you decide to throw caution to the wind and give full-time acting a go, I suggest you begin with a long-term experiment of sorts. Save up some money and take an extended break from camera work, making acting your only focus *for a set period of time*. You and your family can discuss the details of such an arrangement, but anything short of several months won't be long enough. With time to just audition, submit, work non-paying jobs, and look for a representative— without worrying about getting a "real" work call—you'll begin to see not only whether you are getting the response you'd like but how you feel about living the actors' life in earnest. No, three or four months is not long enough to build a career, but it's long enough to get a taste of what building a career would be like. At the end of your experiment, reassess your situation and, with your spouse, make a decision about the next phase of your life.

Nothing is permanent. You can, and probably will, change your mind about what you want to do several times throughout your life. Try not to spend too much time looking over the fence and salivating over the illusion of the greener grass. JA

Dear Jackie,

I have had a very difficult time finding work as an actor and now, to further complicate matters, I found out I'm pregnant. My husband and I are nervous, but thrilled. It will be our first.

Should I just give up acting altogether and find a different career that pays a regular salary?

What will happen to my dream? I have an agent, but should I continue to look for a better representative with a better reputation who will send me out more often? Should I even bother continuing with showcases and workshops? Should I keep doing background and studio audience work, or auditioning for yet more nonunion theatre? At this point, I don't even qualify for SAG-AFTRA health insurance. All the job ads seem like they're for unpaid infomercials and student films, or the roles are for model looking/young/perfect women for sexual situations or nudity at $100 a day.

Am I finished as an actor?
   —Pregnant and Pessimistic

Dear Pregnant,

It sounds to me as if this baby is coming at a perfect time. You are in a rut—tied down to extra and audience work—with an agent who isn't getting you out. Enter your new baby. Use this joyful excuse to take a break from the status quo. Sure, you can let your agency know that you're available for those rare "Pregnant Lady" roles, and do background work when it's convenient. Or you can just let the whole kit and caboodle go for a while.

Agent Hugh Leon of Coast to Coast Talent Group warns that now is not the time to look for a new representative:

> I don't think you need to call it quits because you're pregnant but I would suggest you put your quest for an agent on hold until after you give birth and feel you are ready physically, mentally, and emotionally to put 100% of your efforts back into your career.

100%? Sounds to me like Leon isn't a parent, because—after having kids—nothing gets your full 100% ever again. Your child will change your life and your priorities in ways you cannot now predict or understand. And that's okay.

Los Angeles actor and mom Roberta E. Bassin shares these words of encouragement about balancing a family and performer's life:

> I joined babysitting co-ops. I used to write 1000 postcards waiting for my daughter to take her gymnastics class. She enjoyed going to my theatre company and handing out the tickets. My son had fun helping create characters and reading scripts with me. As they grew, so did my career. It was less of a balancing act and more of a balanced life between family and career. I am very grateful to have accomplished both career and family and not sacrificed one for the other.

Motherhood puts things in perspective, and deepens your capacity to feel. You'll be a better, wiser, more centered actor when you decide you're ready to get back into the game. Stop struggling upstream against unpaid infomercial or nudity gigs and get some sleep before your baby comes. I'm not telling you to give up acting, mind you, just reassuring you that, should you choose to take a breather, the industry will be here when you get back. JA

Dear Jackie,

I am an actor who happens to also be a mother—not a big deal. Like any professional, when I go to work I find childcare. My frustration lies, however, in the amount of times, once someone (be it a director/producer/other actor) finds out that I have children, he/she immediately makes assumptions that are, quite frankly, biased and, in today's professional world, illegal. I've put up with everything from, "You must be thankful to have such a selfless husband (for helping out with the kids)," to outright directives such as "Don't worry about any jobs right now, you should be enjoying your time with your children," as a response to my inquiry about one day of *extra* work on a film set!

This is an industry that revolves around making yourself personable, warm, outgoing, and vulnerable. I think that motherhood has made me a better actor—thus, it would seem to make sense to share this information. Yet, I cannot tell you how many times people who find out I am a mother use the information to edge me out of the competition. Help! What is my best strategy and tactic?

  —Frustrated in Mommywood

Dear Frustrated,

  Human resource departments widely prohibit interview questions about race, marital status, sexual orientation, and children for good reason. Those biases are real.

Try a little experiment. At your next ten auditions, don't tell anyone about your kids. Why should "I have two kids!" come up any more than, "I have a grandma!" or "I love my sister!" Let the fact of your motherhood emerge later, after you've shown yourself to be a focused and tireless professional. At that point, let them marvel at your "selfless" husband, and exhaustion-proof fortitude. Avoid getting sucked into a back and forth about the rights of mothers in the workforce. Enlighten your detractors by example instead of explanation.

I also have children, and have tried to take comments like the ones you describe—which I too get regularly—as compliments. Some people seem genuinely flustered that I can act and teach and mother and write in the same week. Calling my husband a saint for doing his fair share, oohing and aahing over my busy schedule, or warning me not to overdo it seems to make them happy. Sometimes it boosts my ego when they marvel at how I can do it, but usually I just wonder why they can't. JA

What Do You Think?

1   Why might friends and family try to dissuade you from pursuing an acting career? How can you manage this discussion?
2   How will you prioritize your family in relation to your career? Does one come first? If so, which one and why?
3   What are your most important personal relationships? How can you see them being affected by your career pursuits?

4 Should your spouse or partner have a say in which roles you accept? Why or why not? If so, what kinds of things should they be able to weigh in on?

5 Name five aspects of our profession that could present potential challenges to your personal relationships?

6 What are some pros and cons of dating (or marrying) a fellow actor?

7 How might parent/performers balance these two challenging worlds?

8 Do your personal goals align with your professional goals? Where are they at odds?

9 If you got a professional, difficult-to-land audition on the same day you were scheduled to attend a wedding, which would you go to and why? Would that change if you were a member of the wedding party? Why or why not?

10 What are some strategies you might use to balance your home life with your artistic and professional career?

16

THE NATURE OF THE CAREER

Acting can be a wonderful, awful profession, full of rollercoaster-like peaks and dips. It can be hard to navigate, hard to understand, and hard to sustain. It is by turns unfair, thrilling, depressing, healing, colorful, complicated, uplifting, and sometimes just plain weird. The best way to maintain equilibrium as a professional actor is to recognize this unpredictability as an inherent part of the life you've chosen. Expecting things to be fair or logical will never serve you—that way madness lies. If you can learn to embrace the chaos, you'll be better prepared to ride out the ups and downs.

In fact, the random nature of our industry can sometimes work in your favor. Just as you can be overlooked for a part for which you're perfect, you can be also cast in one that probably should have gone to someone else. You can be broke with no prospects on Tuesday, and shooting a major role in a feature film on Thursday.

The journey upon which you've embarked will not unfold along a well-trodden highway with clear roadside markers guiding your way. It will be more like navigating a forest at night. There is no road, it's hard to see where you're going, and you will probably feel lost for a long time. But keep moving forward, learning as you go and making the best choices you can, and eventually, unique and unexpected pathways will emerge.

Much of our business remains out of our direct control, making it easy to be overwhelmed by a sense of helplessness and despondency. Because we are, for the most part, our own supervisors, an acting career requires a considerable degree of self-management, self-awareness, and personal motivation. We know what to do once we're employed, but on a day with no auditions or jobs in sight, how can we make progress? How can we put in a good day's work when we're not at a theatre or on a set?

Each of us must continuously self-inspire and self-direct our careers, managing our own expectations, frustrations, and drive. We have to decide for ourselves when to be strong, push ourselves, and conquer challenges, and when to take a break to restore. We must balance ambition and drive with fun and the occasional self-decreed day off. We need to develop personal methodologies for processing disappointment, disrespect, and unfairness. We must be on alert for career-damaging jealousy, bitterness, and unhealthy forms of competitiveness. As we run our one-person businesses, we have to keep an eye on our own mental health, strive to remain rational, and, maybe most importantly, keep our senses of humor.

It helps to periodically remind ourselves that no one forced us to be actors. We chose this road, and we choose it again and again as the weeks and years go by. As you will discover, attitude matters. In the words of Shakespeare's Hamlet: "There is nothing either good or bad, but thinking makes it so." How you look at things will affect how you experience them, and can make the difference between happiness and misery.

Questions and Answers

Dear Jackie,

About a year ago, I participated in a showcase with other developing actors and since then, every single one of them has booked a job of some sort, except for me. Yup, it has been a big blow to the ego and the psyche. Since we all still keep in contact, it's very difficult for me to engage in conversations when I have nothing to discuss. I've taken many classes—more than any of them—but they're at the level now where if I start to discuss my most recent class, it's met with an awkward silence. I call it the "oh, poor thing" silence. I happen to feel I've grown a lot as an actor even though I get basically no auditions, let alone work. However, they seem disinterested, maybe because they have bigger and better things to talk about. Sometimes I feel my biggest acting job is pretending not to be jealous. I'm not proud of that part of me. I genuinely want to be happy for others' opportunities but it gets more and more difficult when you have none of your own.

I have no idea where my acting will take me and I'm open to whatever happens, because being creative in more ways than one will always be a part of my life and I believe I will find my place. But it sure is hard sometimes. Maybe this is a silly question because it involves uncontrollable human emotion but, how can

I avoid being jealous of the opportunities my acquaintances get and just focus on my own pursuit?

—Happy for Them. Really.

Dear Happy,

It's totally normal to feel jealous and frustrated when your peers exceed you in opportunities, monetary success, or acclaim. We've all been told we shouldn't be jealous of others. We've all been lectured that it isn't nice, it isn't helpful, and it's petty. Yes, yes, I know. But I also know that taming the "green-eyed monster" can be excruciatingly difficult, especially in our fickle, fortune-bending business.

In your case, it sounds as if there's more to the situation than simple jealousy. Frankly, your actor friends sound disrespectful. While they may have booked more jobs than you, there's no reason for them not to celebrate your accomplishments, no matter the size or specifics. Yes, some of these people are doing "better" than you, but in the end that doesn't amount to much at all. The real trick of being an actor is that a) it makes you happy and b) you can support yourself with it or find a livable day job/acting combination. Success can be very fickle and operates outside of logical time constraints—often outside of logic altogether. You may find that in five years you are farther along than any of these people. You may one day see the best actor you know give it all up and become a lawyer or the worst actor you've ever seen land a major role in a new series.

Sometimes friendships take on strange power dynamics, and it sounds as if your group has morphed into a less-than-positive environment for you. This may sound radical, but I suggest you find some new actor friends. How about your peers in the class you are now taking? Make it a priority to spend time with people who don't, however unintentionally, make you feel bad about yourself. It doesn't really matter whether your old friends are trying to make you feel inferior—there's something about the situation that isn't working for you. Forget blaming anyone or beating yourself up, just open up to connecting with other performers. When you have a class success, share it with some of your new friends, and pay attention to their responses. How do you feel afterwards?

You sound as if you have a good handle on your aspirations, concentrating on making a creative life for yourself and winnowing out your place in the arts. Hold tight to that. The more you focus your energy on your own journey, the less you'll waste agonizing about others'. JA

Dear Michael,

How do all these celebrities with no acting credits get cast in movies? What about the starving artist who's been doing this for sixteen or seventeen years? How about the young student who still has to go to classes and build up résumé credits? The dedicated actor goes to auditions week in and week out, and someone with no experience not only gets to audition but gets the role? How is that fair?

—True

Dear True,

You've made a huge mistake in expecting show business to be fair in any way. Indulging in such naiveté only sets one up for a lifetime's worth of bitterness and disappointment. Because, here are the eternal and unchanging truths: there are too many actors, the best actor doesn't always get the job, and no one owes any actor the opportunity to work; roles aren't distributed based on how long you've been in the business, and they're not distributed evenly; there's no point system, no merit badges, and no show business court where overlooked thespians can sue producers for unfairly hiring someone less talented or less experienced; directors get to cast whoever they feel is right for the role, regardless of whether the actor has paid his or her dues. Yeah, it's unfair. Always has been. And if no one communicated that to you before you entered our profession, then I certainly offer my sympathies, but it's time someone did.

I want to encourage you to ponder whether expecting fairness is in your best interest. If you went to work in a coal mine, you wouldn't be justified in complaining about getting your coveralls dirty. If you took a job at a sports arena, it would be strange to object to all the noise. So, here we are in show business, and this particular line of work is neither fair nor logical nor consistent, and that's all part of the package. Does it make any sense at all to expect or demand otherwise?

When we sign on for this actor's life, we sign on for all of it. We sign on for sometimes getting roles we don't deserve, and losing ones we do; for fighting to be noticed among all the other worthy hopefuls; for rejection, as well as, one hopes, acceptance; one minute being shown adoration and the next, being shown the door. And no one, regardless of talent or dues paid, can expect any guarantee of success. MK

Dear Jackie,

I am both an actor and a theatre director—early career in both fields. I have the training, experience, passion, and desire to carve out a career for myself in both of these disciplines. I love them both for totally different reasons and if you told me I had to choose between them it would be like *Sophie's Choice*!

I am about to move to NYC to take my career to the next level, but somehow I'm worried that my dual career might work against me. I'm losing sleep over the fear that if agents and casting directors know that I also direct, they might take me less seriously as an actor, and visa versa.

Am I fooling myself in thinking that I can pursue both simultaneously? What is the industry's attitude towards double-headed monsters like myself? I feel like I might need to make the decision of whether I'm going to pursue both openly, or to swallow hard and put one of these dreams on the shelf.

—Caught In Between

Dear Caught,

You're getting ahead of yourself. At this point you should be thinking about where you're going to live and how you'll find work as either an actor *or* a director, not fretting about an imaginary person's possible problem with your dual career path. Most likely, your reception will depend a little on the person in question and a lot on you. If you are clear that, while you enjoy both of these things, you are reliably able to focus on one at a time, it shouldn't be an issue.

Here's what I mean: I have been around a lot of people who ascribe themselves of many talents, and want others to know about them . . . all of them. You'll be doing a show with them and they'll make sure you know they could direct it better than whoever happens to be directing. They'll be directing you and find it irresistible to give you line readings, because, well, they *ARE* actors after all. They'll be framing you in a shot while also making "helpful" suggestions on your line delivery. People like that can be exhausting. I should know; I have been one of them. It's taken me years to learn to (mostly) keep my inner director hidden when acting.

Anyone can call herself an actor, writer, director, producer, or psychic without completing any course of study, earning any degree, or realizing any professional success. Titles such as "doctor," "contractor," and "firefighter" all require extensive study and fieldwork. Not so with "poet." If you plan to simultaneously pursue acting and directing, create a separate résumé for each. If your credits in one area are lacking, go ahead and list a few from the other, but keep the focus on that for which the résumé was created. If you don't present yourself as a "double-headed monster," that's not how you'll be perceived. JA

Dear Michael,

I wish someone could explain to me why major casting offices put casting authority in the hands of 20-year-old people. Does casting really not require any substantial skill or any knowledge of theatre, which—let's be honest—so many of them do not have, or if they do, it comes from reading *Vogue*? Has the dumbing down of culture really gone that far?

—The Young and the Restless

Dear Y&R,

You've made several enormous leaps in the presumption department. You've equated youth with incapacity, stupidity, and shallowness. Check yourself. That's a lot. I'm sure that all of us prefer auditioning for more seasoned casting directors, who are usually better at giving adjustments or seeing the merit in a unique take on a role. But I must caution you, feeding your own exasperation over a casting person's youth or inexperience is a quick shortcut to "Don't call us; we'll call you." Even if they're completely unqualified, as some *may* be, they're the sentinels, standing watch over the gates to Callbackville. Instead of being resentful, try going to the other extreme. Honor them like trusted, insightful collaborators. Some of them (perhaps rightfully) feel insecure about their lack of experience and knowledge about acting. Be supportive by listening attentively and using their suggestions. You'll put them at ease and make it much easier for them to feel comfortable inviting you to meet the producer . . . who may be even younger. MK

Dear Michael,

I've read in certain books on acting careers that it's important to have deadlines. For example, you'd want a role on *Law & Order* within eighteen months. Or you would want to make $10,000 by your seventh year acting. Do you adhere to this?
—Goal Oriented

Dear Goal Oriented,

In a profession where so many of the puzzle pieces are held by others, I can't see the case for making deadlines. You're challenging yourself to jump through a hoop, but the hoop may not even be there to jump through unless someone else puts it there. If your goal was to learn Italian, setting a deadline would make sense, because *you're* the one assuming the task, and you're the one who can make it happen. But to set as your goal that by a certain date producers and casting directors on a certain show are going to have a role you're right for, give you an appointment, and recognize your work by casting you is, I think, setting yourself up for disappointment.

Besides, there may be other things—better, or maybe just different—headed your way. You want to be open to whatever good opportunities turn up, even if they don't match your preconceived goals. So many of the wonderful things that have happened in my career have been surprises—things I could never have planned on.

Think of yourself like an industrious farmer who doesn't happen to know what crop he's planting. Just work the field like crazy, sow your seeds, do your craft, then wait and see what surprising and interesting things come up out of the ground. MK

Dear Jackie,

Do you just straight up tell people, "I'm an actor," when they ask what you do? I have noticed that their next question is always, "What have I seen you in?" I have no reply to that and it's just awkward for everyone.
—Not Laughing

Dear Not,

Generally, when someone asks me what I do, I say whatever comes to mind. I'm an actor, but I also direct, teach, raise kids . . . Yes, there are times when I lead off with the professor gig only to discover the person is a director and now I appear to be pandering when I add, "Oh, I'm also an actor . . ."

I, too, am plenty tired of the follow up, "What have I seen you in?" to which I have taken to responding, "I do a lot of classical theatre!" which usually ends the conversation. What should I say? "Did you see the commercial with the woman daydreaming because she has so much free time now that she uses such-and-such cleaning product? That's me!"

The truth is that, generally, people don't really care what we do. They are asking to be polite or to make conversation. We could go round and round about whether our self-esteem demands we proudly call ourselves performers whenever possible, but honestly, who cares? Maybe we should all follow George Costanza's[1] lead and call ourselves marine biologists? JA

Dear Michael,

I shot a major national commercial a couple of months ago. It was a great shoot and I was sure a good spot[2] would come of it, and that I'd have nice big residuals coming in. However, it's been months and the commercial hasn't aired. I've slowly been sinking into despair over this. Is there any resource to find out if a commercial is playing, and what shows advertise what products? Also, is there an appropriate way to contact the production company to get a copy for the reel, or even ask what happened?
—Sitting in Traffic

Dear Sitting,

Trust my experience on this one. When you shoot a commercial—or anything for that matter—you're earning only whatever you're paid for the day. That's your paycheck—period, end of story. And it's usually a pretty decent wage compared with other jobs. So take it, call it a day's work, and let anything else be a pleasant surprise. Don't even *consider* what you *might* make on residuals. It's way too common to get edited out (it happened to me only recently) or for the thing not to air at all. Banking on residual income is a certain mistake, both financially and psychologically.

Sure, you could probably track whether a commercial is playing by calling the production company, contacting the client's advertising department, or by asking everyone you know to look for it on TV and online. But then what? What if it isn't playing yet? Are you going to check back weekly? . . . daily? . . . hourly? And what if it is playing? Are you going to hound your agent until the first check comes in, and again in a few months to see whether the commercial is renewed for the next cycle? All this can become quite obsessive. Time to put that focus toward new pursuits.

As for getting a copy, if your spot hasn't aired, advertisers will have their reasons for not wanting it seen. Maybe they're shelving it, with the intention of airing it later (for strategic marketing purposes), in which case they won't want it circulating prematurely. If they've yanked it altogether, they may not want it seen at all.

You really have only two choices: 1) drive yourself crazy, or 2) move on. MK

Dear Jackie,

What are your thoughts on diversity in the media? The majority of audition postings are asking for people who are either white or black. Unless it is a historical or factual piece, why are people so prejudiced? I know this is a big topic and very hard to tackle, but writers, directors, producers, and audiences need to ask themselves this question.

—Just Asking

Dear Just,

Anyone who doubts the seriousness of this problem should visit SAG-AFTRA's website and check the casting data reports (go to EEO and Diversity and then Studies and Reports). The most recent data available as of this writing is from 2007–2008 and lists performers of color at 27.5%. Meaning, at least based on this "eyeball determination" survey, that white performers book 72.5% of Guild jobs.

One major hurdle to changing the status quo is the lack of women writers and writers of color. We've all heard the expression "write what you know." With the majority of Hollywood's writers coming from a white male perspective, it makes sense that we see a lot of white male material. A recent Writers Guild of America (WGA) report on Hollywood employment trends states that men outnumber women writers by nearly three-to-one, and writers of color are all but relegated to "minority-themed" genres. The WGA's 2015 TV staffing report shows that, for TV writing staff, the number of women writers had actually declined from the previous year to 29% and writers of color came in at 13.7%.

The entertainment industry does make occasional overtures towards changing the status quo. Check out the diversity mission on WGA's website (wga.org), where you'll also find a surprising number of opportunities for writers of color and a long list of organizations focused on creating more of those opportunities. SAG-AFTRA, too, has a strong commitment to promoting diversity, evidenced by its diversity committees and resources, which are detailed on its website on the EEO and Diversity page. And every successful venture starring actors of color chips away at the disparity.

Unfortunately, the main driver of most theatre, film, and television is money. Producers tend to cast actors they know audiences have wanted to see in the past, hedging their financial risks. If audiences don't demand a more representative reflection of themselves, they aren't going to get it. When color-conscious casting becomes profitable, it will become commonplace. JA

Dear Michael,

I'm getting a little sick of the lack of roles for people of color. I don't want to just play athletes and criminals all my life. And I'm definitely not trying to play stereotyped roles at *all*. How do I get past the tired old same parts? I am a good actor, but it seems like this business doesn't give me a lot of opportunities to show that.

—"Blacktor" in Brooklyn

Dear "Blacktor,"

There's a lot to say on this topic, including good news, bad news, tough love, and harsh realities.

If you ever want to feel profoundly encouraged about the range and number of roles available for non-white actors, you need only look at how far our profession has come. Film used to be blindingly white, all day, every day. Films with black characters who weren't maids or club entertainers were beyond scarce. And no one thought twice about putting white actors in dark make-up to play "Indians" or Asians. Over the years, that's improved a lot. No, it's not *fixed*. But it's headed in the right direction. Today's producers are consciously trying to include a spectrum of ethnicities in a spectrum of roles. Much credit for that is due to the non-white writers and producers who have carved out more and more space in the industry for new, better, and more varied stories. That's the good news.

The bad news? There are still not enough roles for people of color, the vast majority of content creators are still white men, and there are still stereotypes.

But are all stereotypical roles offensive? Maybe not. I believe there's a difference between the equality and fairness to which we should aspire in society and the misguided idea that equality and fairness must exist in our storytelling. For the most part, writers hope to *reflect* society, not to *correct* it. If we produced only films and TV shows that portrayed a Utopian world, free of stereotypes, without racial disparity, we would be missing opportunities to show things as they are.

I get nervous for actors who flat-out refuse to portray any stereotypes. Just because a character represents something *typical* or *cliché* doesn't mean it's an insult to one's race. Stories of maids and drug dealers and athletes are stories worth telling too. *The Wire*, a legendary HBO series about Baltimore, told gritty and realistic stories of the drug trade, the political world, the police department, the school system, and the media. Many of the characters were black. If black actors had turned down the roles that could be deemed stereotypical, we wouldn't have this very important glimpse into these secret worlds. The show also featured a greedy Jewish lawyer (played by me), an alcoholic Irishman, a tough lesbian, and several corrupt cops and politicians; these are stereotypes too. But no one could ever say such people don't exist. In real life, are there some very effeminate homosexuals? Absolutely. Are there feebleminded old people? Of course. Are there Middle Eastern terrorists? Swindling Jewish businessmen? Snobby French painters? Ditzy models? Loud Italians? Of course. All these people exist. Playing them isn't a betrayal. It's storytelling.

The goal, always, should be to show a spectrum of characters, the noble and ignoble, the leaders and the followers, the stereotypical and the unexpected. Fortunately, that's more and more the case in today's industry as we see characters who fit the cliché as well as those who don't. And that means that accepting a stereotypical role—as long as it isn't advancing bigotry—might be just an opportunity to tell part of the story. Of course, every actor can and should exercise his or her right as an artist to assess whether a role is racist. And anything that clearly betrays a writer's disrespect for a group should be rejected without hesitation.

Finally, the tough love. Show business never has been, and never will be, fair. Not for anyone. An actor's appearance will always be part of what determines how she's cast. Such is the nature of this profession. You can rail against these things all you want and it will still be the case. If you really want to effect change, the best way is to create your own projects and support others who are doing the same.

I agree; we must all keep working toward greater opportunities for—and projects by—people of color, and keep trying to correct the disproportion. It's happening. We're just not there yet. I also urge you to consider accepting *any* role that doesn't do harm or compromise your dignity. MK

Dear Jackie,

Trying to make a living from acting is distracting me from the love of the art. I actually am starting to hate myself. I'm done with building my résumé. I want to feel like a "working actor" and only take professional jobs, but at the same time the artist inside of me just needs to act. How can I handle this dichotomy?

—Sick of Myself

Dear Sick,

A few years back, National Public Radio's *All Things Considered* did a series called "How Artists Make Money." "Starving artist may be a cliché," the report begins, "But if most artists aren't literally starving, it's a fact that few make a real living with the work they love." The series goes on to feature a choreographer who makes money teaching dance and writing grants, a Broadway playwright who writes for television to pay the bills, and a poet working as a corporate executive, among others. Many of the people profiled do use a version of their art, or at least the same skills, to earn a living—the choreographer-turned-dance-teacher, for example—but they can't live solely off the fruits of their artistry.

Although you want to identify yourself as a professional—a working actor—you may need to come up with a system to keep your inner artist fed. You said you were done building your résumé, but that doesn't mean you can't enjoy doing creative, non-paying acting roles that give you a chance to grow. Your paid gigs aren't going to sustain you financially and artistically—at least not at this phase in your career. Give yourself a few opportunities to work without regard to money, at least several times a year. Do a play, a low-budget film, a reading—take the time, without career or financial guilt, to do projects that excite you.

For now, you may need a break. It might do you good to focus on another art or a discipline like yoga, karate, singing, writing, or, I don't know, cross-country skiing. Get your head out of acting for a while—even just a couple of weeks—so you can refresh your point of view.

Finally, if the self hate you mentioned feels real, speak to someone about it right away. The National Suicide Prevention Lifeline can be reached anytime at 800-273-8255 or contact the Crisis Text Line by texting CONNECT to 741741. JA

Dear Michael,

Lately, I've been getting really discouraged. I try not to complain, but I feel like I'm doing everything people say I'm supposed to do for my career, and hardly making any headway. It seems like the one thing no one teaches you is how to keep going when you consistently do good work but don't book anything. I get it. It's a tough business, but right now, it's really getting to me. I'm not asking how to get work. Just how to handle these rough patches.
    —Wrestling with the Blues

Dear Wrestling,

Sooner or later, most of us actors come up against periods like this, when our relationship with our profession isn't working all that well and the acting business isn't our friend. You find you're giving and giving and not getting much back.

At times like these, I have a technique for getting unstuck: shake things up by planning a radical change. I'm talking radical.

Think about moving to a new city. Now, hear me out. I said *think* about it. You may end up doing it—there are other markets out there, other places where actors thrive. But the point isn't to actually move. Just try the thought on for size. It's a mental journey that takes you out of feeling trapped.

Or, think about quitting the business. Now hear me out! I said *think* about it. Seriously consider what else you might do for a living, and look into it. Do research, sign up for a class, look for work. This mental exercise reminds you that you're a whole person apart from being an actor, and it shakes you free from the desperate state of mind that can creep in when you haven't worked in a while. Release your death grip on the idea of making it as an actor and see what happens.

The kind of dip you're going through can be like quicksand; struggling makes you sink faster. The more desperate you get to end the dry streak, the longer it tends to last. Taking determined steps in a completely different direction will open you up and get you breathing again. It's a great reminder that there's a big world out there that has nothing to do with your status as an actor. MK

Dear Jackie,

I'm at a crossroads. I've been in LA for nearly two years and don't really have much to show for it. I've taken quite a few classes and have gone on a good amount of nonunion auditions. I have no representation, but haven't really looked for it. I didn't have experience before coming to LA so I didn't see the need to look for an agent—I'm still building a body of work. I guess my concern is my state of mind living out here and my happiness.

I spent four years in the Marine Corps and I'm extremely capable of living in sub-par conditions. I don't need much to be content, which is actually what I'm afraid of. Since I've been here, I've already lived in five different apartments. To save money to put towards my acting career, I've considered ditching the apartment thing altogether and just sleeping in my car or wherever.

I don't know how someone with no acting background comes to choose acting as a career, but I did. Now that I'm here I'm kind of afraid that I'll stick it out just for the sake of sticking it out and not giving up. If I wasn't trying to be an actor I don't know what else I would do. The thought of being a part of a movie just really grabs me. I guess what I'm trying to figure out is when and how do you know if enough is enough?

—Too Persistent?

Dear Persistent,

Only you will know when it's time to make a change, but I implore you to put your health, happiness, and safety before your career pursuits. Living in five apartments in two years sounds incredibly stressful and difficult. The idea of willingly sacrificing a roof over your head is both extreme and unwise. Actors must present a professional image in auditions and interviews and it will be near impossible to do that without ready access to a shower and a closet of neatly pressed clothes.

I'd wager that at least a hundred people give up their dreams of an acting career every single day. The field is just too crowded for all of us to succeed in all the ways we'd like. It's easy to get caught up in the drive towards our idea of success and lose sight of what drew us to the craft to begin with.

Sit down with a pen and paper and answer the following questions: What do you enjoy about acting? What draws you to it? If you have no acting background, where did you get the inspiration to try it? How do you think being part of a movie will be a positive experience? Have you been happy lately? What was the best thing that happened to you this year? The worst? What do you think will happen if you quit acting?

On that last point, I'd like to reiterate something I say a lot: quitting the pursuit of an acting career is not a failure. It's simply a re-evaluation of how you want to spend your time. When someone quits a job as a banker, people don't question their fortitude. Ex-bankers are free simply to try something new. Why shouldn't actors get the same luxury? I'm often disappointed that the main critics of actors with doubts are . . . you guessed it, other actors, who—in the name of encouragement, go heavy on the "fight for what you love," clichés. But the trick to "making it" isn't always to be the toughest or even the best. There's a lot of randomness and luck in our business and it's natural that some very fine performers tire of the grind.

Quitting gets a bad rap. Leaving something that isn't bringing you joy makes room for something that might. And quitting your LA pursuits doesn't mean you have to quit acting—or even a shot at being in films. Living a happier life in a place where you have friends and family won't prohibit you from keeping up on local production and auditioning when you can. Heck, you'll probably be a lot more "hirable" when you're less stressed.

The bottom line is: if you aren't enjoying your current situation, change it. Yes, building an acting career comes with its share of challenges, but there should be plenty of joy in there as well. If the last two years have been unsatisfying, there's absolutely no shame in doing something else. It's your life. JA

Dear Jackie,

As a performer, I find myself subject to a battle with depression and black moods when not working and sometimes when working. What can a performer do to combat this?

—Down

Dear Down,

In her book, *The Creating Brain: The Neuroscience of Genius*, Nancy C. Andreasen, a psychiatrist and neuroscientist at the University of Iowa, argues that the same attributes that help artists create—such as openness and sensitivity—may also make them more susceptible to mental and emotional challenges. Research is ongoing on the topic, but when we actors spend so much time drudging up various emotions on command, it seems that we'd be more likely to set ourselves off-kilter than, say, a carpenter. Apart from the art itself, add career fluctuations that can drag us through hyper-busy, no-sleep weeks on end followed by stagnant periods with no work in sight, and it can be next to impossible to stay centered.

I contacted two mental health professionals for comment on your question. Both have been actors themselves, so have particular insight into the topic as it relates to our field.

Licensed Marriage and Family Therapist Frann Altman, who also holds a doctorate in clinical psychology and is a longtime SAG-AFTRA member herself, cautioned:

> Anyone who has 'depressive symptoms and black moods' should get themselves to a licensed therapist or psychologist for an assessment. Make sure there is no clinical depression or mood disorder like bipolar. While depression can come and go, bipolar mood disorder is a lifetime disorder and needs attention the same way something like diabetes does. People such as Winston Churchill (who called his depression 'black dog') and William Styron (Pulitzer Prize-winning writer) wrestled with depression that sometimes brought them to their knees, but their brilliance and expression endured. That being said, there is a sense of purpose and creative expression when working. Down time can really cause one to struggle with questions like where is the next job coming from and important meaningful questions like who am I beyond the actor in me. Creating a life that is full and rich off camera is important to explore. Everyone has times when they feel low or sad, but if it impacts your work and your life, it needs more focused attention.

Jeanette Yoffe, an actor and therapist with a masters in clinical psychology, suggests that creative activity should be part of your daily life—even when you don't have a job.

"Get involved," she says. "An actor acts! So take action. Create your own spotlight. Find a theatre company to join or volunteer at, start writing that project you have on the shelf, take a risk."

With a career guaranteed to fluctuate, you may need some steadying forces in your life to maintain balance. Certainly, family, friends, and other hobbies should play a role, and there's a lot to be said for steady income in helping ward off worry, but taking control of your artistic life may help you fight back the dark clouds. As Yoffe suggests, be sure you have a theatre company, inspiring class, or improv group to work out with on a regular basis. Sometimes having an artistic outlet for your feelings can keep them from getting the better of you. And be sure you have friends outside of the acting world to help you keep perspective when times are tough.

All that said, Yoffe echoes Altman's advice: "If you feel your depression is interfering with your ability to function, i.e. difficulty getting out of bed, self-neglect, and/or intrusive or ruminating negative thoughts, seek assistance from a mental health professional immediately." JA

Dear Jackie,

I am an actor, currently training in a college BFA program, and I love my craft. I feel so happy that I am shaping my skills and learning how to be the best actor I can be. Every assignment and audition and show is a great opportunity for me to be able to do something I love, and it's all practice for making what I love into a career.

Here's the problem: recently, I have been learning more and more about the business side of acting, and it sounds like I am going to thoroughly despise this industry! Yes, I understand that no matter what I do for a profession—unless I am working on a farm or off the grid—there will be a business side to it. So why not embrace the crappy business side of acting and run with it? At least I would be doing something I love instead of sitting in a cubicle.

To be honest, I can't answer that question. I have no idea why I am so against things like acting in commercials or networking. I guess it comes from a part of me that feels unclean and ethically wrong supporting major corporations. I don't want to be the face of a product or support the way mass media brainwashes people. There is a strong pull in me to say, "No! I can't become a product!" Maybe I can't play the stupid game of being an actor after all. I want to succeed, but how do I tell myself it's okay to do things I don't want to do?

I don't want to sell out! I want to be an honest, humble, intelligent actor who gets gigs because I'm talented and professional—not because I happen to be the right height and have the right haircut! What do I do?

—Confused

Dear Confused,

It's your right and responsibility to chart your own course. Unlike some careers, where clear signs point you forward and success can be gained from following a well-trodden path, every actor is experimenting, finding success through trial and error—if at all. What works for one actor probably won't work for another. It's what makes this business both amazing and devastating.

Actors worried about "selling out" often point to commercials as the primary culprit. Not associating yourself with a product may seem clear cut, but the issue is less than black-and-white. Commercial casting director and teacher Chris Game makes the point that most actors end up working a day job—selling out in a less obvious—and less lucrative—way. "You're telling me you don't want to do a Coke commercial but you'll work for 'the man' making minimum wage? You'd rather serve jerks like me donuts than use your craft to earn a decent amount of money?" Game understands that some actors don't want to appear as themselves endorsing products they don't believe in, but thinks commercials remain—at the end of the day—just another acting gig.

Whether or not you agree, it's certainly possible to have an acting career without doing commercials. Sustaining a career without networking is a more radical notion. Perhaps, however, you simply have an unrealistic view of what networking really is: collaborating, connecting, and getting to know other people. Some of my students jokingly call it "friend-making," in an effort to remind themselves how innocuous it really should be. You said that in school each "audition and show is a great opportunity for me to be able to do something I love." Well, the people you are meeting at those auditions and in those shows are your "contacts," believe it or not. You're already networking.

It's easy to fall into the trap of thinking that "success" means the same thing to each of us: a golden statue and a face on billboards. That's wildly simplistic. If we are willing to spend time defining exactly what we want, many more of us would succeed in getting it.

An actor's life can take countless shapes. With so many options, defining a particular, personal goal can be a staggering venture. You want to focus on theatre? What kind of theatre? Musical? Classical? Regional? Broadway? Avant-garde? Movement? Puppet? Children's? Would you like to pursue a job with Blue Man Group, a contract with the Oregon Shakespeare Festival, or a role in a Broadway tour? While these gigs all require talent, each demands distinct skills, experience, and training— not to mention a willingness to relocate to disparate places. An actor's daily life in Ashland performing *King Lear* is far removed from that of a Blue Man in Vegas.

At the end of the day, your acting career belongs only to you. It may be that you decide not to mix your art with commerce—and there's no shame in that.

You might be happiest working a day job and doing theatre on your own terms. Great! Who says a "real" actor has to make a living at it? Should we look down on Emily Dickinson's poetry as a "hobby" because she didn't sell her work?

Most likely, you'll find your path by striking a balance between what feels right and what feels like the, as you put it, "stupid game of being an actor." You'll probably figure it out, like we all do, through trial and error. I'm sure looking ahead into such an uncertain, topsy-turvy career is frightening. Take comfort in that you don't have to make any life-altering decisions right now. Enjoy your training and give yourself the chance to wait and see. You don't have to decide what feels right before you've even tried it. JA

Dear Jackie,

I moved to New York City to attend a musical theatre academy and pursue a career in theatre, but the training was too expensive and I had to drop out. I spent a month couch-hopping until I found an apartment in Brooklyn with some coworkers from the restaurant where I bartend. Since then I've had to spend so much time and energy working to make sure I can pay the bills that I've truly neglected my goal. Now, even when I have time to attend an audition, I often opt out at the last minute for no good reason.

Other actors can do it; they go to an audition on four hours of sleep, sing and dance their hearts out, and continue on to work a fourteen-hour shift on their feet, but I find myself making excuses. I feel like a failure. I am only 23 years old but I can feel myself giving up. I thought this was my calling. What happened to that fire I used to feel in my soul? Will it ever come back?

—Dampened

Dear Dampened,

There's not an actor alive who hasn't felt what you're feeling. Building a performance career is a grueling endeavor. Not only are you expected to dance till your feet ache, you've got to smile while you mix a dirty martini with two olives for someone who gets to sit down to drink it. No wonder you're skipping auditions—you're physically, emotionally, and mentally exhausted.

It's time for some practical decisions. The choices you make must support not only your mercurial partner—your career—but also your basic, daily wellbeing. It sounds as if your job is keeping you fatigued. That's not useful for your career—as evidenced by your skipped auditions—but it's not doing much for your health either. Is it possible for you to cut down shifts? Should you look for a new job—one in which *sitting* is allowed? If you don't see an alternative that pays enough for you to afford your apartment in the city, is it possible that's the problem to be fixed? New York is certainly an ideal place for an aspiring musical theatre artist, but we aren't talking ideals here, we're talking balance. Don't limit yourself because of a preconceived notion of how your career should play out. Stay flexible to what you need. "Failure" is a loaded word—one that shouldn't be slapped onto trivial circumstances like a zip code.

On that note—it's possible that skipping auditions is more than just a result of your fatigue. It's possible that you don't enjoy pursuing musical theatre jobs. It's even possible that you no longer enjoy performing at all. I know that might sound appalling at first, I mean, how dare I? But let go of your self-judgment and take some time to consider this possibility. Go for a long walk and give this idea some respect. How would you feel if you never had to audition again?

Having a calling may sound romantic, but it's unnecessarily limiting. I don't believe there's an actor alive so lacking in creativity and imagination that they couldn't find something else equally rewarding to do with their lives. What if, instead of attributing all kinds of magical powers to our field and specialness to our choice of career, we look at it like any other job, one that can be enjoyable and exciting, but that may—now and then—be tiresome, grueling, and just plain unfun? One that we may, while still being an artistic person with lots of valuable and beautiful potential, want to leave behind.

Our culture gives so much emphasis to "sticking with it" and "never giving up" that actors can drown in the "I have to make it" whirlpool. Even performers who know they want change get trapped into thinking they have to succeed in outdated dreams. It's hard to let go without feeling like a "failure." Don't let that happen to you. If you're ready to move on, do so. Only fellow performers who are struggling to stoke their own diminishing flames will judge you, but even they aren't "born to act."

A performer's life is just like every other life. Thrilling in moments, desperate in others, and just plain hard work a lot of the time. Make sure to do that work in a way that brings you joy, whether that means taking one less New York bartending shift per week so you can muster up the chops to dance and sing, devoting yourself to finding a better-paying, less-taxing day job, moving, finding a scholarship at another college, taking a weekend intensive, or even letting your dreams grow and change as you do. JA

What Do You Think?

1   How is an acting career different from other career paths? How is it similar?
2   What did you learn in this chapter that surprised you? Has your perception of an acting career changed? If so, how?

3 Given the nature of this career, what are your reasons for choosing it? After reading this book, have those reasons changed?

4 What positive steps can we take to improve diversity in the various acting media?

5 Describe five techniques for managing the unpredictability of the acting profession.

6 Some actors set deadlines for their careers, to "make it" by a certain age or hit milestones within specific time frames. Having read this chapter, how do you feel about this idea? Is it advisable? Helpful? Why or why not?

7 Is it wrong to play a character that perpetuates a stereotype? Why or why not?

8 Why might there be a link between artists and depression? What are some resources for actors facing depression or suicidal thoughts?

9 Would you ever consider quitting your acting career? Quitting acting altogether? Why or why not?

10 Do you think acting a calling? Why or why not?

Notes

1 George Costanza was a character, played by actor Jason Alexander on the television sitcom, *Seinfeld*, who often pretended to be a marine biologist to impress women.

2 "spot"—industry term meaning a filmed commercial advertisement.

CLOSING THOUGHTS

If you've reached the end of this book and haven't changed professions . . . or majors . . . that's wonderful. You are now armed with greater insight and educated in some very important realities. If you *have* changed your plans, that's *also* wonderful. You've done so as a result of a more enlightened idea of what you want to do with your life. And as we've said several times, choosing another way to pay the bills doesn't negate your artistic expression.

One final word of advice, on the subject of advice: While well-meaning people in and outside of the industry will offer you all kinds of direction and guidance throughout your life and career, it will behoove you to remember that no one else knows what *you* should do. Listen to everyone, take what you like, but never be afraid to ignore advice you don't want to follow. Even ours. In this book, we've done our best to cover a wide spectrum of topics in the best way we know how. But, like everyone else you will ever meet, we're still learning. Cultivate your curiosity, do your own research, and be humble enough to remember that you'll never know everything.

We, your authors, are both artists who are glad we chose to go into the acting business, and we have pursued that business in just about the most different ways possible. We know there are many, many ways to be an actor and we want, most of all, to encourage you to find your own. As overwhelming as it can sometimes be, as unfair, as frustrating, as competitive, as insecure, it is still a very fine line of work.

And finally—we mean this with all our hearts—we wish you the very best of luck. May you find your own way to live the actor's life.

Jackie Apodaca
Michael Kostroff

APPENDIX

Sample Résumé Format

Jennifer Ramos
SAG-AFTRA

Jefferson Talent Agency   Height: 5'2"
www.jeffersontalent.com   Weight: 110
123-456-7890

THEATRE
Our Town	Emily	Neighborhood Players (NYC)
Hairspray	Penny*	Thtr. Downtown (Ames, IA)
In the Heights	Nina	The Space (Bloomfield, NJ)
Weird Stuff	The Muse	Black Box (NYC)
My Life	cabaret act	various venues

*Most Promising Newcomer award

FILM
The Best One	principal	Universal/Ann Ame, dir.
Winter Blues	featured	MGM/Max Clout, dir.
This is My Life	principal	student film/UCLA
Another Movie	supporting	student film/UCLA

TV
Big Deal	guest lead	NBC
Ralph and Gladys	guest star	Netflix
Time Travel	co-star	ABC/Fay Moss, dir.
Weekly Laughs	sketch performer	NBC

TRAINING
BFA in theatre – Southern Oregon University, June 2017
Acting: Fay Missnayme (QB Studios, NY), HS for Talented Kids (Ames, IA)
Voice: Melody Singer, Bea Louder
Dance: Juan Turner (int. ballet), Glide Studios (hip-hop), Grace Foxtrot (ballroom)

SPECIAL SKILLS
Kickboxing, scuba, ballroom dancing (beginner), dialects: New York, Spanish, Puerto Rican, Southern, British, Russian, Irish, singer (mezzo soprano), great with animals, grammar nerd

RECOMMENDED READING

Acting in the Million Dollar Minute by Tom Logan 2005, Pompton Plains, NJ: Limelight Editions

The Actor Takes a Meeting by Stephen Book 2006, Los Angeles, CA: Silman James Press

actor. writer. whatever. by Mellini Kantayya 2013, Brooklyn, NY: Ako Dako Press

An Agent Tells All by Tony Martinez 2005, Beverly Hills, CA: Hit Team Publishing

Audition by Michael Shurtleff 1978, New York, NY: Bantam Books

Audition Psych 101 by Michael Kostroff 2017, Indianapolis, IN: Dog Ear Publishing

How to Agent Your Agent by Nancy Rainford 2002, Hollywood, CA: Lone Eagle Publishing

How to Audition by Gordon Hunt 1977, New York, NY: HarperCollins Publishers

How to Get the Part Without Falling Apart by Margie Haber 1999, New York, NY: Crown Publishing Group

Letters from Backstage by Michael Kostroff 2005, New York, NY: Allworth Press

Notes to an Actor by Ron Marasco 2007, Chicago, IL: Ivan R. Dee

Self Management for Actors: Getting Down to (Show) Business by Bonnie Gillespie 2014, Hollywood, CA: Cricket Feet Publishing; 4th ed.

Seven Deadly Sins the Actor Overcomes by Kevin E. West 2016, Studio City, CA: ShutUp n'Play Productions

What Makes Sammy Run? by Budd Shulberg 1990, New York, NY: Vintage Books

INDEX

Page numbers with "n" refer to endnotes.